Why Visual Basic? Why _____ ?

Visual Basic has revolutionized the world of _____ _____ _____ dows. What took hours using C and other language _____ _____ success is due to a friendly and intuitive interface that s... delivers power and flexibility.

The Beginner's Guide to Visual Basic rises to that challenge. Using a relaxed and visual style, the book takes you quickly and painlessly to outstanding results. It's the book that Visual Basic deserves.

What is Wrox Press?

Wrox Press is a computer book publisher which promotes a brand new concept - clear, jargon-free programming and database titles that fulfill your real demands. We publish for everyone, from the novice through to the experienced programmer. To ensure our books meet your needs, we carry out continuous research on all our titles. Through our dialog with you we can craft the book you really need.

We welcome suggestions and take all of them to heart - your input is paramount in creating the next great Wrox title. Use the reply card inside this book or mail us at:

feedback@wrox.demon.co.uk
or
Compuserve 100063, 2152

Wrox Press Ltd.   Tel: 0101 312 465 3559
2710 W. Touhy   Fax: 0101 312 465 4063
Chicago
IL 60645
USA

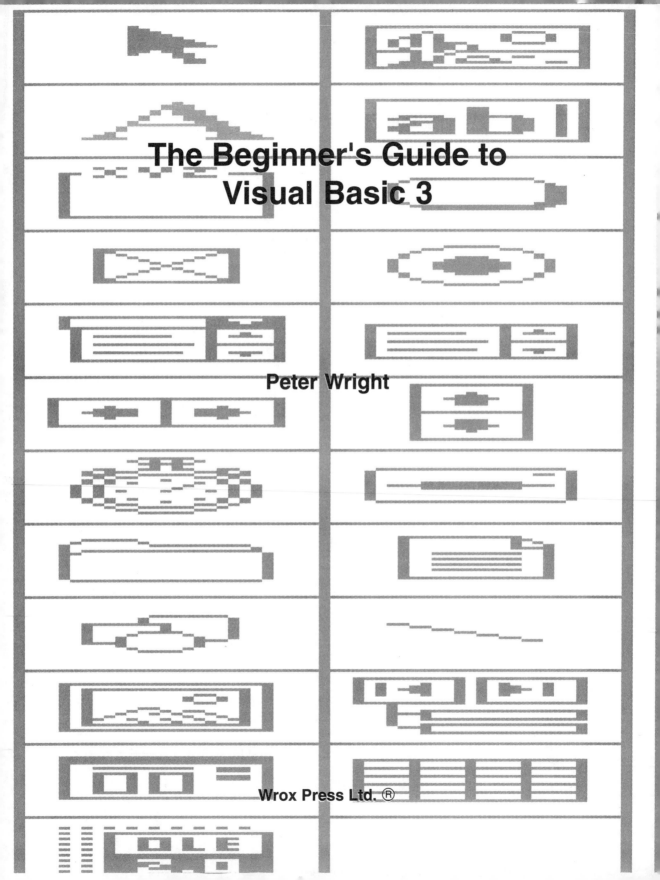

The Beginner's Guide to
Visual Basic 3

Peter Wright

Wrox Press Ltd. ®

The Beginner's Guide to Visual Basic 3

© 1994 Peter Wright

Published by Wrox Press Ltd. 1334 Warwick Road, Birmingham, B27 6PR UK

ISBN 1-874416-19-2

Credits

Author
Peter Wright

Managing Editor
David Maclean

Style Editors
Nina Barnsley
Wendy Entwistle
Luke Dempsey
Rachel Maclean

Technical Reviewers
John Brockett
Ian Cargill
Larry Roof

Production Manager
Gina Mance

Book Layout
Ewart Liburd
Eddie Fisher
Kenneth Fung

Proof Readers
Pam Brand
Sue Thomas

Cover Design
Third Wave

For more information on Third Wave, contact Ross Alderson on 44-21 456 1400

About the Author

Peter Wright is Managing Director of Psynet Ltd, a Windows development company specializing in multimedia, communications and database systems. Currently he and his company are developing a multimedia front-end to the internet as well as a number of CD-based multimedia projects including a CD ROM book creation system, written of course in Visual Basic.

Peter can be contacted by email on Compuserve as 100116,357, on CIX as pwrighta and on the Internet as peter@gendev.demon.co.uk.

Thank You

Technical books like this are rarely written by one person sitting alone in a back room for a few months. Along the way there are tens, if not hundreds of people who's ideas, opinions and thoughts in some way contribute to the book as a whole. I can't, and won't, thank them all but there are a few that deserve my undying gratitude.

Firstly, Wrox Press, the publishers. The help, advice and unerring faith that you have given has been awe-inspiring. In particular though my thanks to Dave Maclean for his patience and tolerance with a particularly stroppy writer.

Thanks also to all the higher echelons of the Compuserve's MSBasic forum. The technical advice and roadsigns you all freely provide always inspire enthusiam for Visual Basic for an invaluable source of help, information and fun.

Thanks also to Steve Dolan, Dave McBain, and Simon Bandy for keeping my feet on the ground, and my nose against the monitor.

Thanks to the following Microsoft Staff for their interest and support: David Deyo, Cornelius Willis, Andrew King, Dilip Mistry. Thanks to Microsoft in general for providing the world with the definitive Windows development tool.

Thanks to our beta testers and technical reviewers: John Brockett, Ian Cargill and Larry Roof.

Finally, my love and thanks to my wife Sharon, and my entry-level humans Chris and Eloise for giving me the reasons for everything I do.

Peter Wright

CONTENTS

Summary of Contents

Contents

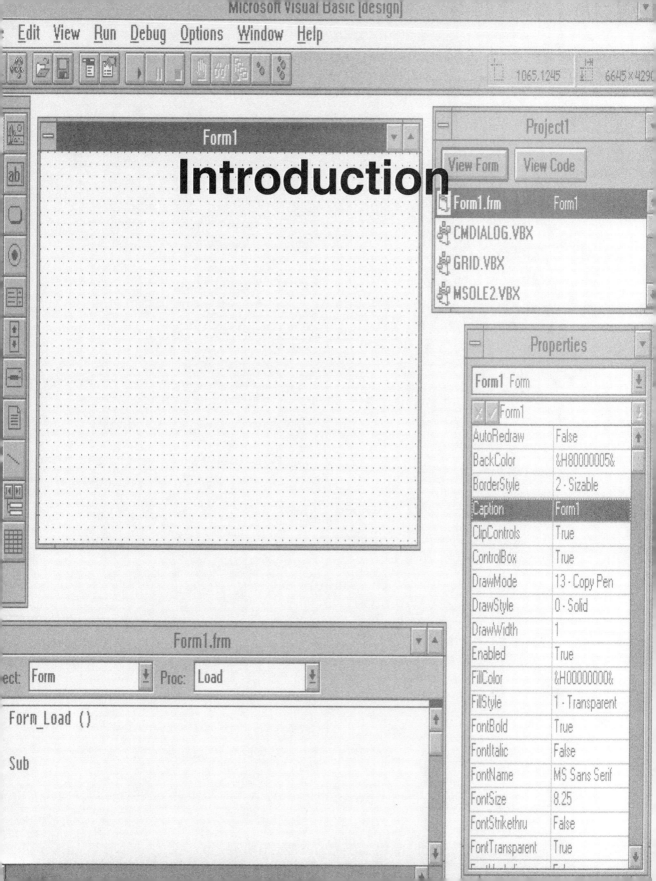

INTRODUCTION

Introduction

Who's This Book for?

This book is designed to teach you how to write useful programs in Visual Basic 3, as quickly and as easily as possible. There are two kinds of Beginners for whom this is the ideal book:

- You're a **beginner to programming** and you've chosen Visual Basic as the place to start. Great choice! Visual Basic is easy, it's fun and it's also powerful. This book will hold your hand throughout.

- You can program in another language but you're a **beginner to Visual Basic**. Again, great choice! Come in from the cold world of C or whatever language you use and enjoy. This book will teach you how Visual Basic does things in terms you'll understand. Along the way I'll give you all the background information you need on Windows Programming to help you to develop really professional applications.

What's Covered in This Book

This book is about the **Standard Edition** of Visual Basic. Newcomers with the Professional edition can also learn a great deal, but an explanation of the Professional-only stuff is beyond the scope of a beginner's guide.

Visual Basic is a big baby. Take a look at the Language Reference Manual that comes in the box. That's a 500 page manual that just lists every word in the Visual Basic lexicon, without even telling you how or when to use it. We're not going to try and look into every nook and cranny of Visual Basic. What we *are* going to do is cut a wide path through the undergrowth to a suitable clearing where we can write our own programs.

Think of this book as a tour guide to Visual Basic country. You're only here for a short period, and it's never long enough (just like a real vacation). What you *don't* want is to go down every street in town. What you *do* want is the big picture, together with enough local understanding to enable you to find your own way around without getting into tricky situations. Sure, we'll look at some of the local highlights together, but these can only ever be a taster.

So what's in the tour? There are some things you have to know, like how Visual Basic programs fit together, and what the main components are. All these fundamental building blocks are covered in detail. We then take a look at what you can actually do with Visual Basic. Just because something appears in Visual Basic doesn't mean it's in the book - we've only included those things that you can usefully use. This book gets you where you want to go.

What's Not Covered in This Book

The things omitted from the book you can live without at this stage in your Visual Basic career. The two big ones that I'll own up to now are File Handling and OLE/DDE.

> File handling is about creating and using data files on your disk. This doesn't mean program files, it means data that a program file will load into itself. Although it's covered a little in Chapter 13, I deliberately haven't spend a lot of time on it. Visual Basic let's you create and use databases easily and quickly. This means that you don't have to use disk files in order to use a lot of data in a program.

> Object Linking and Embedding and Dynamic Data Exchange (OLE and DDE) are two related subjects. They are Windows features that allow you to share and exchange information between programs. The problem is it's every bit as complex as the name suggests. There are whole books that cover just OLE on its own, so in the interests of speed I'm not going to force them on you.

What's also left out of this book are a lot of formal definitions and exhaustive lists of options. Visual Basic is a rich language, and each command has a welter of options. I'm just going to tell you what you need to know at the time. There are lots of good references, like the Visual Basic Manuals and Help Screens, that can give you all the minute detail.

Since this is a beginner's guide, I have specifically ignored the additional features in Professional edition. Whilst they are incredibly powerful and useful, they aren't necessary for everyone. In the words of a famous Vulcan, "the needs of the many are greater than the needs of the few, or the one".

I'm also not going to tell you how to actually use Windows. If you haven't already installed Windows and learnt about the incredible power it has to offer, then now is the time to do so. Throughout the course of the book, I assume you already know the basics of using a Windows program, such as how to select a menu option, or how to double-click something, and so on.

What You Need to Use This Book

Apart from a willingness to learn, you'll need access to a PC running Windows 3.1 and Visual Basic 3. Although many of the examples in the book will work under Visual Basic 2, Visual Basic 3 has a great many features that make life as a developer so much easier.

In order to install and use the samples on the disk (included with this book) you'll need a hard drive with at least 3 megabytes of space. It's also important that you *do* install the samples from the disk as they form an integral part of the book's tutorial style.

To install the examples disk, place the disk in your A: drive and select Run from the File menu in Program Manager. In the box type A:\Setup. From there the installation program takes over.

Conventions

We have used a number of different styles of text and layout in the book to help differentiate between the different kinds of information. Here are examples of the styles we use and an explanation of what they mean:

Try It Outs - How do They Work?

1 Each step has a number.

2 Follow the steps through.

3 Then read How It Works to find out what's going on.

> Advice, hints, or warnings that you really shouldn't ignore, come in boxes like this.

> Background information that you could live without, but is interesting and informative, comes in boxes like this.

> **Important Words** like names and definitions are in a bold type font.

> Words that appear on the screen in menus like the <u>F</u>ile or <u>W</u>indow menu are in a similar font to what you see on screen.

> Keys that you press on the keyboard like *Ctrl* and *Enter* are in italics.

> Visual Basic code has two fonts. If it's a word that we're talking about in the text, say when discussing the **For..Next** loop, its in a bold font. If it's a block of code that you can type in as a program and run, then it's also in a blue box:

```
Sub cmdQuit_Click()
    End
End Sub
```

> If a line of code begins with this symbol ↳ , it means that it is a continuation of the previous line - there just wasn't enough room to fit it on the page. Don't insert a hard return when typing it into the computer.

> All filenames are in capitals, like **CONTROL.MAK**.

These are all designed to make sure that you know what it is you're looking at. I hope they make life easier.

How to Get the Most Out of This Book

This book is designed as a hands-on tutorial. That means you have to get your hands on the keyboard as often as possible. Throughout the book there are Try It Outs! which is where you'll find step by step instructions for creating and running a Visual Basic program. This program illustrates the concept that's currently being explained. Some of the larger Try It Outs! use code that I've already prepared for you on the companion disk.

I also use the Try It Outs! to teach you new concepts when it's better to see it in action first, rather than bury it in the text. After each Try It Out! there is a How It Works section that explains what's going on. As the programs get longer later in the book, some of the How It Works sections themselves get quite large. Please read them through. It's all part of the plan.

There are a lot of what technical writers call forward references in this book. These are where I say 'Don't worry about this difficult concept here. I'll explain it in chapter *whatever*'. This kind of reckless behavior will preclude me from ever entering the Logical Writers Hall Of Fame, but frankly I don't care. What I do really care about is that you have exciting and interesting programs to play with as early as possible in the book, and to do that I sometimes have to ask to you to take things on trust. Where I do use language elements that we haven't covered properly yet I'll tell you. And believe me, they are all there later on, as promised.

When you've finished the book, the one thing you can be sure of is that you'll be hungry for more. You'll have an excellent grounding in Visual Basis, but that's only the beginning. The whole world of Visual Basic development will be at your feet. To help you decide what to do next I've put some unashamedly personal and opinionated advice into Appendix A - **Where Do We Go From Here?**

Tell Us What You Think

We have tried to make this book accurate, enjoyable and honest. But what really matters is what it does for you. Please let us know your views by either returning the reply card in the back of the book, or by contacting us at Wrox Press. The easiest way is to use email:

feedback@wrox.demon.co.uk
Compuserve: 100062,2152

Chapter One

Welcome to Visual Basic

CHAPTER 1

Welcome to Visual Basic

As you will hear time and time again in this book, and other journals, the best way to learn about something as interactive as Visual Basic is to actually sit down at a computer and try things out. In this chapter you will do just that.

You will learn about:

- The Visual Basic desktop
- What makes up a Visual Basic program
- Event-driven programming, and how it works in Visual Basic
- How to write actual code in Visual Basic, and where to put it
- How to design, create, install and run a complete Visual Basic application

A Quick Tour of Visual Basic

First of all, we'll get comfortable with the Visual Basic environment, and then we'll have a go at creating a complete Visual Basic application from start to finish. The program we'll create will hardly be a program at all, but in experimenting with it, you will get an all-round feel for what Visual Basic has to offer.

After a brief tour of the Visual Basic desktop, we will take a good look at **forms**, the mainstay of any Visual Basic program. We'll experiment with properties and even write a small amount of code. After you have created a real Windows application, you will then learn how to save all the components of your program as a Visual Basic project. Finally, you will create an executable program that can be run outside of Visual Basic. Along the way we will look at some of the unique design features that make Visual Basic such an exciting programming tool.

Fasten your seatbelt, we are going on a lightning tour of Visual Basic!

The Opening Visual Basic Screen

When you click on the Visual Basic icon to load and run Visual Basic, a confusing array of windows, icons and scroll bars appears. These are usually overlaying Program Manager.

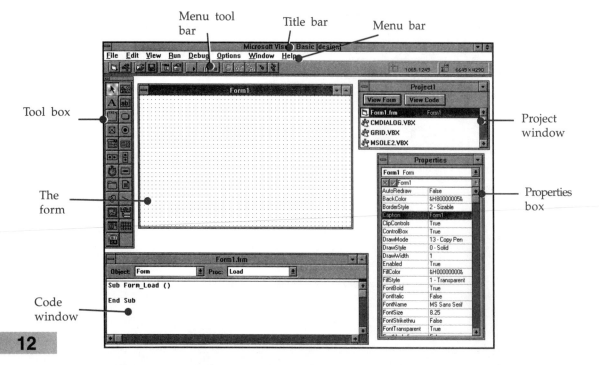

Don't panic if your screen appears different to the one pictured here. Visual Basic remembers how the windows and toolbars were arranged on the screen the last time it was used, and automatically sets itself up in the same way each time you run it. To be honest, the way that Visual Basic overlays Program Manager, or in fact any other program you may have hiding in the background, can be at best annoying and at worst distracting. Many Visual Basic developers prefer to minimize all other windows applications that might be running in order to keep the screen as uncluttered as possible.

Let's take a look at what all these windows and buttons mean.

Visual Basic Menus

At the top of the screen, just as with any other Windows program, you have the title bar and menus.

```
                    Microsoft Visual Basic [design]
File   Edit   View   Run   Debug   Options   Window   Help
```

The title bar shows you that you are currently in Microsoft Visual Basic, and reminds you of exactly what you are doing. On my screen, and hopefully on yours, the title bar reads Microsoft Visual Basic [design]. This means that Visual Basic is currently in design mode, waiting for you to begin designing and writing your new Windows program.

Since it was written by Microsoft, Visual Basic is a truly standard Windows program. The File menu allows you to load and save your work, the Edit menu provides familiar options to cut and paste sections of text, and so on. In fact the only menu headings that may appear unfamiliar are the Run and Debug menus.

All of the menus work just as they would in any other Windows program. If you point at the File menu for example, and click the left mouse button once, a list of options for dealing with files appears.

New Project	
Open Project...	
Sa**v**e Project	
Sav**e** Project As...	
New **F**orm	
New MD**I** Form	
New **M**odule	
A**d**d File...	Ctrl+D
Remove File	
Save File	Ctrl+S
Save File **A**s...	Ctrl+A
Load Text...	
Save **T**ext...	
Print...	Ctrl+P
Ma**k**e EXE File...	
1 \BG2VB\CHAP15\CODE\VALIDATE.MAK	
2 \DEVELOPS\SALES\CONTACTS.MAK	
3 \BG2VB\BUGTRAK.MAK	
4 \BG2VB\CHAP07\CODE\MSGBOX.MAK	
E**x**it	

Don't worry too much at the moment about what all the menu headings and options mean - the easiest way to learn Visual Basic is by trying it out. That's exactly what we are going to do.

The Toolbar

Underneath the menu headings is a rather complex-looking toolbar.

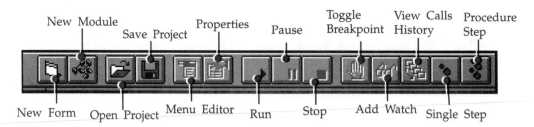

The icons on the toolbar provide an easy way for you to perform common operations without having to plow through the menus. For example, the left-most icon does the same as the New Form item on the File menu, the right-most icon does the same as the Procedure Step item on the Debug menu. Again, don't worry too much about what all the buttons mean at this stage - you'll pick them up with ease as we write a simple program later on.

Forms

In the center of the screen there is a blank window entitled Form1.

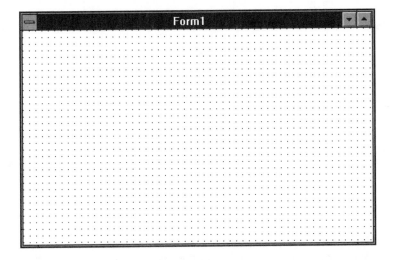

Forms are central to everything you do in Visual Basic. When your program is running, the user sees the forms as normal windows. In these windows the user selects menu options, clicks icons that you have drawn, or enters data into text boxes you have arranged.

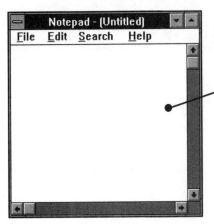

The window in which this typical application operates is derived from a form. It's your job as a programmer to get to such a point from the blank form you see on your screen.

We can compare the process of writing a Visual Basic program to the job of an artist. He starts with a blank piece of canvas. In our case this would be the form. The artist, equipped with a palette of different colors and brushes then begins to lay down images on his canvas. In the same way, Visual Basic programmers lay down **controls**, such as command buttons, text boxes and so on, onto their 'canvas', the form. When the work is complete the artist exhibits his masterpiece to a waiting public, who sees not a canvas sheet, but a painting. When the Visual Basic programs are complete, they are shipped to the user, who sees the elements of a Windows application and not empty and confusing Visual Basic forms.

Visual Basic Program Code

There are two sides to forms: what appears in the form window and what doesn't. Your user sees and interacts with the visible aspect. The invisible aspect is the form **code.** This is program text which you enter to tell the computer exactly what you want the program to do.

If you have never written a computer program before, code is the collection of English-like commands, which tell the computer what to do in a step-by-step way. In the past, programmers spent hours keying in page after page of program code before seeing anything actually work on screen. Thankfully times have changed and the amount of traditional coding required in writing a Visual Basic program is very small.

> If you have already come across other programming languages, such as C, Pascal or even the original BASIC, then you are in for an easy ride. The Visual Basic language is really a hybrid of these languages incorporating many of their best features, as well as features from older languages such as Algol and Fortran. However, the strongest influence in Visual Basic is, as its name suggests, the BASIC programming language. If you have already come across BASIC, the structure of the programs we'll write later on will appear very familiar, even if the commands themselves look somewhat alien.

Try It Out - Viewing the Code Window

It is likely that the window missing from your screen at the moment is the code window. This doesn't normally appear immediately when you start Visual Basic, so let's make it appear.

1 Move the mouse over the form on your screen, and double-click the left mouse button.

Close the window by clicking the control box in the top left corner of the window, or by pressing *Ctrl-F4*.

The code window will appear for whatever control or form you select, in this case your form labeled Form1

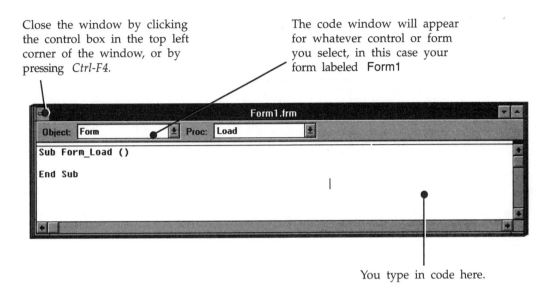

You type in code here.

You can also use function keys to open and close the code window.

2 Move the mouse to the control or form whose code window you want to look at, and click the left mouse button once to select it. Then, press *F7*.

There are two other ways to see what code is present in your program. The first is to use the View Procedures Window.

3 When the code window appears, press *F2*. A dialog box comes up showing you all the files with code in your project, and the names of the code routines within each.

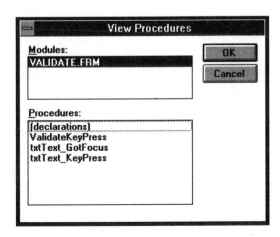

Close this dialog box by clicking the OK button, and then close the code window.

The second way to see the code in your program is to use the Project Window.

4 When the project box appears, click on the name of your form once, and then click on the View Code command button. Once again, the code window pops into view.

The title bar shows the file name of the form you are writing code for.

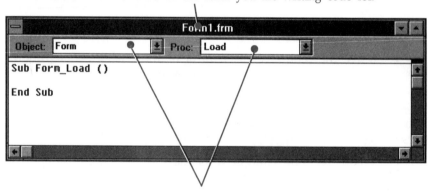

Directly beneath the title bar are two list boxes showing specifically which area of the form this piece of code refers to.

Objects and Events

In Visual Basic the majority of the code you write deals with a combination of two things: **objects** and their **events**.

▶ Objects are the elements that make up your program's user interface. Forms and controls such as command buttons and radio buttons are classed as objects.

▶ Events are the actions which are performed on a particular object, usually as a result of the user doing something. For example, if a user clicks a command button in your program, Visual Basic translates this action into a **click** event, and runs any of the code you have written to handle this event.

Event Handlers

The two list boxes at the head of the code window give you additional information on exactly what you are writing code for. The list box on the left, labeled Object: shows that we are writing code for the form object itself. The list box on the right, labeled Proc: (for **Procedure**) indicates that we are writing code to respond to a form load event. This event occurs when a form is loaded into memory before being displayed on screen. We will look at this more closely later.

Although each control and form in your project can respond to hundreds of different events, you don't need to write a single line of code unless you really want to. For instance, you may not want a command button to do anything when it's clicked - so don't write anything for the click event. You only need to write event code when you really want something to happen in response to the event; Visual Basic is a very undemanding environment, which lets you do as much or as little as you want.

Controls and the Toolbox

The next stop on our whirlwind tour of the Visual Basic environment is the toolbox.

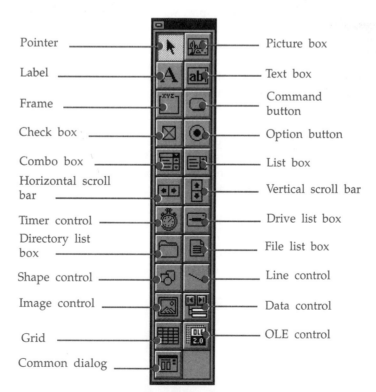

Pointer	Picture box
Label	Text box
Frame	Command button
Check box	Option button
Combo box	List box
Horizontal scroll bar	Vertical scroll bar
Timer control	Drive list box
Directory list box	File list box
Shape control	Line control
Image control	Data control
Grid	OLE control
Common dialog	

The toolbox contains icons for each control you can draw onto your form. Controls put the **Visual** into Visual Basic. You use controls in Windows all the time: typing into text boxes, clicking option buttons and so on. In fact almost every functional element of a Windows program is a control.

Each control, such as text box or command button, has three aspects to it.

> ◗ A graphical representation that you see when you click on a control in the tool box and then place the control onto your form.

> ◗ Properties which govern the way it looks and behaves, determining for example its color, the text that appears as a caption, its shape and size and so on.

> ◗ Event codes which are Visual Basic commands you enter to tell a control what to do when it gets clicked, moved, or dragged over and so on.

Adding Controls Adds Power

If you are using the Professional Edition of Visual Basic you will find that there are a great many more icons in your tool palette than in the above screen shot. The Professional Edition has many more controls than the standard one. Enhanced 3D versions of many of the standard icons are included, as are controls for drawing graphs, playing sampled sounds, communicating over modems, animating icons and many more.

The Professional Edition also has much improved support for databases. It has tools to create help files for your applications. If you plan to develop full-scale, multi-user database applications with on-line help and a very sophisticated 3D look, then you will probably find yourself yearning for the Professional Edition.

One of the strongest features of Visual Basic is the way in which its capabilities can grow through the addition of more powerful controls. Controls that you add in to the standard toolbox are known as **custom controls**, or **VBXs (Visual Basic eXtensions).**

Many companies supply VBXs which greatly enhance Visual Basic. Adding these VBXs to the project makes additional icons appear in the toolbox. The range of VBXs available is staggering, with companies supplying VBXs to do everything from providing enhanced database support, to printing bar-codes, or displaying the latest type of graphics file. Take a look at the toolbox below. This has a number of controls which aren't included with either the standard or professional editions of Visual Basic.

You won't recognize these controls as they are custom controls that I have added into my tool box.

The Project Window

To understand how useful the **project window** is, you need to understand what makes up a project in Visual Basic.

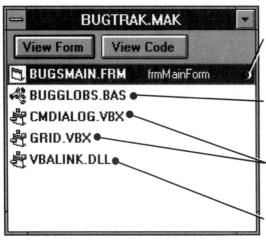

Forms include all the code that is directly attached to that form - and the controls placed on it, provided that these controls are standard parts of Visual Basic.

Code modules are pieces of code that are not directly attached to a particular form, but are still used by the program.

VBXs are not a standard part of Visual Basic, and hence have to be tacked onto your project as an additional item.

This file with a DLL extension is also a VBX.

Each form, module and VBX has its own file name, and is stored on the hard disk as a separate file. For instance, you could have a login form in your project which is stored on disk as a file called **LOGIN.FRM**.

The project file simply tells Visual Basic which of these forms, modules and so on are used in your project. The project's file name can be anything you want, but normally ends in the letters **.MAK**.

The reason **.MAK** is used instead of something more logical like **.PRJ** is simply tradition. It actually refers to a makefile in languages such as C, so Microsoft thought it would be a good idea to keep it as a standard.

The project window simply shows you a list of all the files in your project. By double-clicking the name of a form in the project window, the form appears on screen. By clicking a form and hitting the Show Code button, the form's event code appears on screen.

The Properties Box

Every form and control has properties. Even some objects that you can't manipulate at all at design time, such as the screen and the printer, have properties. Properties control the appearance and behavior of the objects in Visual Basic. These are some of the ways that forms can be customized using their properties.

This text is set by the Caption property.

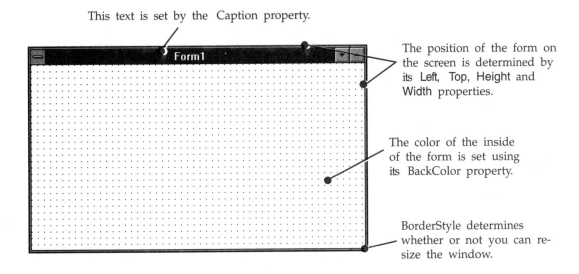

The position of the form on the screen is determined by its **Left**, **Top**, **Height** and **Width** properties.

The color of the inside of the form is set using its BackColor property.

BorderStyle determines whether or not you can resize the window.

The **properties box** allows you to set and view the properties of your forms and controls at design-time. Design-time is before you actually run your program.

The **object box** tells you which control or form you are referring to. You can get a list of all the objects on your form by clicking the little arrow at the side.

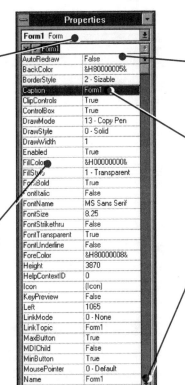

The **settings box** shows the property that is currently highlighted. You type in changes to properties here. It's like an editing window.

This property is highlighted, ready for editing in the settings box.

Each property has a standard name. You can change properties in here at design-time, or with your code at run-time.

Forms have many properties - 43 to be exact! There are more down here that you can get to using the scroll bars.

By far the best way to get to grips with properties is to use them. We will do this in the next section.

Your First Visual Basic Program

Having had a quick look around, it's time to see just how easy it is to produce Windows programs using Visual Basic. The program we will write is extremely simple, but it will serve to illustrate all the major steps we are going to take in subsequent chapters, when we write real Visual Basic programs.

Filling Out the Forms

Forms are not the passive background canvas that our painting analogy suggests. With 43 different properties that can be manipulated, and a host of events to respond to, they are the foundation of your program. In this section, we'll get a glimpse of what forms can do.

Try It Out - Customizing Your Forms

1 If you don't currently have Visual Basic running, then run it by double-clicking its icon in Program Manager.

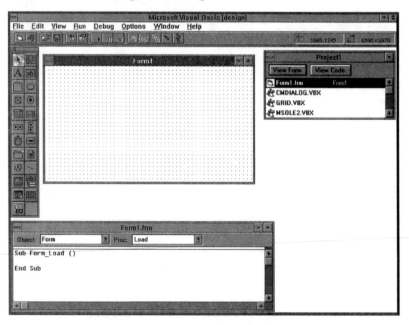

2 Although the form you work with in Visual Basic at design-time is supposed to closely resemble the form in the final program, the reality is somewhat different. To see this run the current project by doing one of the following actions.

Either: Hit *F5*

Or: Click on the run button in the toolbar

Or: Select <u>S</u>tart from the <u>R</u>un menu.

After a short pause the program will run and the main form will be displayed.

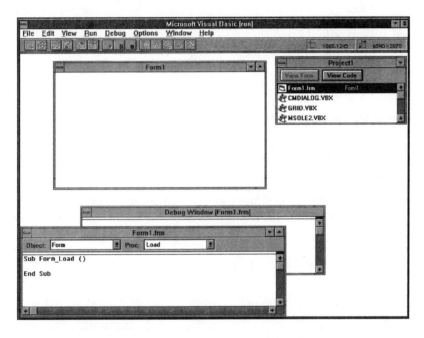

Even though we haven't written any code or placed anything functional on the form, the program can still do a lot.

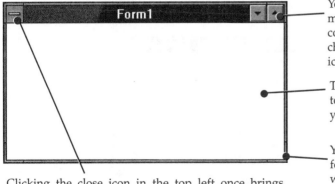

You can also click the minimize and maximize buttons in the top right corner of the form to dramatically change its size, or even turn it into an icon.

The window looks almost identical to the way the form looks when you are in design mode.

You can move and re-size the form just as you would a window in any other program.

Clicking the close icon in the top left once brings up the standard Windows control menu, allowing you to quit the application, switch to a different one, or again change the size of the window.

To write the equivalent program in a language such as C would require in excess of 150 lines of code.

3 To stop the program running either:

▶ Click the stop icon in Visual Basic.

▶ Close the window by double-clicking its control box in the corner.

▶ Press *ALT-F4* which also closes the window.

▶ Select End from the Run menu.

Programming Using Properties

Once the program has stopped running and Visual Basic has reverted to design mode, we can take a look at the properties of our new form. To display the properties box or window:

▶ Click once on the form to select it as the current object. You can tell when a particular window is selected as its title bar is highlighted.

▶ Or, press *F4* to display the properties window.

▶ Or, select Properties from the Windows menu.

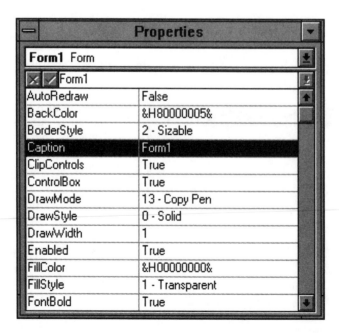

Try It Out - Changing a Property

1 Click on the form to select it and then press *F4* to display the properties box.

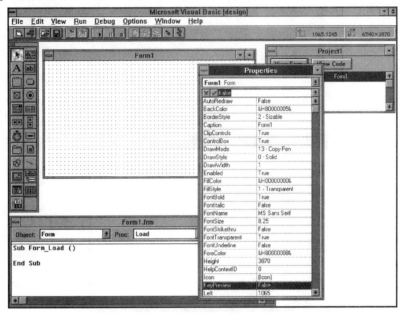

2 Hold down *Shift*, *CTRL* and *C*. This moves you to the first property in the list beginning with the letter *C*. If you keep on pressing *Shift*, *CTRL* and *C* the highlight will move again and soon fall on the ControlBox property.

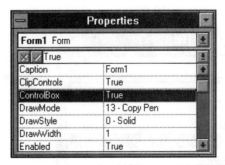

3 To the right of the words Control Box you will see the word True. This means that there is a control box attached to the form at present, so that when the form is run you can click the control box to shut it down.

4   Change this to **False**, either by double-clicking the word **True**, or by clicking the settings box at the top of the properties box and typing in **False**.

5   Try finding the properties called **MaxButton** and **MinButton** and change them both to **False** in the same way.

6   Did you notice that nothing actually changed on the form on screen? Now run the program again, either by pressing *F5* or by clicking the run button.

Notice how different the form looks now.

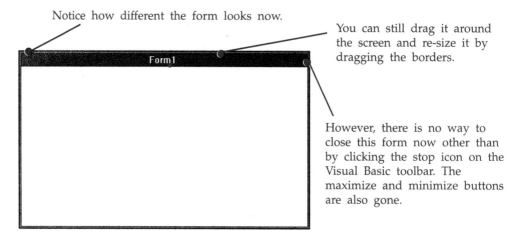

You can still drag it around the screen and re-size it by dragging the borders.

However, there is no way to close this form now other than by clicking the stop icon on the Visual Basic toolbar. The maximize and minimize buttons are also gone.

7   Stop the program. Just to emphasize the point try this.

8   Find the property called **BorderStyle**. The text to the right of the property name should say **2-Sizable**.

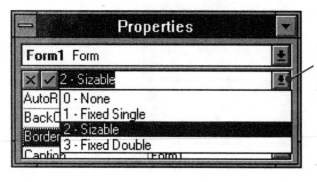

You can see all the alternatives for the property by clicking the arrow at the side to drop down the list box.

9   Keep double-clicking the **BorderStyle** field until it says **1-Fixed Single**. Nothing appears to have changed on the form at the moment.

10 Now find the Caption property. Double-click on the text that says Form1.

11 Press *BkSp* to delete the current caption, then type in a new one.

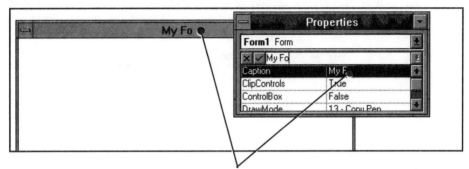

This time your design form does change. The title bar changes as you type a new caption.

The rest of our form doesn't seem so different at design-time.

Your form still appears to have a title bar.

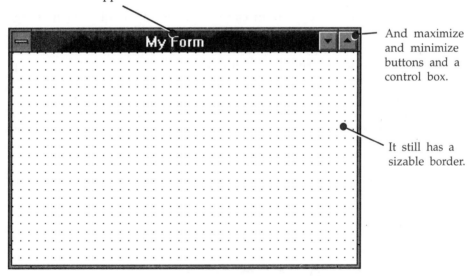

And maximize and minimize buttons and a control box.

It still has a sizable border.

Press *F5* to run your application to see what it looks like at run-time.

12 The result should be a plain white box with a single line border round the outside. There is no way to move this window, re-size it, or close it. Since you deleted the form's caption, Visual Basic automatically decides not to give the form a scroll bar. To stop the program click on the Visual Basic stop icon again.

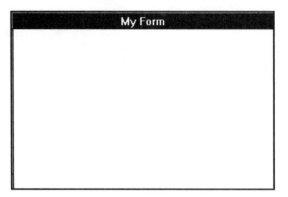

Changing Properties Interactively

Certain properties of your form can be changed without even noticing it. For example, with Visual Basic in design mode, dragging the form to a new position, or changing its size will cause the Width, Height, Top and Left properties to change. This is an important point to remember. By simply moving the form around in design mode, you are actually programming Visual Basic by telling it to display the form in a different position. If you re-size the form then the new size will be adopted by the window in the running program; if you move the form, then the window the user sees will appear in the same position on their screen as the form does on yours.

Of course, simply being able to change the caption of a form, or its border type, doesn't really make for a best selling Windows program. Real functionality can be added to your programs by adding code to handle the form's **events**.

Event Driven Programming

Events are what sets Visual Basic apart from other versions of the BASIC programming language, or languages such as C and Pascal. When a traditional BASIC or C program is run, the computer trots through the program code line-by-line, starting at the top and following a specific route to the end, as defined by the programmer. In Visual Basic the program starts by displaying a form, or by executing a small fragment of code. However, from that point onwards, it's the user who determines which parts of the program code are run next.

A New Way of Thinking

Think about making a cup of coffee. In a traditional programming language you could write a program to make a cup of coffee by doing the following:

1   Fill kettle with water

2   Start kettle

3   Place coffee in cup.

4   Place milk in cup.

5   Wait until kettle has boiled.

6   Pour water into cup.

This is pretty simple stuff to follow. A good way to think of the same task in Visual Basic would be:

1   Show coffee, kettle, water, milk and cup to user.

2   Let user make the coffee.

The user would then be able to use each of the components shown, in whatever sequence he or she wanted in order to make the coffee. As a programmer in this situation, you would just provide small fragments of code to handle specific events. For example, once the user actually turns the kettle on, Visual Basic will run the code you have written to deal with that particular event, which would probably involve heating up the water and such like. The actual order of events required to end up with a cup of coffee is left to the user and not forced on them by the programmer.

Making the Transition

You can write code with Visual Basic in the traditional way but that serves no purpose. Your users will be using your Visual Basic program because they like the flexibility of Windows. They enjoy the freedom to do what they want, when they want. Besides, writing a traditional (let's just call it old-fashioned) program in Visual Basic actually requires a great deal more effort than writing an event-driven one. The net result of all your extra effort is a program that users hate and refuse to use!

Try It Out

Try It Out - Comparing DOS and Windows Applications

1 When you install the sample programs from the disk, a program called **AGE.EXE** is installed along with the Visual Basic stuff. Go to DOS now, CD to the directory where you installed the samples and type *AGE*. Then press *Enter*.

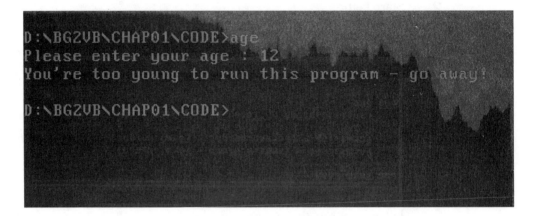

```
D:\BG2VB\CHAP01\CODE>age
Please enter your age : 12
You're too young to run this program - go away!

D:\BG2VB\CHAP01\CODE>
```

2 The program simply asks you to enter your age and displays a message according to the age you enter.

3 Now go back to windows, into Visual Basic and load the **AGE.MAK** project. From the File menu, select Open Project and use the list boxes to select the project and load it.

4 When you have loaded the project, run it in the normal way.

Can you see the difference?!

Where Code Fits in Visual Basic

This diagram illustrates exactly how the user, your form, and your form's event code all fit together in Windows.

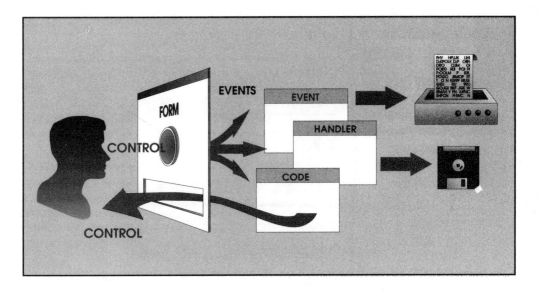

All controls such as the text boxes, command buttons and forms in a Visual Basic program have a set of predefined events which you can add code to. With forms for example, there is a **Load** event triggered the first time the form is loaded up and displayed. You can add code to the **Load** event to do various jobs at set-up time, like positioning the form automatically, or displaying some standard values on the form and so on. There is also an **Unload** event that is triggered when the form is closed down, either because the user wanted it closed, or because you closed it yourself. Each code fragment is called an **Event Handler**.

Your First Visual Basic Event Handler

Time to write some code I think! As we saw earlier, each form has certain events associated with it, one of the most important of which is the **Load** event. The **Load** event is triggered whenever a form is first loaded and just before it is displayed. A common use for this event is to center the form, by placing code in the **Load** event which updates the form's position in relation to the screen, using the form's **Top** and **Left** properties. We will use this feature to create a simple program to tell us today's date in the center of the screen.

Try It Out - Writing an Event Handler

1 If Visual Basic is not running then load it up now. If you have followed the examples so far, and still have the skeleton form hanging around, then start afresh:

2 Select New Project from the File menu.

3 Since we have made changes to the form's properties Visual Basic will check with you whether or not you want to save your work on disk.

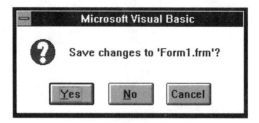

4 Click on the No button when asked if you want to save the form.

5 Click on the No button when asked if you want to save the project.

6 After a short pause you will end up with a new project complete with a clean, new form.

Resize the form so it looks like this.

7   Next, we need somewhere to display the date. The easiest way to do this in Visual Basic is to place a label control onto your form, and then put the value of today's date into it.

> A control in Visual Basic is an object that sits on your form. They have particular functions. This sounds general, but that's just what controls are: general. They range from buttons, to lists, to more specialized controls that access databases. Adding a control to your form allows you to use the facilities of that control in your program. In this case we want to show some text on the form, so the label control will allow us to do that. Chapter 2 gives you a proper introduction to controls. For now, just take it step-by-step, and we'll cover the bigger picture later.

8   To add the label control to your form, click on its icon in the toolbox.

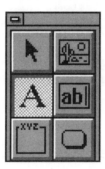

9   Now use the cross-hair cursor to draw a box on the form in the shape and size you want for the label, holding down your mouse button all the time as you draw. Make it about this size:

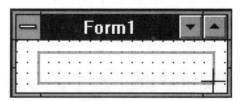

10   When it's the right size, release the mouse button and the label appears.

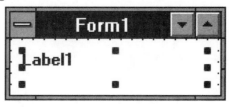

11 Visual Basic has named the control Label1, the default name for a label control. We'll use this name to address the control in our code.

12 Let's run the program now for the hell of it and see what it looks like. Press *F5* or hit the run button.

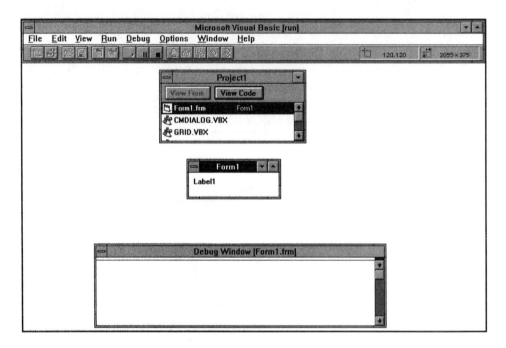

13 Stop the program by clicking the stop button on the toolbar. We now need to add some code to the project to center the form, and to place today's date into the label. When you want to add code to a form, the easiest way to display the code window is to simply double-click the form itself. A code window will appear with the top of the window showing.

14 Clicking the down arrow to the right of the word Load will show a list of all the events that can happen to a form.

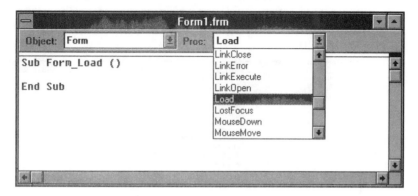

15 For now though just select Load. The main area of the code window shows the code that makes up this event's **sub**procedure. A subprocedure is a piece of code that performs a specific operaton.

16 Click in the code window and type in code so that the subprocedure looks like this.

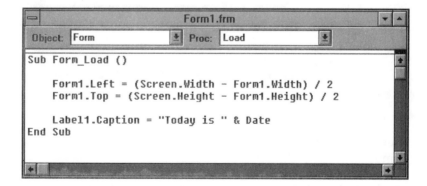

17 The code is explained in detail in the **How It Works** section that follows.

In future I may not show you a screen-shot of exactly how the code window should look; use the Object and Proc list boxes to find the event you need to write code for. You will find it really easy to just bring up a code window, type a couple of screens full of code and then find you have put it in the wrong event. Always check where you are, and where you should be!

18 Try running the program now by pressing *F5* or clicking the run icon (from now on I will assume that you can remember how to run a program). The form will appear on screen as in the other examples, except now it will always appear dead center of the screen. In it is today's date.

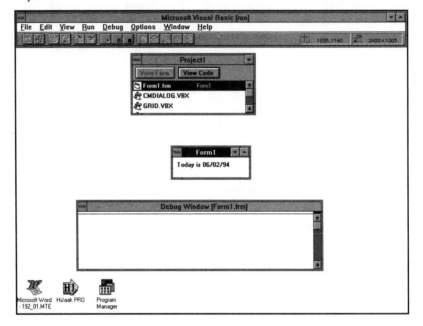

19 Stop the program running by double-clicking the form's control box.

Typing In Code

Newcomers often get concerned about the way their code looks in the code window.

As far as Visual Basic is concerned though, as long as you spell the commands correctly, and put spaces between each command, then it doesn't really care how you go about arranging your code. If you type something incorrectly then Visual Basic will tell you straight away. For example, try to change the minus signs (-) to the word Minus. When you move to the next line, you should see the following:

If you now hit the OK button on this dialog box, Visual Basic returns you to the code window and highlights the offending lines. Change the lines back to how they should be.

As a rule though, indenting using the *Tab* key makes blocks of your code stand out clearly. This is a real help with debugging. Visual Basic gets upset if you treat the code window like a wordprocessor. Single commands, such as each one in the example above, must be kept on the same line. If you reach the right-hand edge of the code window when you are typing, don't panic and don't press *Enter*! The code window will scroll to keep up with your typing. Often, if you do hit *Enter* in the middle of a line of code, Visual Basic will wake you up with an error message complaining that it can't understand what you are trying to say.

However, Visual Basic helps you in a positive way by doing its best to format all your lines of code in a standard way. It spaces out your code, and adds capital letters to words it recognizes. This makes for neater and safer code.

The other important issue when writing event code is not to delete the first or last lines of code; that is, the line beginning with **Sub** and the line that says **End Sub**. If you do delete them, Visual Basic won't know where your code starts and ends, so try to re-type them again yourself. Failing that, drag the mouse over your code to highlight it, then cut the code (select Cut from the Edit menu), re-select the event you want and Paste what you just cut back in again.

Did you notice how Visual Basic makes parts of each line a different color? Colors are used in Visual Basic to show you which parts of a line it recognizes as Visual Basic instructions, which parts are names you have given things (such as Form1 referring to form), and which parts are special Visual Basic symbols, such as the / (slash) symbol meaning divide by. As you type in each line of code, Visual Basic automatically checks it to make sure it makes sense.

How It Works

Let's take a look at the **Form_Load()** event in the last program line by line.

```
Sub  Form_Load()

    Form1.Left  =(Screen.Width  -  Form1.Width)  / 2
    Form1.Top  =(Screen.Height  -  Form1.Height)  / 2

    Label1.Caption = "Today is " & Date

End  Sub
```

The first line **Sub Form_Load()** tells Visual Basic where the code for the load event actually starts. The **Sub** command tells Visual Basic that the code is a **subprocedure.** There is another kind of code block in Visual Basic known as a **function.** We will cover this in Chapter 10. The **Form_Load** bit is the name of the subprocedure. Visual Basic automatically names any event code you write to indicate the object it deals with and the event that will trigger its execution - in this case **form** and **load.**

> Although you can change the name of the procedure yourself it's unwise to do so, since Visual Basic will be unable to relate the event procedure to the appropriate object.

The two brackets () are used to hold something called **parameters**. These are values that are passed to a procedure to allow it to do its job, such as two numbers to be added together. In this case no parameters are needed. Don't worry about this now, it will all be clear later in the book.

The next line sets the **Left** property of the object called **Form1.**

```
Form1.Left =(Screen.Width - Form1.Width) / 2
```

Left is one of the properties of a form that you can select and change with the properties window. In general, if you can change a property at design-time, you can also change it at run-time through your code.

This particular line of code sets the **Left** property of the form by subtracting its width **form1.width** from the screen's width **screen.width.** The result is then divided by two to give the position of the left edge. If that all seems a little weird don't panic! As long as you understand that you can both read and write properties through code then that's the important point. The math is not really crucial to Visual Basic; in fact this particular piece of code is one of hundreds of standard routines you'll probably come across in magazines, books, bulletin boards and so on.

This calculation causes the form's horizontal position to be dead center of the screen. **Form1** is the default name given to our form. We could change it but for now it's OK as it is. Notice the periods in the middle of **Form1.Left** and **Screen.Width.** When dealing with properties in code, Visual Basic must know both the name of the object whose properties you wish to change and the property itself. The two are separated by a period. In the example here we are dealing with two objects, one called **Form1** which is our form, the other called **Screen**, which is what Visual Basic calls the screen (surprise, surprise!). The **Left** property is a number which tells Visual Basic where the left edge of the control should appear.

> The screen is actually arranged like a piece of graph paper with each tiny dot on the screen being numbered from 0 to whatever across the screen from the left, and from 0 to whatever down the screen from the top. I say 'whatever' because the maximum value across or down the screen can change depending on the way you have windows set up on your machine and on which co-ordinate system you are using. Co-ordinate systems are covered much later, in the chapter on graphics. For now, let Visual Basic handle the details in the background.

The next line of code does roughly the same as the previous one, although this time it positions the top edge of the form so that the form is now centered vertically as well as horizontally.

The line of code that inserts today's date into the label looks like this:

```
Label1.Caption = "Today is " & Date
```

There's a lot of things going on here, not all of which it makes sense to explain at the moment. Put simply, the **Caption** property of **Label1** is set to hold a phrase, (or **string** as it's officially known), that is made up of the words **Today is** and today's date, represented in our code as **Date**. The word **Date** is actually a built-in function of Visual Basic that goes and gets the date from the system clock inside your machine, and tacks it onto the end of the string. The **Caption** property of the text box holds the characters that are displayed on the form at run-time. These replace the word **Label1** which was the default value of the property we saw on the label at design time. As I said, there's a lot going on here, but I wanted to throw you in at the deep end and show you how Visual Basic can make a little code go a long way.

Finally, the line **End Sub** marks the end of the subprocedure.

Try It Out - Adding Code to the Form_Unload Event

Now let's add some code to make the form say "good-bye" when it's closed down. First of all, you need to get to the right routine in the code window.

1 If the program is still running then stop it. Double-click on the form to bring up the code window.

2 Click on the downward arrow to the right of the word Load, at the top of the code window. The event list will appear as before.

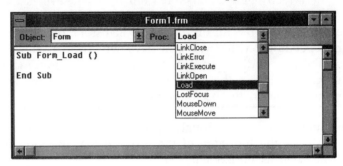

3 Use the scrollbars to find the word Unload, and select it.

4 For the Unload event, the code should read:

```
Sub Form_Unload(Cancel As Integer)

    Msgbox "Goodbye!"

End Sub
```

The **MsgBox** line displays a message box with the word **Goodbye** inside. We'll cover message boxes in full later in the book. Basically though, a message box is a ready made form which you can use to display messages to the user which they must respond to before carrying on. This is great for error messages and the ubiquitous You just formatted your hard disk style of message.

5 Try running your program now. As before the form appears centered on the screen.

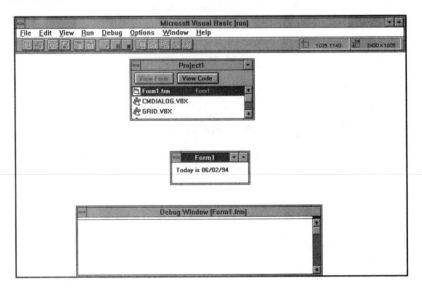

6   If you stop the program by double-clicking the control box on the form, another window appears, (this time a message box), telling you "goodbye".

How It Works

You can change the way the message box looks and behaves from within your program, but our box is the plain vanilla version which contains only text and an OK button. Clicking the OK button will end the program.

Unlike the `Load` event, the `Unload` event does contain some parameters within the brackets, in this case `Cancel As Integer`. The word `Cancel` doesn't really mean anything - it's just a name that Visual Basic has given to the parameter to show what it does. The `As Integer` tells you that `Cancel` is an integer. Integers and other weird names are covered in the section on variables in Chapter 3. For now all you need to know is that integer means whole number. By setting `Cancel` to a number you can cancel the unload event. For instance, your code may not want the form to unload in a real program if the user needed to save some data first. If this all seems confusing then don't worry, it will become clear later.

That's it for our simple application - simple being the operative word here. Although the program hardly seems worth the effort at this stage, you have actually accomplished what would take a C programmer hundreds of lines of code and hours of leafing through extremely technical documentation to accomplish. However, if this was a big project, say a customer order database, or the next best-selling Windows game, you would probably want to think about saving your hard work to disk before something nasty happens and you lose the lot. Let's see how you can do this...

Loading and Saving Your Work

We have already looked at projects and seen that they contain the names of the files and modules that make up your application. How do these forms and modules get given file names, and how does your project get a file name?

Saving Your Project

As with most other Windows programs, Visual Basic has a File menu which contains the menu items to let you load and save. In addition, there is a save button on the toolbar.

 This allows you to save your work quickly at any point without having to fumble about with the menus. Take a look at Visual Basic's File menu.

New Project	
Open Project...	
Save Project	
Save Project As...	
New Form	
New MDI Form	
New Module	
Add File...	Ctrl+D
Remove File	
Save File	Ctrl+S
Save File As...	Ctrl+A
Load Text...	
Save Text...	
Print...	Ctrl+P
Make EXE File...	
1 \BG2VB\CHAP02\CONTROL.MAK	
2 C:\DEVELOPS\VT\VT.MAK	
3 C:\DEVELOPS\PARAMENU\CODE\PARAMNU.MAK	
4 C:\DEVELOPS\PARAMENU\CDSND.MAK	
Exit	

Notice how many options there are to load, open or save something. Normally you would just use the Save Project menu item to save all your forms, including the properties such as position, size, color and so on, along with all your program code.

Try It Out - Saving Your Project

If you haven't followed the examples so far then just load up Visual Basic and we will save the default project it creates.

1 Click on the Save Project menu item and a file dialog box will appear asking you to give your form a filename.

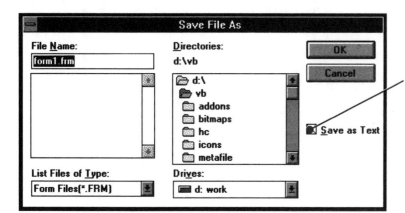

To the right in the dialog box is a check box saying <u>S</u>ave as Text. If you click this to select it, Visual Basic will save your form as a text file, otherwise it will get saved as a Visual Basic only file. The advantage of saving your forms as text is that you can edit them, and the code within them, using any normal text editor if you so desire. You could also go to DOS and print them out directly.

2 If you have more than one form or code module in your project then Visual Basic would put up a file dialog box for each one, and display a name it thinks might be suitable for the form or module. If you want to change the name, click in the File Name text box and type in an alternative.

3 Change the name of your form now. Click in the File Name text box and enter Firstfrm. Don't worry about putting .Frm after the name as Visual Basic will do that for you.

File <u>N</u>ame:

FirstFrm

4 When you are happy with the file name for your form and the directory it will be stored in, click on the OK button.

5 Visual Basic will now display a file dialog box for your project. This allows you to give a name to the project as a whole.

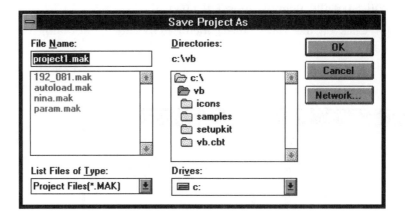

6 We will use this later on to re-load your work. Visual Basic links the file names of your forms into your project so that when you load up a project it automatically knows what all your forms and modules are called, and where they are stored on your computer. Once a project has been set up, you can load and save all the components of your program in one go.

7 For now just type in FirstPrg as the name of the project.

8 As with the form, Visual Basic will automatically tack a .MAK bit to the name. When you are happy, click on the OK button to go ahead and save the project.

9 Take a look at your File menu again. At the bottom of the menu you will now see the name of your project. This makes it very quick and easy to re-load your work whenever you come into Visual Basic; it automatically remembers the names of the last four projects that you worked on.

```
1 FIRSTPRG.MAK
2 H:\BOOKS\192\CHAP04\CODE\BREAK.MAK
3 H:\BOOKS\192\CHAP04\CODE\INSTR.MAK
4 H:\BOOKS\192\CHAP05\CODE\CONTROL.MAK
```

Once you have named all the forms and code modules in your project, saving your work becomes a much simpler task.

10 Try moving the form somewhere else on the screen and then re-select the Save Project menu item. You should notice the disk light come on for a short period of time, but this time Visual Basic won't show you any file dialog boxes. The reason for this is simple; as far as Visual Basic is concerned you have already named your constituent files, so it can just go away and re-save them all with the names you set previously.

> The next item on the menu is the Save Project As item. If you have previously saved your project, this item enables you to re-name it. Be careful though, all you are re-naming is the project itself, the .MAK file Visual Basic loads which contains a list of all your forms and code modules. You aren't re-naming the forms or code modules themselves. Personally, I've never found a realistic use for this particular menu item, but no doubt somebody amongst us will need it.

Working With Individual Project Files

The third section on the File menu enables you to work with individual files within the project.

A<u>d</u>d File...	Ctrl+D
<u>R</u>emove File	
<u>S</u>ave File	Ctrl+S
Save File <u>A</u>s...	Ctrl+A

> You may have a form somewhere in a different project which handles Userids and passwords for example. Rather than re-inventing the wheel, the Add File item could be used to add this file to your project. We'll cover this in Chapter 4.

> Equally, you may have a form in the project which is no longer needed. Selecting the Remove File menu item would remove it from your project. If you remove the first form in your project however, you will find that Visual Basic is no longer able to run your project. You can get around this by telling Visual Basic to look somewhere else for your initial form. We'll try this out later in the chapter.

Removing Files

Adding a file is easy, simply select the Add File item and a file dialog will appear asking you to select the file you wish to add. The Remove File item is a little more problematic. Selecting this option will remove the currently selected form or module.

> A module is a piece of code that isn't attached to a form as an event handler, and just floats about on its own, waiting to be called by name. More on this in Chapter 3 - Writing Code.

For example, if you were working with Form1, meaning it is on screen and is currently selected, then hitting the Remove File option will remove that form from the project.

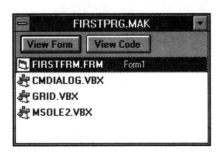

Another way of indicating which file to remove is to bring up the Project window and select a file in the list shown.

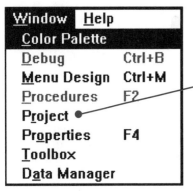

You can display the project window at any time by selecting the Project item from the Window menu at the far right-hand end of the Visual Basic menu bar.

Saving Files

The Save File and Save File As items let you save individual files in your project. You can use these to save work you have done to a form before removing it from your project. As with the Remove File item, these both work with the currently selected form or module. When you save a form, what actually gets written to the disk is a snapshot of the form's properties along with the event handler code attached to that form.

If you just wanted to save the form's code, and nothing else, then the Save Text item is what you need to use. This option saves the code as text only, meaning a plain vanilla ASCII text format. This is useful if you need your code to be edited by another text editor, or if you wish to import it into a wordprocessor document or such like. The Load Text item does almost the opposite - it loads a text file into the current code window. You may have a text file on disk which handles the form's unload event in a standard way. Once you have the code window on screen showing the form unload event you can then use the Load Text menu item to load that text file into the unload event on screen.

Used wisely, the load and save routines in Visual Basic can be used to save you a great deal of time and effort. However, if you do intend to use them, particularly the Load Text and Save Text items, then you need to put a little thought into how your programs are designed and written.

Making an Executable File

So far the program we have written has been run from within the Visual Basic environment by clicking on the run icon, or by clicking *F5*. Visual Basic wouldn't get far as a tool for serious developers if each user of a Visual Basic program had to go into Visual Basic itself to use the application. Visual Basic therefore provides a way to turn your finished programs into, effectively, stand-alone units, that can be run by clicking the appropriate icon in Program Manager, just like programs do in real life.

When your program is complete and ready to go to the users, a long way off yet I know, then it's time to make it a **.EXE,** or **executable file**. Turning your work of art into an **.EXE** is very easy.

Visual Basic follows a slightly unorthodox route to produce code that can be executed by the PC. It lies some way between a compiler and an interpreter. Let me explain.

Compilers and Interpreters

In most of its forms BASIC has been an **interpreted** language. This means that to run a BASIC program you need to have the BASIC system as well. The BASIC interpreter then chugs through each line of your code, telling the PC what to do, as and when required. It's rather like you talking to a Martian through an interpreter. Every time the Martian says something you must wait for the interpreter to translate it into something you can understand.

A compiler works as though the Martian has written down his document, which is in turn translated (compiled) into an English document. Reading the document for yourself is quicker than waiting for the interpreter to interpret.

Strictly speaking Visual Basic is compiled (cue flood of letters from Visual Basic Gurus!). The compiler translates all of your code into an executable file which the PC can work through without any need to ask Visual Basic what it thinks you want to do. In reality though it's more like giving the PC most of your code already translated, along with a phrase book for those bits that aren't. The .**EXE** file which Visual Basic produces tells your PC to look up in a file called **VBRUN300.DLL** those parts of the program which can't easily be translated.

> The compiler or interpreter issue is regularly fought over in magazines and electronic mail services. To my mind, Visual Basic is only *almost* a compiler. More often than not though you will hear it called an interpreted language, with most users aching for the day Microsoft produce a true Visual Basic compiler (the resultant .**EXE** files will run much faster than they do now).

Try It Out - Creating An EXE File

1 To begin with you need to tell Visual Basic which part of your program to run first. Select Project from the Options menu.

2 A dialog box appears, of which one of the items is a entry Start Up Form. Select the form that you want to appear first in your program and hit OK. We only have one form in our little project, so this defaults to Form1.

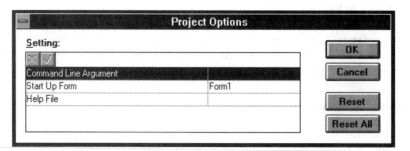

3 Select Ma<u>k</u>e EXE on the <u>F</u>ile menu.

Try It Out!

4 A dialog box appears asking you to enter a file name for your finished program, e.g. **MYAPP.EXE**, **WROXWRITE.EXE.** In the file box that appears type in Test as the program name. Visual Basic automatically adds a **.EXE** to the end of the name and so produces an executable program called **TEST.EXE**.

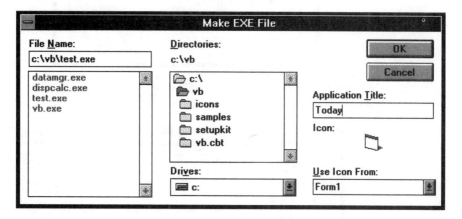

5 You then need to give your program an **Application Name** by typing something into the Application Title box. This is the name of the program that will appear when it's running and you try to switch between it and other applications. It isn't necessarily the same as its file name. Let's call this program Today.

6 Finally, hit OK, and providing there are no obvious bugs in your code, Visual Basic will produce an **EXE** file which you can then run.

Setting Up Your Program in Program Manager

7 Now go to the Program Manager screen and select New from the Program Manager File menu.

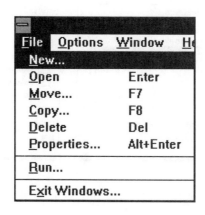

8 The following dialog appears:

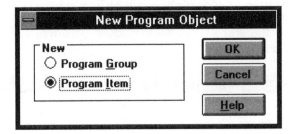

9 Click on the Program Item radio button, then on the OK command button to get to the New Item dialog box.

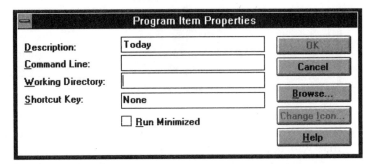

10 Enter a description for the program in the Description text box, in our case Today.

11 Next enter the full name of your. EXE program into the Command Line text box. The easiest way to do this is to hit Browse... and select the EXE file we have just placed into the VB directory.

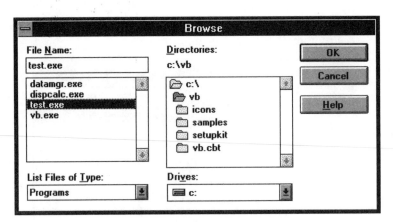

12 Hit the OK button again. Your test program will now appear in Program Manager.

13 You can double-click the icon displayed to run the program anytime now without having to run up Visual Basic first. Let's do it now after all this work.

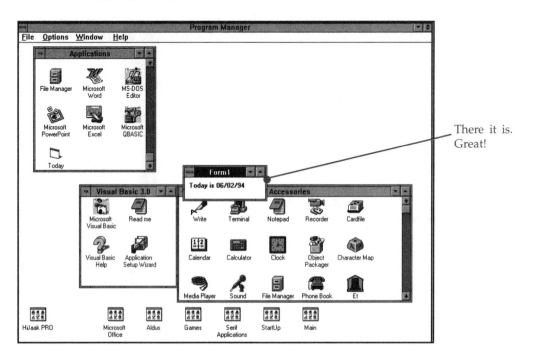

There it is. Great!

Changing the Program Icon

The program icon is a property of the first form to be displayed. The form Icon property holds the name of an icon file which will be displayed if the program is minimized, or when the program is placed within a menu on Program Manager, as it will be when you send out the finished application.

You can set the icon yourself, rather than taking the default one as we just did, by bringing up the properties window of a form, moving to the Icon property and double-clicking it.

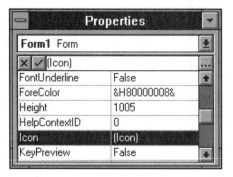

A dialog box will appear asking you to select the name an icon file. These usually end in .ICO.

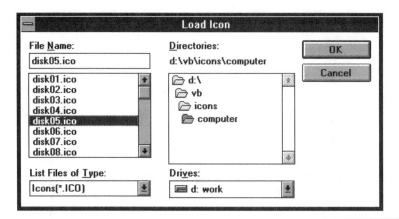

If you installed all the clip art and sample programs that came with Visual Basic, you would find a vast number of icons waiting for you in the Icons directory. Typically this will be **C:\VB\ICONS**.

After that, just go through the same steps as before, and voila! The icon of your choice!

Getting Help

Visual Basic is a complex package. Not only must you master writing programs in the Visual Basic language, but you also need to master the Visual Basic environment, as well as reading the sometimes cryptic messages it can send you. Thankfully Microsoft have supplied one of the best help systems of any development tool.

> You might think it a bit strange for an author to be recommending that you use the Help system as much as you can. You bought the book to teach you Visual Basic and you don't expect to be told to go and look it up on a help screen. However, what you really want from me is the best way to get results, and that is a combination of this book (to teach you the techniques and give you the overview), and the help screens (for the itsy-bitsy references that it is impossible to remember).

Context Sensitive Help

At any point while using Visual Basic you can hit `F1`, your panic button. This will activate the Microsoft Visual Basic Help system where you can obtain help and advice, as well as example program code for anything you come across whilst using Visual Basic.

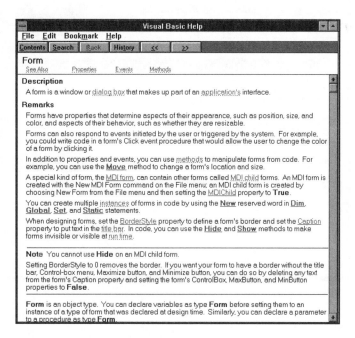

Try this out now. Bring up the form properties window, find the Name property and click on it. Now press F1. Visual Basic will display a page of text describing what exactly the name property is and what it does.

If you are a regular Windows user you have probably come across context sensitive help before. Visual Basic also provides two other routes to help. Open up the Help menu on the Visual Basic menu bar and select Contents. The Visual Basic help contents page appears from the place where you can choose to read complete documents on various aspects of Visual Basic.

Have a play with the help system for a while to get used to how it works. You may notice as you progress through the system that text in green appears. These items of text represent further topics that you can call up help on. By clicking them Visual Basic will whisk you away to another page of the help file to supply further reading, which itself may have green text enabling you to cross reference even further.

Searching for Help

By far the most common way to access help is via the Search button. Try clicking Search now.

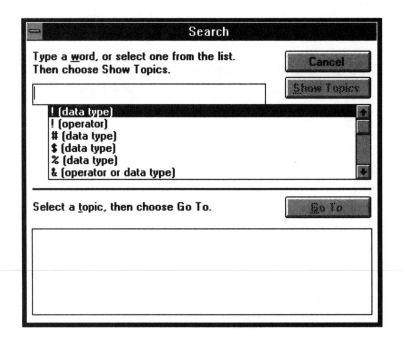

The dialog that appears is named the Search Dialog (original huh?), and it lets you find a specific topic based on a keyword you enter. Type in FORM and press Return. In the bottom section of the help dialog all the topics relating specifically to forms appear; in this case though there's only one. Double-click on it to view the help text itself. A page of help on Forms appear with green text across the top allowing you to jump to specific help on form events, properties, some example code or other related topics.

Summary

We have covered a lot of ground very quickly in this first chapter, so let's just re-cap on what we've done. Over the course of this chapter you have:

- Explored the layout of the Visual Basic environment.
- Learnt how to create a new project by starting Visual Basic.
- Discovered what a form is and what properties can do.
- Run and stopped a Visual Basic program.
- Added code to a form to respond to events affecting that form.
- Loaded and saved your work on your hard disk.
- Created an executable program (.EXE) that can be run without Visual Basic.
- Learnt how to use the Visual Basic help system.

At various points in this chapter you've got a taste of what you're going to learn in future chapters. First on the list are controls and what you can do with them, which is the subject of Chapter 2.

Command1 CommandButton

Command1

BackColor	&H80000005&
Cancel	False
Caption	Command1
Default	False
DragIcon	(none)
DragMode	0 - Manual
Enabled	True
FontBold	True
FontItalic	False
FontName	MS Sans Serif
FontSize	8.25
FontStrikethru	False
FontUnderline	False
Height	495
HelpContextID	0
Index	
Left	1680
MousePointer	0 - Default
Name	Command1
TabIndex	0
TabStop	True
Tag	
Top	480
Visible	True
Width	1215

Chapter Two

Common Controls

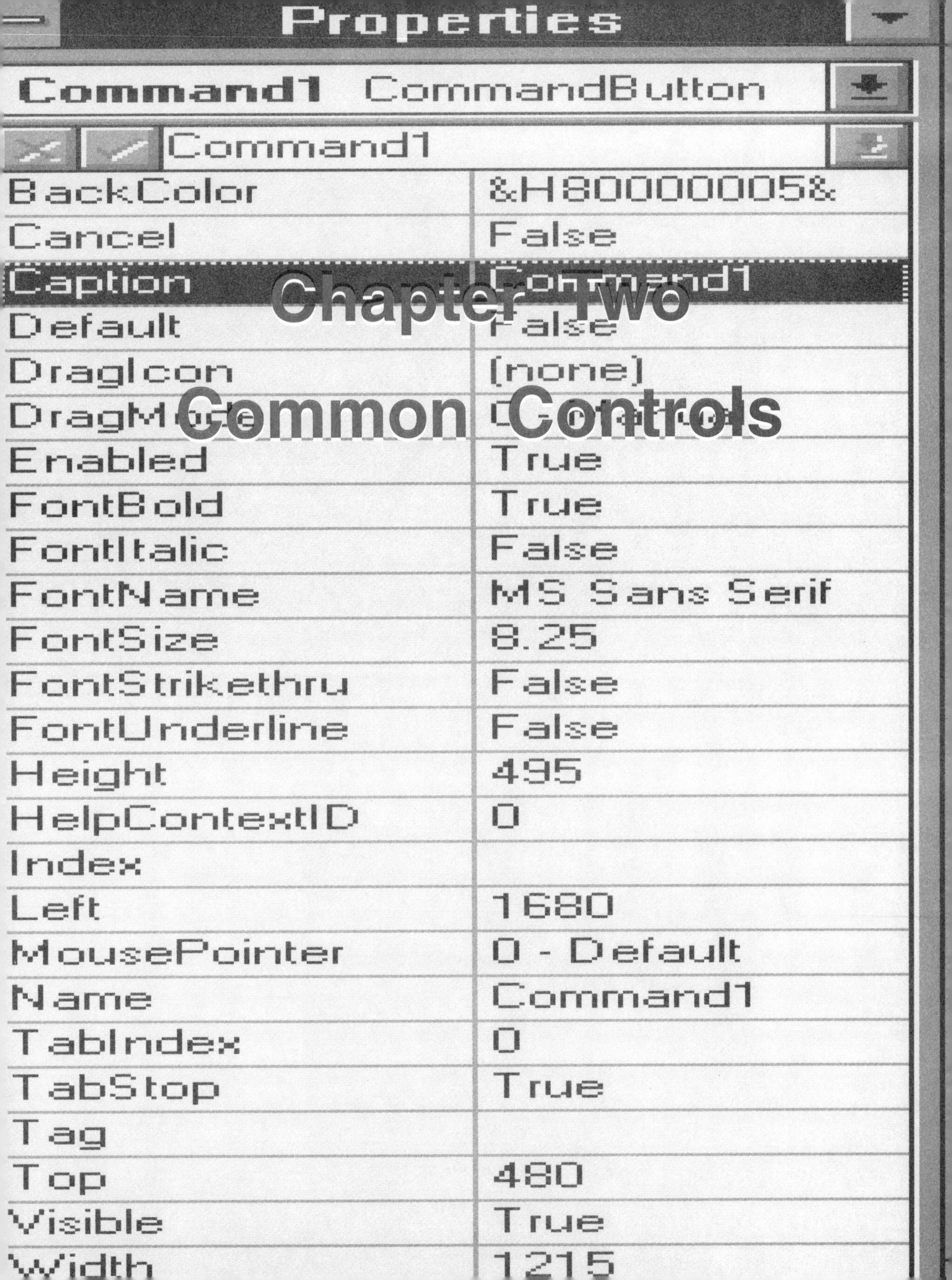

CHAPTER
2

Common Controls

Although forms are the mainstay of any Visual Basic application, they are not much use without controls. Controls are things like the text boxes, list boxes and command buttons that give your user something to interact with. They are also the means by which your program both obtains and displays its data.

In this chapter we'll look at a complete application that contains some of the most common controls. We will see how controls work, and how they fit into a Visual Basic program. You will learn about:

> How to select controls and place them on your form

> What controls really do

> How the command button is used

> Why controls have properties

> Using other common controls such as text boxes, labels, option buttons, image controls and the timer

Working With Controls

In this chapter we will start with the general techniques for selecting and placing the different controls on your form. We'll then look at how the appearance and behavior of controls can be **programmed** using properties, much as we did with forms in Chapter 1.

Once you've got a feel for controls in general, we'll use the command button as an example of a frequently-used control, and we'll run through some of the more common controls you'll use, such as **option buttons**, **check boxes**, **text boxes** and the **timer**. We will also look at some of the problems these controls bring with them, and how to overcome them.

Before we go any further let's take a look at one of the example programs from the disk supplied with this book that illustrates some of the key points about controls from this chapter. If you have not already installed these programs onto your hard disk, then now is the time to do so. Instructions for this are contained in the Introduction.

Try It Out - Controls in Action

1 Using the Open Project item on the File menu, load the project called **CONTROL.MAK**.

2 When you have loaded the project, run it by pressing *F5* or by clicking the run icon in the toolbar.

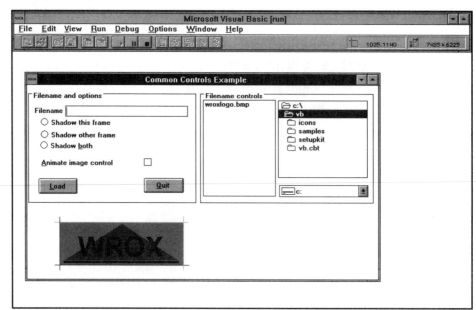

This is a fairly simple program which allows you to view small graphics files and move them around the screen. However, it's a good example to start with as it uses many of the controls supplied with the Standard Edition of Visual Basic. This program is a good illustration of the power of Visual Basic. Although by no means fantastic it does offer the user a great deal of functionality, and only has a tiny amount of actual program code in it. We will see this later.

3 The three list boxes on the right of the form enable you to navigate your hard disk in search of graphics files.

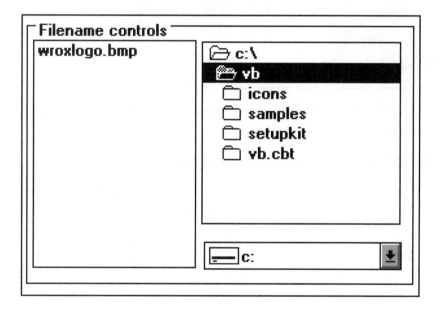

4 Once you have located the right drive and directory, you will see a list of the files you can load in.

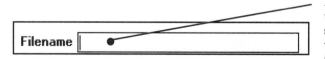

As soon as a file is selected, the text box on the left-hand side of the form is built up with the full name of that file, including the drive and directory that it lives in.

5 Clicking the **command button** labeled Load displays the picture at the foot of the form.

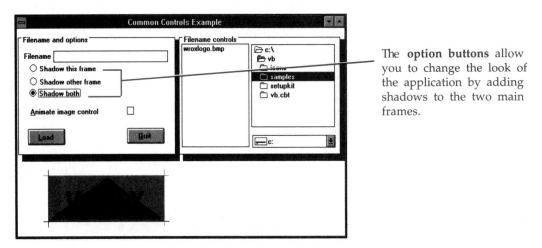

The **option buttons** allow you to change the look of the application by adding shadows to the two main frames.

6 The **check box** lets you animate the loaded image by shifting it left and right across the form.

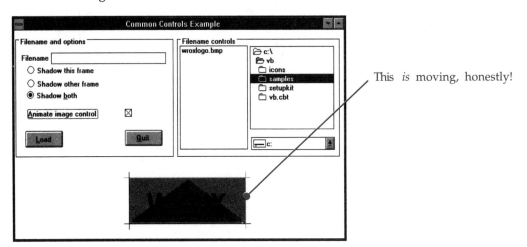

This *is* moving, honestly!

Play around with the program for a while and you should soon find yourself coming up with some questions:

> How does the image get displayed?

> How is the image moved?

> How does the text box know what the three list boxes are doing?

> How does the program check to see if a file exists or not?

Read on, and the answers to these questions and more will be revealed.

The Toolbox

Just as with other aspects of Visual Basic, placing a control such as a command button or a text box onto a form is merely a question of pointing and clicking with the mouse. As we saw in Chapter 1, all of your controls are kept in the toolbox, waiting for you to put them onto your form.

The toolbox can be displayed by selecting Toolbox from the Window menu in Visual Basic.

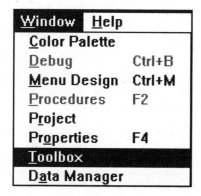

Once displayed you can move the toolbox around the screen by dragging its title bar, just like any other window. You close it by double-clicking the tiny control button in the top left corner of the toolbox window.

Placing Controls Onto Your Form

In Chapter 1, we placed a simple label control onto a form to display today's date. Let's do it again, this time with a command button.

Try It Out - Placing Controls

1   Start a new project by selecting New Project from the File menu.

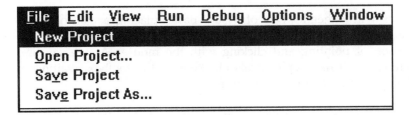

2   Select the control you want by clicking on its icon in the toolbox. Here we want the command button.

3   Move the cursor to the place on the form where you want the control to go.

4   Draw the control by holding the left mouse button down and dragging the mouse. A rectangle will appear on the form representing the size of the control.

5   When you are happy with the size, just release the mouse button and the control will be drawn onto the form in full.

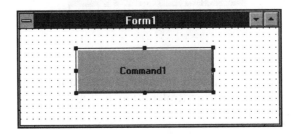

You can now click on the control itself and drag it around until you are happy with its position.

Resizing Controls

Even after a number of controls have been added to the form, it's still possible to move them around or resize them.

Try It Out - Resizing Controls

1 Clicking on a control you have already drawn selects that control and displays the control **resize handles**. These are small black boxes on each edge and each corner of the control.

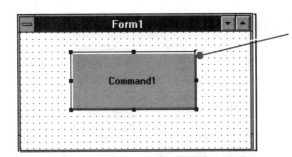

Clicking on these buttons and dragging the mouse around causes the control to change size.

Some controls cannot be changed in size, while others have pre-set minimum heights or widths below which you can't go.

2 Sometimes it's faster to double-click on a control and allow Visual Basic to put it on the form at the default size and position. You can then resize and move it around. Visual Basic lays each control one on top of the other in the default position, so they can be a little hard to find if you don't move each one.

The Alignment Grid

To help you position the controls neatly, Visual Basic provides you with an **Alignment Grid**. This is the grid of small black dots that covers your form. The grid can be changed in size, or removed completely from the Environment item on the Options menu.

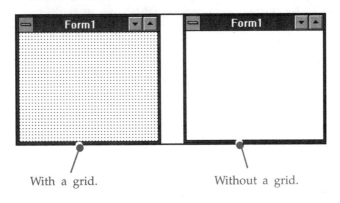

With a grid.   Without a grid.

Try It Out - Changing the Alignment Grid

1   Select the <u>E</u>nvironment option from the <u>O</u>ptions menu.

2   Scroll down the list of options that appears using the scroll bars until it looks like this.

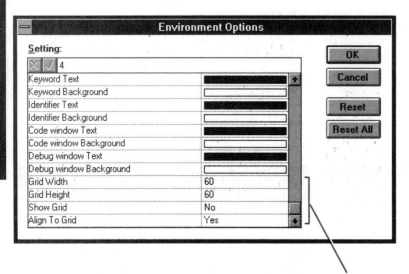

The last four options on this box allow you to set up the size of the grid, decide whether or not you want the grid shown, and whether or not Visual Basic should force you to place controls on grid points (snap to grid). You can change all these options to suit your requirements.

> I tend to use a very fine grid (height and width both 60). This allows me a great deal of flexibility when moving my controls around, yet still lets me line the controls up neatly on the form rather than in a cluttered mess. Some people don't like using the grid at all and turn it off at the first possible instance. Do whatever you feel happy with!

The Environment Options

The environment options can have some dramatic effects on the way you work with Visual Basic, and also how it works with you.

The first option, **Tab Stop Width**, governs how many spaces are inserted into your program code when you hit the *Tab* key. By default, Visual Basic inserts four spaces here. Using the **Tab Stop Width** option you can set this to any amount that suits you.

The next two options determine how Visual Basic treats the program code you write. (Later on when we cover variables and data types you will see how the **Require Variable Declaration** option can be used to automatically check spelling mistakes in your variable names. Don't worry too much about this now.)

The **Syntax Checking** option tells Visual Basic whether or not you want it to check everything you enter in design mode, as you enter it. It can be annoying if you are having a particularly bad typing day to have Visual Basic keep telling you that you have spelt something wrong, or that you have used a Visual Basic command or property in a strange way. Setting this option to **No** stops Visual Basic bothering you with error messages until you finally try to run the program.

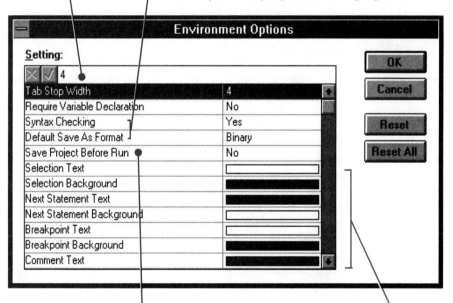

A particularly useful option on the **Environment** dialog is the **Save Project Before Run** option. Visual Basic, like any major application available, has its bugs. Imagine how furious you'll feel if the system crashes and takes all your design work with it, before you've had a chance to save the program! Setting the **Save Before Run** option to **Yes** tells Visual Basic to save any changes you have made to the program before you try to run it.

Most of the remaining options control the colors that Visual Basic uses to show you your program's code. As with the other options you can configure them so that at least Visual Basic's *look* can become your own personal expression!

What is a Control?

If controls were merely nice-looking graphics on your form, then Visual Basic would be little better than a fancy painting program with a programming language attached. The real power of Visual Basic comes as a result of the functionality that is built into each control. What does this really mean?

Controls are Windows

A control is really a window that has a program running inside it. This is no different to what you are used to with your own Windows desktop. To run a new application, you open a new window. This application will take control of that window and invest it with its own appearance and functionality. A Visual Basic control takes control of the window in a rather more extreme fashion than an application, but it's essentially the same.

A control is therefore a lump of pre-written code inside a window which can be dropped into your own program. It incorporates into your own project the functions which that code provides. The software industry has been eagerly awaiting these kind of standard components for many years in order to speed up the process of writing software.

Before Visual Basic introduced custom controls, each programmer would write almost every line of code in an application from the ground up. This meant that there was a large amount of repetition of coding which had no doubt been done by other programmers in other projects. Although we consider Visual Basic to be truly revolutionary, it is only a result of what has happened in every other industry. Your PC is made up of components from dozens of different manufacturers, each specializing in producing one particular part. What makes Visual Basic controls special is not the idea of re-useable software components alone - these have existed in different incarnations for many years. Rather it is the elegance with which each control can be customized to, and integrated with, your particular application.

A custom control, or a VBX (Visual Basic eXtension) is a file on your hard disk that contains the graphical look and feel, as well as all the functionality of the controls that you see on your tool palette. By adding more VBXs to your system you are actually increasing the power and usefulness of your Visual Basic environment. The other side effect of this is that it tends to make each installation of Visual Basic totally unique; every developer has their own preference for which VBXs to use, and which should actually appear in their Visual Basic toolbox.

The VBX is soon to be superseded by the OCX (OLE Control). However, Microsoft claim that the transition between the two will be simple, so don't let that stop you from exploring the exciting world of VBX add-ons.

Events and Properties

You interact with a control by using two types of hook: **properties** and **events**.

▶ **Properties** are a collection of parameters you can set to control the way a control looks and behaves. If controls were people, properties would be characteristics like height, weight, fitness and programming skills.

▶ **Events** are the things you can do to a control that it will recognize, and be able to respond to. Each control has a set of events it understands. You will be relieved to hear that controls respond to a far narrower range of events than people do. We will not have to persuade or encourage controls to do anything; you just click on them with the mouse.

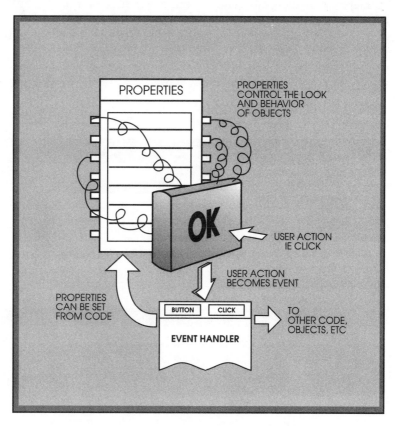

Each control has its own set of properties and events that make it useful for particular purposes. To see how this works, let's take a look at probably the most common control of all, the **command button**.

Command Buttons

Second only in popularity to the text box, and unsurpassed for its sheer simplicity and lack of charisma, is the command button. I talk in terms of simplicity because although command buttons are incredibly useful and enormously widespread throughout the world of Windows, they can only really do one thing - click. You point at them with the mouse, click the left mouse button and voilà, a **click** event occurs!

Events

Of course there are other events that a command button can respond to, but the majority of them all center around whether or not the button is being clicked. Events such as MouseDown and KeyDown are useful in detecting exactly what the user is trying to do to the command button, and with which weapon. Essentially, however, it's all a question of clicking.

To see the code window for the command button, double-click on it as you did on your form:

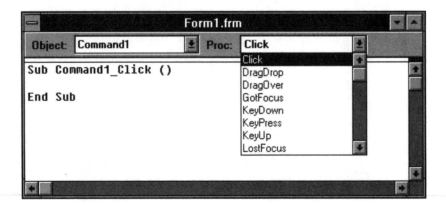

Properties

Once you start to think about controls as windows, it becomes easy to see why they have properties in common with forms:

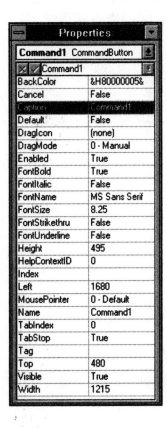

Try It Out - Command Buttons

1 Create a new Visual Basic project - select New Project from the File menu.

2 After the project has been created, select the command button icon from the toolbox.

3 Draw a command button on the form.

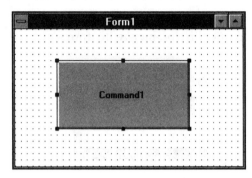

4 Let's actually make the control button do something; this time we'll make it beep whenever it's clicked. To do this we need to display the code window and type in some code.

Notice that the text inside the code window says `Sub Command1_Click()`. This means that we are looking at the code that will occur whenever the command button, Command1 is clicked. We cover code in a lot more detail a little later in the book so don't fret if you can't understand the strange words and symbols. All you need to know is that we are going to be writing code which Visual Basic will run whenever this command button is clicked.

Double-click on your new command button and the code window will pop up.

Type in code so that the code window looks like this.

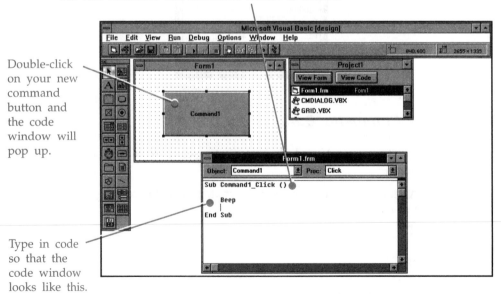

5 Now try running the program by pressing *F5*, by selecting <u>S</u>tart from the <u>R</u>un menu, or by clicking the run icon on the main Visual Basic toolbar.

6 If you now click the command button you will find it beeps, because the code you typed into the command button's click event tells it to.

7 When you have had enough of the program you can stop it by pressing *Alt* and *F4* together.

Returning to the Property Market

Before we go any further, it's worth talking a little more about properties, especially some of the more common ones.

In order to make Visual Basic as easy to learn as possible, Microsoft were kind enough to give most of the controls in Visual Basic similar properties. For instance, all controls have an **Enabled** property, most also have a **Visible** property and so on. This makes it worth speaking generally about properties and controls before delving into specific instances.

Setting Properties at Run-time

We've seen in the last two chapters how to set properties at design-time by using the properties window. It's also possible to set them up from within your program code. In fact this is one of the easiest ways to make your programs come alive.

> **Design-time** is the time when your program is not running and you are placing controls onto your form and writing code. **Run-time** is when you have clicked the run button and your forms and controls respond to events by running the relevant procedures.

Disabling Controls

Imagine the user has just entered some text, the result of which is that you want to disable two command buttons, named Command1 and Command2. In your code you would simply write:

```
Command1.Enabled = False
Command2.Enabled = False
```

Visual Basic would then gray out the command buttons to indicate that they no longer work, and your user would be unable to click them.

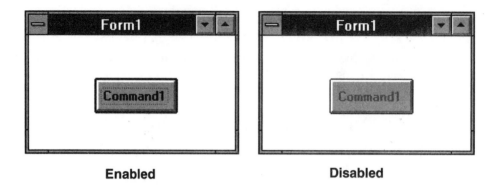

Enabled   **Disabled**

This technique is used in the example program **CONTROL.MAK** to turn the animation of the graphic on and off. Whenever the user clicks on the check box a control known as a **timer** is turned on or off by the following simple instruction:

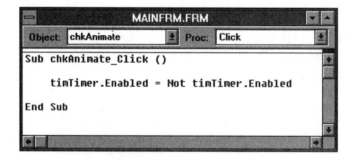

The **Enabled** property can only ever be one of two values: True or False. By saying **timTimer.Enabled = Not timTimer.Enabled** we are actually setting the **Enabled** property to whatever it is not. For example, if the **Enabled** property was true when this line of code was hit, it would change to what it is not - false. It's basically an On/Off switch.

> We'll have another look at the **Enabled** property later in the chapter when we see how it operates with some other controls.

The Name Property

One extremely common property you will come across is the Name property. This is used in order to write code which will differentiate between each of your Visual Basic controls. In other words each control is given a name.

Whenever you create a new control or form in Visual Basic, a default name is automatically given. For example, when you start up a new project in Visual Basic, the default form is called Form1. When you draw the first command button onto that form it will be called Command1, the next will be called Command2 and so on.

Standard Names

There are some common standards for giving a name to your controls. Text boxes for example are nearly always prefixed with **txt**, forms begin with **frm**, option buttons with **opt** and so on.

A full list of these is in Appendix B at the back of the book, but you will come across many of them as we cover the example program in this chapter. At first the names may seem a little strange, but the end result is that your code is a lot easier to read and understand.

For example, you may have typed a line like:

```
optDrive.text = "D:"
```

......which Visual Basic seems to dislike. It's easy to see why, since the name of the control indicates that it's an option button, and option buttons don't have a **text** property.

Of course, if you wanted to name a drive control **optDrive** then that's entirely up to you. Visual Basic only complains if you try to use properties that don't belong to certain controls, such as a **text** property with an option button.

When such a problem is found, Visual Basic simply gives you an error message and lets you go away and fix the error.

In the final analysis, Visual Basic doesn't really care what you call your controls; it's quite happy for you to name them all A, B, C, D etc. However, that doesn't really make your life as a programmer very easy. Sticking to a standard way of naming your controls can make your life a lot more hassle-free, especially when you have to come back to the code in a few months time to maintain it, or to fix a bug. By that time you probably won't have a clue what the code does. The last thing you need at that stage is to waste time trying to figure out what the control and variable names mean.

Text and Caption Properties

Every control on an individual form in Visual Basic has to have a unique name, unless you deliberately place them in a group called a control array. You can assign the name yourself using the standard naming convention, or you just accept the default name that Visual Basic gives you. This is really a private name between you, the programmer, and the control. When you run the program the name will be invisible to the user.

There are, however, two other text labels that can be assigned to certain controls and which will display that text on the screen. These are the Caption and Text properties.

The Caption Property

Captions are usually found on objects such as forms, frames, and command buttons. A caption is simply a piece of text that is displayed on screen to give the object some kind of header or title.

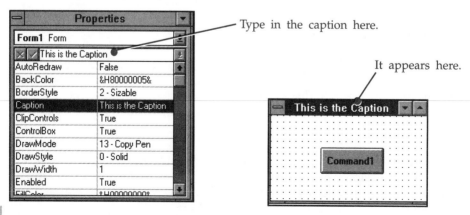

Type in the caption here.

It appears here.

In the case of the command button the text is actually displayed in the center of the command button itself.

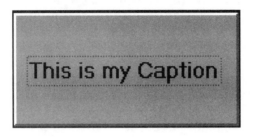

Shortcut Keys

There is another interesting feature of the Caption property, which applies to any control that can have a caption. Look closely at the wording of the caption on the Load button.

Notice how the letter L is underlined. This is called a **hot key**, and it means that by pressing *Alt-L* when the program is running you can trigger the Load button `click` event without having to move the mouse to point and click.

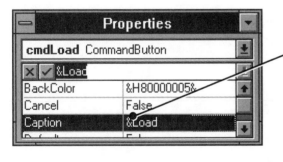

Hot keys can be set up on any control that can have a caption by simply placing an & sign in front of the letter you want underlined.

From a user's point of view this makes your programs much easier to use.

The Text Property

The Text property is somewhat different. This is normally found on controls that can accept data entry from the user such as a **text box** or **combo box**. By setting the Text property, you are actually telling Visual Basic what to display on screen in the text entry area. To see how this works, let's take a look at the text box control.

Text Boxes

Text boxes are one of the most common controls found in any Windows program. They provide an area on screen into which the user can enter information and where you can also display information to the user.

The area inside these controls behaves like a DOS text screen of old. Like many of the other controls in Visual Basic, much of the hard work with text boxes is done for you. In a great many cases all you need to do is simply place a text box onto a form before your users start entering data. Visual Basic and Windows automatically handle all the complex stuff such as displaying the characters which the user types, inserting and deleting characters, scrolling the data in the text box, selecting text, cut and pasting text and so on.

It's so easy in fact, there's nothing stopping us trying it out!

Try It Out - Text Boxes

1   Start a new project in Visual Basic by selecting <u>N</u>ew Project from the <u>F</u>ile menu.

2   Select the text box control from the toolbox.

3   Draw the text box onto the default form.

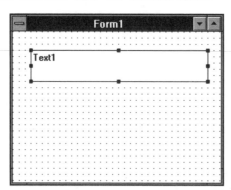

By changing the various font properties of the text box you can dramatically alter the way that text appears. This allows you to provide emphasis on screen where needed. Let's try it now.

4 Make sure that the text box you just drew is still selected. If it isn't then click it once. Bring up the properties window by pressing *F4*. Change the Text property to something substantial.

5 Now find the FontName property in the text box and double-click it. Visual Basic moves to the next font on the system and changes the way the text looks in the text box.

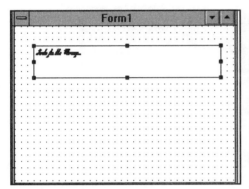
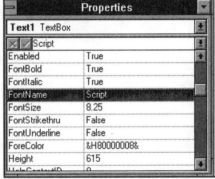

6 A bit small I reckon. So move to the FontSize property. At the top of the properties window there is a combo box. When you select a property that has a number of choices available, you can click the arrow on this combo box to see the options. Click the arrow now to bring down a list of available font sizes. Select a nice large number to blow up the size of the text.

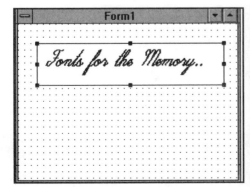
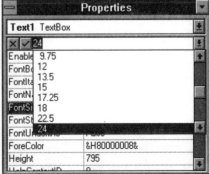

7 The FontBold, FontItalic, FontStrikeThru and FontUnderline properties work in a slightly different way. Instead of having a large list of options available to you, you have only two: True and False. You can switch between these two settings by simply double-clicking the property in question.

8 Some properties have their own separate dialog boxes to help you choose an option. The BackColor and ForeColor properties change the color of the background, and of the text itself, and show a color chart for you to choose from.

9 Find the BackColor property and double-click it. A color dialog appears.

10 Select a color you think would look good as the background.

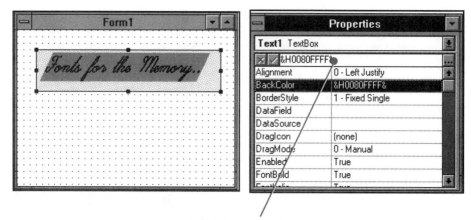

This number tells Visual Basic which color you've chosen. You don't need to worry about it at the moment. We'll learn all about it in Chapter 8 - Graphics.

Visual Basic gives you a lot of freedom to use color. Be careful that you don't either use too little color, in which case your forms can get lost on a busy desktop, or too much color, when it becomes confusing to the user.

Text Box Properties

The most important property of a text box is the Text property itself. In the example above, we changed this at design-time. At any point in time, the Text property can also be examined by your program to see exactly what is in the text box on screen, or to change that text on the fly.

The example program **CONTROL.MAK** displays the file you selected with the list boxes, by placing the filename into the Text property of the text box.

To see how it works re-load **CONTROL.MAK** and double-click on the file list box to display the code we want:

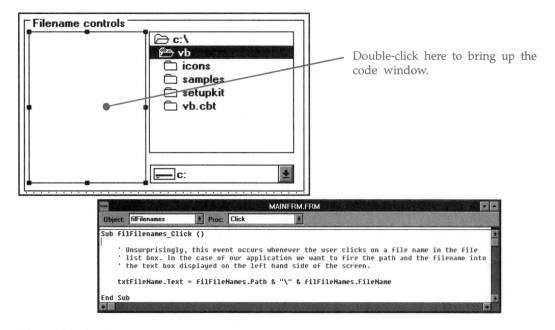

Double-click here to bring up the code window.

How it Works

The **&** signs tell Visual Basic to join different pieces of text, known as **strings,** together to form one big string. In this case, that involves piecing the file list box **Path** property together with the \ sign and finally the file list box **Filename** property. We'll look at those properties later when we cover the file list box in detail. For now though, if the **Path** property has **C:\TEMP** in it, and the **Filename** property has **TEST.BMP** in it, then the text box will show

        C:\TEMP\TEST.BMP

The code window above illustrates the difficulty of reading and printing very wide code text in Visual Basic. There is no simple solution to this. We will adopt a special symbol (↳) at the end of a line that has been broken, to show that you need to type this into Visual Basic as one line. So if we put this line in the main text of the book, it will look like this:

```
txtFileName.Text  =  filFileNames.Path  &  "\"  &
↳ filFileNames.FileName
```

Checking User Input

In fact the only thing text boxes can't do without your help is check the data that the user enters. Problems occur because a text box allows the user to key in more information than can be displayed, and to enter alphabetic data when your program only really wants numeric information and so on.

By default the text box allows you to type in data that is larger than its width. When this happens the text box scrolls to show you the next section. You can even scroll it yourself by placing the cursor inside the text box. Point at it with the mouse, click the left mouse button and then use the arrow keys to move left and right. This can be great when you need such a feature, but it can make your interface look badly planned to the user.

Visual Basic provides a property to help us get round this. Setting the **MaxLength** property to anything other than 0 limits the amount of data that can be keyed in. Try it out by setting the **MaxLength** property to something silly like 5 and then running the program. Now when you select a file name, only the first 5 characters of it will be displayed in the text box and the program no longer works reliably. Stop it, and change it back to zero.

Text Box Events

I keep on saying **displays data** and **enters data** for the text box when really it would be more logical to say that a text box holds and displays **text**. Well, despite the somewhat misleading name, text boxes don't only hold text. They can hold punctuation marks, numbers, arithmetic symbols; in fact, anything you can produce through a **KeyPress**, the text box can display. This can become a little bit of a problem, if for example you needed the user to enter a number, and nothing else but numbers.

Try It Out - Checking Input to a Text Box

Let's look at program that does check what is entered into a text box.

1   Load up the **DETAILS.MAK** example project.

2   This program has just the problem we were discussing. It prompts for your forename, and your age, but it doesn't prevent you from entering numbers in your forename, or letters in your age.

3   We're going to fix that now. We also need to check that when the user hits the <u>O</u>K button they have actually entered data in to both the name and age text boxes.

Adding Code to the KeyPress Event

The best way to check data as it's entered is using the **KeyPress** event. This is triggered for a text box whenever the user presses a key that's displayed in the text box and tells us the **ASCII** code for the key pressed.

Each character on your keyboard has a specific unique number, called the ASCII (pronounced ass-key) code. Using this we can check that the right keys have been pressed and we can also tell the KeyPress event to ignore certain keys. Convenient isn't it?!

To help you, Visual Basic also has a complete list of these ASCII codes built in. Select Search from the Help menu and enter the word ASCII. Visual Basic will search its help topics and display the results. The result, called the ASCII character set, shows you a complete list of all the characters and their associated codes.

Try It Out - Trapping Key Strokes

To enter code in the **txtForeName_KeyPress()** event, first stop the program running.

1 Double-click the Forename text box to bring up the code window.

2 When the code window appears, click on the arrow next to the word Change.

3 Select KeyPress from the list shown. The code window should now look like this:

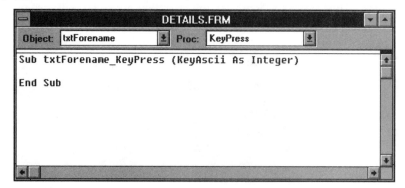

The first line of code

```
Sub txtForename_KeyPress(KeyAscii As Integer)
```

marks the start of the event code. It tells us, and Visual Basic, where the code for dealing with the **KeyPress** event starts, and also lets us know the name of the control whose **KeyPress** event we are writing code for. The **KeyAscii** bit in brackets is called a **parameter**, but let's take one thing at a time!

4 Conveniently, the ASCII codes for the numbers 0 to 9 all run in sequence, so our event code to catch them is fairly simple. Let's add a line to the event to check which key was pressed and deal with it. Change the event code so that it looks as follows.

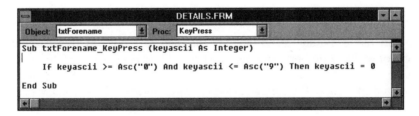

How It Works

The first line of the **KeyPress** event has the phrase **KeyAscii As Integer** in it.
KeyAscii is called a parameter. This is a way for Visual Basic to give your
code a value which it can use to figure out what is going on; you'll come
across it frequently!

In the **KeyPress** event, **KeyAscii** holds the ASCII number of the key that was
pressed. For example, if the user had pressed the *A* key then **KeyAscii** would
equal 65. The line

```
If keyascii >= asc("0") and keyascii <= asc("9") then keyascii = 0
```

uses the **KeyAscii** parameter to check whether the key pressed was valid. It
does this using the Visual Basic **asc** function.

> A function is a piece of code, in this case built into Visual Basic, that takes
> something from your code, processes it away on its own, then returns a new
> value. The `asc` function allows us to get at the ASCII value for a symbol; so,
> saying `asc("0")` will give our code the ASCII code for 0.

We can then compare whatever is held in **KeyAscii** against the value returned
by **asc** to determine whether or not the key pressed was numeric or not.

Finally the **>=** symbol means **is greater than or equal to** and the **<=** symbol
means **is less than or equal to**. Armed with this knowledge the line of code
actually reads: **If the parameter KeyAscii is greater than or equal to the
ASCII code of '0', and KeyAscii is less than or equal to the ASCII code of
'9' then set KeyAscii to 0**.

Setting **Keyascii** to 0 in the **KeyPress** event has the effect of canceling the key
just pressed. If you run the program now and try typing numbers into the
Forename text box, you will find that they will simply be ignored. All the other
characters work fine though.

Try It Out - Verifying Input to the Age Field

We can use a similar technique for the age text box. In this case we need to keep only the numbers and ignore everything else.

To enter code into the **txtAge_KeyPress()** event.

1 Stop the program running.

2 Double-click the age text box.

3 When the code window appears, select the **KeyPress** event.

4 Key in the Event Handler code:

Now if you run the program you will find that the age text box only accepts numbers, and ignores spaces, letters or any other character you decide to hit. In addition, because the **MaxLength** property has already been set to 2, you won't be able to enter an age of more than 2 digits in length - the chances of a 100+ year old reading this book and using Visual Basic is pretty remote so I'm confident I can get away with this.

Try It Out - Checking For an Empty Text Box

Now all we need to do is check that the user has actually entered something in the text boxes when the OK button is hit. We have already seen that the Text property lets us see what is in a text box, so if the Text property equals "" then obviously the user has entered nothing. In Visual Basic "" is how you would check to see if a piece of text actually contains nothing. This is commonly called an empty string.

1 If the program is running, stop it and double-click the command button to bring up its click event code. A few lines of code, and the program is complete.

```
Sub cmdOK_Click()
    If txtAge.Text = "" then
        Msgbox "You must enter your age"
        Exit Sub
    End If

    If txtForename.Text = "" then
        Msgbox "Enter your name please"
        Exit Sub
    End If
End Sub
```

2   The code checks the value of each text box to see if anything was entered. In either case, if nothing was entered, a message box is put on screen with an error message in it. Then, the **Exit Sub** line exits the event code. Event code like this is normally called a **subprocedure**. We cover subprocedures later in the book.

3   We can make the program even better by using a command called **SetFocus** to move the cursor to the offending text box. Focus is a tricky subject best discussed in a separate section, so I'll leave that to the end of the chapter.

Label Control

The **Label** control is the perfect complement to the text box. The text box is one of the few controls that doesn't have a caption of its own, so a label is used to place some text on the form near to the text box to show the user exactly what the text box represents.

Label Properties

The style of the label font can be changed with the FontName, FontSize, FontBold and FontItalic properties, just as we did with text boxes earlier on. You can even add a border around a label to make it appear to all intents and purposes the same as a text box. This is done by changing the BorderStyle property in the same way that you did with the form in the last chapter.

Properties	
Label1 Label	
Label1	
FontSize	8.25
FontStrikethru	False
FontUnderline	False
ForeColor	&H80000008&
Height	495
Index	
Left	720
LinkItem	
LinkMode	0 - None
LinkTimeout	50
LinkTopic	
MousePointer	0 - Default
Name	Label1
TabIndex	0

Label Events

Labels are lightweight controls; they use less system resources (such as memory) as they need less processor power to manage. This is because Visual Basic doesn't have to worry too much about the user entering data in them, resizing them and so on.

However, while they may be lightweight from a Windows management point of view, they're up there with the best of them when it comes to event handling.

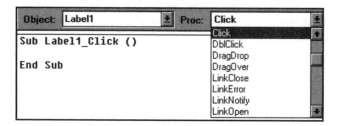

Labels can respond to the full set of events, with the obvious exception of events such as **Change,** since the data in the label caption wouldn't normally need to be changed. One of the most common events coded for labels is the click event. For example, in a banking application you may have a client's personal details such as address on the screen. Adding code to the click event of the label that says **Address** could be used to bring up another form showing the other addresses that the customer may have lived at over the years.

Other programs tend to use label click events as backdoors - ways into a program if all else fails. I recently came across one such program which, if you double-clicked the **Password** label on a particular form, allowed you to change or re-set the password - very convenient for forgetful users!

Check Boxes

Check boxes allow you to present On/Off, True/False options to users. Think back to school - remember the old multiple choice questions? Well, a check box is similar to the squares that you ticked to indicate your answers.

You can see a check box in action in the **CONTROL.MAK** project. Load it up and take a look at the form. On the left hand side there is a single **check box** and a number of round option buttons.

○ **Shadow this frame**

○ **Shadow other frame**

○ **Shadow both**

Animate image control   □

In this example the check box acts as an On/Off switch for the animation of the picture box. Click on the check box and the animation starts. Click it again and you turn the animation off. Of course, check boxes have many other uses, other than simply acting as switches. A personnel system could use check boxes to indicate if an employee is still with the company or not. A banking system could use a check box to freeze or unfreeze a customers account - in fact I think I know a bank that uses this.

Try It Out - Check Boxes

1 Create a new Visual Basic project.

2 When the default form appears, select the check box from the toolbox.

3 Double-click the check box icon to draw a check box on the form at the default size and position.

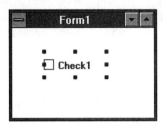

4 By default the caption of a check box appears to the right of the box. You can change this by changing the Alignment property.

5 Bring up the properties window and find the Alignment property. By default it is set to Left Justify, meaning that the box, not the text, is on the left. Double-click this property to change it to Right Justify.

6 The text moves automatically.

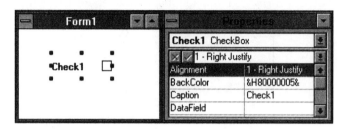

7 Add a couple more check boxes to the form so that the form now looks like this. Don't forget to change the alignment property of each.

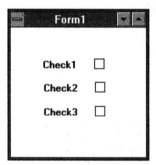

8 Now try running the program. You can select any of the check boxes independently of the others.

Check boxes are independent of each other which means that checking one does not affect any of the others on the form. This is very different to the way that option buttons work, as you will see a little later.

Check Box Events

There aren't many events that can be used with a check box, and by far the most important is the **click** event. This triggers both when the user points and clicks on the check box and when the user presses the hot-key combination. You can add code to the click event to do something based on the status of the check box at that point in time. However, you can't just insert the action you want performed into the click event directly, as the clicking action could either **select** or **de-select** the option depending on what state the check box was in beforehand.

To really make use of check boxes, you have to use the **Value** property.

The Check Box Value Property

The current status of a check box can be examined using its **value** property.

Values of Check Box	Value Property
0	Unchecked
1	Checked
2	Grayed out, Disabled

Let's write a small program to look at the Value property of a check box while the program is running.

Try It Out - Checking the Check Box

1 Create a new Visual Basic project, and draw a check box onto the default form. Add a caption as shown.

2 Still in design mode, double-click the check box to bring up the code window.

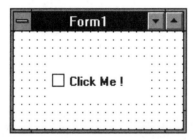

3 Type in a message box line so that the code window looks like this.

```
Sub Check1_Click()

    MsgBox "The value is now " & Check1.Value

End Sub
```

4 Try running the program now.

5 Each time you click on the check box, a message box will appear showing you what is in the **Value** property of the check box. If the check box is checked then **Value** will be 1. If it is not checked then the value is 0. The only value you won't see here is 2, which you get when the check box is disabled.

> The ability of the check box to be grayed out can be the cause of some very worrying bugs. Let's imagine you let the user check the box and then disable it to prevent them doing it again - at that point you can't determine in your program whether or not the check box was actually checked or not, since the value you will get from the Value property will be 2. Beware of this!

Option Buttons

Option buttons are a close cousin to the check box. They are also an On/Off switch for various options. The difference is that a list of option buttons is **mutually exclusive**. In the example program, **CONTROL.MAK**, they are used to get details from the user of how the program should look and behave, that is to register preferences. Because they are essentially On/Off switches they are ideal for this. They are very useful in database type applications to let the user quickly choose one from a number of options in a list.

> All the option buttons on a form, or in a frame (more on these later) work together; clicking one option button clears all the others. It's like the station selector on a radio, where pressing the button for a new station makes the old one pop out. In fact, they are also known as radio buttons.

Try It Out - Check Boxes

1 Create a new Visual Basic project.

2 When the default form appears select the option button from the toolbox.

3 Double-click the option button icon to draw an option button on the form at the default size and position.

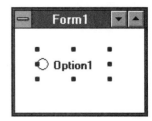

4   Like the check boxes we saw earlier, the caption of an option button always appears by default to the right of the button. Just as with the check box this can be changed by using the option button Alignment property.

5   Bring up the properties window and find the Alignment property. Double-click this property to change it to Right Justify.

6   Add a couple more option buttons to the form so that the form now looks like this:

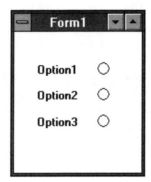

7   Now try running the program.

Any option buttons placed directly onto the form, or into the same frame, cancel each other out. If you select one, all the others are deselected. Try it out; with the program running try clicking on each of the buttons in turn and you'll see the result.

Control Arrays

The fact that option buttons operate as a group mean that they are usually used in something called a **control array**. It's a complex name but the idea behind it is very simple; all the buttons have exactly the same name (in the example they are all called `optShadow`). In order to tell the difference between them, a property called Index is used to give each option button a unique number, starting at 0. Then, in the click code, Visual Basic gives you the index number of the button just pressed.

Normally Visual Basic does all the numbering with the Index property for you. You simply add a new control to a form with the same name as another. Visual Basic pops up a dialog box asking you if you want to add this new control to a control array. Answering 'yes' causes Visual Basic to assign a new index number to the new control. Control arrays can be a complex subject, but they are also very useful.

If you need to set the properties of an individual member of a control array, then all you need to do is tell Visual Basic the option button name, here **optShadow,** and its index number in brackets, **optShadow(0),optShadow(1),optShadow(2)** and so on.

Control arrays allow you to deal with a group of buttons on a form very conveniently; instead of having 3 option buttons with 3 click events all doing roughly the same thing, you have just 1 click event handling all 3 buttons.

Option Button Click Events

You can see this in the example program by double-clicking one of the option buttons to see the click event I wrote for it.

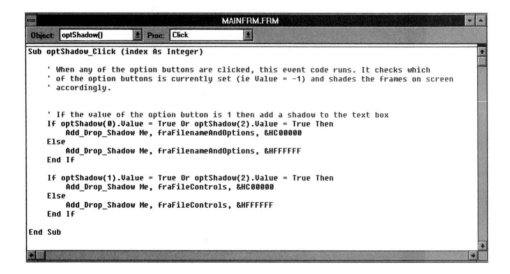

```
MAINFRM.FRM
Object: optShadow()        Proc: Click

Sub optShadow_Click (index As Integer)

    ' When any of the option buttons are clicked, this event code runs. It checks which
    ' of the option buttons is currently set (ie Value = -1) and shades the frames on screen
    ' accordingly.

    ' If the value of the option button is 1 then add a shadow to the text box
    If optShadow(0).Value = True Or optShadow(2).Value = True Then
        Add_Drop_Shadow Me, fraFilenameAndOptions, &HC00000
    Else
        Add_Drop_Shadow Me, fraFilenameAndOptions, &HFFFFFF
    End If

    If optShadow(1).Value = True Or optShadow(2).Value = True Then
        Add_Drop_Shadow Me, fraFileControls, &HC00000
    Else
        Add_Drop_Shadow Me, fraFileControls, &HFFFFFF
    End If

End Sub
```

Although it may look quite complex, the code for the option button click event is fairly straightforward. It simply examines the **Value** property of the option buttons to see which is pressed and calls a routine of my own called **Add_Drop_Shadow** to draw a shadow either in white, which just rubs out any previous shadow that was visible, or in blue, depending on the status of the buttons.

Unlike the check box, the **Value** property of an option button can only be one of two values: the True or False values we encountered earlier. This makes for some fairly easy code to both read and write.

Picture Boxes and Image Controls

Visual Basic provides two controls specifically for displaying graphic images: the **Image** control and the **Picture** control. These controls are both very powerful and each has advantages and disadvantages over the other. In this section you will get an overview of both, how they work and what they can be used for. Later, in Chapter 8 - Graphics, we will go into each of them in much more detail. For now, however, it's just a brief glimpse.

Using the Image and Picture Controls

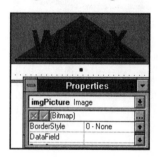

The most important property of both the picture box and the image control is the **Picture** property, which determines the image file that is loaded into the control. By displaying the properties window and double-clicking the Picture property, Visual Basic will display a file requester and ask you to select a file which you want displayed in the control.

Image File Formats

You can load a number of different kinds of graphics files into the picture and image controls.

Image File Type	File Extension	Description
Bit Map	***.BMP**	The traditional Windows format for graphics. Windows Paint is the usual source of these images which can be used for everything from clip art to icon symbols.
Windows Metafile	***.WMF**	Normally a graphic file drawn with a **structured** drawing package, such as Microsoft Draw. Good for clip art in a program since MetaFiles take a lot less memory than any other format.
Icon	***.ICO**	Small Icon graphic, like those found on toolbars.

Try It Out - Changing the Image

Let's try changing the file displayed in the image control of **CONTROL.MAK**. When the program first loads, it displays an image called **WROXLOGO.BMP**.

1   Click on the Wrox logo to select the image control.

2   Bring up the properties window by pressing *F4*.

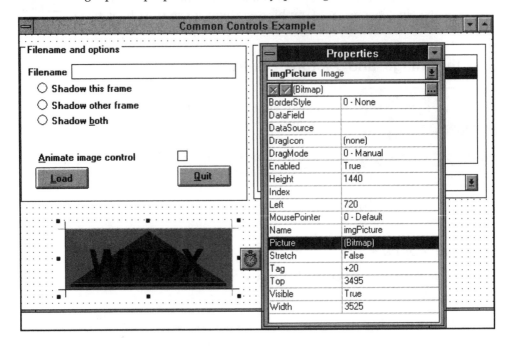

3   Double-click on the Picture property to display the file selector box.

4   Change the Picture property to one of the sample images supplied with Visual Basic (usually in the **\VB\ICONS** directory).

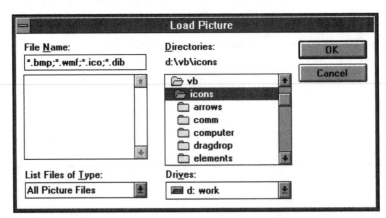

You will see the image change instantly to the newly selected one.

Try It Out - The Picture Control

To see how the Picture control works, set up a new project:

1   Open the File menu and select New Project.

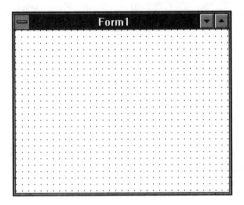

2   Double-click on the picture control in the toolbox to place it on the form in the default position.

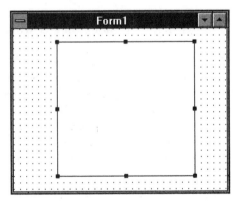

3   Bring up the properties box for the picture control by selecting the control and pressing *F4*.

4   Double-click on the Picture property in the properties box to bring up the file dialog.

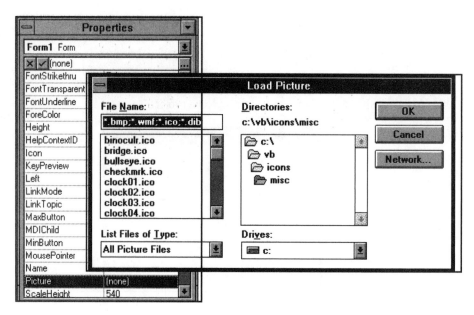

5   Select an image file from the relevant directories as before.

Image and Picture Controls Compared

On the surface the picture and image controls appear similar. The difference between the two controls is rather subtle and is worth some explanation.

An **Image** control is one of a collection of controls known as **lightweight** controls, some of the others being the line control, shape control, and label. In a nutshell, lightweight controls require less system resources (such as computer time, and memory) to manage them than other controls do; for example, the picture box, the command button or the heaviest of them all, the grid. The reasons for this are fairly complex, but from our point of view it is the limitations of the Image control compared to the picture control that are of interest.

> **Images** cannot be placed on top of other controls, unless they are first placed inside a container object such as a frame or picture box. Also they cannot receive focus at run-time. We cover focus a bit later as I have already said, but you can see what it is by running the example program. The control with the focus is the one that is highlighted in some way, or which currently displays the cursor. If you click on the text box then it gets the focus. If you press *Tab* then you will see the focus move from control to control.

> **Picture Boxes** are much more functional than Image controls. They can be drawn anywhere and they can receive the focus, which makes them very useful for creating your own graphical toolbars. They can also act as container controls, which means you can place other controls inside them, almost like a form within a form.

In Chapter 8 - Graphics, you will learn how to really put these two controls to work.

The Timer Control

The animation of the graphic image in the example program is achieved using a special control known as a timer. In nearly every other language available, animation like this is achieved using a **loop** - the section of the program that moves the image runs over and over and over in an indefinite cycle. The timer control provides Visual Basic programmers with a lot more flexibility than having to create your own loop.

In a nutshell the timer control doesn't actually do anything for the user or provide any kind of interface for the user to see. What they do, they do in the background, firing off timer events with monotonous regularity. If you need something to happen in your program at regular intervals, say every tenth of a second, or every 5 seconds, then the timer control is the control for the job. All you need to do is place the code you want executed at regular intervals into the timer event.

Timer controls are invisible controls. Although they are drawn on the form in the same way as any other control, they do not actually appear to the user when the program is running. They do, however, sit on the form at design-time.

Timer Properties

The property called Interval defines how often the timer triggers its own special Timer event. The interval is actually a number representing milliseconds (thousandths of a second). In the example program the interval is set to 10 which means that the timer event will occur every 10/1000 of a second.

The Enabled property turns the timer on or off. You can toggle between the two states, True or False, by double-clicking on the entry in the properties table.

You can also switch the timer on from your code by the line:

```
Timer1.Enabled = True
```

Timer Events

The only event that occurs to the timer control is the **Timer** event. When this event occurs in **CONTROL.MAK**, the code in the event updates the **Left** property of the image control in order to move it across the screen. As before you can see the code for yourself by double-clicking the timer control to display the timer's code window.

```
                              MAINFRM.FRM
Object:  timTimer        Proc:  Timer
Sub timTimer_Timer ()

    imgPicture.Left = imgPicture.Left + Val(imgPicture.Tag)

    If imgPicture.Left < 200 Or imgPicture.Left > (frmMainForm.ScaleWidth - imgPicture.Width)
        imgPicture.Tag = 0 - Val(imgPicture.Tag)
    End If

End Sub
```

For now that's all you need to know. The intricacies of the coordinate system is covered fully in Chapter 8 - Graphics later in the book whilst the `Tag` property is discussed in Chapter 12 - Object Variables.

More Common Properties

Many of the controls presented in this chapter have properties in common. We looked at some of the simpler ones at the start. Having gained more knowledge about specific controls, we can now get a better understanding of more advanced properties such as **Enabled**.

The Enabled Property

Check boxes can have three states from the user's point of view. These are **selected**, **de-selected** or **grayed** (meaning disabled). A check box, like most other Visual Basic controls, has an **Enabled** property to control whether it's able to be selected on the form at run-time. The **Enabled** property can only ever be one of two values as far as Visual Basic is concerned - True (meaning on), or False (meaning off).

> If you have programmed in C or Assembler before then you will be used to the words True and False. For the rest of us, this may seem awkward - why not simply use the words Yes and No? This is unfortunately one of the many areas of programming where jargon has crept in from the bad old days of binary and machine code programming. It stems from something called **Boolean logic**.

Setting Enabled at Runtime

Once you have set the **Enabled** property at design-time, Visual Basic lets you change that setting from your code while the program is running. This is useful, for example, to remove some items from a list of options by putting the **Enabled** property of their option boxes to **False**. To directly assign the state of the **Enabled** property, you would write something like this:

```
optStayInBed.Enabled = False
```

If you want to reverse the current condition of the control, without having to keep track of its current state, then the **Not** operator simply flips backwards and forwards from **True** to **False**. If, for example, the timer called **timTimer** was previously **Enabled**, then by saying

```
Not timTimer.Enabled
```

Visual Basic knows that the effect we are after is **whatever the timer is not**. The only other alternative is **True** so Visual Basic sets it to that.

Enabling Different Controls

Although the **Enabled** property is used mainly to turn an object off, the actual effect on screen varies enormously. Text boxes, command buttons, list boxes, menu items, all tend to appear grayed out, indicating to the user that they no longer function.

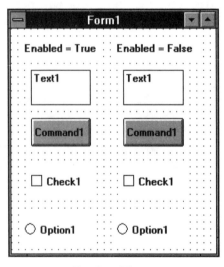

Design-Time

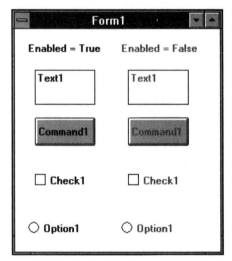

Run-Time

Try It Out - Enabling Controls

You can see this in the example program **CONTROL.MAK.** All the controls on this form are grouped into what are known as **Frames**. These are container controls that can have other controls inside them, and cause these interior controls effectively to inherit some of the properties of the frame in which they reside. We will cover Frames in more detail when we discuss container objects in Chapter 8 - Graphics.

1 Load up **CONTROL.MAK** and show the main form.

2 Click on the right-hand frame.

This is the frame.

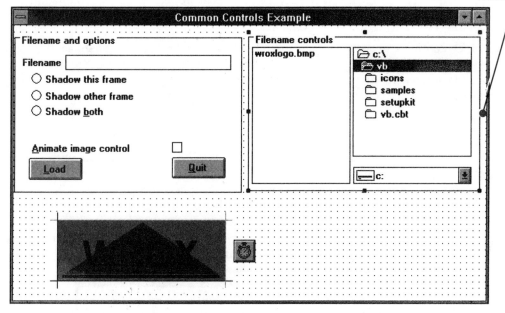

3 Press *F4* to bring up the properties window.

4 Find the **Enabled** property and set it to False.

Run the program to see the effect of the frame grayed out.

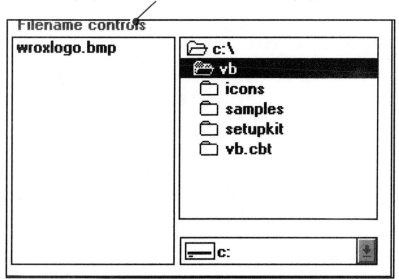

5   Try and use one of the controls inside the disabled frame - it doesn't work! Although the directory list box will appear enabled, you won't be able to select anything. The same applies for the other two list boxes.

Another common property which operates in a similar way to **Enabled** is **Visible**. Setting this property to False has the effect of removing the control from the screen. In the case of a container object such as a form or frame all controls within it would also disappear when the program is run.

Focus

Earlier on we mentioned focus - surprisingly this has nothing to do with karma or the summoning of an inner force to accomplish a goal! In Windows, focus tells us which control is currently selected when the program is running.

To see it work, run the example program, **CONTROL.MAK,** and press *Tab* a few times. You will see the highlight move from control to control. Wherever the highlight lands, that is the control which currently has the focus.

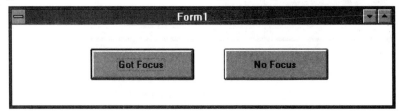

The TabIndex Property

Focus is really useful on a form that has a lot of separate fields requiring data entry. Many experienced typists prefer to move about the form using the *Tab* key, rather than taking their hand off the keyboard to use the mouse. You control the order in which the controls receive the focus using the TabIndex property.

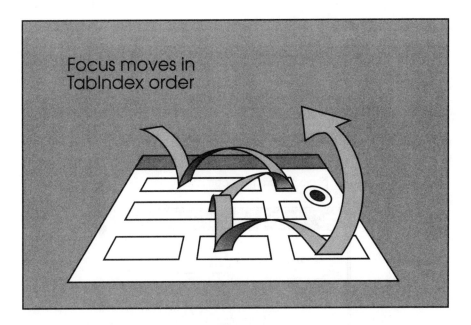

Focus moves in
TabIndex order

You can see this at work in the **CONTROL.MAK** project. Load the project and run it. When the application is running, keep pressing *Tab* and you will see the highlight move from control to control starting with the text box, then moving down the option buttons, over to the file controls and finally down to the two command buttons. If you stop the program running and bring up the properties window for those controls, you will see the TabIndex starts at 0 with the text box, 1 for the first option button and so on.

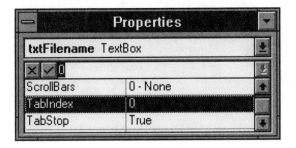

Whenever you change a TabIndex property, Visual Basic automatically re-orders the rest. Again you can see this if you bring up the properties window for the Load command button. Set the TabIndex of this to 0 and re-run the program. This time the Load button gets the focus first, then the text box, option buttons and so on.

Using Focus at Run-time

You can also move the focus from within your program code. For example, if the user enters some bad data, you can move the focus back to the offending control by using the **SetFocus** command.

Try It Out - Controlling Focus

You can also track whether or not a control has focus through the **Gotfocus** and **Lostfocus** events. Now, this is where the problems start to creep in.

1   Load up the project called **FOCUS.MAK**

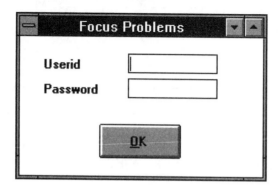

2   The program has two text boxes, one for a Userid, the other for a Password.

3   There is event code attached to Userid for the **Lostfocus** event.

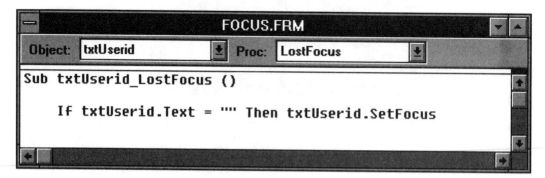

4   If the control loses focus, meaning the command button was clicked, or the user moved to the Password box without entering any data, then the **Lostfocus** code sets the focus back onto itself.

5 Run the program and try moving off the Userid box without entering anything. You will see the cursor snap straight back into the Userid box, forcing you to enter something - no problems there!

Now imagine we want to do the same to the Password box.

6 Double-click the Password box to bring up the code window, and select the **Lostfocus** event. Now change the code so that it looks like this:

```
Sub txtPassword_LostFocus()
If txtPassword.Text = "" then txtPassword.Setfocus
End Sub
```

Now we have a problem. For one control to lose focus, another has to gain it. If you run the program now and try moving off the Userid box, the program will hang up; it will lock itself into a loop which you can only stop by pressing *Ctrl Break*.

What happens here is that as Userid loses focus, so Password gains it. The Userid box then says 'Hang on...you didn't enter anything', and then grabs focus back, causing the Password box to lose focus itself. The Password box then does exactly the same as the Userid box just did.

For this reason many programmers do not use the Lostfocus or GotFocus events at all, and especially not for text box validation. The preferred route is to use the KeyPress or Change events. However, if you must use Lostfocus then there are ways around the problems, as you will see later.

Summary

In this chapter you learnt about the more common controls and how to apply them. You learnt the following:

▶ How to use text boxes, option buttons, check boxes, command buttons, timers, picture and image controls.

▶ How to change properties in your code.

▶ How to validate a text box.

▶ The basics of control arrays using option buttons.

▶ The problems that come with text boxes, option buttons and control focus.

In Chapter 5 - Advanced Controls, we will go on to look at the controls in **CONTROL.MAK** that we didn't cover in this chapter, such as list boxes and the file controls. Before that, let's learn more about writing the code that responds to the events that controls can generate.

Chapter Three

Writing Code

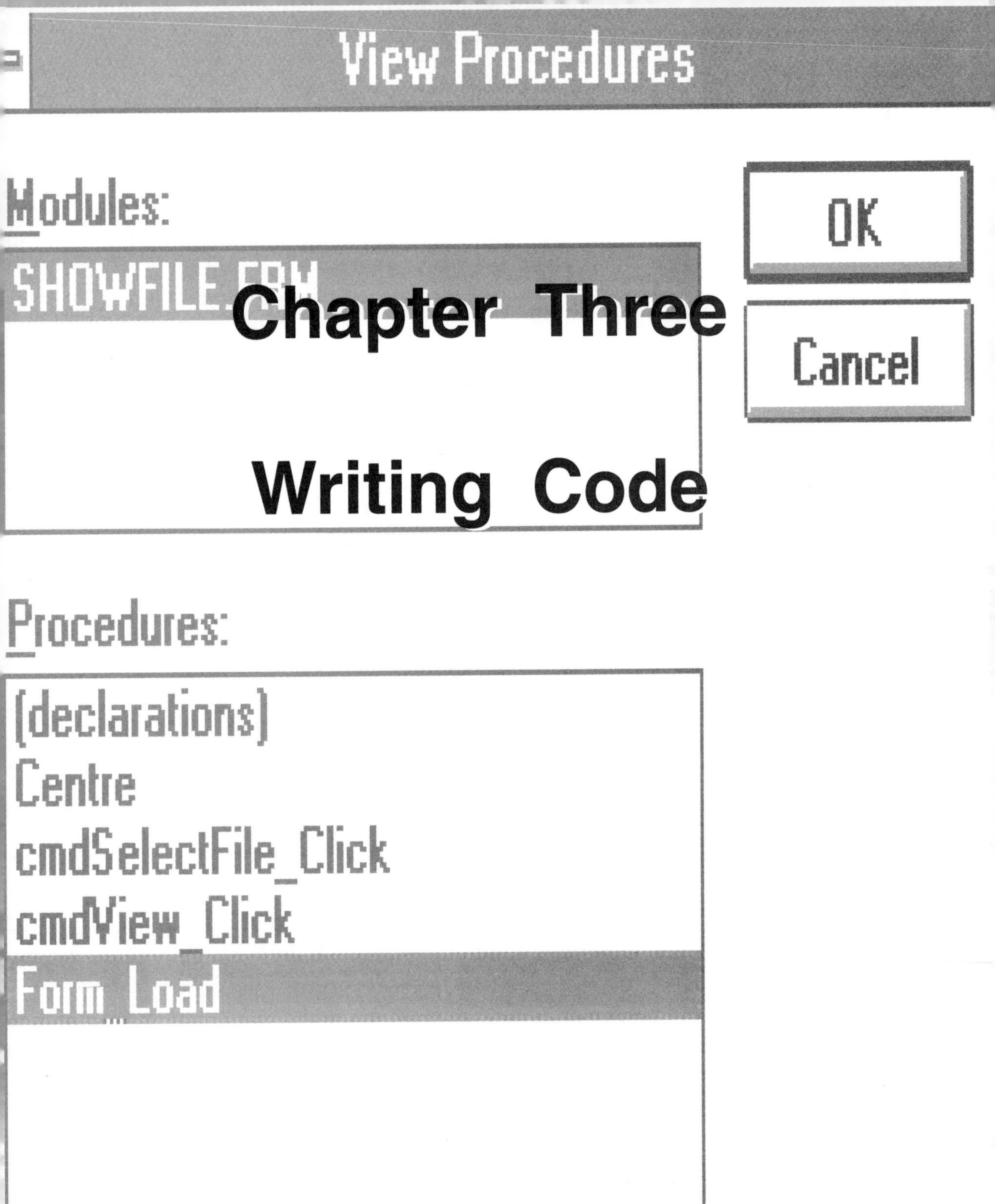
View Procedures
Modules:
SHOWFILE.FRM
OK
Cancel
Procedures:
(declarations)
Centre
cmdSelectFile_Click
cmdView_Click
Form_Load

CHAPTER 3

Writing Code

It's now time to bring your programs to life and make them think for themselves. Designing forms and adding controls isn't enough. Among other things, your programs need to be able to make decisions and run different bits of code dependent on what the user does.

In this chapter we'll look at some of the building blocks of Visual Basic programming. If you've programmed in BASIC, C or Pascal before, then most of this will be familiar.

You will learn:

- How to make choices using `If..Then`
- How to select from various options
- How to loop using `For..Next` and `Do..While`
- How to combine all these language features into working Visual Basic programs

Writing Code in Visual Basic

In the first two chapters you gained an understanding of the main components of a Visual Basic program:

▶ **Forms** are the framework on which you build your interface.

▶ **Controls** are the building blocks from which you construct that interface.

▶ **Event** procedures are the glue that binds these components together and make it into a system that achieves what you want.

One of our objectives in this book is to try and get you up and running fast, with practical and interesting programs. To do this, we've thrown you in at the deep end. You saw your first lines of code in Chapter 1, using the `Form_UnLoad` event to display a message box wishing you good-bye. In Chapter 2, you saw even more code in the `CONTROL.MAK` project. We explained some of this as we went along, the rest we've kept under wraps for the moment.

Now, I'm afraid, the party's over and it's time to get down to some serious programming. The next two chapters are about the techniques you need to write effective event handler code.

▶ In this chapter we'll explain how to structure your program code so you can make choices and respond to different events and conditions.

▶ In Chapter 4, you'll find out how to represent data in your code, and what you can do to that data to get your required results.

These two subjects are fundamental building blocks for programming in Visual Basic. You will learn all sorts of other things along the way, including the rich set of built-in functions that Visual Basic offers. We'll throw all of these in as and when appropriate. For now though, if you are going to get to grips with writing code in Visual Basic, you need to understand its structure, and the data within it. So, let's make a start!

Making Choices in Programs

Two of the most important parts of any programming language are its decision making capabilities and its branching capabilities. These terms need some explanation.

Decision Making

In an event procedure your code will normally start to run at the first line of code and proceed down through the rest of the event code until it meets either an **Exit Sub** or an **End Sub** statement. The word **Sub** is short for **subprocedure**, which is the name Visual Basic gives to a single block of code. For example, many applications include a Quit command button. When this button is clicked the application shuts down. The simplest event code you would find for this command button being clicked is:

```
Sub cmdQuit_Click()
    End
End Sub
```

Decision making takes place when the program code decides to perform a particular action *providing* that a certain condition is met. As a programmer, you first of all have to test the condition, then write the code that needs to be executed in response.

Think about the Quit command button again. Although the event code does the job just fine, it could make a safer exit. What would happen if the user hit the Quit button by accident? The application would close down and your poor users could lose a lot of work which they had forgotten to save. Decision making can get around this problem:

```
Sub cmdQuit_Click()

    If WorkSaved = False then
            MsgBox "Save your work first!"
    Else
            End
    Endif
End Sub
```

With just a few extra lines of code, and a line of decision making code, your users become happy bunnies. When they hit the Quit button, our code checks to see if their work is saved. It does this by checking the value of a variable called **WorkSaved**. If the work has not been saved then our old friend the **MsgBox** is used to display a message to that effect. Otherwise, the application ends as before.

If you want to run this fragment of code yourself, then add the line **WorkSaved = False** directly before the **If** statement. It's really intended to work as part of a larger program where the value of **WorkSaved** would have been set elsewhere.

Branching

Branching occurs when the program code takes control of itself and decides that the next line to run is in fact ten lines back, or ten lines further on.

Decision making and branching are closely related. The code won't normally branch to a different line unless a decision has been made saying that it should do so. Think about a trip to the beach. Given that everything goes to plan you:

1 Drive to the beach.

2 Find a pleasant spot.

3 Relax for the rest of the day.

4 Pack up your stuff.

5 Drive home.

Decision making comes into play if you live in a country such as England, which has no roof! In that case you:

1 Drive to the beach.

2 **If** the weather is rotten, **Go to** step 6.

3 Find a pleasant spot.

4 Relax for the rest of the day.

5 Pack up your stuff.

6 Drive Home.

The same techniques apply with Visual Basic. You lay out your code in the order you want things to happen. You then use condition statements like **If** to check things are OK. If they aren't, then the **Goto**, **GoSub** or **Call** statements can be used to branch to another part of the code.

Over the course of this chapter you will learn everything you need to know about **If** statements, **Goto**, **Gosub**, and **Call** - so don't panic if it isn't all completely crystal-clear straight away.

It is possible to branch off to another part of the program unconditionally, without first having tested any condition. However, this is regarded as bad programming practice and I'll explain why in the course of this chapter.

Decision Making

There are various ways to make choices and selections in code. They all come back to the same basic action - testing whether or not something is true. The different ways, one of which is **Select Case,** are designed to handle different instances of this process in a more elegant way than having a long list of **If** statements. However, behind the scenes they amount to the same thing.

Testing for Conditions With If

The simplest way to make a decision in a program is using the **If** statement. You may remember that we used this in some of the other examples in the book. Hopefully, everything that you've seen already will now begin to fall into place. Let's try out some code to see how the **If** statement works.

Try It Out - The Basic If Statement

Many business applications have some form of security built-in to prevent unwanted users from playing around with information they shouldn't have access to. Normally, you use the **If** statement to check the user's name and password before letting them go any further.

Let's see how to do this.

1   In Visual Basic, start a new project. From the File menu, select New Project.

2   After a short pause the project will be created and the default form, called Form1, will appear.

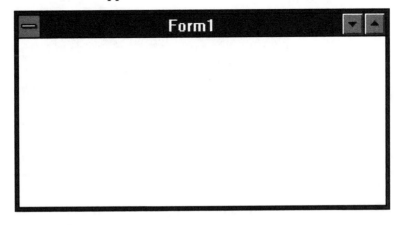

3 Bring up the properties window for the form. Pressing *F4* is the easiest way to do this. Change the Caption property to Please enter your password.

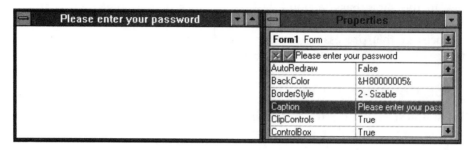

4 Draw one text box and one command button on the form. Resize the form, and move the new controls around so that your form looks something like this:

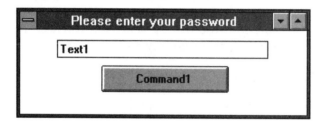

5 Select the TextBox and bring up its properties window. Find the PasswordChar property and set it to *. See how the text box caption is replaced by ****.

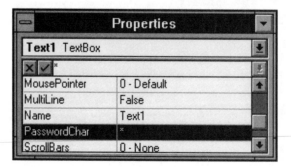

6 Then, find the Text property and blank it out: select the property by clicking on it, then press the *BkSp* key on your keyboard, followed by *Enter*. This removes the ***** from the box.

7 Select the command button, bring up its properties window and set the Caption to OK.

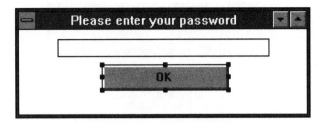

8 Now we can write some code. When the program runs we want the user to key in their password, then hit the OK button. At that point, an **If** statement will check the password and display the results in a message box on the screen.

9 Double-click the command button to bring up the code window. Type in code so that the command button's click event looks like this:

```
Sub Command1_Click ()
  If Text1.Text = "noidea" Then
        MsgBox "Great - password accepted!"
        Unload Form1
        End
    Else
        MsgBox "Sorry, that's wrong, try again!"
        Text1.SetFocus
        Text1.Text = ""
    End If
End Sub
```

This program is on the disk called PASSWORD.MAK

How It Works

Now try running the program. If you typed all the code in correctly then the program will run after a short pause. Click in the text box and type Fred.

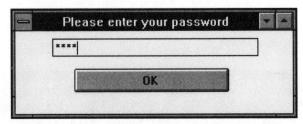

Stars appear in place of the keys you press on the keyboard. This is what setting the PasswordChar property to * does for you.

Having entered Fred, click the command button and a message box appears telling you to try again.

Get rid of the message box by clicking the OK button, then type noidea into the text box and click the command button again. This time the password is accepted and the program ends.

The **If** statement in the above example consists of a number of parts:

> Straight after the word **If** there is the condition we want to test. In this example the condition is **Text1.text = "noidea".**

> Immediately following the condition is the **Then** statement which tells Visual Basic what to do if the condition is met.

Take a look at the code again. Translated into plain English it says: **If the value of the textbox is "noidea" then unload the form and end the program.**

The **Else** statement, and the code following it, tells Visual Basic what to do if the condition is not met; so in the example, this part of the command actually means: **otherwise, display the message "try again", move the cursor back to the text box.** The **Else** part of the statement is optional. You could just have an **If** statement that only does something if the condition is met, but which does nothing if it is not.

The two lines of code:

```
Text1.SetFocus
Text1.Text = ""
```

set the focus back onto the text box and clear the previous text ready to accept your next attempt.

By default, comparing text in Visual Basic is case-sensitive. This means that it matters whether you use capitals or lower-case letters in the text. If you had typed NoIdea then it would have been rejected as an incorrect password. You make Visual Basic case insensitive by adding the `statement` `Option Compare Text` to your code. To return to the default you need to use `Option Compare Binary`.

Defining the Conditions You Want to Test

This actually leads us nicely on to **conditional expressions**. It's pretty obvious what the = sign means in the example above, but what if you want to test for two numbers not being equal, or a number that is higher than another? By changing the equals sign in the example, you can test for many different conditions.

The complete list of symbols that you can use to test conditions are:

Symbol	Meaning
=	Is Equal To
<>	Is Not Equal To
>	Is Greater Than
<	Is Less than
>=	Is Greater Than or Equal To
<=	Is Less than or Equal To

For example, `If Age > 21 then Admit_Entry`, would read as **If age is greater than 21 then admit entry**. Here `Admit_Entry` represents some code you want executed if the condition is true.

The code `Admit_Entry` can either be a few lines of Visual Basic code tucked right there in the same event handler, or it can be code contained in its own module, separate from this handler. In the second case, this block of code is called a **subprocedure**, and simply writing its name, `Admit_Entry`, causes Visual Basic to jump to that code and execute it there and then. Modules and subprocedures are inherently bound up with controlling program flow, and we'll look at them in more detail later in this chapter. Before that, let's finish our review of the ways to test conditions in Visual Basic.

Testing Multiple Conditions

This is all fairly straightforward stuff - but what happens when you need to test for more than one condition before doing something. An example could be a correct password and the person's age to be greater than 21.

Visual Basic lets you use the words **And** and **Or** in order to make your complex conditions easier to read in code. In this example we could have an **If** statement that says:

```
If Age > 21 And Password = "noidea" Then Admit_Entry
```

You can also use brackets to group conditions together. Normally with an **If** statement you check for a number of conditions and tell Visual Basic whether you want to do something if all the conditions are met (using **And**) or if only one condition is met (using **Or**). You can group those tests into one by using brackets around some of the tests on the **If** line. For instance you could have a line like this:

```
If Age > 21 and Password = "noidea" or Password ="Supervisor" Then
  Do_Something
```

It's not immediately obvious what this line of code does. Does it do something if the **Age** is greater than 21 and the password **= "noidea"** or **"Supervisor"**? Does it do something as long as the password **= "noidea"** and the age is greater than 21, or the **Password = "Supervisor"**? Confusing isn't it!

By using brackets the code becomes much more readable and the results a great deal more predictable:

```
If (Age > 21 and Password = "noidea") or Password = "supervisor" Then
  Admit_Entry
```

This **If** line will do something if the password is **"supervisor"**, or both the age is greater than 21 and the password is **"noidea"**. The brackets separate the tests into smaller groups, so the **If** line treats:

```
(Age > 21 and Password = "noidea")
```

as one test, call it test A, and:

```
Password = "Supervisor"
```

as another test, call it test B. The **If** line will then work as long as A *or* B is met.

Multi-line If Statements

It's already obvious that the line of code gets longer and longer as the condition gets more and more complex. There is another way to use the **If** statement which can help make the code a little more readable.

Using the multi-line **If** statement, the code following the word **Then** is spread over one or more separate lines. A new command, **EndIf**, tells Visual Basic where exactly the conditional code ends. Let's try the example again:

```
If (sPassword = "noidea" and sUserName = "Peter") or LoggedIn = True Then

    Allow_Access
    Update_User_Log
    Display_First_Screen

Endif
```

By using the multi-line **If,** you can not only make your code a lot more readable, but you can also place a lot more functionality into the **If** statement. In this example, providing the appropriate conditions are met, three subroutine calls are made instead of just one.

Multi-line If...Else Statements

Just as with the single line **If,** the multi-line version lets you use the **Else** statement to give Visual Basic an alternative course of action:

```
If (Password = "noidea" and UserName = "Peter") or LoggedIn = True Then
    Allow_Access
    Update_User_Log
    Display_First_Screen
Else
    Deny_Access
    Erase_HardDisk
    Electrocute_User
Endif
```

Multiple Alternatives Using ElseIf

Under normal circumstances you are limited to having just two possible outcomes with an **If** statement:

> The code that executes if the condition is met.

> The code following the **Else** that executes if the condition fails.

The multi-line version provides yet another benefit; the ability to perform further tests as an immediate result of a prior test, using **ElseIf**. Instead of the normal **Else** statement you can use **ElseIf** to build complex decision making code that can take any number of courses of action.

```
If <condition> Then
    :
    :
Elseif <condition> Then
    :
    :
Elseif <condition> Then
    :
    :
Else
    :
    :
Endif
```

The code following the last **Else** statement is run, providing all the other conditions on the **If** and **Elseif** lines fail.

Try It Out - Multi-line If Statements

1   Load up the example **MULTVIEW.MAK** project from the sample programs provided. This project allows you to select a file and then view it using one of the other programs on your system.

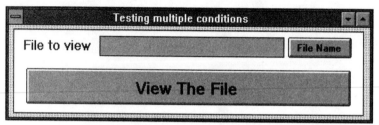

2   Run the program. Click on the File Name command button to select a File to view. This displays a common dialog, a built in piece of code included with Windows. We'll cover these in detail in Chapter 8 - Dialogs. For now, don't worry about how it works in detail.

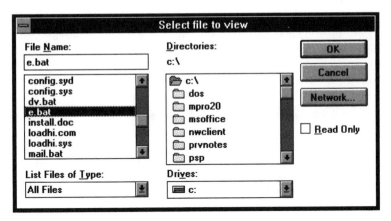

3 Once you have selected a file, click on the View The File command button and MultView will load up the appropriate program and display the file.

The program does have some problems. If you select a file ending in **.BAT** then nothing happens. You'd expect it to load that file into Notepad in the same way as **.TXT** files. Also, in this age of multimedia, the program is unable to deal with **.WAV** (sound samples) files, **.MID** (Midi soundtrack) files and **.AVI** (realtime video) files. Let's add these features and make the program tell us when something has gone wrong.

4 In design mode, double-click on the View The File command button to display the code that recognizes the various files.

```
Sub cmdView_Click ()

    ' This sets up a variable, a place in memory to hold some data.
    ' The As String bit tells Visual Basic that we are going to store
↳Text in this area.
    Dim sExtension As String
    Dim ReturnValue

    sExtension = UCase(Right$(txtFile, 3))

    If Dir$(txtFile.Text) = "" Then
        MsgBox "Sorry, I couldn't find that file!"
        Exit Sub
    ElseIf sExtension = "TXT" Then
        ReturnValue = Shell("Notepad " & txtFile.Text, 1)
    ElseIf sExtension = "WRI" Then
        ReturnValue = Shell("Write " & txtFile.Text, 1)
    ElseIf sExtension = "CRD" Then
        ReturnValue = Shell("Cardfile " & txtFile.Text, 1)
    End If

End Sub
```

Looks daunting doesn't it. The first three lines, excluding the **Sub** line, set up some variables. These are places in memory to temporarily hold data. We cover variables in the next chapter.

The line:

```
sExtension = Ucase$(Right$(txtFile.Text, 3))
```

takes the right-hand 3 letters of the selected file name, the file extension, and makes sure that all the letters are changed to uppercase. The result is then stored in the **sExtension** variable. If you selected **AUTOEXEC.BAT** for example, then this line would take the **BAT** bit, change it to **BAT** and store **BAT** in **sExtension**.

The main part of the code is the **If...Then** statement. This is a multi-line **If** which first checks whether the file selected actually exists, and then checks the three **sExtension** variables to see if it recognizes the file type. If it does, then the appropriate program is loaded up using the **Shell** command and the selected file is shown.

How It Works

DIR$** allows us to check whether a file exists. The **DIR$ command returns either the name of the file if it is found or **""** if it's not. So the line:

```
If Dir$(txtFile.Text) = "" then
```

will do something if the file name in the text box can't be found on the disk. **Shell** is a command in Visual Basic which lets us run another program. The program name and any other parameters are held in the brackets after the word **Shell**. For example:

```
ReturnValue = Shell("Notepad " & txtFile.Text, 1)
```

runs up Notepad and displays your computer's **AUTOEXEC.BAT** file. The **1** in the code tells Visual Basic that when the program is run it should be displayed in front of our Visual Basic program. You could equally well have **Shell** run a program out of sight in the background, or just display a minimized icon for it.

Shell actually returns a value to your code which you can check to see if everything worked OK. In this example though, we just dump whatever **Shell** returns into the **ReturnValue** variable.

Try It Out - Adding More File Types

1   In the code window click on the line above the words **End If** and type in this:

```
ElseIf sExtension = "WAV" or sExtension = "MID" or sExtension = "AVI" then
    ReturnValue= Shell ("MPlayer " & txtFile.Text, 1)
ElseIf sExtension = "DIB" or sExtension = "PCX" or sExtension = "BMP" then
    ReturnValue= Shell("PBrush " & txtFile.Text, 1)
Else
    MsgBox "Sorry, I don't know how to handle this file type"
```

2   These **ElseIf** lines tell Visual Basic how to deal with sound, video and graphics files. As you saw before, the code after the **ElseIfs** will only be run if all the initial **If**, and the other **ElseIfs** fail.

3   Now if you run the program you'll be able to deal with graphics files and multimedia files, such as **WAV**s and **MID**s.

The bottom **Else** command which you entered displays a message box. **Else**, as opposed to **Elseif**, normally lets you tell Visual Basic what it should do if the **If** fails. In this case though, **Else** tells Visual Basic what to do if the **If** and **ElseIf** lines all fail.

> I'll make no bones about it, this is a difficult program to throw at you now. Don't worry if it doesn't all fall into place immediately. A lot of what's in it will be covered in later chapters. I just wanted to give you a useful application here and now. To save you typing, the finished program is on the disk as **SHOWDONE.MAK**.

Putting Code into Modules

Once you start to use multi-line **If** statements, the code you write for all the possible conditions can be huge. Worse than that, you may want to branch to the same code in many different situations, the result being that you type in the same piece of code over and over again.

Imagine, for example, that you wanted to check the characters that your user was inputting into a text box, like we did in Chapter 2. If you only have one text box, then that's no problem. Unfortunately, most real-life forms have lots of data entry points, so you could end up typing in the code for each one. There has to be a better way, and sure enough there is - **modular programming**.

Try It Out!

So far in this book, all the code we have written is directly contained in the event handlers of various controls and objects. As these objects are themselves placed onto forms, all our code has been inside forms. Modules are very different. Whereas the code in a form normally relates specifically to that form, code in a module is **global**. It can be called on by any other code in your project, and is not normally tied to any one control or form. So in the case of checking text box input, you could create a global module called, for example, **CheckInput**. You are then able to call that central routine whenever you need it.

Functions and Procedures

In breaking down your program into modules, you have a choice between **functions** and **procedures**.

▶ Functions usually consist of code that does something specific and then returns a result to the part of the program that called it. The **Sin()** function in Visual Basic does exactly this. You pass a number to it, and it gives you back a result which is the sine of the original number.

▶ Procedures on the other hand, don't tend to return results. They just do something. The **Load** method in Visual Basic is actually a procedure. There is no way to check whether the form is actually loaded or not: Visual Basic handles everything for you.

So far, all the Visual Basic code you've written is for event procedures. A command button is pressed so Visual Basic runs the **Command1_Click()** event **procedure**. Your code in that procedure usually does something like changing the display, but you don't tend to pass anything back to Visual Basic.

A stand-alone Visual Basic procedure is really just an event handler that is invoked from within your own code, rather than in response to an external event.

The Big Picture

Forms, modules, subprocedures and functions are all related. Just what exactly are they? Well, you already know about forms; these are the elements of your programs onto which you can draw controls to build up a program's user interface.

Behind all the graphic excitement you have event code. This is code which does something in response to the user triggering an event, such as clicking on a command button, moving the mouse and so on. These events are actually called subprocedures.

Think about making a cup of coffee. **Making_Coffee** is the application. Filling up the kettle, putting coffee in the cup, and stirring the coffee are all subprocedures. You don't have to learn how to fill the kettle each time you want to make some coffee. **Filling_The_Kettle** is stored in your head as a subprocedure. It's the same in your Visual Basic application. If you have a common block of code that is used over and over, then put it in a subprocedure.

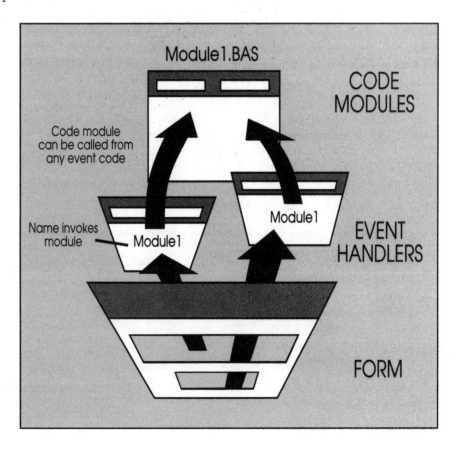

Functions are very similar to subprocedures except for the fact that they return results. When you make a cup of coffee you may not be able to find the coffee jar (because you're so lazy you never make any coffee), so you call out to the **Wife_Find_Coffee** function to locate the coffee. You can then get the **Get_Coffee** subprocedure to go to wherever the **Wife_Find_Coffee** function told you to go.

Imagine a form which has no visual manifestation, just subroutines and functions! If you can picture that, then you can picture a module. Modules provide a way for you to write code which can be used throughout your entire system. Normally, subprocedures and functions in a module are **global,** meaning that they can be called by code anywhere else in your application.

If you're still a little confused, don't worry. We'll cover functions, subprocedures and modules in a lot more detail as you work your way through the book.

Try It Out - Adding Subprocedures

Let's add some more code to the **MULTI-VIEW** project we saw earlier. By default the form appears on your screen wherever Windows and Visual Basic think it should. Wouldn't it be nice if we could just call a subprocedure that automatically centers the form?

1   Load up the **SHOWFILE.MAK** project again. When the form appears, press *F7*, or double-click the form to bring up the code window.

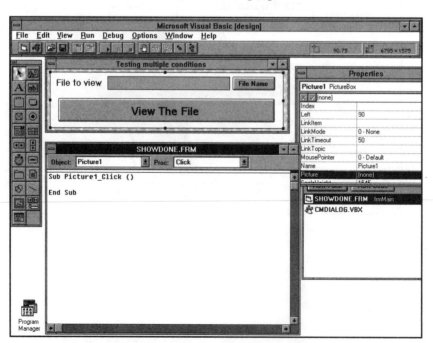

2 To add a new subprocedure simply move the cursor to the bottom of any code you see.

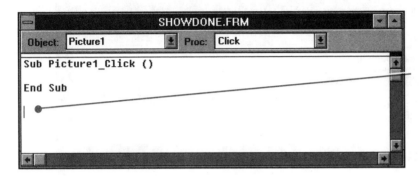

Make sure that you click beneath the words **End Sub,** as these mark the end of the event code you are looking at.

3 Type this line in and press *Enter:*

```
Sub Center
```

4 The code window will instantly clear and Visual Basic will present you with a blank code window ready for the new subprocedure. Visual Basic also automatically puts in an **End Sub** for you to mark the end of the subprocedure.

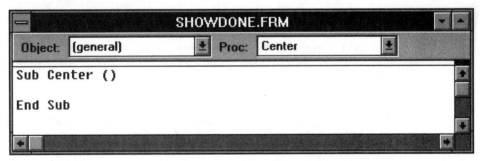

5 Type in code so that the **Center** subprocedure looks like this:

```
Sub Center ()

    frmMain.Left = (Screen.Width - frmMain.Width) / 2
    frmMain.Top = (Screen.Height - frmMain.Height) / 2

End Sub
```

6 Now use the object combo box at the top of the code window to select Form.

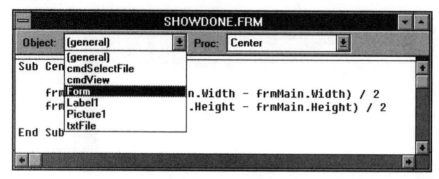

7 As soon as you select **Form**, the form **Load** event code is displayed in the code window, instead of your new subprocedure. Your subprocedure is still there, just not visible.

Change the form **Load** code to say:

```
Sub Form_Load()

        Call Center

End Sub
```

8 The **Call** command tells Visual Basic that we want to call a subprocedure. In our case **Call Center** tells Visual Basic to run the subprocedure called **Center**.

Call is really a hang over from the days of Visual Basic 1 and 2. Although you can use it, and it does make your code a lot easier to read, we could equally well have said:

```
Sub Form_Load ()

        Center

End Sub
```

Since **Center** is not a keyword Visual Basic knows that we are trying to call a subprocedure.

Keywords are words that mean something in Visual Basic. They are used for things such as commands. You can't use them in your code for your own purposes.

9 While you are still in the code window you can press *F2* just to make sure that all your event procedures and your **Center** subprocedure are still there.

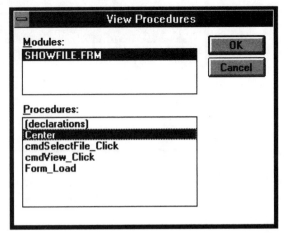

10 You'll see a list of all the event code in the program, along with your new **Center** subprocedure at the top of the list.

11 If you run the program now, you'll see that the form loads up positioned dead center of the screen.

Where's the Form?

When you use modules you can actually choose not to show any form at all when your program starts. Instead, you can run code in a module directly. If you want to interact with your users, however, you'll have to create a user interface on the fly. Modules are normally used as a backup to forms. They provide common code which all the forms can use. Just to illustrate the point though, let's write a program with no forms at all.

Try It Out!

Try It Out - A Program With No Forms

1 Load up Visual Basic and start a new project.

2 All new projects in Visual Basic are created with a form already in them. From the Window menu select Project and the project window will appear showing you a list of all the files in your project. The top one is Form1.

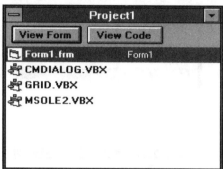

3 Select this line by clicking it once, then from the File menu select Remove File. The form will vanish from your project for ever.

4 There are a number of ways that you can create modules. You can either select New Module from the File menu, or click on the new module icon on the Visual Basic toolbar.

5 As soon as you create a module, a code window pops up for it. Remember, modules are forms but without the visual side.

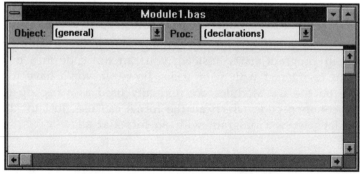

6 For a program with no forms to run, you need to have a subprocedure called **Main** in a module, to act as the replacement for your main form. Click in the code window now and create a **Main** subprocedure.

Visual Basic names this Main in the Proc: window.

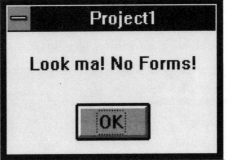

7 Whenever you create a project that has no forms, Visual Basic instinctively knows to run the **Main** subprocedure when the program starts to run. If you click the run button now, up comes the message box.

8 However, there will be times when you'll need to run a **Main** subprocedure in an application that does have forms. When this happens, you need to actually tell Visual Basic to load up your module first, rather than the first form you created. You do this using the Start Up Form option. Bring up the dialog by selecting Project from the Options menu.

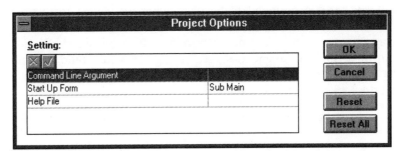

9 Here the Start Up Form option is set to Sub Main, meaning that the **Main** subprocedure will be run before anything else. If you had a project with a number of forms, then you could select any of these forms to be run first instead.

Getting Selective

If you play around with conditions and **If** statements long enough you'll soon end up tying yourself in knots with code consisting of line upon line of extremely similar looking **If..Then...Else** statements. **If** is great for one-shot tests and simple two-state decision making (If a Then b Else c). When things start to get really messy, then that's the time to reach for the **Select Case** statement.

The Select Case Statement

There does come a point in any program where the **If** command is simply not up to the job. Imagine, for example, a menu on screen, not your normal Windows style menu, but a simple list of numbered text entries. Let's say there are seven of them. If the user presses number 1 on the keyboard then you want the first subprocedure to run. If they press 2 then a different one kicks in, and so on.

Using **If** you would have something like this:

```
If KeyPressed = "1" then
     Call Sub1
else if Keypress = "2" then
     Call Sub2
else if Keypress = "3" then
     Call Sub3
else if Keypress = "4" then
     Call Sub4
     :
     :
```

Looks a mess doesn't it? If computers are so great at making repetitive tasks simple, then there must be a more elegant way of doing this kind of test. There is, by using the **Select Case** command.

Select Case is designed to be used when you need to test a single property or variable against a number of values. Picture the scene where you've got a control array of five command buttons which all use the same **Click** event, but all display different messages. Using **If** you would end up with an **If..Elseif** combination as long as your arm. However, with **Select Case** the world looks a much brighter place.

Try It Out - Select Case in Action

Remember the awful multi-line **If** statement in **SHOWFILE.MAK**. Using **Select Case** that code could be so much nicer. Before we launch into a fully blown breakdown of how it all works, let's type some code.

1 In Visual Basic, load up the **SHOWFILE.MAK** project again. When the form appears, double-click on the View The File command button to see its code.

2 With the exception of the first **If Dir$(txtFile.Text) = ""** statement, all the other **ElseIf** lines relate to the **sExtension** variable, checking the extension of the selected file and running the appropriate program. This is ideal hunting ground for **Select Case**. (Finger ache time).

3 Change the code so **Select Case** is used, like this

```
Sub cmdView_Click ()

' This sets up a variable, a place in
' memory to hold some data.
' The As String bit tells Visual Basic
' that we are going to store Text in this area.
    Dim sExtension As String
    Dim ReturnValue

    sExtension = UCase(Right$(txtFile, 3))

    If Dir$(txtFile.Text) = "" Then
        MsgBox "Sorry, I couldn't find that file!"
        Exit Sub
    End If

Select Case sExtension
 Case "TXT"
    ReturnValue = Shell("Notepad " & TxtFile.Text, 1)
 Case "WRI"
    ReturnValue = Shell("Write " & txtFile.Text, 1)
 Case "CRD"
    ReturnValue = Shell("Cardfile " & txtFile.Text, 1)
End Select

End Sub
```

4 All that's involved here is moving the **EndIf** line to underneath the words **Exit Sub**, then changing all the **EndIf**s to **Case,** and adding a **Select Case** statement.

5 **Select Case** tells Visual Basic that we want to check against one specific variable, in this case **sExtension**. The **Case** lines that follow tell Visual Basic what to do if the variable equals the value following the word **Case**. So far the code doesn't look that much more compact or easy to follow. We haven't added in graphics or multimedia support yet!

6 To add graphics and multimedia support to the program, we need to check for any one of three possible selections. For graphics we need to see if the file extension is **PCX**, **DIB** or **BMP**. For multimedia we want **WAV**, **AVI** and **MID**. Using multi-line **If**s this meant some pretty messy **If** XXXX = XX or XXXXX = XXX or XXXX = XX lines.

7 Add these lines to the routine, just above the **End Select** line:

```
Case "BMP", "PCX", "DIB"
    ReturnValue = Shell("PBrush " & txtFile.Text, 1)

Case "WAV", "MID", "AVI"
    ReturnValue = Shell("MPlayer " & txtFile.Text, 1)
```

8 The **Select Case** statement now looks like this:

```
Select Case sExtension
  Case "TXT"
    ReturnValue = Shell("Notepad " & txtFile.Text, 1)
      Case "WRI"
        ReturnValue = Shell("Write " & txtFile.Text, 1)
      Case "CRD"
    ReturnValue = Shell("Cardfile " & txtFile.Text, 1)
  Case "BMP", "PCX", "DIB"
    ReturnValue = Shell("PBrush " & txtFile.Text, 1)
  Case "WAV", "MID", "AVI"
    ReturnValue = Shell("MPlayer " & txtFile.Text, 1)

End Select
```

9 By separating values after the word **Case** with a comma, you can give Visual Basic a list of values to check in order to run the same piece of code. To **Select Case**, the command actually means OR. So the graphics **Case** line reads: **In case of BMP, PCX or DIB do this**. As I'm sure you can appreciate, this is so much easier to read.

10 The only thing the program still doesn't do is display a message if the file type isn't known. Just as you can still use **Else** on a multi-line **If** to handle *any other value*, **Select Case** has **Case Else** for just this purpose.

11 Move the cursor to just above the **End Select** line again, and enter this:

```
Case Else
    Msgbox "Sorry, I don't know how to handle this file type"
```

12 If you run the program now you should find it works exactly the same as the Multi-line If version. The major difference between the two is that this version is a lot easier to read, maintain and change.

Selecting Options Based on Different Conditions

So far you have seen how we can use **Select Case** to check a single value or a range of values against a variable. However, it can do much more than that. Each **Case** statement, just like a standard **If** statement, can be used to compare the variable against a range of values. The syntax is somewhat different to a standard **If** statement though.

With **Case**, each of the values you want to check for is separated by a comma. So, if you wanted to see if a variable contained the numbers 2, 5 and 10 you could write:

```
Case 2, 5, 10
    'Here is the code
    'That you want to execute
    'If these values are true.
```

In addition to this, the **Case** statement can also check running ranges of numbers, such as 1 to 5, or 100 - 200. Let's say you wanted to check if the variable contained a number in the range 10 - 15; your **Case** statement would look like this:

```
Case 10 To 15
    Here is the code
    That you want to execute
    If these values are true.
```

Another difference to the normal **If** statement is that **Case** statements can't contain the name of the variable you are checking, so you couldn't say **Case Index > 10** if the **Index** is the name of the variable in the **Select** statement. In its place, though, you can use the word **Is**. **Is** refers to the variable you're checking, so it is quite legal to write:

```
Case Is > 100, Is <= 500, 999
```

This checks for values greater than 100, or less than 500 or equal to 999. Unlike the **If** statement you cannot just say **variablename > 100**. Remember that the variable name is held on the **Select Case** line. The **Is** keyword checks the value of the variable against the condition, so **Is > 100** means: **if the variable IS greater than 100**. As before, the commas mean **or**, so the above line actually says: **If the variable IS greater than 100 or IS less than or equal to 500 or equals 999 then do something**.

Selecting Strings

The use of **Case** when dealing with text is exactly the same. If you use the **To** clause, Visual Basic does an alphabetic comparison on the two strings:

```
Select Case sPassword
    Case "Apples" To "Pears"
            :
            :
End Select
```

This example would cause your case code to run if the value of the **Password** string falls alphabetically between **"Apples"** and **"Pears"**.

When you do comparisons between text strings Visual Basic deals with the comparison in a semi-intelligent way. First of all it looks at the case of the letters in the string. A capital letter, such as G, is treated as coming before its lowercase equivalent g. So if you were to compare Peter and peter, in alphabetical sorting Peter comes first.

This type of comparison happens for every letter of the string. The result is that Visual Basic handles strings properly so that Apple comes before Pear, Aardvark comes before Arachnid and so on. Beware though, that Aardvark is quite different to aardvark as far as Visual Basic is concerned.

For My Next Trick - Loops

Conditional statements such as **If** are great for running pieces of code that are based on a condition once only. However, the real beauty of computers has always been their ability to do a great many repetitive operations in a fraction of the time it would take a human to do the same thing.

This is where loops come into play. Think back to your schooldays. You've just entered class late for the 12th time and neglected your homework for the 10th time. The teacher is naturally a little upset and in a fit of fury orders you to write down "I must stop being a complete failure" 1000 times. There we have it - a boring, odious task which a computer could perform with no hassle. The only thing to remember here though, is that the well-programmed computer probably wouldn't have been late for class in the first place.

A **For** loop is what we need here. This enables us to run a block of code a set number of times. In the case of our little childhood problem, the code in question would simply write the words "I must stop being a complete failure" 1000 times.

Try It Out - The For Loop

1 Start a new project in Visual Basic.

2 Double-click on the form (Form1) to display its code window.

3 Select the **Form_Load** event code.

4 Type in some code so that your **Form_Load** event looks like this.

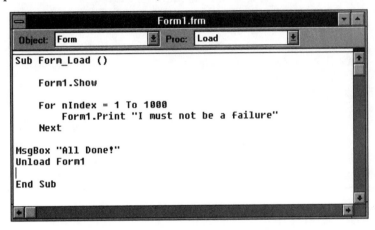

```
Sub Form_Load ()

    Form1.Show

    For nIndex = 1 To 1000
        Form1.Print "I must not be a failure"
    Next

MsgBox "All Done!"
Unload Form1

End Sub
```

5 Run the code and you'll see the message appear on the form 1000 times. A message box then appears telling you that the program has finished. We'll cover the **Print** command in more detail in Chapter 8 - Graphics, but for now this is quite straightforward.

The line `For nIndex = 1 to 1000` is the start of the `For` loop we're interested in. The `Show` command before that just makes sure the form is visible before we start to `Print.` If it wasn't, nothing would appear.

Loading a form with the `Load` command simply sets aside some memory to hold the form's graphics, code and controls. It doesn't actually make the form appear on screen.

The form will normally come into view at some point after the end of the form's `Load` event. I say "at some point," because the code in the load event could go off and do a hundred or more other things such as setting up variables to hold data, or doing some calculations in loops. The form will only become visible when Visual Basic has the time.

The `Show` method gets around this, by forcing Visual Basic to bring the form into view. It's always good, from a user's point of view, to put a `Show` command in a form's `Load` event. If something appears on screen almost straight away, your users won't start panicking and think that your program, Windows, or both have crashed. It's all a matter of psychology; if users can see something happening then they stop counting the seconds it takes for your program to actually do something useful. You could take another approach and `Show` a small form containing a message such as Please Wait - Loading Data.

How the For..Next Loop Works

Of all the looping commands in Visual Basic, the `For...Next` combination is the only one that has been inherited from the first ever version of the BASIC language. This is because `For...Next` is easy to use and is surprisingly powerful.

The `Next` statement shows where the loop actually ends. All code placed between the `For` and the `Next` commands is run on each pass or iteration of the loop.

How Index Variables Control For Loops

`For` loops use a numeric variable (`Integer`, `Long`, `Double` etc.) as a **counter** to keep track of the number of times the loop actually needs to run. In loop-speak this variable is often called an Index.

A variable is a container for a piece of data. You can assign labels, called variable names. You can change the value of a variable at run-time, which is why it's useful for counting loops.

By saying `For nIndex = 1 to 1000` we are telling Visual Basic to load the variable **nIndex** with the number 1 to start with, and add 1 to it at each pass through the loop's code until it equals 1000. As soon as the variable goes outside the range 1 to 1000, the loop exits and the code following the **Next** statement is run.

You should place the name of the index variable straight after the word Next (i.e. Next nIndex). This can make the code a lot easier to read and follow, particularly if you have a number of For loops nested inside each other. In our example there is only one For loop, so it's obvious that the Next command relates to this.

Controlling the Index Variable

In our example, the **For** loop increments the index variable by 1 on each iteration. This is the default setting for a **For** loop. It can be changed by placing a **Step** statement at the end of the **For** statement. **Step** tells Visual Basic how many to add to the index variable on each iteration. We can see that:

```
For nIndex = 1 to 1000 step 50
```

tells Visual Basic to start with the value of 1 in **nIndex** and add 50 to the index variable on each pass. As before the loop will exit as soon as the value of 1000 is exceeded in **nIndex.**

By far the most common use for **Step** is in creating decreasing loops. Visual Basic will automatically add 1 to the index variable every time, so a statement like:

```
For nIndex = 1000 to 1
```

wouldn't actually work. The statement:

```
For nIndex = 1000 To 1 Step -1
```

would work, since the **Step** clause tells Visual Basic to add -1 to the index variable on each pass.

Leaving a For Loop

Visual Basic provides a command for leaving a **For** loop prematurely. Placing the command **Exit For** inside a loop will cause it to stop immediately and the code to continue running from the line directly following the **Next** statement. It works in much the same way as **Exit Sub** does to leave a subprocedure.

It's a long standing tradition that index variables in **For** loops are usually called I or J, or even X and Y. Despite what other books or magazines might have you think, this is extremely bad programming practice.

If you defined a variable then you undoubtedly had a reason for doing so. Furthermore, if you have started a **For** loop then there was a reason for that as well. Always give any variable a meaningful name. If you have a **For** loop that is counting records in a file then call the index variable **nRecordsInFile**. If you have taken the time to bring a variable to life then take the time to christen it properly too. When you return to your code to make changes to it in a month or a year's time, the variable name will make the code much more readable. You should be able to get a hint from the index variable's name as to exactly what the loop itself is doing.

This bad naming practice stems from the limited choice of variable names that were available in Fortran, a language that was a predecessor of BASIC. In Fortran, all integer variables began with the letters I,J,K,L,M or N. The X and Y names presumably come from terse mathematicians.

The Do Loop

The **For** loop is a venerable remnant of the original BASIC language. Visual Basic is an evolutionary product that has adopted many of the best commands and attributes of other leading languages such as C and Pascal, and married them to its BASIC roots. The **Do** loop illustrates this point well, as it's based on a similar structure found in Pascal.

The **Do...While** loop is an alternative way to repeat a block of code. You can achieve the same results using various combinations of **For..Next** loop, but sometimes using **Do...While** makes your code more elegant and intuitive. At the end of the day however, it's a question of style.

There are 3 types of **Do** loop; those that run for ever, those that run until a condition is met, and those that run whilst a condition is being met. The three are covered using the **Do...Loop, Do...Loop Until**, and **the Do...Loop While** commands. We'll have a look at them now.

Do..Loop While

Let's go back to the password example from earlier on in the chapter. It's OK to electrocute the illegal user and throw them out of the system, but sooner or later you'll run out of living users. You really want to give the user a second, or maybe even third chance. Enter stage left the **Do...Loop While** loop.

Try It Out - Three Tries for the Password

1 Load up the **PASSD01.MAK** project. Try it out for yourself by trying to enter a password.

2 On the third wrong attempt, the program ends.

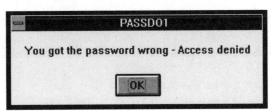

Try It Out!

3 Take a look at the code by pressing the View Code button on the project window.

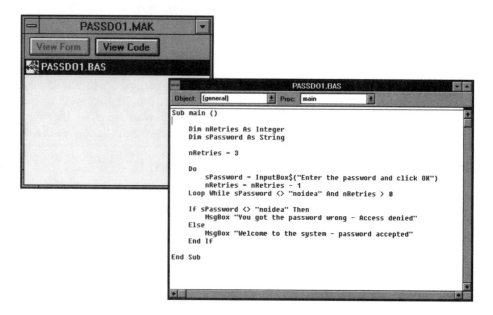

```
Sub main ()

    Dim nRetries As Integer
    Dim sPassword As String

    nRetries = 3

    Do
        sPassword = InputBox$("Enter the password and click OK")
        nRetries = nRetries - 1
    Loop While sPassword <> "noidea" And nRetries > 0

    If sPassword <> "noidea" Then
        MsgBox "You got the password wrong - Access denied"
    Else
        MsgBox "Welcome to the system - password accepted"
    End If

End Sub
```

How It Works

First of all we need to declare 2 variables. This tells Visual Basic what these variables are going to be used for. Here, **nRetries** is a number that counts the attempts that have already been made at guessing the password, while **sPassword** contains the text string that is the current guess:

```
Dim nRetries As Integer
Dim sPassword As String
```

Dim is used to declare or dimension these variables. Don't worry about this too much, as we'll discuss it in more detail in the next chapter.

The **Do** command marks the start of the loop code. Just as **Next** marks the end of a **For** loop, the **Loop** keyword closes a **Do** loop. The **While** clause tells Visual Basic to run the code as long as the users keep getting the password wrong and the user still has a number of retries left.

The first line of the loop places an input box on the screen with the words Enter the password and click OK on it:

```
sPassword = InputBox$("Enter the password and click OK")
```

An input box is another of Visual Basic's built-in features like the message box. This time it accepts input from the user and then puts that input into a variable of your choice, in this case **sPassword**.

We then reduce the number of tries left by one:

```
nRetries = nRetries - 1
```

Providing the password was wrong, and there are retries left, the line:

```
Loop While sPassword <> "noidea" And nRetries > 0
```

then sends the program back round the loop again.

When the loop ends, one of two conditions must be true. Either you ran out of tries, in which case the first message box is displayed:

```
MsgBox "You got the password wrong - Access denied"
```

or you got the password right, in which case the second message box is displayed.

```
MsgBox "Welcome to the system - password accepted"
```

> Input boxes and message boxes are covered in detail in Chapter 7. What's important here is the **Do..Loop While** code.

Do..Loop Until

Maybe three attempts to get a password right still isn't enough. Maybe your users are management personnel, or worse still, executives. Enter stage right the **Do...Loop Until** loop.

If we use Do.. Loop Until we can keep the loop going as long as it takes for the user to enter the right password. Load up **PASSDO2.MAK** and take a look at this code:

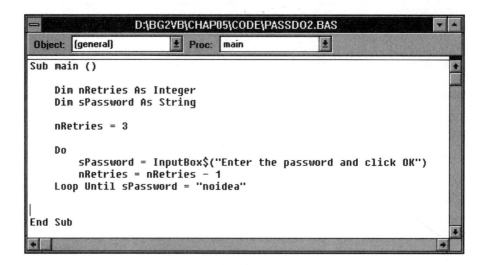

If you try running the code you should notice how the **Until** clause keeps the loop going until the user finally gets the password right. To stop the program running press the *Ctrl* and *Break* keys.

Where to Test in the Loop

It's worth noting at this point that the **While** and **Until** clauses we have so far placed after the **Loop** keyword, can also be put straight after the **Do** command. Apart from the obvious syntactical differences, doing this actually changes the way the code itself runs.

Placing the clauses **While** or **Until** after the **Loop** statement causes the loop code to run at least once. It encounters the **Do** keyword, does its business and then looks at the **Loop** line to see if it needs to do the whole thing again. Placing the clauses after the **Do** statement means that if the condition is not met then the loop code is ignored totally, and the next line to run is the one immediately following the **Loop** command:

```
Do While 1 = 2

    ' This code will NEVER run

Loop
```

Finally, just as with the **For** loop, the **Exit** keyword can be used to drop out of a **Do** loop prematurely. In this case the exact statement you need is **Exit Do**.

If you have a loop that does nothing but calculation, (in other words it never updates the screen or asks for user input), then it's possible that your loop can grind any other Windows programs that are running to a halt. The reason for this is that Windows allocates a little time to each program running when the current program calls windows to do something, like update a form.

If your code is quite happily chugging away in a loop doing nothing but calculations, then Windows isn't going to get a look in. The DoEvents command is a way around this. Place a DoEvents command in your loop and whenever it is encountered, your program will tell Windows to do anything it has to before your code can continue. In this way any other programs that are running will be able to run quite happily, and all will be well for your users.

Chapter 11 - Interacting With Windows explains how you can use DoEvents and something known as the Idle loop to not only create system friendly programs, but also to create extremely responsive programs your users will love. There's nothing worse than the Microsoft approach to development where users with low-powered machines are punished with slow load times, painful screen re-paints and so on. Idle loops enable you to get around some of these problems.

The While...Wend Loop

The final type of loop in Visual Basic is the **While..Wend** loop. To be totally honest, I see no reason at all why Microsoft included this loop in Visual Basic, other than to keep the C and Pascal programmers happy. It's exactly the same as the **Do...While** loop, but without some of the flexibility that particular loop offers. Indeed, even the Programmers Reference manual states that it's better to ignore **While..Wend** and head straight for the **Do... While** loop.

For this reason you'll only see **Do** loops used in the more complex code examples later in the book. For those of you who desperately want to use the **While...Wend** loop, here is our password code rewritten:

```
While sPassword <> "Noidea"
    sPassword = InputBox$("Enter password")
Wend
```

It's basically the same as a **Do... While** loop, except that the word **Do** is missing and the **Loop** statement and the end of a **Do...** loop has been replaced by a **Wend**. The other difference between the two types of loop is that you can't exit a **While** loop using an **Exit** command. The only way out is to change the variable that the **While** loop is testing against so that you make the condition fail and the loop stop.

Jumping Around With Goto

There have been hundreds of pages of press and book coverage devoted to the evils of the famous **GoTo** command. For those who have never heard the term, **GoTo** is a command which lets you jump from one part of your code to another. It's as simple as that. Not a voodoo doll in sight!

The History of the Crime

In the early days of BASIC, before subprocedures and functions came along, **GoTo** provided an easy way to break your code into manageable chunks. You could write some code to perform a common function and use **GoTo** to run it from anywhere within your program simply by saying **GoTo**, followed by the line number that the code you want to run began at.

The problem with **GoTo** was that your code could soon end up looking a real mess with **GoTo**s all over the place and no real indication of where they actually lead to in functional terms, or why.

When procedures and functions came along, under the banner of structured programming, the aging **GoTo** command was dropped like a proverbial hot brick amidst comments such as "It promotes spaghetti code" or "It increases the likelihood of bugs creeping into the system". Anyhow, you can write a program without ever touching **GoTo.**

When to Use GoTo

The fact of the matter is that **GoTo** can be a useful command. Visual Basic's built-in error handling command **On Error** actually works very well when used with **GoTo**. When your Visual Basic program is running for the first time, errors will normally occur. You may come across values in your controls which are too big for Visual Basic to handle. In a database program your code might have trouble actually talking to the database, especially if your users belong to the typical breed that have a habit of deleting things with their eyes shut.

On Error provides a way for you to catch these errors in your subprocedures and run a piece of code to handle them, rather than having your program crash all over the floor. For example the line:

```
On Error GoTo ErrorHandler
```

tells Visual Basic that in the event of an error occurring in the program it should go to the part of the procedure named **ErrorHandler** and run the code from there.

> Handling errors that crop up during run-time is a whole subject in itself, and is extremely important if you are going to distribute Visual Basic applications to other users. Take a look at Chapter 10 - Writing Code That Works, for a full explanation. In that chapter you'll see how everything else in the book can be used to create a large, useful program. It goes without saying that this program must be able to handle errors!

If you have a valid and legitimate reason to use the **GoTo** command then by all means do so. Used wisely it won't ruin your program and it won't damage your street credibility. Once again though, always use the right tool for the job.

Jumping to a Label

Before you can use **GoTo** you need to define a label. A label is a name you can assign to a point in your code. You define labels by simply typing a name on a line and placing a full colon : immediately after it.

If you define a label, called **Code1** for example, you can jump to the code following your label by saying **GoTo Code1.**

```
Sub A_Subroutine()

    GoTo EndOfCode
        :
        :
        :
EndOfCode:
        :
        :
End Sub
```

Problems start to occur when you have a **GoTo** followed by another **GoTo** and so on and so forth. A sure-fire way to test for overuse of the **GoTo** command is to try drawing straight lines on a listing of the code in your project between all the labels and the **GoTos** that call them. If you end up with a jumbled mess of criss-crossing lines then you've overdone it and would be well advised to simplify your code. This line-drawing approach is where the term "spaghetti coding" comes from.

Just one more analogy before we close the subject of **GoTo**. Two men with a hundred thousand nails each and a thousand small pieces of timber are given identical plans to build a house. The first man builds a tumble-down shack which quite literally tumbles down. For generations afterwards the man's offspring refuse to use wood and nails to build houses since they are unsafe to live in. The second man however builds a fine house out of the materials and lives happily ever after.

The moral of this tale is that it's not the tools and materials that a man uses which create disasters, it is his naiveté and lack of skill. A badly written program is a badly written program, not an indictment of the tools used to write the program in the first place.

Summary

In this chapter you've learnt about loops, decision making and jumping. These are three of the most fundamental aspects of writing Visual Basic code. We have covered:

- How to define conditions in **If** statements and loops

- How to write single-line and multi-line **If** statements

- How to add code modules to your project

- How the **Select Case** statement can help you check one variable for a range of values

- How to use a **For** loop to run parts of your program a specific number of times

- How to use **Do** loops, and the significance of the **While** and **Until** clauses

- How to make safe use of the **GoTo** command

In the next chapter, we'll learn about how to represent data in your Visual Basic programs. You've already used simple data-like strings and loop counters; now you'll learn about what other kinds of data Visual Basic supports.

Chapter Four

Making Data Work For You

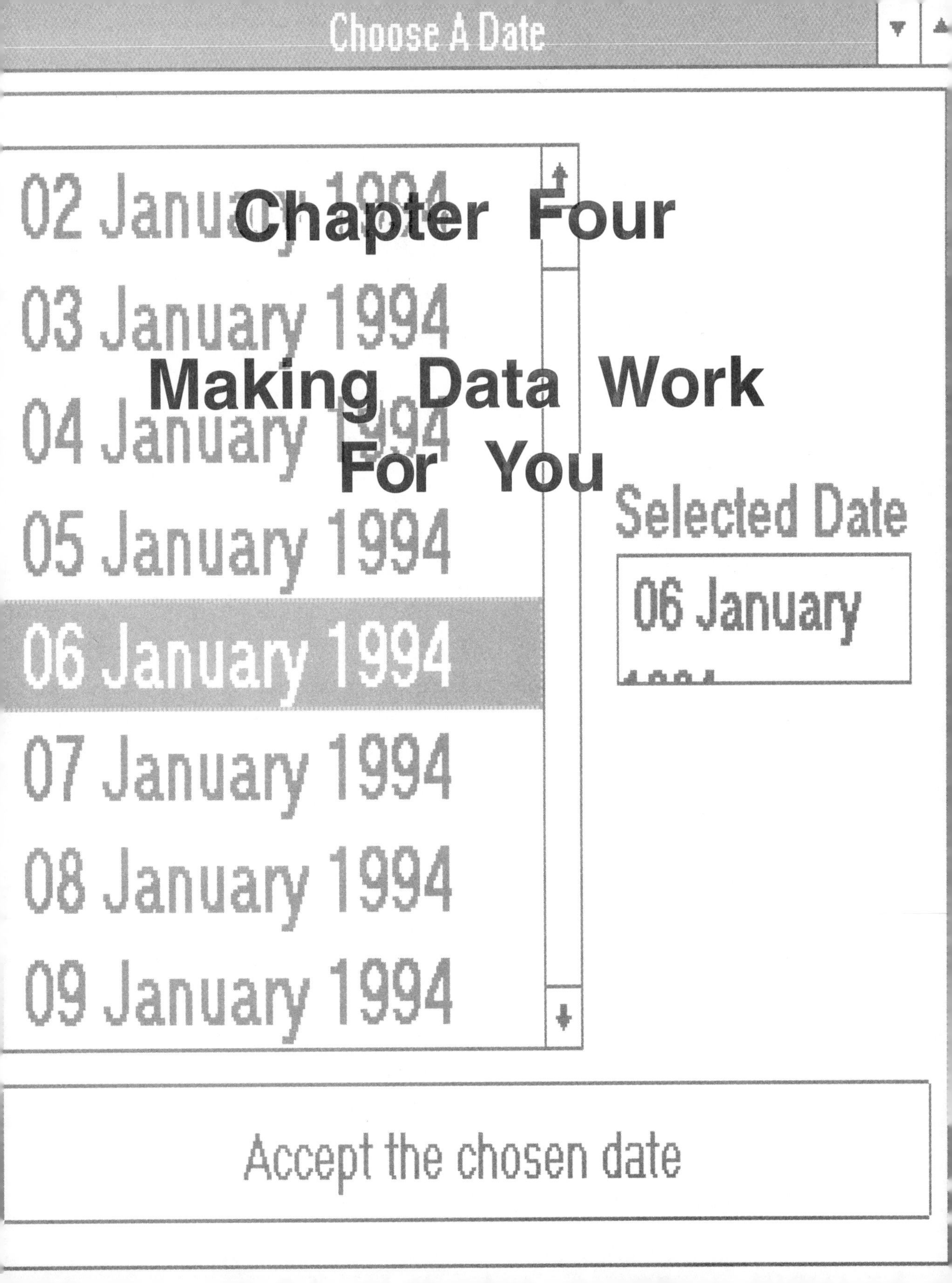
Choose A Date
02 January 1994
03 January 1994
04 January 1994
05 January 1994
06 January 1994
07 January 1994
08 January 1994
09 January 1994
Selected Date
06 January
Accept the chosen date

CHAPTER 4

Making Data Work For You

The programs you write focus around one thing - data! From a programmer's point of view there are two aspects to handling data. Firstly there's the user interface; the forms you create and the controls you draw on them. This interface must allow the user to enter the data your program needs easily and efficiently. After that, however, your program has to process that data to produce the results you want.

Visual Basic incorporates a number of ways in which you can both hold and manipulate data inside your applications. Once the work is finished, you can either kick the results back out to the user interface, or store them somewhere more permanent, such as on the hard disk or on paper.

This chapter is about how to handle data once it gets inside your program. You will learn:

- What kinds of data Visual Basic can work with

- How to use scroll bars to input numeric data

- How to use date and time information in your programs

- What strings are, and what you can do with them

- How to build your own data objects using Visual Basic

- When variables are valid in a project with more than one form and when they are not

Data and Visual Basic

A variable is a space set aside in your applications where you can store temporary information. This could be anything from a piece of text to represent a user name, to a simple number holding a count of the number of times a user has performed a certain operation. The overriding theme here is that variables are *temporary* stores for your data. They are used to hold the information your program needs to do the job in hand. As soon as your program ends, your variables vanish, taking the data they contain along with them.

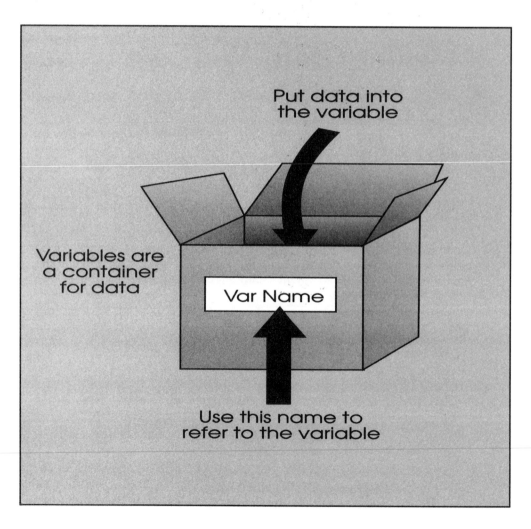

Using Variables

When you first set up a variable you have to give it a **name**. From then on you can examine the data in that variable, change it, delete it and so on by referring to it by name. You don't have to worry too much about the work Visual Basic has to do behind the scenes in terms of actually storing the data somewhere.

Let's look at an example. Imagine you need to store someone's age somewhere. You could create a variable called **Age** and store a value in it by typing:

```
Age = 24
```

Later, the number stored in **Age** could be used in calculations to get further numbers to store in other variables, or it could even be assigned to a control property. You may, for example, have a form containing a text box to display someone's age called **txtAge**. You could then display the contents of the **Age** variable in the textbox by simply saying:

```
txtAge.Text = Age
```

If you've ever done any programming before, you won't need much introduction to variables. Even if you are new to programming, then you'll find the concepts here straightforward. In fact, having made it through the first three chapters of this book, you have come across almost as many variables as you will ever need. For example, in Chapter 3 - Writing Code, we used a variable **nIndex** as a **counter** when creating a loop:

```
For nIndex = 1 to 20
     'Do Something Here
Next nIndex
```

In this kind of simple context, variables are really quite intuitive. What we'll do in this chapter is focus on the ways that Visual Basic uses data, and only examine in detail those features that are peculiar to Visual Basic.

Declaring Variables

In many BASICs, including Visual Basic, simply having a command that says **Age = 24** is enough to create a variable called **Age** which can hold numbers. Similarly, saying **Name = "Peter"** is enough to create another variable, this time called **Name**, which can hold text, or more specifically alpha-numeric characters. This is known as **implicit** declaration.

The **explicit** method of creating a variable is slightly more verbose. We have to first tell Visual Basic that the variable exists by declaring it using the `Dim` command. With `Dim` you have to give your variable a name immediately, and you also have the choice of telling Visual Basic what kind of data that variable will hold. This is known as setting the **data type**.

> Explicit declaration, while it may be a little more long-winded, is actually the best method to use. It prevents confusing bugs at run-time that are difficult to track down and even more difficult to fix. I'll show you a good example of this when we look at how to manage variables in projects that have more than one module or form. We'll do this at the end of the chapter.

Choosing the Explicit Declaration Option

The way Visual Basic expects you to define variables is determined by the Environment menu item on the Options menu. Select this menu now to see the Environment settings dialog appear as below:

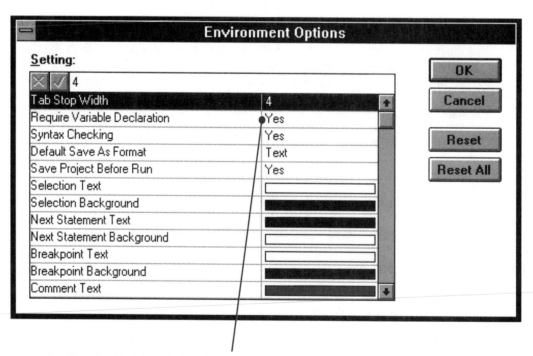

The Require Variable Declaration option toggles Visual Basic between automatically declaring variables for you, **implicit variables**, and needing variable declarations from you before a variable can be used, **explicit variables**.

For this option to be effective you need to make sure that it's set to Yes or No before you create a new project. The reason for this is that Visual Basic then inserts the words **Option Explicit** as the first line of code in any module or form. It's this **Option Explicit** command that makes Visual Basic force you to declare your variables before use.

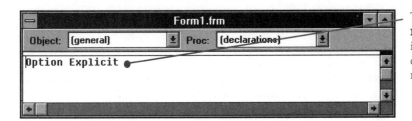

The words **Option Explicit** are inserted at the head of every code module.

> To make the change effective, you have to create a new project after changing to the explicit declaration option. Changing this option on an existing project will only affect new forms and modules that you create.

Constants

Variables, as the name suggests, are places in your program where you can hold items of data that are going to change. You'll frequently find a need for a more stable kind of run-time storage. This is what **constants** are for. They're rather like a variable in a bomb-proof glass case; you can look at it but there's no way you're going to mess with it.

Constants are great for improving the readability, and hence maintainability, of your code. Imagine a game for instance, where you need to use a simple **For** loop to move ten aliens around the screen:

```
For nAlien = 1 to 10
    Call MoveAlien (nAlien)
Next
```

There are no problems with this on its own, but what if the rest of the program had other loops that went from one to ten to do various other tasks? There could be loops to check if an alien wants to fire, die, or make a sound. What's going to happen when someone tells you the game is too easy and you need to put twenty more aliens in it?

Under normal circumstances you'd have to trot through all the code in your program hunting for loops from one to ten. If you'd used a constant then you would only have one line to change.

```
' To increase the number of bad guys, change this constant declaration
Constant NUMBER_OF_ALIENS = 10

For nAlien = 1 to NUMBER_OF_ALIENS
    Call MoveAlien (nAlien)
Next
```

Notice how the name of the constant is typed in capitals. Visual Basic is laid back about what you want to call your constants and variables. It is common practice though, to set up constants with names that are all capital letters. That way, just by reading through the code, you can easily see which parts of your program are using variables and which are using constants.

Types of Data in Visual Basic

If Visual Basic is the only programming language you've used, or even if you came here from QBasic, then you could be forgiven for being oblivious to the idea of there being different types of data. So far, almost all the variables we've looked at have behaved the same, regardless of the kind of data they store, be that words, numbers or whatever.

In fact, you've been living on borrowed time. Visual Basic, like most languages used by the big boys, does have **data types**. This means that you can create variables that will only accept one type of data. These are the traditional fare of **typed** programming languages like C and Pascal. When you program in Visual Basic, you are in fact using an additional feature called **variant data types** which allows you to avoid this kind of typing.

A Variable for all Seasons - The Variant

So far in this book we have used variables known as **variants**. These are variables which are named in the same way as any other variable, but which are a jack of all trades when it comes to actually storing information. You can store literally anything in a variant and it won't moan at you. From a beginner's point of view this is great. You could store text in a variant variable one minute, numbers the next, and dates a short while later. You wouldn't have to worry about whether or not the variant can cope, or whether you are matching the right type of data to the right variables.

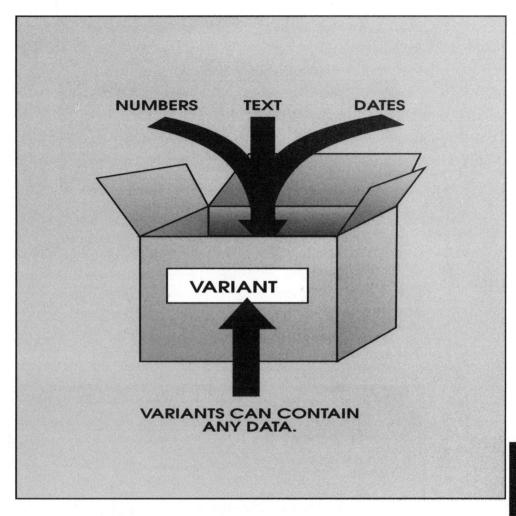

Try It Out - Variants and Typed Variables

Variants have a number of specialized uses apart from being the lazy programmer's data stash. For example, you can check the contents of a variant to find out what kind of data a user has entered. This is done by using the **IsDate** and **IsEmpty** functions.

Let's try out the **IsDate** and **IsEmpty** functions with a short example.

1 Load up the **VARIANT.MAK** project from the samples included with the book.

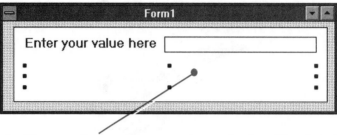

This is a label with no caption, so you can only see it when it's selected. Use the *Tab* key to get there.

2 We want to use this invisible label to show a message displaying the type of data entered into the text box as it is being entered. Double-click the text box to bring up the code window with the text box **Change** event.

3 Type in code so that the **Change** event looks like this:

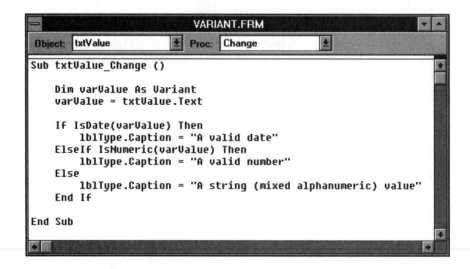

```
Sub txtValue_Change ()

    Dim varValue As Variant
    varValue = txtValue.Text

    If IsDate(varValue) Then
        lblType.Caption = "A valid date"
    ElseIf IsNumeric(varValue) Then
        lblType.Caption = "A valid number"
    Else
        lblType.Caption = "A string (mixed alphanumeric) value"
    End If

End Sub
```

4 Now try running the program and keying something into the text box. As you key in values, the label beneath the text box shows you the type of data you have entered.

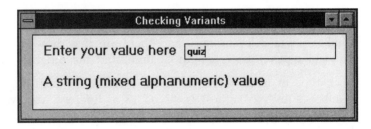

5   Try keying in text, mixing text with numbers, or entering a date. The **IsDate** and **IsNumeric** functions can detect what you're doing, and your code can use these functions to show on screen exactly what's going on.

How It Works

The **IsDate** and **IsNumeric** functions return either **True** or **False** to your code, depending on whether or not the value in the variant can be converted to either a numeric variable or a date variable. In our example a multi-line **If** is used to check first for a date, then a numeric value. If both checks fail then the program assumes that what you've entered must be a mixed text and numeric value which can only be stored in a string variable. We'll look more closely at strings later in the chapter.

In the example, the value of the textbox is actually copied into the variant **varValue** before any of the checks are done. This is actually good programming practice. Visual Basic can deal with values in variables a lot quicker than it can with values in properties, such as the text property of the text box.

In practice the text property is a variant itself, although Visual Basic always treats the data in it as text. This means that you can actually use the **IsDate** and **IsNumeric** functions on the text box if you want to check data that the user is entering without having to key in extra code to copy the property to a variable:

```
If IsDate(txtValue.Text) Then
```

This will work just as well as the other alternative we used in the example.

> The name `varValue` uses the prefix `var` to indicate that this is a variant type variable. See Appendix B for a guide to Visual Basic naming conventions.

When to Use Variants

This flexibility has a price though, and there are two drawbacks to using a lot of variant data types. One is length of time, and the other is safety.

▶ Each type of information in Visual Basic (be it text, numbers, decimal numbers, Yes/No values) is stored in a different way. Variants know instinctively how to cope with each type of data, but first of all they have to go through a short process to determine what the data actually is. You don't see this happen, but the net result is that variants can actually slow your program down.

▶ Variable typing is not just an excuse for over-complicated programming. It can play a big role in preventing errors and it does this by allowing you to restrict the number of things you can do to a variable that has been made to be a certain type. You can't, for example, find the square root of a name. We'll look at how this actually works a bit later on, but for now just remember that the more Visual Basic knows about your data, the more it can help you.

So why use variants? Firstly, because they make life incredibly easy, and secondly, because often you don't have a choice not to. Many of the control properties you come across are variants themselves (remember the Text property of a textbox?) as are many of the values returned to you by Visual Basic commands and keywords. For these reasons it's important to understand variants and how they work, even though it's best to avoid them wherever possible. Variants are the only type of variable that can really handle **date** and **time** information well.

Checking the Contents of a Variant

Since variants can hold almost any kind of data, Visual Basic has a special function we can use to determine what kind of information is in the variant. The **VarType** function returns a number that corresponds to the data type stored in the variant at that time.

Try It Out - Checking the Contents of a Variant

1 Load up **VARIANT2.MAK**. This is the same as the earlier example but with a few changes to the text box **Change** event.

2 Try typing in a proper date:

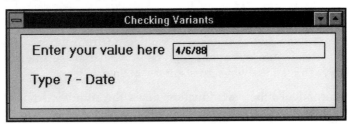

3 Stop the program and double-click on the text box to bring up the code window. Now take a look:

```
Sub txtValue_Change ()

    Dim varValue As Variant

    If IsDate(txtValue.Text) Then
        varValue = CVDate(txtValue.Text)
        ElseIf IsNumeric(txtValue.Text) Then
        varValue = Val(txtValue.Text)
    Else
        varValue = txtValue.Text
    End If

    Select Case VarType(varValue)
        Case 5
            lblType.Caption = "Type 5 - Double"
        Case 7
            lblType.Caption = "Type 7 - Date"
        Case 8
            lblType.Caption = "Type 8 - String"
    End Select

End Sub
```

How It Works

Instead of putting the text box value into a variant straight away, the code first checks to see if the value is either a date or a number. This is true if it's a date:

```
    If IsDate(txtValue.Text) Then
```

And this is true if it's a number:

```
    ElseIf IsNumeric(txtValue.Text) Then
```

Remember that at this point **txtValue.Text** is just a string with any possible combination of letters and numbers. Depending on whether Visual Basic thinks the string is a date or a number, one of two conversions is performed:

▶ The **CVDate** function takes a valid date from the **txtValue.Text** and converts it into a variant of type 7. Visual Basic then places it into **varValue** and always treats it as a date.

▶ Alternatively, the **Val** function takes the number from the variant and outputs a double precision number which can be stored in a variant, or in most of the other number data types.

> Both **CVDate** and **Val** will convert strings as well as variants. Unfortunately there are no functions in Visual Basic to find out what kind of number it is that's held in a string or variant. You have to put up with **Val** and just convert unknown number types to double.

At this point, **varValue** contains either a date, a number, or a string. These are the only possible things you can type into a text box. Next, the **VarType** function looks at what kind of variant **varValue** is, and then returns a number that describes exactly what's in it. The possible return values, and what they tell us about the type of variant are:

Value	Name	Contents of the Variant
0	**Empty**	There is no data in the variant
1	**Null**	The variant has no value, which is different to it being empty
2	**Integer**	A whole number between -32768 and 32767
3	**Long**	A whole number between -2,147,483,648 and 2,147,483,647
4	**Single**	A normal, everyday decimal number
5	**Double**	A decimal number which is either *very* big, or has a huge number of decimal places
6	**Currency**	Decimal number with 2 decimal places
7	**Date/Time**	Combination value
8	**String**	A piece of text

All that remains is for a **Select Case** block to print out the corresponding message:

```
Select Case VarType(varValue)
        Case 5
                lblType.Caption = "Type 5 - Double"
        Case 7
                lblType.Caption = "Type 7 - Date"
        Case 8
                lblType.Caption = "Type 8 - String"
    End Select
```

Numbers in Visual Basic

Variants are great, but as we said earlier, it's not good programming practice to use them, due to their lack of discipline and system overhead. The alternative to using variants is to define a data type for a specific kind of data.

Visual Basic has a number of different data types for storing numbers. The type you use depends on whether you want to store whole numbers (1, 2, 3, 4) or decimals (1.234, 2.345), and on how big or small you expect the numbers to get.

Integers and Longs

Integer and **long** variables allow you to store whole numbers. Integers are the fastest of all the data types available in Visual Basic, and are excellent for use as counters in loops for precisely that reason. However, integers can only hold a number between -32768 and 32767. For this reason they are not that suitable for holding numbers such as account numbers, or ID numbers in a database, where you could possibly have hundreds or thousands of records. For larger whole numbers, the long data type should be used, which allows you to play with numbers from -2,147,483,648 to 2,147,483,647.

More Precise Numeric Types

When **decimal** values are needed, for instance in scientific applications, you'll need to turn to **single** and **double precision** numbers. To be honest, **single** is probably as far as you will need to go, allowing you to store decimal figures in the billions range, and at very high precision. If you know anything about scientific notation then the exact range is -3.402823E38 to 3.402823E38. If you need to go above and beyond that, and deal with extremely high precision numbers, or numbers in the zillions, then opt for the **double** data type.

Predictably, handling double variables takes a lot of work on the part of Visual Basic, so using them can be slow.

The final numeric data type is the **currency**. Despite the name, currency variables have little to do with cash or a country's currency value. Instead, the currency data type is a numeric data type with a fixed number of decimal places, in this case four.

If you do a calculation that results in a value with more than four decimal places, or if you store a value with more than four decimal places in a currency variable, the extra decimal places are simply truncated - cut off in their prime. So the number 123.456789 becomes 123.4567.

Since currencies are nothing more than single and double values with a fixed decimal point. There's not that much more to tell. If you intend to have calculations in your program that need a fixed number of decimal places, then use the currency. Otherwise, integers, doubles, singles and longs are all perfectly adequate.

Declaring Numeric Variables

Declaring any of these number variables is straightforward. Simply type **Dim** followed by the name you wish to give the variable. Finally type **As** followed by the data type.

```
Dim nNetPay As Currency
Dim nDragCoefficientOfHullAtWarp1 As Double
Dim nUnitsSold As Long
Dim nCounter As Integer
Dim nRoyalty As Single
```

You can also declare variables using the keywords **Static** and **Global**. Both of these tell Visual Basic something about the life and scope of your variable. We'll cover these later in the chapter in a specific discussion on those topics.

Working With Numbers

As you would expect, Visual Basic lets you do arithmetic with numbers. You can add them using + and subtract with -. Many newcomers to programming get a little confused when it comes to division and multiplication. Take a look at the keyboard and you'll see there's no multiply or divide sign. Instead you use * to multiply and \ and / to divide. Why two divides?

Just as you can have decimal and integer variables, so you can divide to produce decimal and integer results:

> The / sign does decimal division; doing 5/3 in code will give you the answer you would expect - 1.666666666667.

> Doing 5\3 in code gives you 1; the decimal part of the number is truncated (cut off) to give you an integer result.

Integer division runs quicker in code than its decimal equivalent. It's worth bearing this in mind if you need to do division inside a loop of any kind. The loop will run significantly faster with an integer division \ than it would with a decimal division /.

Using Scrollbars to Input Numbers

In the introduction to this chapter, we differentiated between data flows in and out of your program, and the way that data is then manipulated inside your code. Good programming makes these two work in unison, so that the user interface you create gets the data you need from the user in the most direct and intuitive manner. Choosing the right tool for this is half the job.

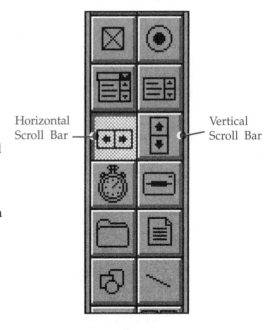

Horizontal Scroll Bar

Vertical Scroll Bar

If you want numbers from your user, then you have a number of choices of control. For numbers that have a defined and specific value, such as your age, a text box is the best choice. If, however, you want the user to alter the value of a variable bit by bit, then scroll bars are ideal.

When to Use Scroll Bars

Scroll bars are ideal when your user has to give you a ball-park value, and they want immediate feedback about the result. They are put to good use by the Paintbrush palette that comes with Windows. Load up Paintbrush, and open the Edit Colors dialog box from the Options menu.

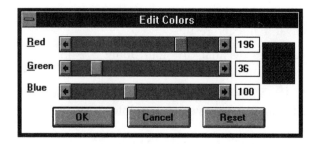

As you change the sliders, so the color mix changes. You don't really care whether the value is 63 or whatever, what you care about is the result, which you can see change as you alter the sliders.

How Scroll Bars Work

For many beginners scroll bars can be a little daunting. They are not something that you can easily relate to the real world and they provide a very abstract method of obtaining information from your users. For this reason many beginners ignore them totally, assuming that something that looks complex really is complex. In reality, nothing is further from the truth. Indeed, scroll bars are one of Visual Basic's easiest controls to master.

Visual Basic provides two scroll bars for you to use, a horizontal one and a vertical one. Play around with them to get a feel for what properties and events must be lurking in there.

Click on here with the mouse and drag it along. The number changes.

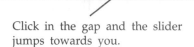

Click in the gap and the slider jumps towards you.

The arrows also move the slider.

Let's see how this all works in real code.

Try It Out - Using Scrollbars

1   Start a new project in Visual Basic.

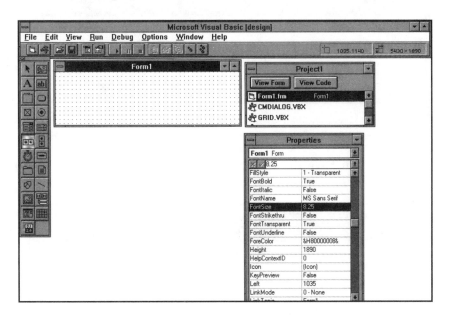

2   Select the horizontal scroll bar button and draw a scroll bar onto your form as shown.

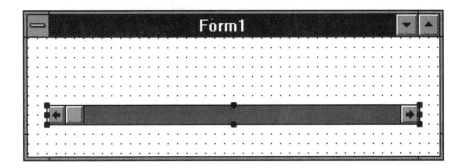

3 Now place a label above it on the form.

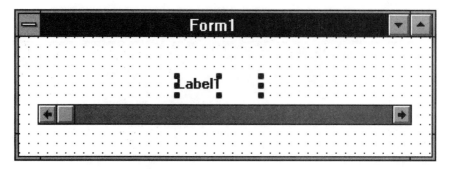

4 When you have drawn the label, bring up its properties window and give it a BorderStyle of 1, and erase the Caption.

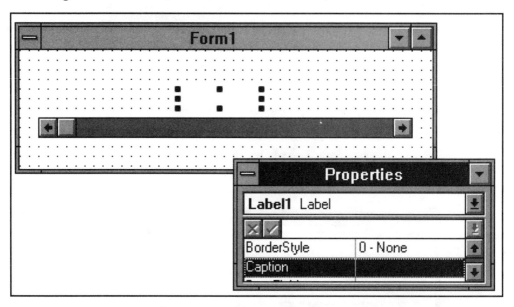

Setting the BorderStyle like this puts a single line border around the label so that it looks almost identical to a text box. This is a great way to display data in simulated text boxes that the user can't change.

5   In order for Visual Basic to determine what the position of the slider relates to, we need to tell the scroll bar what its maximum and minimum values are. Select the scroll bar and bring up its properties window.

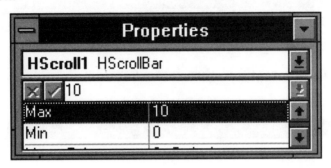

6   Find the Min and Max properties of the scroll bar and set Min to 0 and Max to 10. This gives our scroll bar a range of 0 to 10.

7   At run-time, if the user clicks in the area between the slider and an arrow, a value called LargeChange is added to the current slider value to make the slider jump. Find the LargeChange property and set it to 5. This will cause the slider to jump in steps of 5 if the user clicks between it and an arrow.

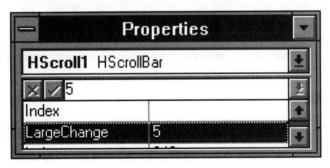

8   Finally, when the user clicks an arrow, a value called SmallChange is added to the current slider value. Find this property and set it to 1.

9   By setting the Min, Max, LargeChange and SmallChange properties we have told Visual Basic how the scroll bar should work. The next step is to display the current value of the scroll bar in your label whenever the scroll bar is changed.

10 Double-click on the scroll bar to bring up its code window. By default the **Change** event appears. Type in this code:

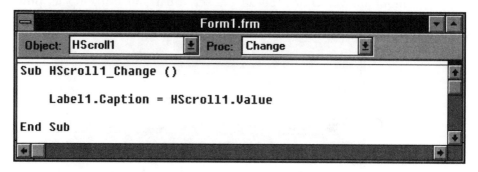

11 Now run the program.

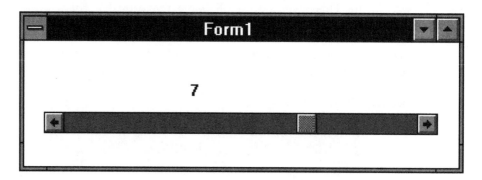

How It Works

With the program running you can see the effect that the properties we set have on the scroll bar. When the slider is at the left end of the scroll bar, the value is 0; at the right hand end it is 10. These are the values you placed into the Min and Max properties.

If you click between the slider and an arrow, the value of the scrollbar changes by 5. Click on one of the arrows though and the value changes by 1. These are the values you put into the LargeChange and SmallChange properties.

The change event you added code to places whatever is in the **Value** property of the scroll bar into the caption of the label. The change event occurs whenever a change occurs to the scroll bar, for example when an arrow is clicked, or when the slider is dragged and released.

There is an alternative place to put this code. The **Scroll** event reflects the changes to the scroll bar as they happen, rather than after they have happened, as is the case with the **Change** event. Stop the program running and bring up the code window for the scroll bar once again. This time, use the Proc: combo box to select the **Scroll** event.

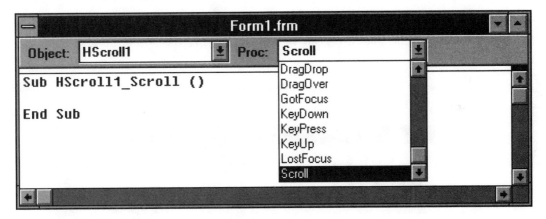

Add this line of code:

```
Label1.Caption = HScroll1.Value
```

Now run the program again and try dragging the slider around. This time, each time the slider moves the label changes, regardless of whether or not you've actually let go of the slider.

A more interactive view of what sliders can do for you is shown in Chapter 8 - Graphics. In Windows, colors are held as numbers, with each part of the color (Red, Green or Blue) being represented as a number between 0 and 255. This is ideal hunting ground for the slider, as you'll see later.

The Date and Time Data Type

Date and time values are handled rather uniquely in Visual Basic in that both are combined together into a single value. Visual Basic handles the conversion from this single value into a meaningful number for us to read automatically. Since date and time values can only be held as variants, setting up a variable to deal with them is easy:

```
Dim varDateTime
Dim varDateTime As Variant
```

Try It Out - A Visual Basic Clock

The current date and time can be obtained using the Visual Basic **Now** keyword.

1   Start a new project and place a label onto your form. Make the FontSize property nice and big.

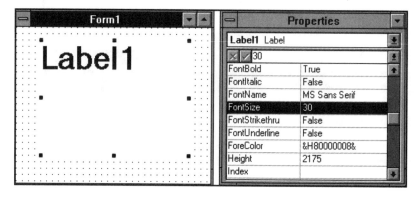

2   Double-click on the form itself and when the form **Load** event pops up change it so it looks like this:

```
Sub Form_Load ()
    Form1.Show
    Label1.Caption = Now
End Sub
```

3   Run it. Hmmm... not so easy.

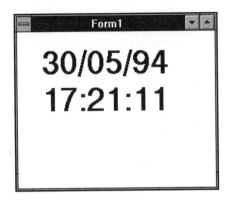

4   The time doesn't change of course. All it does is load the current time into the label at form load time. To make the time change you need to use a timer event to change the caption of the label at regular intervals.

Breaking Now Down into Parts

Obviously much of the work you do with date and time values will inevitably involve breaking a value down into its component parts, for example **Day, Month, Year, Hour,** and **Minute**. Luckily, the categories I just listed are also the names of Visual Basic keywords which allow you to break a date and time field down into these parts. For an example of how some of these functions work, load up the **CLOCK.MAK** project and take a look at the timer event code.

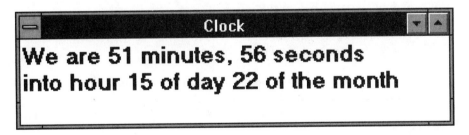

The value of **Now** has been broken down in order to space out the display, and to leave off information that wasn't really necessary. It does act as a good illustration of some of these functions though. All of them work in roughly the same way. You just state:

```
<variablename> = <functionname>(<date and time>)
```

and away Visual Basic goes.

This is not what you actually type in. In practice you would substitute each of these for your own variable name and so on.

```
nHour = Hour(Now)
nDay = Day(#01/01/94 12:00#)
nYear = Year (#01/01/1994#)
        :
        :
```

You've probably gathered by now that it's also possible to feed dates to these functions explicitly, without needing to use the **Now** variable. If you do want to specify a date in your code, all Visual Basic needs is for you to surround it with hash signs #. Then, providing the date is a legal date, that is it matches the date settings in the Windows Control panel, then the date will be accepted and used.

Dates are strange things to deal with. Unlike strings and other number variables, specific parts of a date variant mean specific things. You may want to pull a day number out to find out what day of the week a specific date falls on. You may have the day, month and year stored in separate variables and want to bring them all together in a date variant. Visual Basic has a range of functions specifically to help in all these cases.

Converting To and From Date Variants

The **DateSerial** function allows you to convert a day, month and a year value into a date variant. For example:

```
Dim varDate As Variant
varDate = DateSerial (1970, 03, 04)
```

This code puts the 4th of March 1970 into the variant **varDate**. The format of the **DateSerial** function is **DateSerial (<Year>, <Month>, <Day>)**. This can be an extremely useful function as you will see in the Try It Out section in a few moments.

Earlier on you saw how to use the **IsDate()** function to see if the value in a variant can be converted into a date. The actual conversion of the date is where the **DateValue** function comes into play:

```
If IsDate(varText) Then varDate = DateValue (varText)
```

The format of the **DateValue** function is straightforward, you simply say:

```
<variable name> = DateValue ( <variant or property> )
```

You'll see this in action later in the chapter.

You may at this point be wondering what the point of the **DateValue** function really is. If you can hold a string in a text variant, or even in a string variable, and check to see if it's a valid date, what's the point of going to all the trouble of converting the date to a date variant? The answer is math!

Working With Variant Dates

Once you have a valid date in a date variant you can then use the **DateAdd** and **DateDiff** functions to do some simple math on it. If you want to know what the date will be in two weeks time, use the **DateAdd** function. If you want to know how many days difference there is between today and the date an invoice was printed, then you use the **DateDiff** function.

Both functions work in a very similar way, in that you need to tell them the units you're dealing with. For example:

```
varDate = DateAdd ( "d" , 7, varDate)
```

adds 7 days to the date in the **varDate** variable.

```
NDifference  = DateDiff ("d", varDate1, varDate2)
```

puts the difference in days between the dates in **varDate1** and **varDate2** into **NDifference**. The **"d"** in both cases is known as the interval and could be any one of the following:

Symbol	Unit of Time
yyyy	Years
q	Quarters
m	Months
y	Day of the year (1 is 1st January etc.)
d	Days
w	Weekday
ww	Weeks
h	Hours
n	Minutes
s	Seconds

Try It Out - A Pop-Up Calendar

There is one other function which doesn't relate specifically to dates, but which is very useful when dealing with them. This is the **Format** function. With **Format**, you can take a date and change its format. You can choose a short date format (01/01/94), a long date (1 January 1994), and many more.

You pass the variable you want to format to **Format**, along with the type of formatting that you want. **Format** then returns a variant which you would typically display on screen.

1   Load up the **DATE.MAK** project and run it.

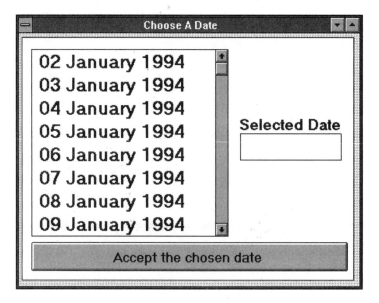

2   The program displays a list box with a list of all the dates in 1994 in it. If you scroll down the list box and click on a date, then the date is copied over to the label on the right of the list box, but in a different format. Try it.

> A list box is a kind of text box with extra functions built in. We'll cover them in detail in the next chapter.

3   To see how this works, stop the program from running and double-click on the list box to bring up its **Click** event.

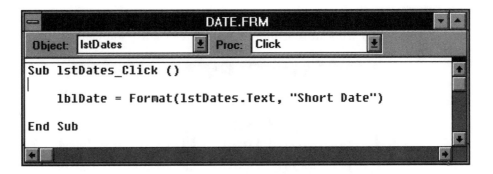

4 This code takes the date you select and formats it for the label. The dates in the list box are displayed in long date format with the full year and the full name of the month displayed:

    02 January 1994

5 Short format is used to display the selected date in the label. There's no need to add the caption property to the **lblDate** name as Visual Basic assumes that's what you mean.

    01/02/94

6 Let's change the format command so that it looks like this:

```
lblDate = Format(lstDates.Text, "Long Date")
```

7 Now run the program and the date will be copied to the list box exactly as it appears in the list box. Unfortunately it won't all fit in the label.

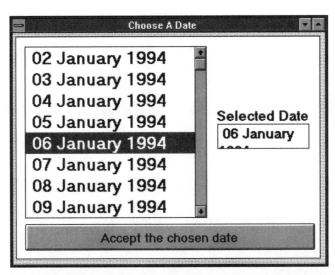

8 Now try changing it to **Medium Date**. Visual Basic automatically knows how to truncate the month to a three-digit abbreviation.

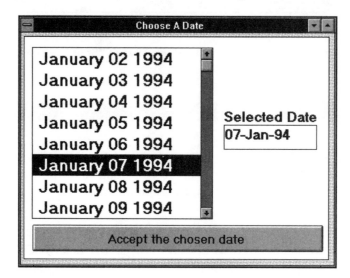

The Null Value

The **Null** value and keyword are rather special. The **Null** value is used to indicate **unknown** data, and is most commonly found in database applications. Consider filling in a paper form. The form asks you for your surname, but you leave it blank by mistake. When the form gets processed by the company that uses the form they get a blank surname area. Since your surname can't realistically be nothing, they tell their database that your surname is unknown. In Visual Basic we use **Null** for just that purpose.

Only variants can hold **Null** values. If you try to assign **Null** to a string variable then you'll get an error. You can assign **Null** to a variant with the simple phrase **<variable> = Null.** Checking to see if a variant contains **Null** is a slightly different matter, and requires the use of a Visual Basic function called **IsNull.** Here's an example:

```
If IsNull(VarVariable) Then MsgBox "Variant is null"
```

The **IsNull** function returns a value of **True** or **False,** so it makes code like the line above pretty easy to read. I could have written:

```
If IsNull(VarVariable) = True Then MsgBox "Variant is null"
```

but that begins to make the code a little cryptic.

The **Empty** value is in some ways similar to the **Null** value. Where the **Null** value indicates unknown data, **Empty** indicates that a variable has never had a value put into it. The **IsEmpty** function can be used to test for this, in the same way that **IsNull** can test for the **Null** value.

Strings

String variables are predominantly used to store and manipulate text. Numeric variables can only hold numbers, whereas strings can hold both numbers and figures, although they are both treated as text. The following are all strings:

```
sFirstName = "Peter"
sAddress1 = "28 Code Gulch"
sDateOfBirth = "5/8/88"
```

Declaring Strings

Strings can be declared in a number of ways. Most of the built-in data types that Visual Basic supports have a special abbreviation code attached to them. In the case of strings, this is the **$** sign. This abbreviation is actually known as a **type declaration character**. Despite its long name it does a straightforward job. If you dimension a variable and attach the appropriate type declaration character to the end of the variable name, then Visual Basic will automatically create a variable of the required type.

Let's say we wanted to create a new string variable to hold someone's name. Using the long-hand method, we'd have to write:

```
Dim sName As String
```

With the shorthand method the amount of code is reduced, but so too is the readability of the code:

```
Dim sName$
```

> The small **s** at the start of the name tells you this is a string. Take a look a Appendix B for a guide to naming variables.

Use Quotation Marks for Text

Whenever you place some data into a string variable you must enclose the data in quotation marks. This lets Visual Basic see which parts of your program are supposed to be variable names, and which parts are constants (numbers, letters, text and so on). It's an important point to remember and actually brings us back to the option-explicit phrase we met a while back. Without the option-explicit phrase, a line like:

```
sFirstname = Peter
```

would compile without any problems. Visual Basic would assume that **Peter** is a string variable, the contents of which you want to copy to the string variable **sFirstname**. This is far from what we actually wanted to do though, which was to place the name **Peter** in the string variable itself:

```
sFirstname = "Peter"
```

Had the option-explicit facility been turned on, then the first example wouldn't have got past the Visual Basic compiler. You'd have been given a Variable not defined error message.

Explicit Declaration Prevents Bugs

Why is it so important to have this option turned on, especially as implicit variables require less code and thought than explicit ones? Well, take a look at this code:

```
Sub Problem_Proc()
    sO10 = Inputbox$("Enter your name")
    msgbox "Your name is " & sO10
End Sub
```

This is a very simplified piece of code, but it has a pretty serious bug in it. If the subprocedure was embedded in a couple of hundred other lines of code, the bug could become very hard to track down. Basically, the code is supposed to get the user to enter their name and then display their name on screen in a **MsgBox**. The variable used to store the name that the user enters is called **sO10.** However, no matter how hard you try, the program will not work. Instead it will keep on displaying the message Your name is, but without any name!

The reason for this is that I have misspelt the variable name in the **MsgBox** statement. In the first line of code I implicitly created a variable named s**o1o** (letters s**o**, number **1** and number **o**). However, in the **MsgBox** code I refer to a variable called s**o1o** (letter s, number **o**, number **1**, letter **o**). Visual Basic doesn't care; it just goes ahead and creates two variables, each with very slightly different names. If I'd been using **Explicit** variables the program wouldn't have run and Visual Basic would have pointed the bug out to me immediately.

Working With Strings

Dealing with text in string variables can become a little tricky, so Visual Basic has a full set of very useful string handling functions which allow you to break down the string and examine parts of it.

The first function is **StrComp** which is designed to compare two strings and return a number telling you what the comparison is between them.

Try It Out - Comparing Strings With StrComp

1   Start a new Visual Basic project and remove the default form from the project by selecting Remove File from the File menu.

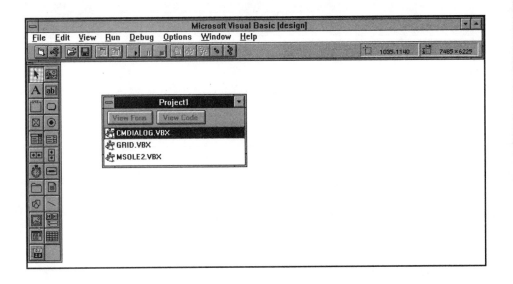

2 Create a new module by selecting New Module from the File menu.

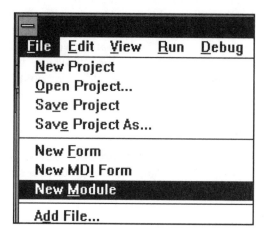

3 In the code window that appears type in code so that the code window looks like this:

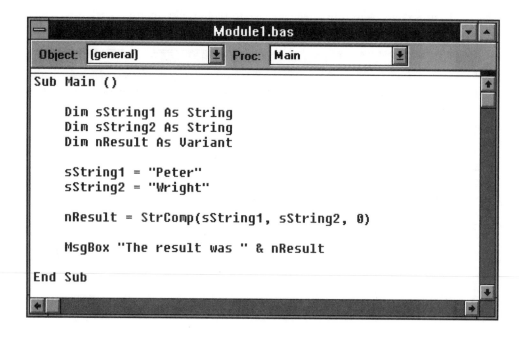

4   If you now run the code a message box appears telling you that the result of the comparison is **-1**.

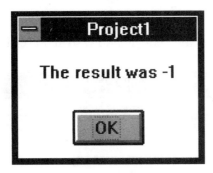

The finished program is on the disk called COMPARE.MAK

How It Works

The numbers returned by **StrComp** can be tested using **If** statements or **Select Case** to determine how the strings compare. The results will be **-1** if the first string precedes the second alphabetically (A comes before B and so on), **0** if they are the same, **1** if the first string comes after the second alphabetically, or **Null** if one of the strings compared was **Null**. Because **StrComp** can return a null value you can easily see why we declared the **nResult** variable as a **Variant**.

Changing Case

The number **0** at the end of the **StrComp** statement tells Visual Basic to do a **case-sensitive** comparison:

```
nResult = StrComp(sString1, sString2, 0)
```

If the number was anything other than **0** this code would do a **case-insensitive** comparison. The **LCase$** and **Case$** functions enable you to change all the letters in a string to either upper-case or lower-case. Both functions return a string to you which you can assign to a string variable using the **=** sign. There are two alternative functions, **UCase** and **LCase** which return variants of type 8 (strings) so you can assign them to variant variables.

Try It Out!

Try It Out - Changing Case

1   Start up a new project. Remove the form and add a new module to it, as we did in the previous example.

2   Enter code into the code window so it looks like this:

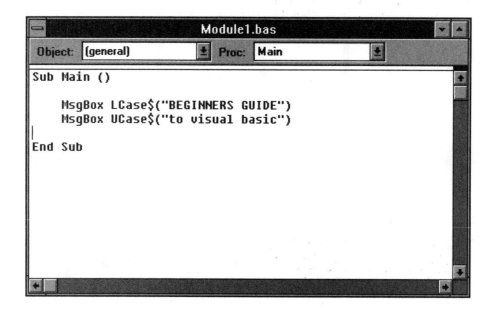

3   Run this code. See how the **LCase$** and **UCase$** functions invert the case of all the letters passed to them.

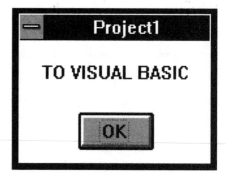

4 The first message box says beginners guide, whilst the second says TO VISUAL BASIC. They are somewhat different to the actual strings passed to the two message box functions.

Searching Strings

The two things you'll need to do most frequently to strings are searching and dissecting. Visual Basic comes with a daunting array of functions especially for doing just these things; **Mid$**, **Left$**, **Right$** and **Instr**.

The simplest of these is **Instr**, pronounced in-string. **Instr** allows you to search one string to see if another appears in it. If a match is found, Visual Basic returns a number to your code which is the number of the letter in the first string at which the second appears. If the search fails then all you get back is 0.

Try It Out - Using Instr to do Simple Searching

1 Load up the **INSTR.MAK** project. There's no code in this, just a form with some controls on, waiting for you to add the good bits.

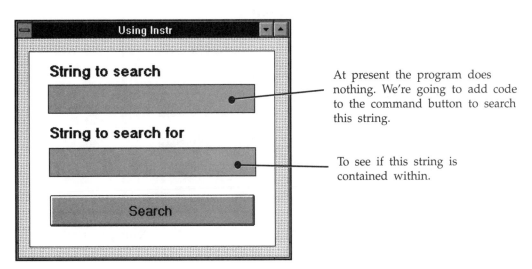

At present the program does nothing. We're going to add code to the command button to search this string.

To see if this string is contained within.

2 Double-click on the command button to bring up the code window.

3 Type in code so that the command button click event looks like this:

```
Sub cmdSearch_Click()
   Dim nIndex As Integer

   nIndex = Instr(txtSource.Text, txtSearch.Text)
   If nIndex = 0 Then
       MsgBox "The search string could not be found!"
   Else
       MsgBox "The search string was found starting at position " & nIndex
   End If

End Sub
```

4 Now run the program.

5 Enter source text in the top text box and then add the string text you want to search for in the bottom textbox.

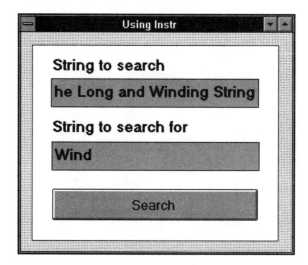

6 Hit the Search button and a message box appears telling you whether or not the text was found, and at which position in the top string it was found.

How It Works

Let's take a look at the code that makes **INTR.MAK** useful. The first line declares an integer variable **nIndex** to hold the position of the second string **txtSearch.Text**, in our second string, **txtSource.Text**.

```
Dim nIndex As Integer
```

This value will be zero if no match was found. The next line is the one that counts as it contains the **Instr** function:

```
nIndex = InStr(txtSource.Text, txtSearch.Text)
```

You simply assign **Instr** to a variable to hold the result. In this case that variable is **nIndex**. The two strings you're dealing with are held in brackets straight after the **Instr** function. The first string, be it a variable, property (as here), or a piece of text in quotes (e.g. "Source String"), is the string you want to search. The second string is the value you want to search for.

The remaining lines examine the value that **Instr** returned and display the appropriate message box. If **nIndex = 0** then **Instr** couldn't find a match and so The search string could not be found! is displayed. Otherwise, the value of **nIndex** is displayed.

```
If nIndex = 0 Then
    MsgBox "The search string could not be found!"
Else
    MsgBox "The search string was found starting at position " & nIndex
End If
```

Instr is great for doing simple searches. However, if you really want to pull some strings apart then you need to look to the **Mid$**, **Left$** and **Right$** functions. Using these three functions you can write code that can examine portions of a string.

Try It Out - Taking Strings Apart

Your users may have just entered their forename followed by their surname. Using the **Left$** and **Right$** methods we can separate these two words.

1   Load up the **BREAK.MAK** project and run it.

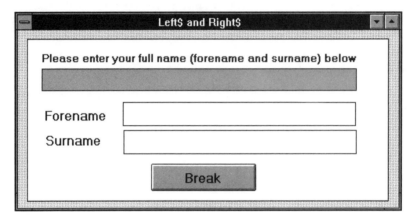

2   At the top of the form is a text box where our users will enter their name. As soon as the command button at the bottom of the form is pressed, code which you will write in a moment splits the name entered into its forename and surname parts.

3   Stop the project, and double-click on the command button to bring up the code window for its click event.

4   Type in code so that the **Click** event looks like this:

```
Sub cmdBreak_Click ()

    Dim nPosition As Integer

    nPosition = InStr(txtName.Text, " ")

    If nPosition = 0 Then
       lblForename.Caption = txtName.Text
       lblSurname.Caption = ""
    Else
       lblForename.Caption = Left$(txtName.Text, nPosition)
       lblSurname.Caption = Right$(txtName.Text, Len(txtName.Text)-
   nPosition)
    End If

End Sub
```

5 Now run the program and enter your name. When you press the command button at the bottom of the form the name is split into two parts.

How It Works

The first two lines of code should be pretty familiar. The **Dim** line sets up an integer variable which we use in the next line to find the first space in the name entered. Most people enter their forename and surname separated by a space, so we can use **Instr** to search for this.

The **If** clause checks to see whether or not any spaces were entered. If none were entered, so that **nPosition = 0,** then the program assumes that no surname was entered and copies the text you just typed into the **Forename** box only.

Providing a space was entered in the name though, these two lines of code are run:

```
lblForename.Caption = Left$(txtName.Text, nPosition)
lblSurname.Caption = Right$(txtName.Text, Len(txtName.Text) - nPosition)
```

The first line uses the **Left$** method to pull some text from the left of the string entered. The number of characters to pull and the string to pull them from are passed as parameters to the **Left$** method. In this case the string is the text property of the text box, and the number of characters to pull is held in the **nPosition** variable. Remember, we used **Instr** to find the space. If a space was found 5 characters into the string and we pull the 5 left-most characters from the string, then we'll actually get everything up to and including the space.

The **Right$** function works in exactly the same way. You tell it which string you want to pull characters out of, and how many characters to pull. The difference, as you probably guessed, is that **Right$** pulls characters from the right-hand side of the string, whereas **Left$** pulls them from the left-hand side. Previously, we used the **nPosition** variable to determine how many characters to get. This won't work with the **Right$** function. If the string is 25 characters long and the space is the 5th character in, then saying **Right$(text,5)** wouldn't give us the desired answer, so some math is needed.

The **Len()** method can be used to find out how long a string is. So if the space was found at character 5, and the string is 25 characters long, **Len(Text) - 5** gives us 20. In the code above, this would mean that we'd pull the rightmost 20 characters out of the string. It looks complex initially but it's really very straightforward.

The Mid$ Function

The third function, which I mentioned earlier, is the **Mid$** method. Where the **Left$** and **Right$** methods can be used to pull text from the left and right-hand sides of a string, **Mid$** lets you pull chunks out from anywhere in the string, but most commonly from the middle.

Mid$ works in a similar way to the other two commands. You pass it the text you want to pull stuff out of. However, instead of just telling it the number of characters to pull, you tell it which character to start at, and how many characters you want to pull.

Try It Out - Extracting Strings Using Mid$

We could have done everything we just did using only the **Mid$** function. Take a look at this.

```
Sub cmdBreak_Click ()

    Dim nPosition As Integer

    nPosition = InStr(txtName.Text, " ")

    If nPosition = 0 Then
        lblForename.Caption = txtName.Text
        lblSurname.Caption = ""
    Else
        lblForename.Caption = Mid$(txtName.Text, 1, nPosition)
        lblSurname.Caption = Mid$(txtName.Text, nPosition + 1,
    Len(txtName.Text) - nPosition)
    End If

End Sub
```

The two lines that have changed are:

```
lblForename.Caption = Mid$(txtName.Text, 1, nPosition)
lblSurname.Caption = Mid$(txtName.Text, nPosition + 1,Len(txtName.Text) -
↳nPosition)
```

The first parameter you pass to **Mid$,** just as with **Left$** and **Right$,** is the text you want to manipulate; in this case **txtName.Text**. The next parameter is the first character you want to pull. Finally, we pass the number of characters that **Mid$** should return. The string returned is saved in the two labels on the form, just as before.

Collection of Data

In a larger application, such as a payroll system, or even a game, by far the most important data you'll need to deal with will be held in groups of one kind or another. For example, you may not want to deal with employees by holding their name, address, IRS number and so on in different variables, when it's much more convenient to deal with an employee as a **group** of related data. The **Type** command in Visual Basic lets you create such groups.

In a game you may need to keep track of which aliens are alive, and which are dead. This kind of group is called an **Array**. This is a list of variables all with the same name and data type.

Lets look at the **Type** command first.

Type Declarations

As I've already said, the **Type** command lets you define a group of variables and give them a common name. You could have an employee type to hold an employee's name, address and so on. In a game you might have a **Type** defined to hold information about the bad guys, such as the name of the graphics file that holds their image data, their co-ordinates, energy and such like. If you are used to C or Pascal then you'll feel at home with **Types**. In C you have the **struct** keyword which does the same thing, whilst in Pascal you have **records**.

Take a look at this fragment of code:

```
Type Employee
    nEmployeeNo As Long
    sSurname As String
    sForenames As String
    varBirthDate As Variant
EndType
```

This declares a type called **Employee** which holds some of the data you might associate with an employee. Declaring a type like this only declares a template for a new variable. It's like telling Visual Basic "This is what a variable of type Employee would look like". Having created the **Type** you then have to create a variable from it:

```
Dim CurrentEmployee As Employee
```

This declares a variable of type **Employee**, which has already been set up by the **Type** statement. **CurrentEmployee** doesn't itself hold any data that we are interested in. In code we want to see what is in each part of the **Employee** data. You do this by placing the name of each **element** of the type after the new variable name:

```
CurrentEmployee.nEmployeeNo = 1
CurrentEmployee.sSurname = "Wright"
CurrentEmployee sForenames  = "Peter"
```

Arrays of Data

A type groups a collection of possibly different data types together under one name. **Arrays** on the other hand let you create lists of a single data type. What you get with an array is really a number of variables, all with exactly the same name but with different data. So you could have an array to hold the values of cards in a deck. Each element of the array, or individual item of data in its own right, is differentiated from the rest by something known as an **index**. Index simply means an identifying number.

If you want to declare an array instead of a variable it's easy. You just put brackets after the variable's name, with a number inside them saying how large the array should be:

```
Dim nArray(100) As Integer
```

In this example an array is set up called **nArray**. The array consists of 100 integer numbers. You can get at these numbers to see what they are, or to set them to different values like this:

```
nArray(2) = 50
nArray(50) = nArray(0) + nArray(99)
```

Have a look at the last line of code in that example. The first element of an array is numbered 0, with the last being one less than the size of array that you asked for. So, if you set up an array of 100 elements, these are numbered 0 to 99.

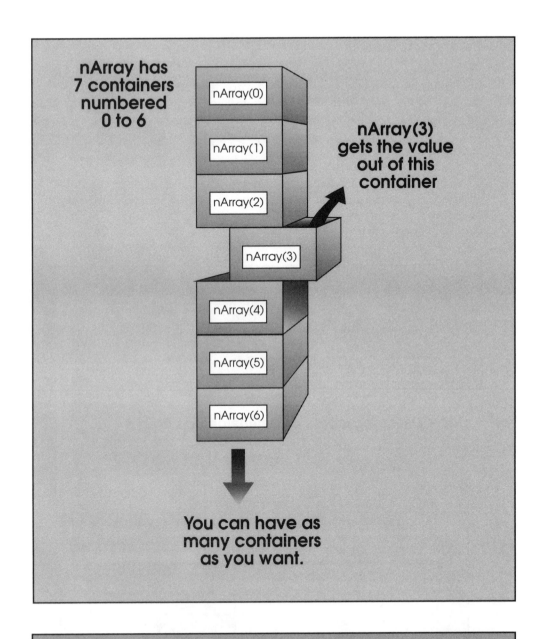

nArray has
7 containers
numbered
0 to 6

nArray(0)

nArray(1)

nArray(3)
gets the value
out of this
container

nArray(2)

nArray(3)

nArray(4)

nArray(5)

nArray(6)

You can have as
many containers
as you want.

Arrays don't always have to start with an index number of 0. You can declare an array to start at any number you like. For example, `Dim nArray (-12 to 28)`.

Re-Dimensioning Arrays

Arrays have been with us since BASIC first hit a computer screen. However, something Visual Basic can do which very few other versions can, is change the size of an array once it has been declared. Previously, if you asked for a 100 element array, that's what you got. If you needed to change its size then you'd have to stop the program and change the code. This can get very annoying!

In Visual Basic you can **ReDim** an array to change its size up or down. In addition, if you use the **ReDim** command in conjunction with the word **Preserve,** you can even change the size of an array without destroying the data contained inside it.

> One of the most common uses for this is in games, or any other application that needs to deal with random data. Being able to change the size of an array at run-time is often used for increasing the number of bad guys in a game, or adding more bullets to the screen. In a serious application it's great for creating random amounts of data to throw at a program for testing. Each piece of data could be held in an array, with the exact number of items of data determined at run-time, changing the array with **ReDim.**

Try It Out - Declaring and Re-Dimensioning Arrays

1 Start a new project in Visual Basic.

2 Double-click on the default form to bring up the code window.

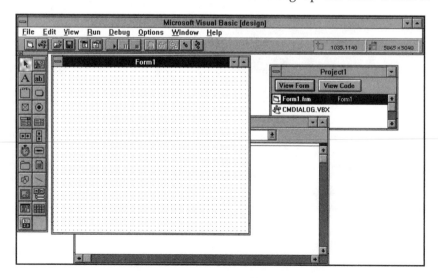

3 Type in code so that the `Form_Load()` event looks like this:

```
Sub Form_Load ()

    Dim nRandoms() As Integer
    Dim nLoopCounter As Integer
    Dim nArraySize As Integer

    Form1.Show

    Randomize
    nArraySize = Int(Rnd(1) * 10)
    ReDim nRandoms(nArraySize)

    For nLoopCounter = 1 To nArraySize
        nRandoms(nLoopCounter) = Int(Rnd(1) * 1000)
        Form1.Print "Element " & nLoopCounter & " = " &
 ⤷nRandoms(nLoopCounter)

    Next

End Sub
```

Each time you run the program you see a random number of random numbers printed onto the form. The array is also resized randomly to hold these numbers.

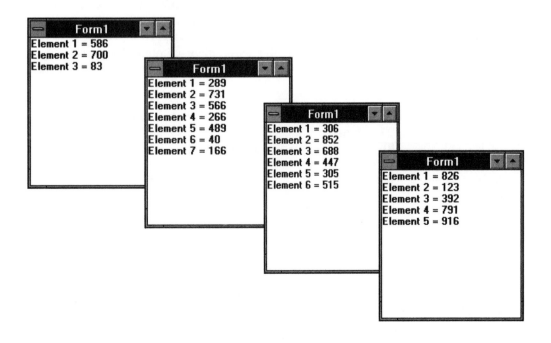

How It Works

The first line of the code

```
Dim nRandoms() As Integer
```

sets up an array with no elements in it. Two other variables are then set up; one to hold the size of the array **nArraySize**, the other **nLoopCounter**, to hold a counter to step through each element of the array later on.

After showing the form, the **Randomize** method is used to set up Visual Basic's random number generator. We'll look at random numbers later, in the chapter on graphics, so don't worry about exactly what this and the **Int(Rnd(1) * 1000)** statements in the code do. The net result is that a random number between 0 and 10 is put into **nArraySize**. This is used in the next line to **Redim** the array.

```
ReDim nRandoms(nArraySize)
```

The rest of the code steps through each element of the array, using the **For** loop to put a random number into each element and then print that element on the form.

The line **Form1.Show**, as you saw in the previous chapter, forces Visual Basic to display the form on screen as soon as possible. Remember, the **Load** event just loads the form up into memory, it doesn't actually display it. We need to **Show** the form in order to **Print** on it. Without the **Show** command, all you would see at the end of the program would be a blank form. Try removing the line yourself to see this.

There's a bit of a problem with using **ReDim** in this way. Imagine the situation where you have 100 employee names held in an array and you suddenly decide you need 101. You could **ReDim** the array to make it bigger, but when you do a **ReDim,** any data in the array is lost forever. We need to find a way of **preserving** the data held in the array when it's resized.

Preserving Array Data

You may need to **Redim** an array and preserve the contents of it quite frequently. You may have an array of record IDs in a database for instance. What happens when the user adds a new record to the database? The answer is that you use the Visual Basic **Redim Preserve** keywords.

Redim Preserve works in exactly the same way as the **Redim** statement on its own, the only difference is that you now say **Redim Preserve** instead of **Redim.**

```
Dim nArray(100) As Integer
Redim Preserve nArray(200)
Redim Preserve nArray(400)
```

Now the data already in the array will still be there after you change its size.

Multi-Dimensional Arrays

It's possible to have multi-dimensional arrays, where there is more than one index. All you do is add another number to the declaration like this:

```
Dim nMultiArray(100,100) As Integer
```

You can then address each element of the array as you would a one-dimensional array, only this time there's another index to change.

Variable Scope

Variables have a limited visibility and the data they hold can only be accessed whilst the variable is still in view. The most obvious time that a variable goes out of view is when your program stops. When you restart it, all your variables are set back to their initial values.

This is known as **scoping**. As long as a variable is **in scope,** you can write code to change it, display it and so on. When the variable goes out of scope all the information becomes unavailable and the programmer can no longer write code to deal with that variable. Ending an application makes all variables go out of scope, but there are less extreme cases than this. Variables that you declare in one module are normally only in scope when that module is running. It's possible to circumvent this by creating **Static** or **Global** variables, but on the whole, variables live and die with their parent modules.

This can be a little confusing, so let me explain some more. You have four types of variable scope. **Global, Form/Module** level, **Local** and **Static.** Imagine that you are looking out of a submarine periscope from inside a particular module. Global variables are those that you'll always be able to see. If the world is your program then no matter where you are, the periscope will always show you the sky and the water; no matter where you are in your program you can always see, use and update global variables.

Module level variables can be thought of as icebergs. It doesn't matter where you are in the two polar regions, you will always be able to see icebergs. Module and form level variables are always available to you if you are running code in the same form or module they were declared in.

Local variables are like seagulls in the sky. As far as you are concerned they exist only while you have the periscope fixed on them. In your programs, local variables and their contents only exist in the subroutine or function in which they were declared.

Static variables are like seagulls which have landed on your sub. They are always in the same position each time you bring the scope round to a certain angle. As soon as you move the scope off them they no longer exist, but move it back and they're still sitting there just as before. In your program, static variables, like local variables, can only be used in the procedure or function they were declared in. Move out of the subroutine or function and the variables can no longer be used. However, when you come back to that subroutine the statics are still there, with exactly the same values as before. Local variables change; they lose their contents and have to be rebuilt.

A variable's scope is determined by where and how the variable is created. We've already seen how to use **Dim** to declare variables. Using **Dim** creates local variables whose scope is within the module in which they are created. In order to understand what this really means, we need to take a look at how to create projects that have more than one form.

Multi-Form Projects

All the projects we have looked at so far only have one form. Any variable that is declared on that form using **Dim** is **local** to that form, and can be accessed by event handlers for any object that is also on the form. In the previous chapter, we learnt how to create subprocedures that can be called from code within a form, even though they are contained in a separate module.

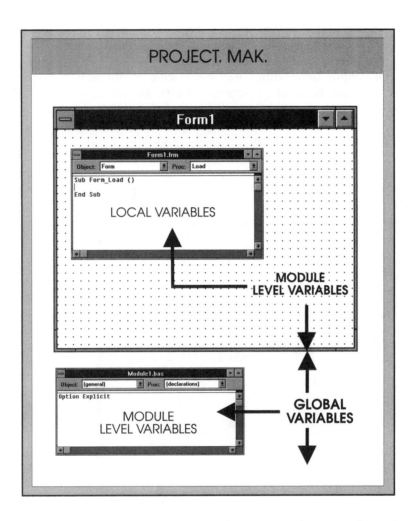

It's also possible to create projects that have more than one form. In this situation, variables in one form that are declared in the normal way are not accessible to code in other forms. To see how this works, let's create a simple pop-up calendar on it's own form.

Try It Out - Adding a Calendar Sheet

Scoping can cause some real problems, as you'll find out if you spend any amount of serious time with Visual Basic. One of the problems is that there is no direct variable type which you can use to get one form to pass values to another. The same goes for the controls and properties of a form. Code in one module or one form can't get at the properties and controls of another form unless that form is loaded up.

This can often be a real pain as you may want to pop up a form to select a date from a calendar. When the date is selected you may want to unload the calendar form to save memory. But how does the first form know when the calendar form has finished? How can we make the calendar form tell whoever called it, that all is now OK? Lets find out!

1 Start up a new project and draw a label on the form.

2 Now draw a command button underneath the label and change its caption to Choose a Date.

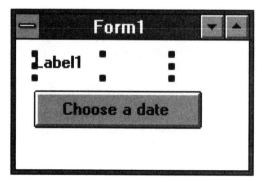

3 When the command button is clicked, we want a second form to load up and display the calendar from the example earlier in the chapter. The calendar should then set the label on the original form to the date selected.

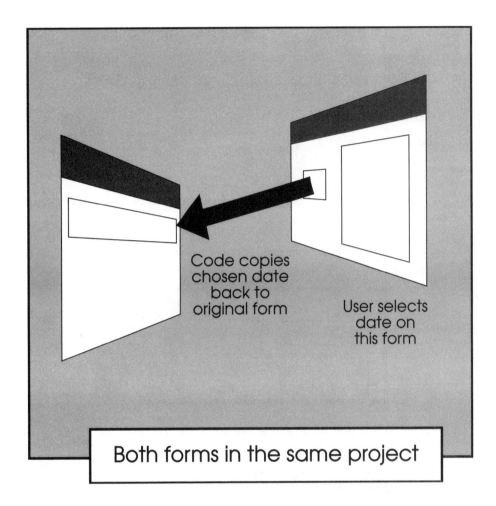

Code copies
chosen date
back to
original form

User selects
date on
this form

Both forms in the same project

4 From the File menu choose Add File, and when the dialog appears select the **DATE.FRM** file from the samples that came with the book. You'll see the name of the form appear in the project window.

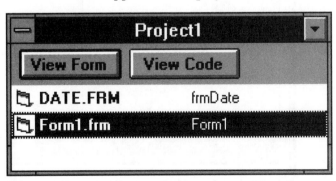

5   Now we need to type a bit of code. Double-click the command button you just drew to bring up its code window with the click event.

6   Change the click event so that it looks like this:

```
Sub Command1_Click()

    frmDate.Show

End Sub
```

7   This will cause the Date form to load and show itself whenever the command button is clicked.

8   Now select Project from the Window menu and the project box will appear.

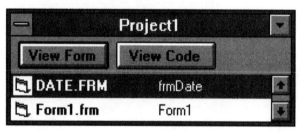

9   Double-click the **DATE.FRM** entry to show the calendar form we made earlier.

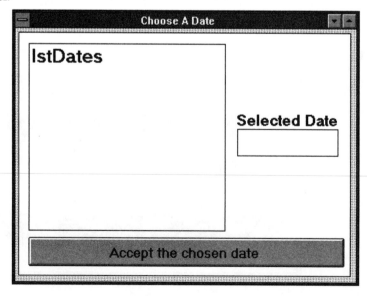

10 Double-click the Accept the chosen date command button to view its **Click** event, and change it so that it looks like this:

```
Sub cmdAccept_Click ()

    Form1!Label1.Caption = lblDate.Caption
    Unload frmDate

End Sub
```

11 Now if you run the program, your form will appear. Click on the Choose a date button and the calendar form will appear. If you now select a date and click Accept the chosen date the form will vanish and your label on the first form will show the selected date.

How It Works

The line that accomplishes this transfer of the date from one form to the other is:

```
        Form1!Label1.Caption = lblDate.Caption.
```

Providing the form you want to address is currently loaded, you can change its properties by putting the form name before the control followed by an exclamation mark.

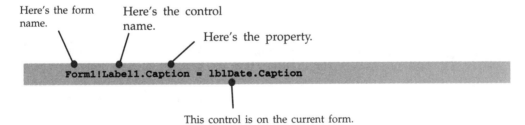

Here's the form name. Here's the control name. Here's the property.

```
        Form1!Label1.Caption = lblDate.Caption
```

This control is on the current form.

This line says on **Form1**, change **Label1**'s **Caption** so it's the same as the **Caption** on this form's **lblDate** label.

This is the easiest way to pass values between forms. Another approach is to use something called **Modal** forms. However, this is a subject all of its own and is covered in Chapter 6 - Dialogs, later in the book.

Local Variables

A variable declared within a **Sub** procedure or a **Function** with the **Dim** keyword is said to have **local** scope. It can only be accessed by code within the same **Function** or **Sub** procedure. This gives rise to some interesting problems. Because a local variable can only be accessed from within the **Sub** or **Function** it was **born** in, it's possible to have more than one variable in a program with the same name and all with different values. This little gem of a bug-haven is known as **name shadowing**.

Try It Out - Same Name, Different Place

1 Load up Visual Basic, delete the default form, and create a new code module.

2 Bring up the code window and enter the following:

```
Sub Main()
    Dim nNumber
    nNumber = 12
    Call Proc2
    MsgBox nNumber
End Sub

Sub Proc2
    Dim nNumber
    MsgBox nNumber
End Sub
```

If you now try running the code you'll see a message box procedure. Click on the OK button and another message box appears with the number 12 in it. This is the value of the **nNumber** variable in the **main** subprocedure. Confused? Just imagine what it gets like with a couple of hundred instances just like this.

To summarize then, local variables are created in **Sub** procedures and **Functions.** They can only be accessed from within the routine they were created in. Identically named variables in other functions live a totally separate existence and have their own values.

Module Level Variables

In contrast, **Dim** can also be used to create variables which can be used by all the code in a form or module. Each form or module has a section outside of any procedure or function which is known as the **declarations** section. It's here that **module-level** variables can be created. You can see this section by bringing up a code window on any form or **.BAS** module and selecting (general) from the object combo at the top of the code window.

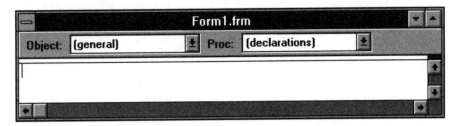

Creating a variable here using the **Dim** statement makes that variable and the data it holds accessible by every procedure in this particular form or module. Procedures in other forms or modules can't see these form level variables, and as before, can have identically named form level variables of their own.

Static Variables

The information held in a **module-level** variable is static. This means it remains in existence for as long as your application is running. There are ways of killing off **module level** variables in forms, but we'll look at how to do this in Chapter 13 - Object Variables.

The **Static** keyword can be used to create a similar type of variable. **Statics** hold their data for as long as the application is running, but are only visible and able to be used by the code in the procedure in which they were created. So really they are safe local variables. They obey the same rules as any other local variable but they don't forget their data when the sub-procedure or function ends.

Statics are declared in exactly the same way as if you were using **Dim**, but instead of actually typing **Dim**, you type **Static**:

```
Static nNumberOfRuns
```

A typical use of a static variable is as a counter that needs to be referenced from outside its module. An example of this would be when keeping track of the number of times a subprocedure has been called before.

Global Variables

The final scope of variable you'll come across is the **global** variable, which you can create, surprisingly enough, with the `Global` keyword. Global variables can only be created in the declarations section of a code module. Forms can't create global variables at all. The data held in a global variable is accessible by every line of code in the application and can therefore be quite useful for maintaining information used throughout your application.

A common use of globals is to hold the name of the program's current user. Any code which needs to access this can then do so with no problem at all. As with **static, local** and **module** level variables, you create a `global` one by typing the word `Global` followed by the name of the variable.

```
Global sUserId
```

Each type of variable scope brings its own problems with it. Global variables are considered to be too unstructured and uncontrolled to use too much in any one program. If all your variables were global then the chances are that a bad piece of code in one procedure could cause many others to function badly by updating a global variable with the wrong value.

While local variables are better in theory, they can also cause their fair share of problems. Too many local variables in a procedure can cause an Out of stack error message to crop up which will crash Visual Basic. This isn't normally a problem and only affects procedures that have an extremely large number of variables defined in them.

Statics can solve the stack problem since they use their own private area of computer memory to store their values and it's totally separate from that used by the local variables. Static variables, however, can cause problems if you forget that in a procedure a static never forgets its data. You should never assume that a static variable will be empty or contain empty values.

Variable Scope Quick Reference

Type	Declaration	Where	Scope
Local	`Dim varName as varType`	In each event procedure or module.	Can only be used in the procedure in which they are declared.
Module	`Dim varName as varType`	In (general) (declarations) section of the form or module.	Can be used in all procedures in that module.
Global	`Global varName as varType`	In (general) (declarations) section of the form or module.	Can be used in all modules in the whole project.
Static	`Static varName as varType`	In any location.	Scope depends on where it is declared. Data is preserved out of scope.

Summary

In this chapter you've learnt how to represent and use data inside your Visual Basic programs. We covered:

▶ How to declare variables, and the benefits of forcing explicit declaration.

▶ The use and limitations of the variant data type.

▶ What other kind of data Visual Basic understands, including numbers, dates and strings.

▶ How to use Visual Basic's rich set of string handling functions.

▶ When and how variables are in and out of scope, and how to deal with data in a project with multiple modules.

In the next chapter we look at some of the more advanced controls in the toolbox which are particularly suited to handling data input and output.

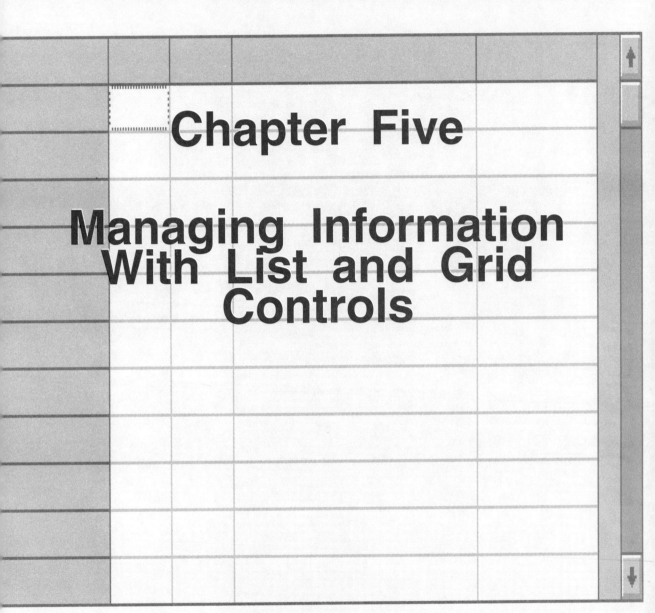

Chapter Five

Managing Information With List and Grid Controls

CHAPTER 5

Managing Information With List And Grid Controls

This chapter discusses some of the more complex controls in the standard edition of Visual Basic. These are all concerned with data input and output. Each control offers its own facilities for managing lists and blocks of information. In Chapter 2 we had a quick tour of some common controls. We then looked at how to write code and saw the kind of data you can use with Visual Basic. This will equip us well to make the most of the more powerful controls.

In this chapter you will learn:

- What a list control is
- What combo boxes and list boxes are
- How to add, select and remove items from list boxes
- How Visual Basic adapts list boxes to work as file controls
- How to use the grid to manage more complex data

List Controls

Many applications, particularly those dealing with data, need to present lists of information to the user. A personnel system for example, may need to present the user with a list of job categories or department names when entering personnel into the system. A strategic space game may need to present a list of appropriate weapons to the player on the Fire control screen. More commonly though, your users will want to navigate easily through the directories on a disk. All these facilities can be easily implemented in Visual Basic through the use of various types of list boxes and combo boxes.

When you're dealing with tables of data (as opposed to lists), spreadsheet-like facilities can be added to your application using the grid control. The most common use for this kind of facility is for entering data into a table structure of the kind used in a database.

Each of these controls is quite straight forward and well adapted for its purpose. They can make laying down the skeleton of your application seem easy. To make them all operate effectively and in unison you need to write some interesting code. This chapter tells you how to do just that.

What's on the Menu

Visual Basic offers a rich variety of list and file controls. So that we know where we're going in this chapter, let's have a look at what they do.

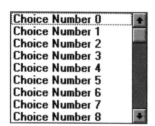

List boxes allow your user to choose a control from a list of options that you put up in the list box window. The user can only choose what you allow them to see.

Combo boxes come in three styles:

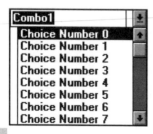

The **drop-down combo**, style 0, is like a text box with a list attached. The user can either type in their own entry, or select one from the list. The user has to actually choose to show the list of options by clicking on the down arrow.

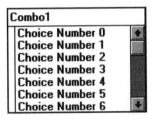

The **simple combo**, style 1, always shows the list of options to the user, but again, the user can enter their own selection.

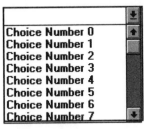

The **drop-down list box**, style 2, is a hybrid of the list and combo boxes. The user can only select from the list of options, but this isn't displayed until the arrow is clicked.

The **file, directory** and **drive list** boxes are all customized versions of list and combo boxes that are provided as separate controls to make life easier. They can be combined together to create complete file dialog boxes, like this example from Chapter 2.

Text box for filename selected

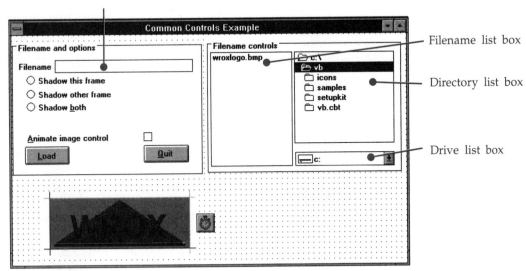

The **grid** is a powerful control that has many potential applications. It can handle large blocks of data, and using some tricky coding, you can give it the kind of functionality that is more reminiscent of a spreadsheet.

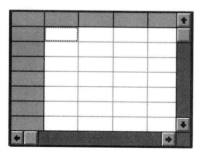

List Boxes

List boxes are ideal when you want to present a list of choices to the user, and restrict their choice to that list alone. If you only have a short list of choices, you could in theory use a collection of option boxes, but the list box is a far better choice because:

▶ The list of options looks like a continuous list, so it appears to users as though they are picking one option from a list.

▶ You can control how much space the control takes up on your form by sizing the box at design-time.

▶ You can add and remove items from the list easily from your code.

Let's have a look at using the list control.

Try It Out - Creating List Boxes

1   Load up the **LIST.MAK** project from the program disk. This project appears to consist of a single blank form, but there is code in the **Form_Load()** event which adds items to the list box you'll create in a moment. If you try and run it now it won't work. We have to build the form first.

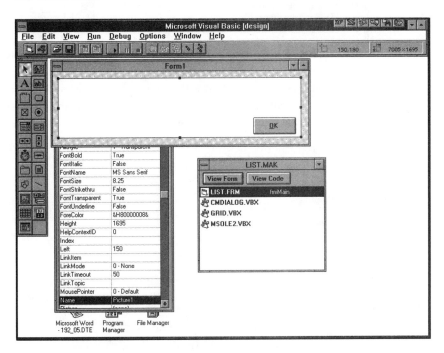

2   Select the list box control from the toolbox and draw a list box on the form.

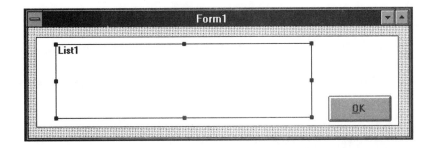

3 Run the program when you have drawn the control as shown.

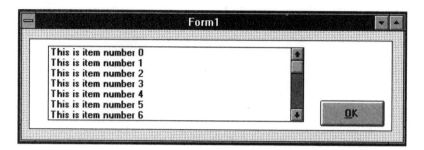

4 The list box displays the items that have been added by the code in the **Form_Load()** event. Because there are too many items to display in the box, Visual Basic adds a scroll bar down the side.

5 Stop the program by pressing the OK button on the form. This stops the program by executing this code:

```
Sub cmdOK_Click ()

    Unload frmMain

End Sub
```

By default all Visual Basic programs cease to run as soon as all the forms in them have been unloaded. In our case there is only one form, so in the OK button **Click** event, saying **UnLoad frmMain** closes down the application. You could also stop the program from running by saying **End** instead of **Unload frmMain**, but traditionally the former is a better approach. By unloading a form you guarantee that once a form is finished with, the memory it took up is released ready for use by other Windows applications.

How It Works

In this short example, I had already added code to the **Form_Load()** event that filled up the list box with items when you ran the program. This code used the **AddItem** method to create the list. If you bring up the **Form_Load()** event in the code window, you can see how this works:

```
Sub Form_Load ()
    Do While list1.ListCount < 100
        list1.AddItem "This is item number " & list1.ListCount
    Loop
End Sub
```

The **Do While** loop tells Visual Basic to run the following lines of code up to the **Loop** statement until a certain condition is met. In this case the **Do While** loop will run until there are 100 items in the list box, as denoted by the listbox's **ListCount** property. The **ListCount** property always holds the exact number of items in the list; the actual items though are numbered from 0 up.

> One of the quirks of these kind of controls, like arrays, is that the item numbering always starts from 0. In this example, the number of the last item will always be ListCount - 1.

The **AddItem** line places a new item in the list box, made up of the string **"This is item number "** followed by the **ListCount** property of the list box. The **&** sign is used whenever you want to tag something onto the end of a string. For example:

```
Print "Peter " & "Wright"
```

prints **Peter Wright** onto the form. In our example it works like this:

```
List1.AddItem "This is item number " & List1.ListCount
```

This line says that the string we want to put into the list box is **"This is item number "** followed by the value of the listbox **ListCount** property. If this property contains the number 5 then the string you'd see on screen will be **"This is item number 5"**. You'll come across the **&** sign used in this way a lot more as you explore Visual Basic.

Sorting Items in a List Box

By default the items in a list box are displayed to the user in the order in which they were added to the list. So if you had code that said:

```
List1.AddItem "Zebra"
List1.AddItem "Camel"
List1.AddItem "Elephant"
```

Then your list box would look like this:

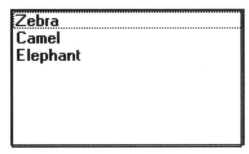

As list boxes go, this is fine. It appears with all the items in and the user can make a selection without any problems. Well almost. Users are funny creatures who tend to expect a little more of your applications than they actually put in the program specifications. If you had a list of 1000 clients displayed in a list box, in a random order like this, they would get upset fairly quickly.

The solution is close at hand. List boxes have a property called Sorted, which you can change between True and False simply by double-clicking it in the properties window.

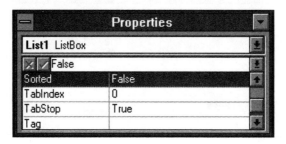

By setting the Sorted property to True, any items you add to the list are automatically sorted. This gives our users the desired result:

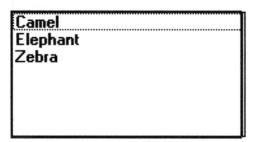

Sorting, however, does have the rather unfortunate drawback in that it takes Visual Basic a little longer to add each item to the list. If you're dealing with large lists, say hundreds of items rather than tens, this can add a lengthy delay to your program code.

One way to get around this delay is to build the list box using an idle loop before the list comes into view. This is one of the subjects we'll look at in Chapter 11 - Interacting With Windows.

Selecting Items in a List Box

Once you've put this list of options up in your list box, the user needs to be able to select one, or maybe more than one of them, and you need to be able to get that selection into your code.

Detecting When the User Makes a Selection.

Let's start by taking a look at some of the events that both list and combo boxes support, to enable you to detect when something happens to a list box. By far the most useful event to use is the **Click** event. This event occurs whenever the user selects an item from the list, by using the mouse, or by using the arrow keys to move up and down the list. Once a click event occurs you can then examine the text property of the control to see exactly what was selected.

Try It Out - Using the Click Event with List Boxes

1   Load up the **LIST.MAK** project again. If it's still loaded then you don't have to reload it to do this example.

2   Make sure you have a list box on the form as before.

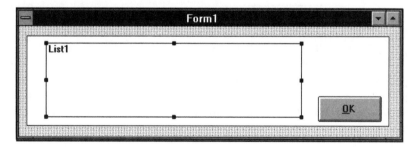

3   Double-click on the list box to bring up the code window for it. Select the **Click** event.

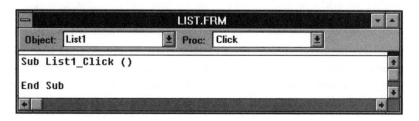

4   Add a **MsgBox** command so that your event code looks like this:

```
Sub List1_Click ()
    MsgBox " Selected : " & list1.Text
End Sub
```

5   Now run the program. Whenever an item on the list is selected, the click event occurs and displays a message box showing you the item you chose.

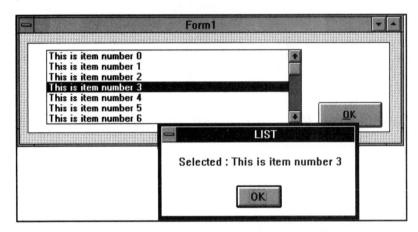

The **Text** property is an extremely simple way to find out what was selected. It works for all styles of list boxes and combo boxes. The property contains the currently selected item from the list. If no item is selected then the text property will contain a blank string "". In combo boxes though, as you'll see later, the **Text** property could also contain text the user has entered rather than selected. As far as list boxes are concerned, it's the value of the item selected.

Identifying Specific Entries in the List

The **Text** property is OK for working with a selected item. It can also be useful to address individual items in the list box, for example to insert a new item at a particular point in the list.

As with most other information about list boxes, this can be pulled up from a property, in this case called **ListIndex**. All list type of controls maintain an array. **ListIndex** is analogous to the index of a user-defined array of the type **variable(index)**.

Try It Out - Using ListIndex to Find the Number of the Item Selected

1 If the original program is still running, stop it to get back to Visual Basic design mode.

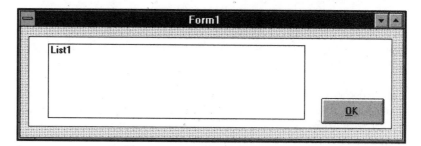

2 Double-click on the list box to bring up the code window again, and see the **MsgBox** statement that we typed into the **click** event.

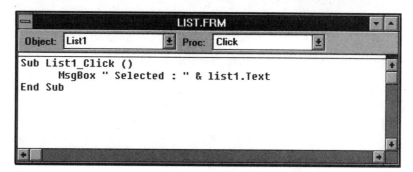

3 Change the code so that it looks like this:

```
Sub List1_Click()

    MsgBox "You have selected Item number " & List1.ListIndex

End Sub
```

4 If you run the program again now, clicking an item in the list will show you the value of the **ListIndex** property, which is also the number of the item you selected.

The **ListIndex** property can also be used to remove specific items from a list, or to add them to above the currently selected item.

Try It Out!

Removing Items From a List Box

The **RemoveItem** method as the name suggests, allows you to remove items from the list. Unlike the **AddItem** method you must specify the number of the item you want to remove, after the word **RemoveItem**. Typing:

```
List1.RemoveItem 5
```

removes item number 5 from the list box. Since items in the list box are actually numbered from 0 upwards, item 5 is actually the 6th item in the list. Aren't computers wonderful?!

ListIndex is commonly used with the **RemoveItem** method to remove the currently selected item from the list. You may, for example, have a command button on a form that says Delete Current Item. The click event for that button could be:

```
Sub cmdDelete_Click

    List1.RemoveItem List.ListIndex

End Sub
```

Try It Out - Removing Items From a List

In addition to using **RemoveItem** to get rid of entries in the list, you can also use the **Clear** method to rapidly get rid of all the items in a combo box list. Simply say:

```
list1.Clear
```

The items will vanish almost immediately. Let's try an example.

1   Create a new project in Visual Basic and draw a list box and two command buttons onto the form like this:

2 Bring up the properties window of each command button, by clicking on each and pressing *F4*. Change the Caption property of Command1 to Clear and Command2 to Remove.

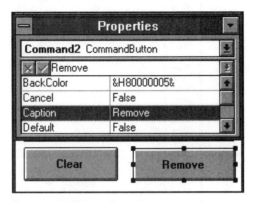

3 Add some code to the form **Load** event to add 100 items into it. Double-click on the form itself, not on the list box or either of the buttons. This brings up the code window. Type in code so that the **Load** event looks like this:

```
Sub Form_Load()

    Do While List1.ListCount < 100
        List1.AddItem "Item " & List1.ListCount
    Loop

End Sub
```

4 Close the code window down and double-click the Clear command button. This is where we'll use the **Clear** method to empty the list box.

5 Change the button **Click** event by adding the line:

```
List1.Clear
```

6 Close the code window again, but this time click on the Remove command button and add the following line to its **Click** event:

```
List1.RemoveItem List1.ListIndex
```

7 That's all there is to it. Now run the program:

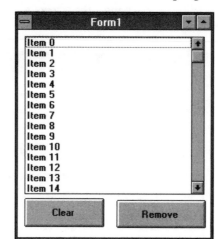

8 Try selecting an item in the list and pressing the Remove button. The selected item will vanish and the ones below it will automatically shuffle up to fill the gap.

9 Now try hitting the Clear button. All the items in the list box are immediately cleared out leaving you once again with an empty control.

> If you try and remove an item without giving an index number, you'll get a syntax error. If you try and remove an item using an index that doesn't exist, you'll get a run-time error.

Selecting Multiple Entries

In all the examples so far, we've used a method of selecting items from lists known as **simple select**. With simple select, the user can only ever select one item at a time. List boxes do however allow users to select more than one record. With an order entry system for example, you could have a list box showing you which invoices are waiting to be paid.

Using **multi-select** your users could click on each invoice in the list that was paid off today, and remove them from the list all at once. This would be so much easier than forcing the user to select each item individually, and then to click a delete button after every one.

The Multi-Select Property

The mode you use for making selections from a list box is controlled by the MultiSelect property. This has three settings:

Setting	Meaning
Setting 0	Allows the user to select only one item at a time. This is the default setting.
Setting 1	**Simple multi-select.** Each item the user clicks is selected, so click on three items and all three become selected. To de-select an item just click it again.
Setting 2	**Extended multi-select.** With this method, clicking an item normally works the same as Setting 0. Holding down *Shift* when you click selects all the items between the previous selection and the current one. Holding *Ctrl* down while you click makes the list box work in the same way as Setting 1.

These can only be set from the properties window at design-time.

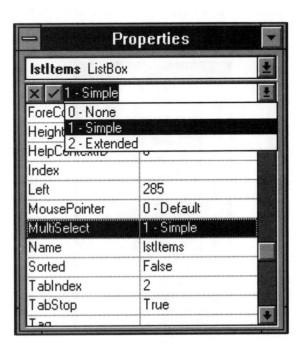

Try It Out - Simple Multi-Select

1 To see how this works, load up the **SELECT.MAK** project and run it.

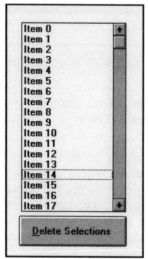

2 The form contains a single list box with 500 items in.

3 Underneath this is a large command button marked <u>D</u>elete Selection. The program lets you select more than one entry in the list simply by pointing and clicking.

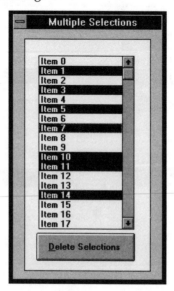

4 When all the entries you want to delete have been selected, press the command button to delete them.

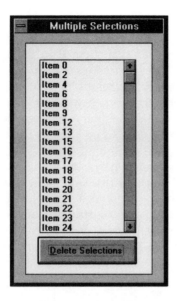

How It Works

When the command button is pressed, the following loop goes through the entries in the list, examining the **Selected** property to see whether the item has been marked. If it has, the **RemoveItem** method is used to get rid of it:

```
Sub cmdDelete_Click ()

    Dim nEntryNumber As Integer
    nEntryNumber = lstItems.ListCount

    Do While nEntryNumber > 0

        nEntryNumber = nEntryNumber - 1
        If lstItems.Selected(nEntryNumber) = True Then lstItems.RemoveItem
    nEntryNumber

    Loop

End Sub
```

First, a variable called **nEntryNumber** is set up to hold the number of the item in the list that is to be checked. The total number of items in the list is then placed into this variable. We have to check the last item in the list first and work backwards, since every time you delete an item the **ListCount** property goes down by one. If you tried to work up through the list you'd tie yourself in knots, as your code could end up trying the check items that no longer exist.

The **Do While** statement makes the code between it and the **Loop** statement run until a certain condition is met. In our case it runs for as long as the item we've just checked is greater than item 0 in the list.

The code inside the **DO** loop decreases the entry number each time around and checks the **Selected** property to see whether or not the item has been selected. If it has been clicked with the mouse, then **Selected** is **True** and the item is deleted.

When you check the **Selected** property, you need to include the number of the entry you want to check in brackets straight after the word **Selected**. In our case the item number is held in a variable called **nEntryNumber**, so that is placed in the brackets instead of a straight number. Again, it's possible to think of **Selected** as an array of boolean values, each of which can be either True or False, depending on the state of the corresponding item in the list box's own array.

> After a multi-select, the Text property of the list box contains the last entry selected.

Try It Out - Extended Multi-Select

There's also a way to select multiple items without having to laboriously click each one. This is known as **extended multi-select**. Let's see how it works.

1 Stop the last program running.

2 Bring up the properties window for the list box.

3 Find the SelectMode property and change it to 2 - Extended to turn the select mode to extended multi-select.

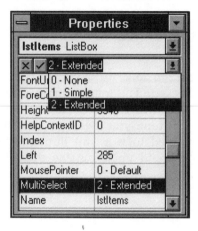

4   Run the program again.

Now when you select items, the list box appears at first to have its multi-select capabilities turned off.

5   If you select the top item, and then another further down, the top item becomes de-selected. In extended multi-select mode you need to use some keys in conjunction with the mouse.

6   Click on the top item in the list, then holding down the *Shift* key, click on another item much further down. All the items between the top one and the next one are selected automatically.

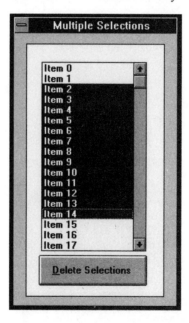

7   Now try selecting another item even further down, this time holding the *Ctrl* key down while you click. This selects an item in a similar fashion to the way simple multi-select works.

Once the items are selected, the corresponding elements of the `Selected` array are set to True, enabling you to process the data as you wish.

Displaying Multiple Columns of Entries

List boxes have a further advantage over combos in that they can display multiple columns of information. This facility is controlled by the list box Columns property.

Try It Out - Multiple Columns

1   Open the project **SELECT.MAK**.

2   In design mode, bring up the properties window for the list box.

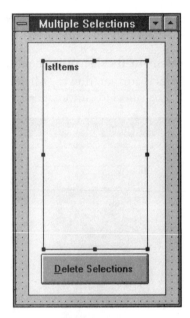

3 Find the Columns property.

4 Type in the number 2 into the Columns property.

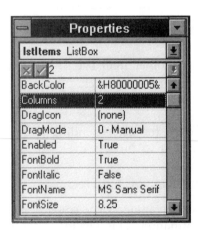

5   Run the program again.

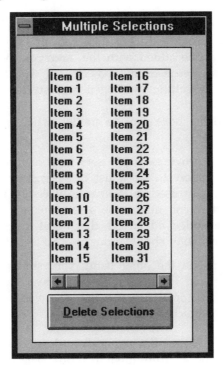

How It Works

The program works the same way as before, but now the information fills the list box by taking up two columns instead of one. The scroll bar that previously lived on the right-hand edge of the list box now lives on the bottom of the box, allowing you to scroll across the columns rather than up and down the list.

> The Columns property determines how many columns are visible in the list box at one time, not the total number of columns.

Combo Boxes

Combo boxes are extremely close cousins to list boxes. Everything you can do to a list box you can also do to a combo box. Items can be added with the **AddItem** method, removed with the **RemoveItem** method, cleared with the **Clear** method and sorted by setting the Sorted property to True.

If combo boxes and list boxes are so similar, what is the advantage of each?

▶ A combo box provides your users with an area to enter data, or the **option** to see a list of suggestions. Combo boxes are usually used in the same places in your application that you might use a text box for user input, but with the added advantage that a list of possible options is available, should your users need it.

▶ List boxes are, on the other hand, very similar to a grid without columns. The list is always shown, and the user can only select items from the list. There is no data entry portion attached to a list box.

Combo boxes come in three flavors; a **drop-down combo box, a simple combo box** and a **drop-down list box**. These flavors, or styles can be selected by changing the **Style** property of the combo box when it's on the form.

Try It Out - Creating Combo Boxes

1 Load up the **COMBO.MAK** project. Like **LIST.MAK**, this project consists of a single blank form. Again though, there is code in the **Form_Load** event which adds items to the combo box you'll create in a moment.

2 Select the combo box control from the toolbox and draw a combo box on the form. If you try and change the height of the box, it will snap back to one line deep.

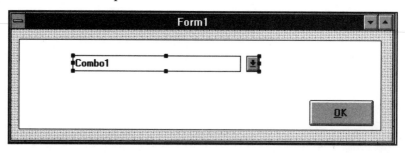

3 Run the program. When the form loads up, you can either type text into the text area of the combo, or click the down arrow to display a list of possible options.

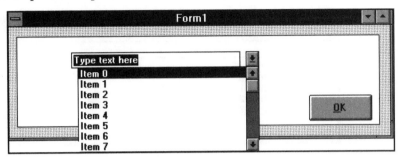

4 The combo box won't force you to select one of the items if you enter some text of your own. This is called a **drop-down combo** box and is the default style for a new combo box.

5 Stop the program now. When you're back in design mode, select the combo box and then bring up its properties window.

6 Find the Style property and change it to Style 1 - Simple Combo.

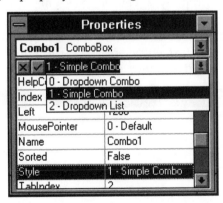

7 See how the downwards arrow on the combo box on the form vanished automatically. Now resize the combo box so it looks like this.

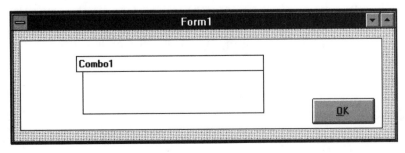

8   Run the program again. As before, you can type any text you want into the combo box, or select an item from the list. Unlike the last time though, the list is displayed all the time.

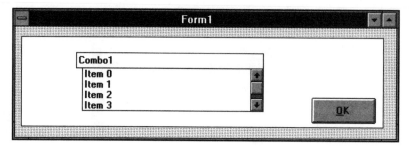

9   This, as you probably guessed when you set the Style property, is called a **simple combo** box. Because the list is always displayed, you must size the combo box at design-time so that the list is visible. If you don't, then your users will be unable to select anything from the list.

10   Stop the program, and once again bring up the properties window for the combo box.

11   Find the Style property again, but this time change it to 2 - Dropdown List box. This type of combo box looks almost identical to the drop-down combo box, with the difference being that the down arrow is flush against the text entry area. The drop-down combo box has its arrow icon a short distance away from the end of the text entry area.

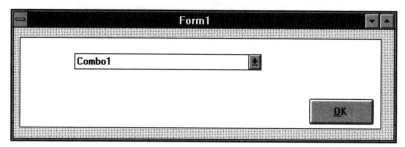

12   Run the program again. This type of combo box, the drop down list box, will only let you select items that are in the list; you can't enter any old free-form text. To see the list of items, press the button.

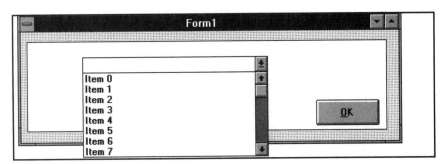

13 However, if you type in the letter I, the combo box will automatically find the next entry in the list beginning with I and display it. Keep pressing I and you'll display the next entry and so on.

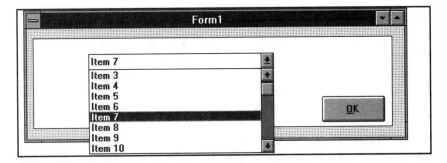

This only works here because all the entries in the list begin with the letter I. If they began with the letter A for example, you'd have to press A to cycle through the items.

Combo Box Events and Properties

Although there are a great many similarities between combo boxes and list boxes, there are quite a few differences between the events and properties they both support. Let's look at the events first.

A combo box consists of two parts: a text entry box and a drop-down list. Because of this you'll find that a combo box has a **Change** event, just like a text box. You can use this to see when the user has actually changed the text in the text box by typing something in. It's worth noting that the **Change** event only occurs when the user types something into the text box part of the combo, and not when the user selects a new item from the list.

The **DropDown** event is another new one, allowing you to catch the point in time at which the user clicks the arrow causing the drop-down to occur.

Finally, list boxes allow you to catch **MouseMove**, **MouseDown** and **MouseUp** events. With these it's possible to always see where in the list box the mouse is currently pointing, and to catch the points at which the user presses and releases a button. No such events are available with the combo box. This isn't really too much of a problem. List boxes present lists of information to the user, so being able to detect the mouse events can be quite handy for popping up information about selecting items without actually selecting them. Combo boxes on the other hand only use the list to present a list of valid choices to the user. There's really no need for such techniques.

On the properties side, combo boxes don't have a Selected property. With a list box, Selected is handy for letting the user do multiple item selections. Since combo boxes only ever let you choose one item at a time, there's no need for a Selected property - just check the Text property to see what the user wants to do.

The Text property with a combo box kills two birds with one stone. When you use it you can not only see which item the user has selected, but also whether they typed something in instead of doing a selection. You can use this property to see what they typed.

The File Controls

Visual Basic provides three controls in the tool box specifically for dealing with disks, directories and files. All three are customized versions of list boxes and combo boxes that have code built into them to connect to the file system. They're all used in the example program **CONTROL.MAK** in order to obtain the name of a graphic file from the user.

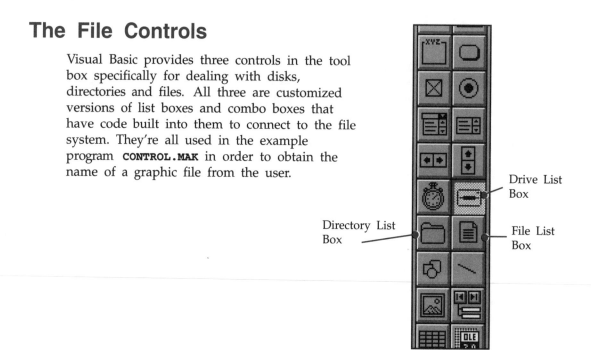

Drive List Box

Directory List Box

File List Box

Using the File Controls

Let's take another look at **CONTROL.MAK** to see how these controls behave in use. In particular, look at the way they interact. Despite their apparent complexity these controls are extremely simple to set-up and use. There's just a little bit of code needed to glue them together.

Try It Out - The File Controls

1 Load up **CONTROL.MAK** and run it.

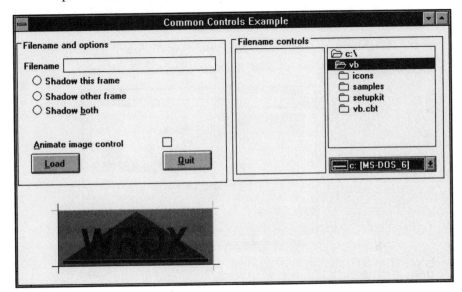

2 To be able to load a certain image, Visual Basic has to know the drive, the directory and the name of the file itself. This is known as the full **pathname**. The controls work together to hand Visual Basic this full pathname.

3 First of all, you have to choose the drive by selecting one from the drop-down combo box.

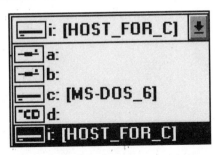

4 Next, you choose a directory from the directory list box. You will see that by changing the drive you updated this box. Something must be connecting the two.

5 Highlight the directory you want, and double-click on the folder. What happens? A list of files appears in the file list box.

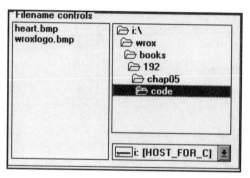

6 To load in the file you want, highlight it and press Load, or double-click directly on the name.

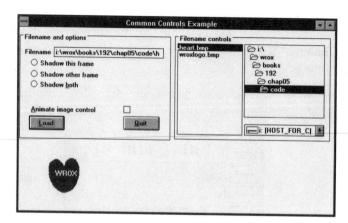

Whenever you use the file controls to load a file into Visual Basic, what you're doing is creating the full pathname and handing it to another control, in this case the image control, to load in the file. The process of building that pathname is handled by the three file list controls.

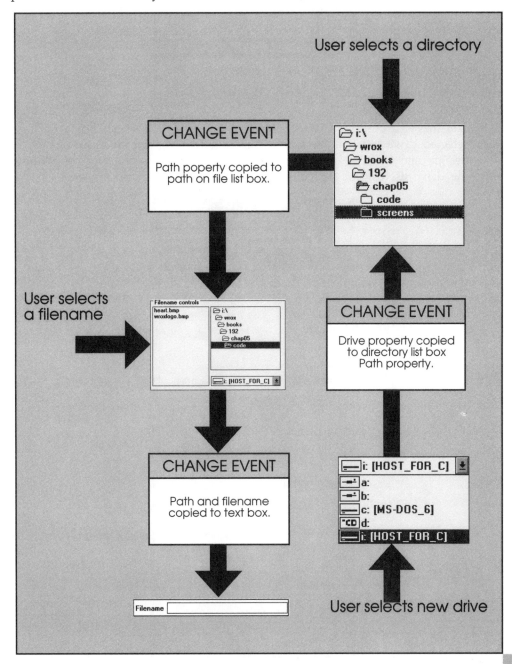

The Drive List Box

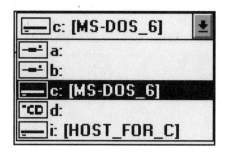

The drives drop-down list box has a property **Drive** which holds the currently selected drive letter at all times. This is not a property you can change at design-time from the properties window. All the properties in the window for the drive list control are concerned with its cosmetic appearance.

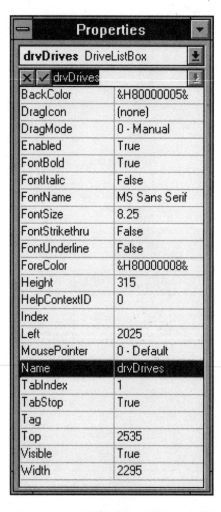

Whenever the drop-down list box is clicked, indicating that a new path has been selected, the contents of the **Drive** property are copied to the **Path** property of the directories list box. Double-click on the drive control in **CONTROL.MAK** to see the event handler that does this.

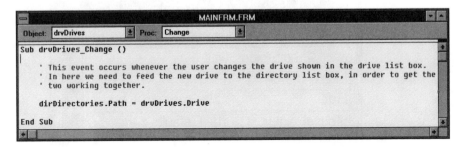

```
                              MAINFRM.FRM
Object: drvDrives          Proc: Change

Sub drvDrives_Change ()

    ' This event occurs whenever the user changes the drive shown in the drive list box.
    ' In here we need to feed the new drive to the directory list box, in order to get the
    ' two working together.

    dirDirectories.Path = drvDrives.Drive

End Sub
```

The Directories List Box

The directories list box also has a property called **Path.** This holds the current path, made up of the drive letter and directory name of the currently selected directory in its list box. Getting a selection in the directory list box to update the file list box is similar to the way the drive and directory boxes are linked. In addition, just as with a normal list box, you can both read and set the **ListIndex** property to find out which item in the list box is currently selected, and to move the highlight from one item to another through your code.

In the example program **CONTROL.MAK**, when the user clicks on a directory in the list box, a **Click** event occurs, during which the contents of its **Path** property are copied to the file list box **Path** property. This causes the file list box to **rebuild**, displaying all the files in the given directory:

```
Sub dirDirectories_Change ()

    filFileNames.Path = dirDirectories.Path

End Sub
```

Selecting Files by Type

The program **CONTROL.MAK** shows a list of graphic files in its file list box. These are files ending in **.ICO, .BMP** or **.WMF**. This feature is set up using another property of the file list box known as the Pattern property.

The Pattern property accepts a list of wild-card file name patterns. So, in order to list only **ICO, BMP** and **WMF** files, set the pattern property to this.

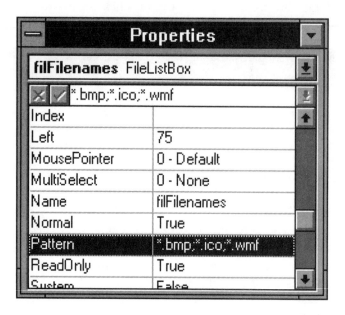

Only files whose names match these wild cards will be displayed in the file list box.

File Attributes

Like the controls you draw on a form, files on PCs have properties associated with them. These are more commonly called **attributes**. Attributes govern things such as whether or not a file is read-only, reserved for system use only, or archiveable. Archiveable files are ones which have been changed since they were last backed up.

Sometimes it's useful to display some or all of these types of files in the list box. A backup program might need to show only those files which have been changed since they were last backed up, and hence require backing up again.

The properties of the file list box (archive, hidden, normal and system) allow you to do just that. Each property can be set to either true or false to change the types of files which the list box will show. For example, setting the archive property to true and setting hidden, normal and system to false, will only show files which need backing up in the list box.

By default, the file list box shows normal files, and archivable files.

Building a Complete Filename

The final link in the chain is to build the complete pathname by adding the filename to it from the file list box. Once this is done, we can pass it to the image control to load the chosen file. The full filename is held within the file list box in two parts; the filename itself, and the path in which the file lives. The two properties used to hold these are called the **Path** and **Filename.**

Both **Path** and **Filename** are run-time properties of the file list box. This means you can only read or set them at run-time. This is why they won't be visible if you bring up the properties window for a file control. As with any other property you can set them at run-time. For instance, to change the path when the user selects a different directory in a directory list box, you can write:

```
FileList.Path = "C:\Pathname"
```

To create the full pathname to pass to the image control, the contents of these two properties are strung together to create the full string using the **&** operator we used earlier to join strings together.

When a filename is clicked in the file list box, the two properties are strung together with a \ sign in the middle to make the filename valid. For example, if the selected path is **C:\TEMP** and the filename is **Peter.Txt** then the result will be **C:\TEMP\Peter.Txt**. The resultant string is then put into the text box with the code you saw a while back, using the file list box **Click** event:

```
Sub filFilenames_Click ()

    txtFileName.Text = filFileNames.Path & "\" & filFileNames.FileName

End Sub
```

That's really all there is to it. With just three lines of code, all three list boxes work together and update a text box to display the sum total of their efforts.

Selecting From Lists by Double-Clicking

Another useful event when dealing with lists of data is the **DblClick** event. This is triggered whenever a user double-clicks on an item in the list box. For many users this is the most convenient and logical way to tell a Windows program that they want to not only choose an item, but also to perform some kind of operation on it.

In **CONTROL.MAK** the code has already been written in the **Load** command button click event to handle the loading of a file. All we need to do is catch a double-click on a filename, and run that code from the **Load** command button **click** event, even though the button itself won't have been pressed. This saves you, the programmer, some typing and makes the program a great deal more usable.

Try It Out - Adding a Double-Click Event

1 Bring up the code window for the file list box and find the **DblClick** event. The code looks like this:

```
Sub filFilenames_DblClick ()
End Sub
```

2 We want the double-click to load the file up in the same way that the Load command button does. This is fairly easy to do since the Load button click event is nothing more than a subprocedure. We call this subprocedure by changing the file list box double-click event to this:

```
Sub filFilenames_DblClick ()

    cmdLoad_Click

End Sub
```

3 If you run the program you can double-click on a filename to load that file up, rather than having to first select the file and then click the Load command button.

Avoiding Crashes with File Controls

One of the difficulties of dealing with the file system is that disk drives are physical devices, and are prone to the same kind of erratic behavior that plagues all machinery. Fortunately disks are more reliable than your Ford Edsel, but they do go wrong, especially if users insist on doing things like switching to drive a: when there's no disk in the drive.

The sample program **CONTROL.MAK** is not bullet proof. Try and load a file from the a: drive without putting a disk in.

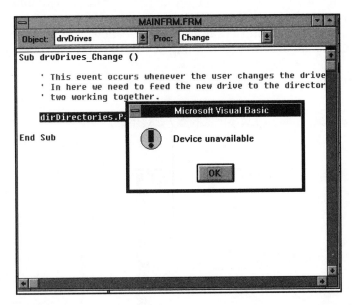

This is clearly unacceptable, but what can you do about it? Visual Basic provides a way to jump to certain bits of code that will respond to errors. In this situation we could put up a dialog box to request that the user puts a disk in the drive, and then retry the code again. This is called **Error Handling**, and is covered in detail in Chapter 10 - Writing Programs That Work.

The Grid Control

The grid control is one of the more powerful and flexible controls that come in the standard edition toolbox. However, this power and flexibility comes at a price which you pay with the amount of work and coding you have to do to adapt the control to your particular requirements. We've already covered a great many of the properties and events that control grids, as they have a lot in common with list boxes.

Using Grids

Grids are great for presenting multiple columns of related information to the user, or for displaying tables of information, such as you might find in a spreadsheet or accounting application. Grids allow you to show two dimensions of information, something which list controls don't permit.

A grid consists of a number of distinct parts.

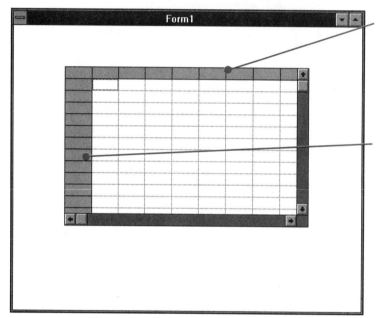

At the top of the grid you can have a number of fixed columns. Usually these contain headings your user will want to see all the time, such as the months in a year, or the days in a week.

You can also fix columns down the left hand side of the grid for the same purpose. In a project management program for example, you may have the left hand columns fixed to show the user the names of the resources available to them, or the names of the various stages of a project.

The information you display in the grid is split into **rows** and **columns,** with each individual piece of data in the grid being called a **cell**. If you've used spreadsheets at all you'll already be very familiar with these terms.

Normally the number of rows in a grid is **dynamic,** meaning it can change at run-time. This allows you to add and remove entries to the table from your code. The number of columns is usually fixed throughout the application, although it doesn't have to be.

Before you can start to use a grid, you need to do some work to get it into the right format.

Try It Out - Setting Up a Grid

1   Create a new project in Visual Basic.

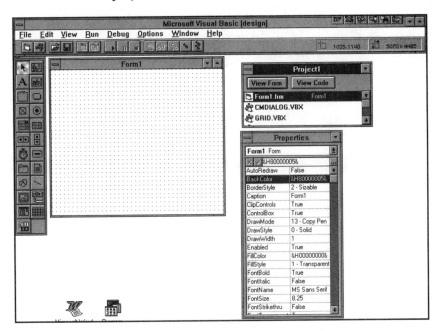

2   Before you can start to do anything with grids you need to make sure that the **GRID.VBX** file is in your current project. Bring up the project window by selecting Project from the Window menu.

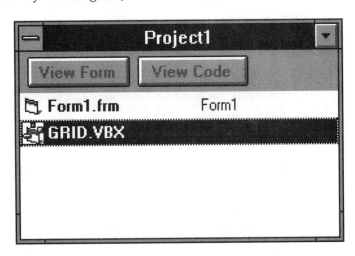

3   If you can't find the line that says **GRID.VBX**, then press *Ctrl-D* to add a file to the project. **GRID.VBX** is in your **WINDOWS\SYSTEM** directory.

> Why is the grid control a separate VBX, unlike most other controls in Visual Basic? The reason is that it's not that great, and Microsoft obviously expect you to go out and buy your own replacement.

4   Bring up the default form, Form1, on the screen and select the grid control from the tool palette and draw a grid on the form, so that it looks like this.

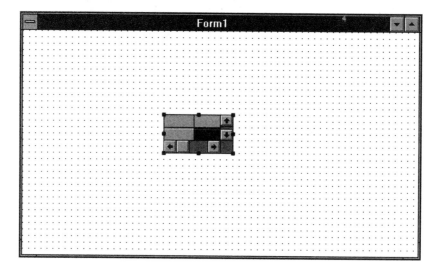

5   Resize the grid to fill almost all the form, and press *F4* to display the properties window.

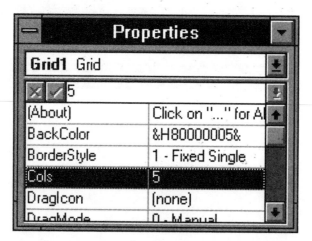

6 Find the Cols property. This determines how many columns there are in the grid. Change it to 5 and press *Enter*.

7 Now find the Rows property. This determines how many rows the grid will load up with. Change it to 50 and press *Enter*.

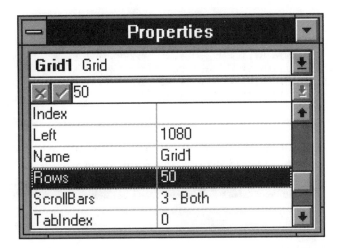

8 So far the grid looks like this:

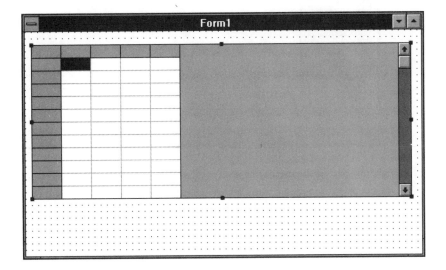

9 So far the grid columns are out on their own, not quite fitting the overall width of the grid. We can change that through code. Double-click on the form, not the grid, to bring up the **Form_Load()** event code. Then add the following code to set the column widths to suit whatever information we might want to put in the grid:

```
Sub Form_Load ()

    Grid1.ColWidth(0) = Form1.TextWidth("X") * 10
    Grid1.ColWidth(1) = Form1.TextWidth("X") * 5
    Grid1.ColWidth(2) = Form1.TextWidth("X") * 5
    Grid1.ColWidth(3) = Form1.TextWidth("X") * 20
    Grid1.ColWidth(4) = Form1.TextWidth("X") * 10

End Sub
```

10 If you now run the program the widths of each column on the grid are set to the desired size as the form loads.

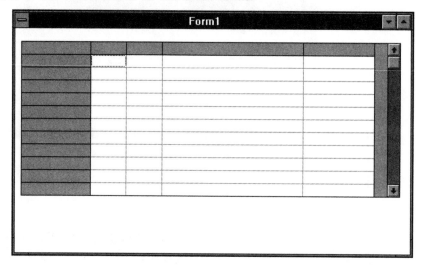

11 We've covered quite a lot of ground in this Try It Out, and we'll build on this as we continue. It's generally a good idea to save large projects that you work on to protect your work. From the File menu select Save Project. Visual Basic will then give you two dialogs. The first one asks you to give your form a name. Call it **TIO.FRM**. The second asks you to give your project a name. Call it **TIO.MAK**.

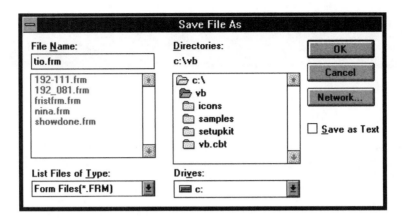

How It Works

In order to decide how wide to make the columns, we used the `TextWidth` function. `TextWidth` gives us a number which is the width of the character, or characters, specified in the brackets. Here we just chose `x` at random, it could have been any character:

```
Grid1.ColWidth(0) = Form1.TextWidth("X") * 10
```

This function returns a width, which is then multiplied in our code to set up the columns to show first 10 characters, then 5, then another 5, and finally 20 and 10.

The column widths can only be set at run-time as they are held in an array. `ColWidth(0)` is the width of the first column, `ColWidth(1)` is the width of the second, and so on. The actual number you enter to determine the `ColWidth`, depends on which coordinate system you are using. Coordinate systems are a topic in their own right. If you have a mad craving for instant information about these, then take a peek at Chapter 8 - Graphics, where it's covered in more detail.

For now though, the easiest way to set up the `ColWidth` property is to decide the maximum number of characters you'll want to display in a column. Then use the `TextWidth` function, as you saw above, to determine the number for the `ColWidth` function.

The `ColWidth` property then sets up the column widths using the numbers we've just worked out. The brackets straight after the `ColWidth` property specify which column we want to change.

Just like items in a list box, the cells in a grid are contained in an array. Each column and each row has its own index number, numbered from 0, not from 1, as is the case with all arrays.

We set up the Cols property of the grid earlier to display 5 columns; these are then numbered from 0 to 4.

When you run the program and the grid appears, you'll see how the left column and the top row are both different colors to the rest of the grid.

These are the **fixed** areas of the grid. If you try scrolling around the grid using the scroll bars, you'll find that this row and column refuse to move.

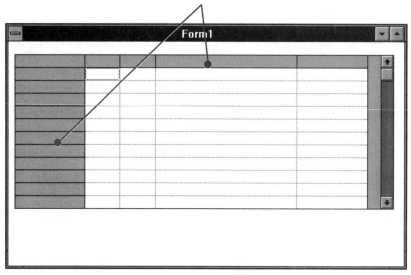

Let's now find out how to turn them both off.

Try It Out - Unfixing Rows and Columns

1   If the last program is running, stop it by selecting <u>E</u>nd from the <u>R</u>un menu, or by clicking the stop icon on the Visual Basic toolbar. If you saved it, and quit Visual Basic, load it up again. Remember you called it **TIO.MAK**.

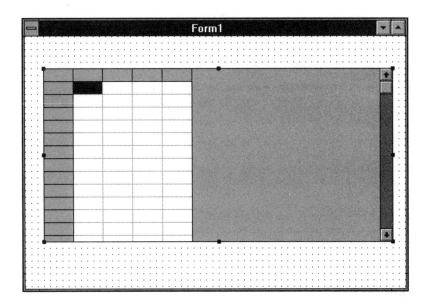

2 Select the grid and then bring up the properties window by pressing *F4*.

3 Scroll through the list of properties to find the FixedCols and FixedRows properties. Set both of these to 0.

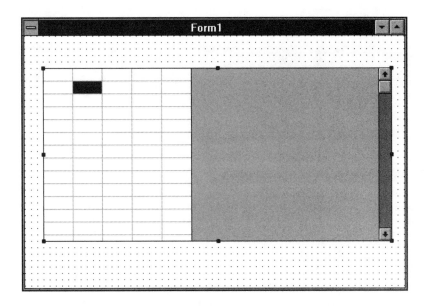

Did you notice that the grid's appearance changed instantly, with the different colored row and column vanishing as soon as you set each property? The FixedRows and FixedCols properties each contain a number that tells Visual Basic how many columns or rows to fix. Changing either of them to 2 for instance, would display 2 rows or columns as fixed. In the example though, changing them to 0 automatically turns off these features of the grid.

Using fixed rows and columns you can add column headings or row numbers to a grid so they can't be scrolled out of sight by the user of your application. A good example of where they're used can be found in Microsoft Excel, to display the column letters and row numbers of a grid.

You can change the values of these properties at run-time, setting them to 0 to remove them if you want. A grid however must always have at least 1 non-fixed row or column.

Adding Items to the Grid

Once we've set up the grid with the appropriate number of rows and columns, the next step is to add data to it.

Although it's a powerful control, the standard grid that comes with Visual Basic has one fatal flaw - it's **read only**. It can only display information to the user. It can't accept any input directly. You can't click on a cell and start to type something into it in the same way that you might with a spreadsheet.

To add and edit data in the cells of a grid, you need to either move a text box over the offending cell and edit the cell contents, or use a totally separate form and set of controls to do the editing. We'll look at both methods here.

First of all, we'll use an input box to get the data from the user, and write some code to insert that data into the grid. After that, we'll use a floating text box to make it look as though you're entering data directly into the grid.

For obvious reasons grids are one of the most popular type of third party VBX (Visual Basic eXtension). You can build a lot more functionality into a grid, including the ability to enter data directly into it. Another major drawback of the built-in Visual Basic grid is that it can't be linked directly to a database, as you'll see later.

I personally use a grid called TrueGrid, from Apex software. Not only does it allow you to color the rows and columns of a grid individually, but you can also build a fairly complete database browser/updater with very little code indeed. Equally good options are Sheridans Data Widgets Grid, and Farpoint's Grid VBX.

There is project on your program disk waiting to have data entered into it. Let's take a look.

Try It Out - Placing Data into the Grid Using an Input Box

1 Load up the **GRID1.MAK** project and run it.

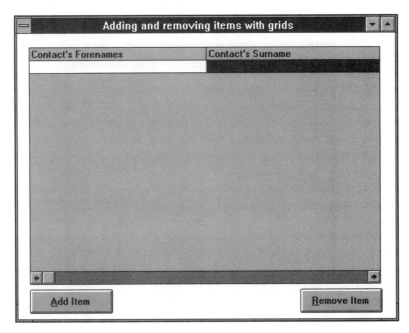

The program contains one form consisting of a number of names, split into a forename and surname. At the bottom of the form are two command buttons allowing new names to be added to the form, and existing names to be removed from the grid.

2   Try adding a few names to the grid. Click on the Add Item button and enter a forename. Press OK after you've typed it in.

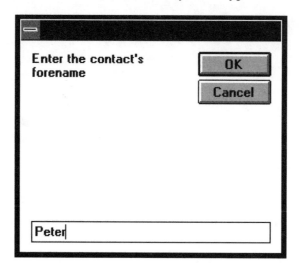

3   Add the surname.

4 The name then appears in the grid.

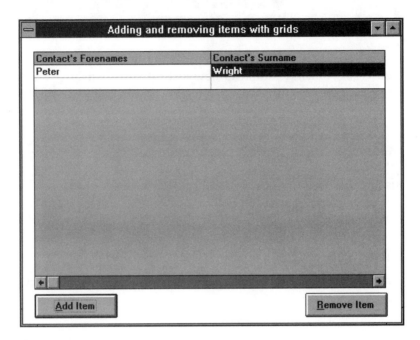

5 Enter in a few more names to make it realistic.

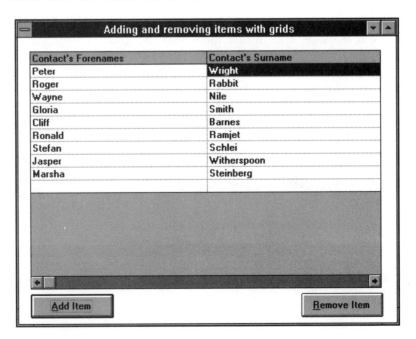

Don't stop this program running at this point. If you do, you'll lose all the data. We want to use this data for more Try It Outs shortly.

How It Works

The Add Item command button is obviously doing something clever to insert these names into the grid. The code in the Add Item button click event looks like this:

```
GRID1.FRM

Object: cmdAdd        Proc: Click

Sub cmdAdd_Click ()

    Dim sColumn1 As String
    Dim sColumn2 As String

    sColumn1 = InputBox("Enter the contact's forename")
    sColumn2 = InputBox("Enter the contact's surname")

    grdContacts.AddItem sColumn1 & Chr$(9) & sColumn2, grdContacts.Rows - 1

End Sub
```

This piece of code does two things. First of all it gets the two parts of the name from the user, and inserts them into the grid.

The first four lines of the event code get that input from the user. Two variables, **sColumn1** and **sColumn2** are defined as strings using the **Dim** command. The two input box lines display a Visual Basic **input box** on the screen. This is a kind of ready-made dialog box which allows you to get information from your users without having to go through all the hassle of defining a new form especially for the job. Input boxes and various other forms of dialog boxes are covered extensively in Chapter 7. Put simply though, each input box displays a message, such as Enter the contact's forename, and stores whatever the user enters in one of the variables defined at the start of the event.

The line that most interests us is the **AddItem** line.

```
GrdContacts.AddItem sColumn1 & chr$(9) & sColumn2, grdContacts.Rows  - 1
```

AddItem is a **method** that works with both list type boxes, as we saw earlier, and also with grids. The correct syntax for **AddItem** is:

```
<control>.Additem <data to add to the list>, <row to add the data to>
```

The **<control>** part is the name of the grid, list or combo box to which we're going to add something. In our case, the grid has already been named **grdContacts**, so that's the name placed before the **AddItem** method.

With grids, there can be more than one column of information. The **AddItem** method works with complete rows, so you use the **CHR$(9)** statement to separate the data that's going to go into each column.

Each time you press a key on the keyboard Visual Basic translates this key into a number, called an ASCII code. Another name for this is a character code. **CHR$** allows us to use these codes in our program rather than straight symbols like "A" or "0". This is particularly useful when we need to tell Visual Basic to use a special character such as *Tab*. You can't type a *Tab* directly into program code - all that happens is that you get 4 spaces on the screen. **CHR$(9)** tells Visual Basic that we want to use a *Tab*, whose ASCII code is 9.

We have two columns of data, and the information we want to put in those columns has already been stored in the variables called **sColumn1** and **sColumn2** by our **InputBox** commands. So, to add these to the grid in separate columns we just say:

```
AddItem sColumn1 & Chr$(9)& sColumn2
```

You've seen the **&** sign before. It's used to join more than one text string together, in this case it joins **sColumn1** to the **Chr$(9)** code. This tells Visual Basic that after putting the forename into the grid, the next bit of information we send goes in the next column, the surname column.

This can be a bit confusing, so an example might help a little. Here's what would normally happen:

1   The user clicks the Add Item command button.

2   Visual Basic displays an input box asking the user to enter the person's forename. The user types in Peter and our code puts this into a variable called **sColumn1.**

3   Visual Basic now displays a second input box, asking the user to enter the person's surname. The user types in Wright and our code places this into the second variable, **sColumn2.**

4   The code now tells Visual Basic to add an item to the grid. First it tells it to add whatever is in **sColumn1**, in this case the word Peter.

5   Our code then sends the **AddItem** method the **CHR$(9)**. Visual Basic sees this, and moves from the first to the second column.

6   The code then tells Visual Basic to add whatever's in **sColumn2**, in this case the word Wright.

The final bit of the **AddItem** command is the code **grdContacts.Rows - 1**. At the end of the **AddItem** method you can tell the grid where you want the data added. The grid has a **Rows** property which we can use to see how many rows are in the grid. When the grid first loads up there's a blank line on it by default. Adding the new item after this line would look bad in our case, as we'd end up with a blank line followed by some data. Data followed by a blank line looks much better and is an accepted method of showing the user that the grid can still accept further information. We therefore place the item *before* this last line.

Try It Out - Moving Around the Grid

1   Run the program and click on a cell in the grid. A border appears around the selected cell - this is commonly known as the marquee.

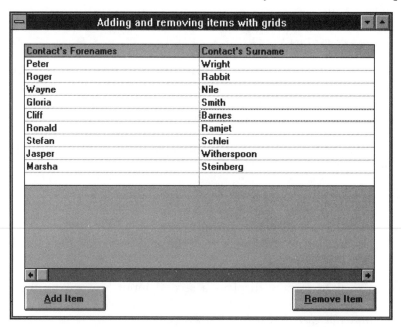

2 You can move across columns using the left and right arrow keys on the keyboard. You can also move up and down rows on the grid with the up and down arrows keys.

3 The *Tab* key moves you off the grid onto one of the other controls on the form. As soon as the grid loses focus the last cell you selected is highlighted in a different color.

Removing Items From the Grid.

You'll be pleased to know that removing items from a grid is a whole lot easier than adding them. The **RemoveItem** method can be used to delete a row from anywhere in the grid, the beginning or the end, it really doesn't matter.

Try It Out - Removing Data From the Grid

1 With the contacts program still running, move the marquee to a record you've already added. Then click on the Remove Item button to see how it works.

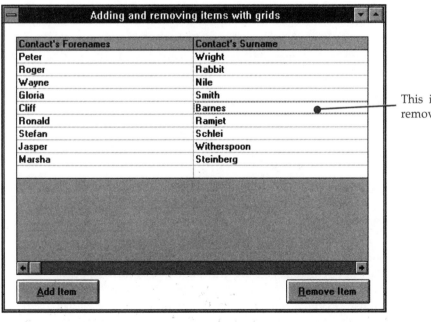

This item will be removed.

2   To see how this works, stop the program, and in design mode double-click the Remove Item command button in our example project. Take a look at the code when the code window appears.

The full syntax of the **RemoveItem** method is:

```
<control>.RemoveItem <row number to remove>
```

Remember that I said the grid always knows which is the current cell? Its location is always stored in the **Row** and **Column** properties of the grid. In our **RemoveItem** code we just need to tell Visual Basic to remove the current row:

```
grdContacts.RemoveItem grdContacts.Row
```

I told you it was easier than adding items to the grid, didn't I! You could also remove items from the grid by reducing the **Rows** and **Cols** properties of the grid. Unlike the **RemoveItem** method however, this only gets rid of the bottom rows of the grid, or the rightmost columns of the grid. This isn't very useful if you want to get rid of something in the middle of a grid.

Getting Data From the Grid

So far we've seen how to put data into the grid, and remove it from the grid at a later point. What about actually using the data in a grid? A prime example of when you might want to do this can be see in our contacts grid. All the grid does is list people's names. There may be a separate form used to display a person's full details, for example their name and address. How would we know which form to pull up for a particular cell?

Try It Out - Getting Data From a Grid

1   Load up the **GRID2.MAK** project and run it.

2   At a superficial level the program looks identical to the earlier example. However, if you now double-click on a cell in the grid, a separate form pops up showing you the information in both columns of the grid.

3   Run the program to see how it all fits together.

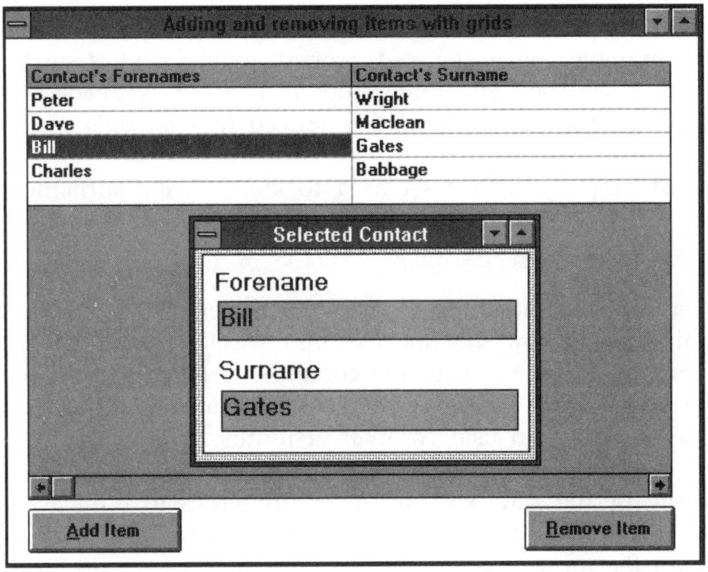

4   When you've had enough, stop it and double-click on the grid to see its double-click event code:

```
Sub grdContacts_DblClick ()

    Dim sForename As String
    Dim sSurname As String

    grdContacts.Col = 0
    sForename = grdContacts.Text
    grdContacts.Col = 1
    sSurname = grdContacts.Text

    Load frmDetail

    frmDetail!lblForename.Caption = sForename
    frmDetail!lblSurname.Caption = sSurname

    frmDetail.Show

End Sub
```

Try It Out!

How It Works

Two variables are declared at the top of the program to hold the currently selected surname and forename. Don't panic if you're not exactly sure what these mean or how they work, all will be explained in the next chapter.

To get at the value of a cell in the grid we can use the **Text** property, just as you would with a text box. However, before we can start to look at the text property of the grid, we need to ensure that we're looking at the right cell.

The **Col** property can be set to move the highlight to a different column. So, in the example above, the **Col** property of the grid is set to **0**, the first column. If we copy the **Text** property into our **sForename** variable we can be certain that the value obtained is indeed the contact's forename.

The **Col** property is then set to **1** to move to the surname column:

```
grdContacts.Col = 1
```

We haven't done anything to the **Row** property so we're pulling values out of columns on the row that the user has selected. Once the **Col** property has been set to **1**, the value of the contact's surname can be copied into our **sSurname** variable. These two values, forename and surname, are then displayed on screen using a **MsgBox** routine.

You can use the **Col**, **Row** and **Text** properties to update cells in a grid as well. That's how the column titles are set when the form loads up. Double-click on the form in design-time to see the code for its **Load** event:

```
grdContacts.Row = 0
grdContacts.Col = 0
grdContacts.Text = "Contact's Forenames"

grdContacts.Col = 1
grdContacts.Text = "Contact's Surname"
```

Here we first set the **Row** to 0, the topmost row in the grid. The code then moves through the two columns setting the **Text** property and thus setting up our column titles.

The values are passed to the two labels on the separate form with the lines:

```
frmDetail!lblForname.Caption = sForename
frmDetail!lblSurname.Caption = sSurname
```

You saw how this works in the last chapter when we passed information from one form back to the calling form. This one works in the opposite way. First of all the **Detail** form is loaded.

Loading a form doesn't actually display it, it just loads it up. Once the form has been loaded we can tell Visual Basic to change the caption of the two labels on the form, **frmDetail!lblForename** and **frmDetail!lblSurname**, to the values in our two string variables. Once these values have been loaded the **Show** command is used to actually bring the form into view.

Summary

This chapter has shown you how to present a lot of data to the user in an efficient, organized way. You've also learnt how the user can then interact with that data in an intuitive way. This ability to make data transparent to users is one of the great benefits of Windows. In the old text interface days, users had to work with data through layers of forms, making it much harder for the user to visualize the complete set of data.

These are all important tools that will be used a lot in later chapters such as Chapter 9 - Databases. It is this ability to manipulate data that has made Visual Basic so popular for business applications which so often involve a great deal of shoveling data about.

If you want to see a real-world application of the grid control, take a look at Chapter 13 - Putting It All Together. This is a complete application that can be used to record bugs in a system and uses a grid for its main form. Take a look!

In this chapter you learnt:

- How to use list and combo boxes
- How the file controls, drive, directory and file list boxes work and fit together
- How grids work
- What you can, and can't do with a grid, and why it's probably better to go out and buy a better grid as a VBX

In the next chapter we'll learn how to add menus to your Visual Basic programs.

File

Open

Save

Save As

Delete

Exit

CHAPTER 6

Menus

Menus are an integral part of any Windows application. Visual Basic makes the process of creating and modifying menus a breeze when compared to old-style Windows programming. However, there is still a big difference between a good and a bad menu structure, as any frustrated Windows user will tell you.

In this chapter you will learn about:

- What a good Windows menu should look like
- How to create simple menus using the menu editor
- Adding options to drop-down menus
- Using shortcut and access keys
- Cascading menus
- Creating dynamic menus
- How to add code to menu events

You Already Know Menus

If you've used PCs for any length of time then you should be familiar with what a menu is. (Windows users can't get away from them!). In this world of graphical user interfaces, point and click icons, and highly intuitive mouse driven programs, you still can't beat a good text-based list of options which open up the power and features of your application to your users.

A Great Windows Menu

This book is being written using Word 6 for Windows, which in many ways is the archetypal Windows application. If you look at how the Microsoft applications programmers have implemented this excellent product you can learn a lot about creating well-crafted Windows applications.

Consider the Word 6 for Windows menu bar.

Each word you see on the menu represents a group of functions. For example, click on the <u>F</u>ile option and a list of **menu items** appears which relates to things you can do with files (in a *virtual* sense!).

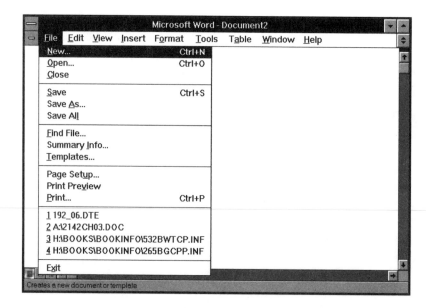

In this chapter we'll explore the two types of menus that Visual Basic provides (drop-downs and pop-ups). We'll also find out how to create them, control them and generally make use of them in your applications. There is one control that all Windows applications seem to have, and that's the menu bar. Ignore it at your peril; but use it well and your users will love you forever!

Drop-Down Menus

The standard type of menu (and the easiest to develop) is the drop-down menu. In its simplest form you simply pick some categories for your program functions, such as file handling, editing, and program options, and place these category names onto a menu bar. All you need to do then is add functions to each category of menu items that drop down when the menu heading, such as File or Edit, is clicked.

This is what we want as our end product:

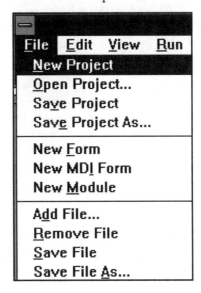

Don't panic! We're going to work through each stage step-by-step.

How Drop-Down Menus Work

If you are a programmer who has come to Visual Basic from some other language, then you may be a little daunted at the prospect of having to provide such menus in your programs. Questions like 'how do I know if the mouse is over a menu heading?', or 'how do I place a menu list over the form and redraw the form when the menu goes?' are probably making you break out in a cold sweat already. Worry not - Visual Basic (or more to the point Windows) does it all for you.

Menus, just like command buttons, option buttons, pictures and frames, are controls. Once you've set up the menu control, then you only have to worry about handling the events that each menu item can trigger - in the same way as if you were using a command button. Windows automatically takes care of drawing the menu, re-drawing the covered parts of the form when the menu vanishes, displaying and positioning sub-menus, and so on. In fact, menus are one of the easiest controls you'll come across in Visual Basic; the most time-consuming part is typing in all the text that form the menus themselves.

Creating Menus Using MenuEdit

Unlike other controls, the menu control isn't found in the standard Windows toolbox. Instead, Microsoft in its wisdom chose to place it as an icon on the main Visual Basic toolbar.

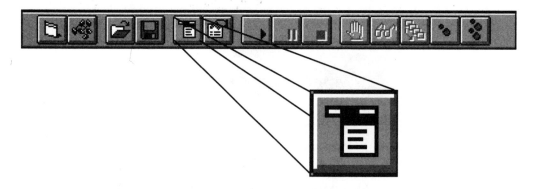

Alternatively, you can select the Menu Design item from the Window menu:

Window	Help	
Color Palette		
Debug	Ctrl+B	
Menu Design	Ctrl+M	
Procedures	F2	
Project		
Properties	F4	
Toolbox		
Data Manager		

The Visual Basic Menu Editor

Setting up a menu is done via a fairly complex looking dialog box called the menu editor. If you have a form visible, click the menu icon and you'll be launched into the menu editor.

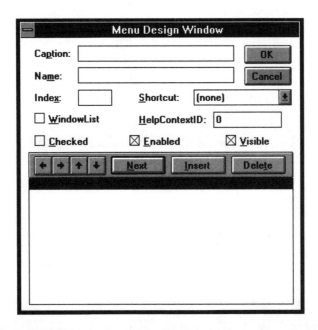

If you don't have a form visible then the menu editor icon is actually disabled, so there's no way that either you or Visual Basic can get confused about what's actually going on in the development environment. Visual Basic adds the menu you create to the form which is currently selected.

Try It Out - Creating a Simple Menu

Most Windows applications have a File menu which allows your users to open and save data, exit the application, and so on. Actually creating the menu with the Visual Basic menu editor is a simple task:

1   Start up a new project in Visual Basic and make sure that the form (Form1) is visible.

2   Click on the menu editor icon on the Visual Basic toolbar.

Try It Out!

3 When the menu editor dialog appears, enter &File in the Caption property, and mnuFile as the Name property.

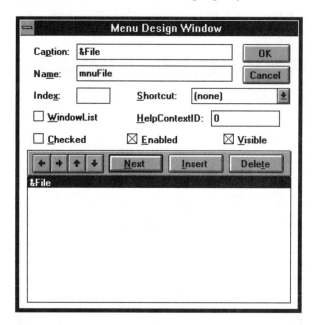

As with any other control's caption you can assign the menu item a hot-key by putting an & in front of the letter in the caption that you want to be the hot key. You can use any key in the word, not just the first one. Going back to the File example, you can usually select a File menu by pressing *Alt* and F together. The user knows this because what he or she actually sees on screen is the word File, with the F underlined. The way you set this up in the caption is to simply say that this item's caption is &File.

4 Now press *Enter*. Visual Basic will store the menu item in the list area at the bottom of the dialog and move the highlight down to the next line.

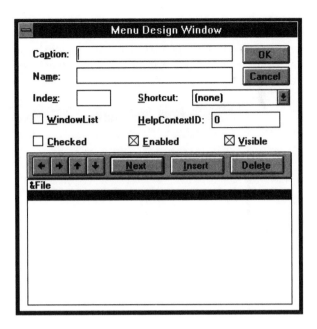

5 Use the same process to enter Open and Save As menu items. First enter &Open for the Caption and mnuOpen as the Name. Then enter Save &As (note the space!) as the Caption, and finally mnuSaveAs as the final Name property. The Name and Caption properties are the bare minimum you can specify when creating a menu. We'll look at the other optional properties in a moment.

6 If you now hit the OK button, Visual Basic checks the dialog to make sure you don't have any errors in the properties. When it's satisfied Visual Basic will create your new menu structure on the visible form, in this case Form1.

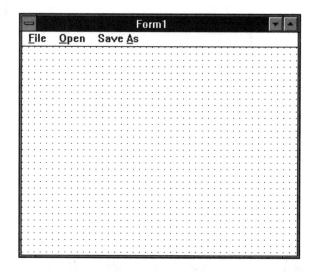

> If you pressed the *Enter* key after entering the last menu item, before you add an item name, you will have created a blank menu item and Visual Basic will respond with an error message: Menu control must have a name.

Well done, you've just created your first Visual Basic menu!

Try It Out - Creating a Drop-down Menu

The menu we've just created isn't exactly a classic piece of Windows design.

Ideally the Open and Save As options shouldn't actually be visible at this point. Instead they should be drop-down items that become visible when you click on the word File, as in this more typical Windows menu layout:

Try It Out!

Let's fix it by creating a proper drop-down list of options from a single menu header.

1   Click on the menu editor icon again to re-load the menu dialog and display the list of menu items you've created.

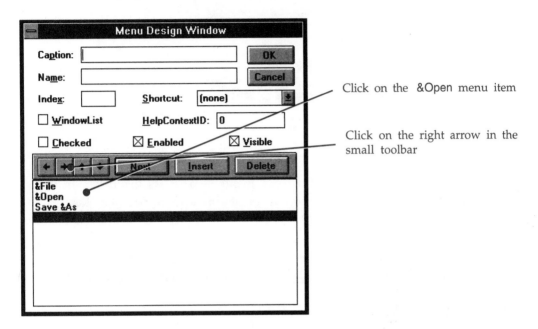

Click on the &Open menu item

Click on the right arrow in the small toolbar

2   The &Open option will shift to the right. This indicates that it's now an option from the &File option.

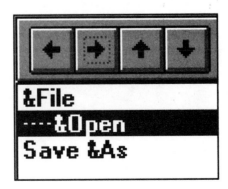

3   Do the same for the Save &As item.

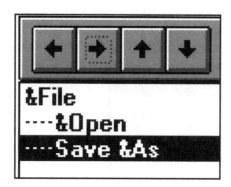

4   To view your finished menu structure, click OK.

5   The form will now only show one menu item on its menu bar. In this case you'll see the &File option all on its own. Click once on this heading to see the menu underneath it.

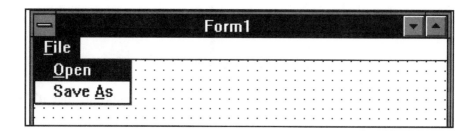

The process of aligning the menu items to create the right structure is called outlining.

Try It Out - Editing Your Menu Structure

Of course, when you come to write your own applications, it's rare to find all parts of the development process whiz by as smoothly as following a Try It Out section. It's easy to miss menu items off, or get them in the wrong order. Thankfully Visual Basic's menu editor lets you go back and make changes.

1 Click on the menu editor icon again. The menu edit form appears, but this time showing the menu we just created. If it's not still loaded, then it's on the disk called **MENUDES.MAK**.

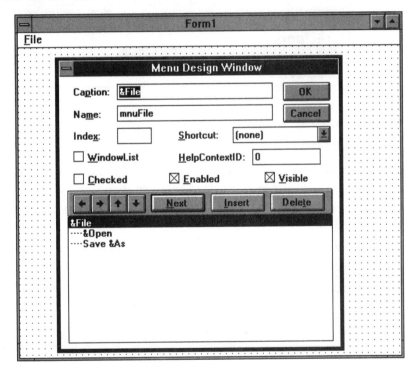

2 To the right of the four arrows in the menu editor there are three more command buttons: Next, Insert and Delete. Let's see what they do:

3 Click on the top item in the list, the &File item, to highlight it. Click on the <u>N</u>ext button and the highlight moves down to the next item in the list - &Open. When you reach the bottom of the menu, <u>N</u>ext creates a new blank item ready for you to add a new menu option.

4 Now click on the Save &As item. If you click the <u>I</u>nsert button you'll place a new menu option above the current one. Do it now.

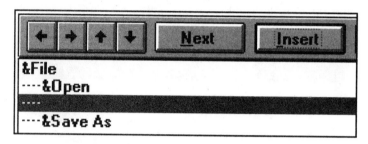

5 The Save &As option drops down a line and a new item is added immediately above it.

6 The <u>D</u>elete button does just the opposite of insert, removing the currently selected item from the list. Click it now and the new blank item will vanish, and Save &As will move back up to its original position.

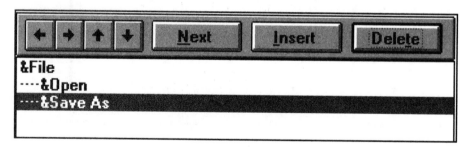

You've already seen how the right pointing arrow can shift menu items across the menu structure. The left, up and down arrows work in a similar way.

7 Click on the &Open menu item, then click the left arrow.

8 The item shifts to the left, so that if you pressed OK now you'd have a File and Open menu with Save &As underneath Open. Don't press OK yet though.

9 With the &Open item still selected, click the up arrow and it will move up to the top of the list. The effect this has on the final menu is that &Open now appears on the title bar before &File.

10 To put the menu back to normal, click on the right arrow, then click on the down arrow.

Try It Out - Nested Menus

At last our menus are starting to look the way they're supposed to. One further layout option is to place menu items in lists branching off from another menu item. This is called **menu nesting** and can be done as many times as you like. Take a look at this menu:

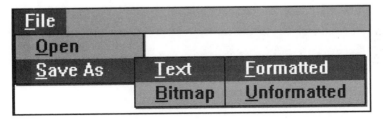

You can create nested menus in the same way that you create normal menus; you simply add new items to the list and shift them to the right of the one you want them to be nested under.

1 With the menu editor still visible, click on the Save &As item and press the Next button to create a new menu item.

2 Set the caption of this new item to &Text and the name of the menu to mnuText.

3 Repeat this process to create three more items with their captions and names set like this:

&Bitmap	mnuBitmap
&Formatted	mnuFormatted
&Unformatted	mnuUnFormatted

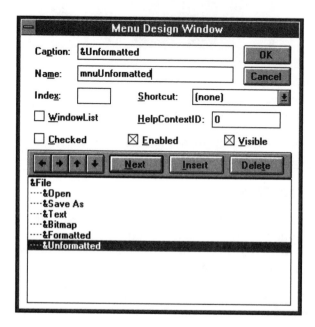

4 The actual order of these items is wrong. We want Formatted and Unformatted to appear underneath the Text item. Click the &Formatted item and press the up arrow once.

5 Now do the same for the Unformatted item.

6 We need to **nest** our new menus to make them appear as sub-menus of other menu items. Click on each of the four new items and press the right arrow.

7 This makes all the four new menu items appear as a sub-menu of the Save &As item. The next step is to make the Formatted and Unformatted items appear as sub-menus of the &Text item.

8 Shift the Formatted and Unformatted items right again.

9 If you press OK you'll find that your menu structure is the same as the one you saw at the start.

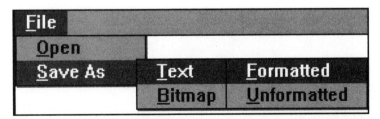

Menu Properties

We said earlier that a menu is a control, and like other Visual Basic controls you can change the appearance and behavior of a menu by manipulating its properties.

Just as the menu control isn't accessed in the normal way by clicking on an icon from the toolbox, its properties aren't accessed through the properties window either. Instead, the properties are all constantly displayed in the menu editor window itself.

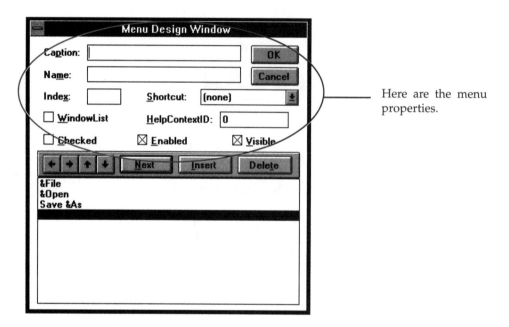

Here are the menu properties.

The normal flow of work when designing menus is to first create a menu item, then set its properties, then move onto the next item. So far we've only dealt with the Caption and Name properties, which are mandatory. We've ignored the middle section of the dialog in the interests of speed, but now it's time to go back and see what we can do with properties.

The properties can be set at design-time using the MenuEdit dialog box, or at run-time from within your code.

Name	Description
Caption	The text of the menu that the user will see.
Name	The name which you'll use in your code to address this menu and to identify the event code for each menu item.
Index	Used to form control arrays. This is where more than one menu item has the same name property, so a number in the Index property is used to address each item individually.
Shortcut	The menu can be invoked either by clicking it with the mouse in the normal way, or by pressing the shortcut key; for example, *Ctrl-C* is usually the same as a Copy menu item.
WindowList	This is used in Multiple Document Interface (MDI) applications. These are applications that have one main form and smaller subforms contained with it (like Program Manager). The WindowList property tells Visual Basic to display the captions of the windows in this menu item.
Checked	Clicking on this property, or setting it to **True** in code, causes a tick, or **check mark** to appear beside the menu item. This is great for lists of options.
Enabled	If this is clicked or set to **True**, then the menu can be selected by the user. Setting it to **False** by clearing the check box causes the menu item to appear **grayed out**, meaning the user can't select it.
Visible	Clicking the check box to set this to **True** causes the menu or item to be visible at run-time. Clearing the check box makes it invisible.

Menu Name Properties

The second property, Name, should be fairly straightforward by now. It's a property that allows you as the programmer to decide on the name, which you can use in your code to refer to a menu item, as you would with any control.

Let's say you had a menu heading of File. You could change the name of this to something else. Then in order to change any other property of that menu item, you would use the following code:

```
mnuFile.<property name> = <a value>
```

One of the greatest hassles when dealing with menus is deciding what to call them. Each menu item is a control and each menu item needs to have its own caption and name. With a big menu structure, such as the one in Word 6 or even Visual Basic, deciding on unique names for each control can become a real hassle.

There are two ways to approach this problem. The first solution, and the one which the Visual Basic Programmer's Guide advocates, is to create control arrays of menu items. Here each item under a certain heading has the same name and is part of a commonly named control array.

The other approach, and the one I prefer, is to give each menu heading a name starting with mnu and ending in the name of the menu heading. For example, if you have a File heading, then its name would be mnuFile. Each item of the menu is then named with the heading name (or an abbreviated version of it) followed by a cut down version of the caption. So, if under your File heading you have a Save As option, it would be named mnuFileSaveAs. This is simple, easy to understand, and a whole lot less likely to melt your brain!

The Menu Index Property

Index is another familiar property and is used to uniquely identify a menu item that is part of a control array. Using the Index property it's possible to set up a number of menu items all with the same name. You'll see how this can be used later in Chapter 12 - Using Object Variables, where it's used to create menus that are built up using code, like the list of recently opened projects that Visual Basic shows you in its File menu:

Load Text...	
Save Text...	
Print...	Ctrl+P
Make EXE File...	
1 \BOOKS\BG2VB\CHAP05\CODE\GRID2.MAK	
2 \BOOKS\BG2VB\CHAP05\CODE\GRID1.MAK	
3 \BOOKS\BG2VB\CHAP05\CODE\CONTROL.MAK	
4 \BOOKS\BG2VB\CHAP05\DAVEONLY.MAK	
Exit	

Enabling Menu Items

The **Enabled** property determines whether or not the menu option is actually available to be used. It appears grayed out if the **Enabled** property is not set. The **Visible** property indicates whether this particular menu item should appear on the menu at all.

Take a look at this screenshot:

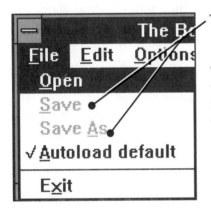

These items have their Enabled properties set to False.

This shows menus which are disabled and menus which are invisible. OK, you can't actually see the invisible ones, but that just shows how effective it can be!

Later in this chapter you'll see how to create pop-up menus. By creating an invisible menu you can create menus that the user can't see until you decide to pop them up onto the screen using some code. Another use of the Enabled and Visible properties is for when you need to build some kind of access **security** into your programs. Menu items that you don't want certain users to be able to use can be either made invisible or disabled.

Assigning Shortcut Keys

The **Shortcut** property is rather novel. Hot-keys created with & only work if that particular menu item is visible when *Alt* and the appropriate letter are pressed. Think back to the menus we created earlier.

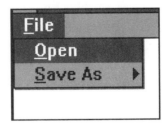

The <u>O</u>pen item was created with a text property of &Open. The <u>O</u> of <u>O</u>pen is underlined in the menu, meaning that we can access it by pressing *Alt* and *O* together. This only works however, when the <u>F</u>ile menu is actually dropped down and visible. <u>S</u>hortcuts allow you to do this even when the menu isn't visible.

By assigning a key combination to the Shortcut property you can actually call the menu option from any point in the program by simply pressing the shortcut keys. You may have come across some of the more standard shortcuts in Visual Basic; *Ctrl-X* to cut something, *Ctrl-V* to paste it, and so on. It's a good idea to try and stick to standard shortcuts.

Try It Out - Assigning a Shortcut Key

Assigning a shortcut to a menu item is as simple as point and click; point at the arrow to the right of the <u>S</u>hortcut combo box and click on one of the key combinations listed. Let's try it.

1   Load up the **EDITMENU.MAK** project. This has two menus, <u>F</u>ile and <u>E</u>dit, with items on each of them. We're going to assign shortcut keys to the <u>E</u>dit menu items.

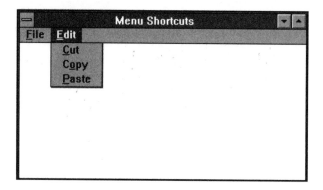

2   When the main form appears, click on the menu editor icon on the Visual Basic toolbar.

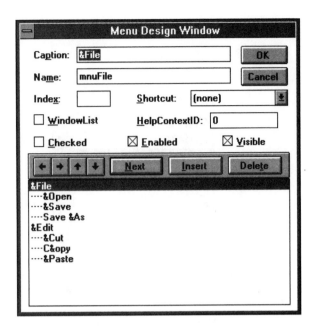

3 We need to add shortcuts to the C̲ut, C̲o̲py and P̲aste items. C̲ut will be *Ctrl-X*, C̲o̲py will be *Ctrl-C* and P̲aste will be *Ctrl-V*.

4 Click on the C̲ut item, and click on the down arrow beside the S̲hortcut combo box.

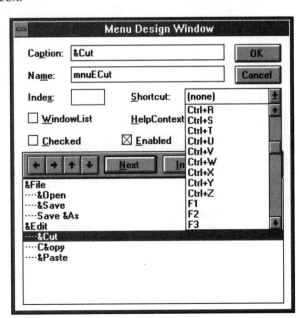

5 Scroll down the list until you find *Ctrl-X* and select it by clicking it with the mouse.

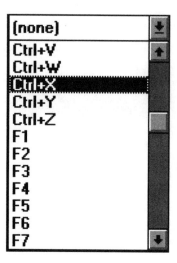

6 The menu editor dialog will now change to show you that the S̲hortcut selected is *Ctrl-X*.

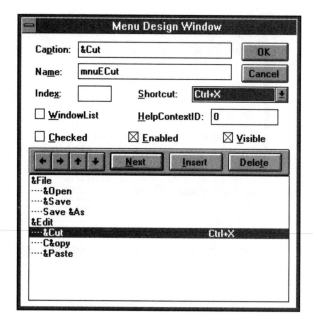

7 Using the same process select the *Ctrl-C* shortcut for the C**o**py menu item, and *Ctrl-V* for **P**aste. These are all standard shortcut commands for the **E**dit menu items that Microsoft recommend.

8 When all the shortcuts are set, click on the OK button on the menu editor and take a look at your new edit menu.

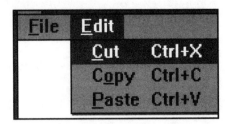

9 Now run the program, and instead of selecting menu items by pointing and clicking with the mouse, press *Ctrl-C, Ctrl-V* or *Ctrl-X*. Each time a message box will pop-up showing you which menu item you've selected. You can check this by selecting the **E**dit menu items themselves. The same message boxes appear.

> You can't add a shortcut key to a menu item that isn't indented.

The **W**indowList Property

Later on in the book, you'll come across **Multiple Document Interface (MDI)** applications. An MDI application is similar to a Windows File Manager, or Program Manager. It has a main background form, with smaller **child** forms inside. Visual Basic lets you set up menus for the background forms and for the child forms.

Whenever a child form gets clicked on by the user the MDI background form changes its menu to match that of the child form. This is a very common approach used by most Windows applications. Nearly all of Microsoft's own programs work this way. As an example, take a look at this screenshot of Word 6 in operation.

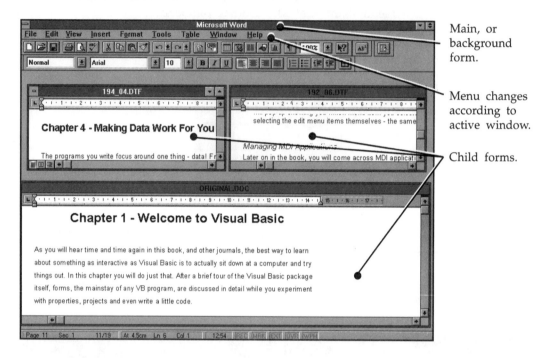

Main, or background form.

Menu changes according to active window.

Child forms.

To understand MDI applications you also need to understand object variables. An object variable is a variable that contains not a number or text string, but a Visual Basic object, in this case a whole form. We cover object variables, and therefore MDI applications, in Chapter 12 - Using Object Variables.

Menu Separators

The final menu design feature we need to look at are separators. If you have a drop-down menu that has a large number of items on it, it makes sense to break up the items into logical groups. On the Visual Basic File menu, the options are grouped according to whether they apply to projects or files.

Try It Out - Adding Separators

Separators are just as easy to create as any other menu item. Simply enter a dash for the item Caption, and a dummy name such as mnuDash1 as the Name property. Visual Basic automatically interprets a menu item with a dash (-) for a Caption as being a separator line.

1 Load up the **FILEMEN.MAK** project. This is a simple application with a File menu containing Open, Save, Save As and Exit options. What we need to do is add a separator bar just above the Exit option.

2 When the main form appears, click on the menu editor icon on the toolbar.

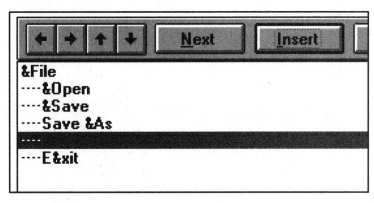

3 We want to add the separator bar above the Exit option, so click on that option in the list and then click the Insert button. Pressing *Alt-I* does this just as well.

4   For the Caption of the separator bar, just enter a dash. The only gripe I have with the way Visual Basic handles separator bars is that you still need to give each one a unique name. In the name property enter mnuFDash1 to show that this is the first dash on the File menu.

5   Press OK to finish editing, then on the form take a look at the File menu.

Adding Code to Menu Items

Selecting a menu item triggers a click event. As a developer you can add code to respond to that event. To bring up the code window for a particular menu item, single-click on the item on the form at design-time.

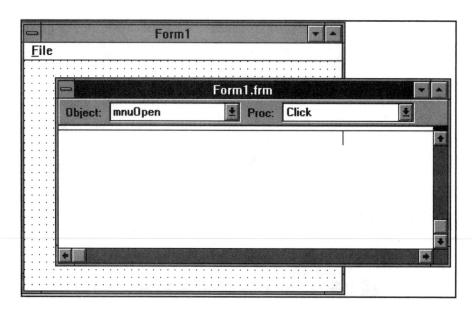

Try It Out - Adding Code to Menu Items

If you want to play around with menus a little more, load up the sample project **DROPDOWN.MAK** and use the menu editor to see exactly how the menus are created. Don't be afraid to experiment with nesting or unnesting the sub-menus; if you *do* make a horrendous mistake you can simply load the project in and start again.

Actually adding event code to a menu item is as easy as it is to add code to a normal control.

1　Bring up the form from **DROPDOWN.MAK**.

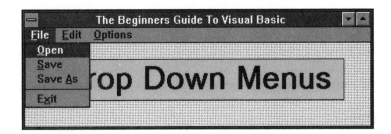

2　To bring up the event code window for a menu, just select it in the combo box. Select Open from the File menu:

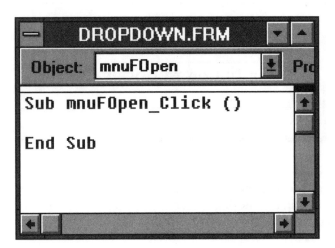

3 Let's add some code to make this menu item pop-up a message box. Change the **mnuFOpen_Click**() event so that it looks like this:

```
Sub mnuFOpen_Click()

    MsgBox "You selected Open from the File menu"

End Sub
```

4 Once this is done run the program. Select Open from the File menu, and the message box you've just added appears.

Pop-Up Menus

Once you have created your menu structure, you aren't limited to simply displaying drop-down menus. Visual Basic provides a command you can use which displays a menu anywhere on the screen, whenever you want.

What's a Pop-Up Menu?

Load up the **POPUP.MAK** sample program and run it.

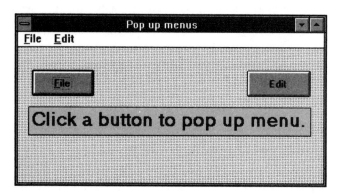

Here we have a program with a single form and a very familiar menu layout. There are also command buttons on the form which have similar captions to the menu headings. Clicking on one of these command buttons will **pop-up** the appropriate menu underneath the command button.

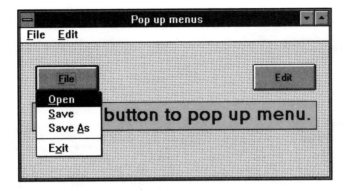

Creating Pop-Up Menus

The command which implements this menu is the ingeniously named
PopUpMenu command (and you thought learning Visual Basic would be tough!).

Load up the **POPUP.MAK** project and double-click on the command button
named File to see the code.

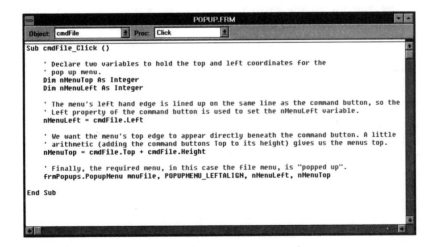

The first four lines of code after declaring the subprocedure are used to set up
two variables, **nMenuLeft** and **nMenuTop**, which will locate the top-left corner
of the pop-up menu on the form. These are then set to the bottom-left corner
of the command button:

```
nMenuLeft = cmdEdit.Left
nMenuTop = cmdEdit.Top + cmdFile.Height
```

After this only one line of code is needed to actually display the menu:

```
frmPopups.PopupMenu mnuFile, POPUPMENU_LEFTALIGN, nMenuLeft, nMenuTop
```

This line tells Visual Basic that the **PopUpMenu** is a menu from a form named **frmPopups**.

> This is the only form in our project so it isn't really necessary to tell Visual Basic that this is the form we're using. I've included it in the example simply because the **PopUpMenu** command can pop-up menus which actually belong to different forms. In that case you would place the name of the form that holds the menu *before* the **PopUpMenu** command.

The next part of the command, **mnuFile**, is the name of the menu I want to pop-up. This is the name that is typed into the menu editor <u>N</u>ame field.

Immediately following the name of the menu, you need to tell Visual Basic a number, (known as a **Flag**) which it then uses to determine how you want the menu displayed. Instead of using straight numbers however, I've included the **CONSTANT.TXT** file in the project so I can use the constants in that file to make the code more readable.

> Including the whole of **CONSTANT.TXT** in your code isn't a good idea. Global constants, just like global variables, eat a great deal of precious memory and Windows resources.
>
> A much better approach is to load **CONSTANT.TXT** into Windows Write. As you work through your program and find a need for stuff from **CONSTANT.TXT**, go to Write, select the text you want, and select <u>C</u>ut from the <u>F</u>ile menu. Then in your Visual Basic code window find the appropriate declarations section and press *Ctrl-V* to paste the declarations back into your code. You'll get to do this for yourself in the next chapter.
>
> I've included a new copy of **CONSTANT.TXT** on the disk. This includes declarations for pop-up menus that should be in the original that came with your copy of Visual Basic, but weren't.

In this case, **POPUPMENU_LEFTALIGN** indicates that I want the left-hand edge of the menu to appear at the X coordinate which I specify later in the command. I could have said **POPUPMENU_CENTERALIGN**, or **POPUPMENU_RIGHTALIGN** to have the menu centered on the **nMenuLeft** coordinate or positioned with its right edge on the **nMenuLeft** coordinate. It's really just a question of personal taste and how much screen space you have on which to actually display the menu.

The last part of the **PopUpMenu** command is the **nMenuLeft** and **nMenuTop** coordinates, which are used to position the menu on the screen. Coordinate systems are covered later, in the section on graphics. For now though, try to think of the screen as being divided up into a number of dots *across* the screen and a number of dots *down* the screen, rather like very fine graph paper. The **nMenuLeft** and **nMenuTop** coordinates tell Visual Basic how many dots across the screen (**nMenuLeft**) and how many dots down the screen (**nMenuTop**) are required to display the pop-up menu. Again, if you have a major craving for more instant information, then check out coordinates systems in the graphics chapter later in the book.

For simplicity though, you don't have to specify the flags or the **nMenuLeft** and **nMenuTop** coordinate parts of the **PopUpMenu** command. If you don't, the menu will appear by default at the location of the mouse pointer.

PopUpMenu is a new command to Visual Basic 3. When I first came across it I found it difficult to see where I'd actually *use* it. After all, what's the point of displaying pop-ups when you can have drop-downs with no code at all? The answer to this is simple. You can have pop-up menus which are not visible on the menu bar. For example, Excel 5 uses this feature to display a special pop-up whenever the right mouse button is clicked. The code in Excel 5 decides what the user is currently doing, such as entering numbers or a formula, and displays a menu specific to that operation.

You can do the same in Visual Basic 3 by coding the **MouseDown** event of a form or control to display an appropriate pop-up.

Dynamic Menus

As well as using the design-time menu editor to create and change your menu structure, it's also possible to create new menu items at run-time. This is great for creating dynamic menus such as the Visual Basic File menu, which automatically shows you the last four Visual Basic projects you worked on, cutting out the need for you to traverse your hard disk with the open project dialog box.

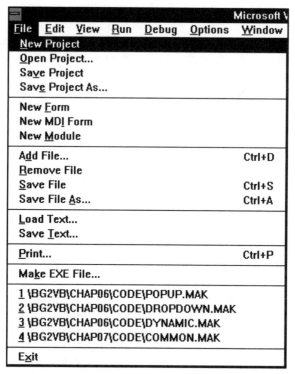

Adding Menu Items at Run-time

Dynamic menus such as this all revolve around control arrays which we covered briefly in a previous chapter. We'll take a look at exactly what is involved by creating a dynamic File menu of our own. Let's do this by extending a project already on your disk.

Before we begin, load up the **DYNAMIC.MAK** sample project and take a look at the file menu.

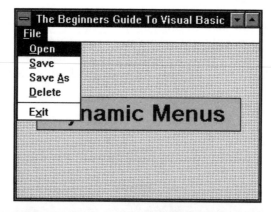

It's a standard File menu with options to Open, Save and Save As. What we need to do is add the previous filenames to the bottom of the menu, separated from the rest of the menu options by a separator bar.

The theory is that we create a control array of menu items that starts with one element - the separator bar. Then, at run-time, we simply **Load** new instances of the control array, in the same way that you'd **Load** a form in. Visual Basic automatically numbers the new control array elements and displays them on the menu. Let's try it out.

Try It Out - Showing the Last Used Files on the Menu

Make sure you still have **DYNAMIC.MAK** loaded in with the main form showing. We're going to make the file menu of this program display the most recently opened files below a separator bar at the bottom of the menu.

1 Click on the menu editor icon on the toolbar to display the menu editor dialog.

2 Move to the bottom of the menu item list and create a separator bar named **mnuFileList**. Do this by moving to the last item, and clicking on the Insert button. Then place a dash in the Caption box, and type in the Name.

At this point we have two problems. Firstly, Visual Basic doesn't yet know that this is a control array. Secondly, the bar will appear even when there are no files to list underneath it. This looks untidy.

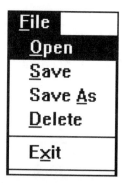

3 Make the separator bar menu item invisible by clearing the Visible checkbox.

4 To tell Visual Basic that this is actually a control array, place the number 0 into its Index property.

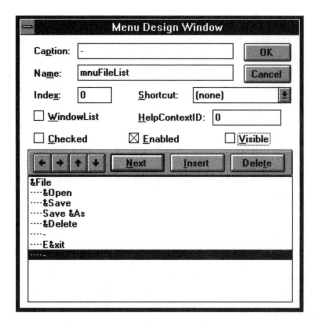

We now have a one element control array; the one element is our separator bar named **mnuFilelist**.

We need to create the code to add items to the menu at run-time.

5   If you go into the code window and look at the **Declarations** section of the form you'll see a level variable defined:

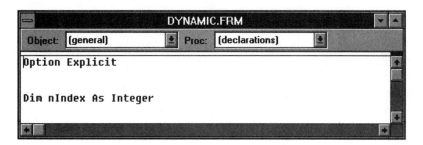

We'll use this variable to keep track of the number of items in our array. In the form **Load** event there is an additional line of code to set this variable to 1, to show that there is currently one item in the array. Don't panic yet, we'll cover menu arrays in a few moments.

6 Take a look at the **mnuFOpen_Click** code. Bring up the code window by opening up the <u>F</u>ile menu at design-time, and clicking on the <u>O</u>pen option. **mnuFOpen** is the name of the menu item. It's not as confusing as it looks. Since it begins with **mnu** its easy to tell in our code that we're dealing with a menu. The **F** part of the name tells us this is a sub-menu of the <u>F</u>ile menu. Finally the word **Open** lets us know exactly which menu item we're dealing with, the **Open** item. This is a common way of assigning names to menus, and you'll see it a lot more throughout the course of the book.

7 There's already code in the **Click** event to use a common dialog to select a file name:

```
Sub mnuFOpen_Click ()

    On Error GoTo OpenError
    dlgOpen.CancelError = True
    dlgOpen.DialogTitle = "Select the file to open"
    dlgOpen.Filter = "All Files (*.*)|*.*)"
    dlgOpen.FilterIndex = 1
    dlgOpen.Action = 1


    '_____

    ' Insert menu code here

    Exit Sub

OpenError:
    On Error GoTo 0
    Exit Sub
End Sub
```

Most of this code deals with a feature of Windows and Visual Basic known as the **common dialog**. Common dialogs are built in to Windows to make all routine dialog boxes look the same to the user. We'll cover these in a lot more detail in the next chapter, but for now it's safe to ignore this part of the code. All we need to do is use the filename that the user selects from the common dialog to set up the filename as a menu option.

8 In the **mnuFOpen_Click** code you'll see a comment line stating:

```
' Insert menu code here
```

9 This is the line in which we need to put some code to make the <u>F</u>ile menu grow dynamically. Directly below this line, type the following code in.

```
frmDynamic.mnuFileList(0).Visible = True

Load frmDynamic.mnuFileList(nIndex)
mnuFileList(nIndex).Caption = dlgOpen.FileName
mnuFileList(nIndex).Visible = True
mnuFDelete.Visible = True

nIndex = nIndex + 1
```

Your code window should now look like this:

```
Sub mnuFOpen_Click ()

   On Error GoTo OpenError

   dlgOpen.CancelError = True
   dlgOpen.DialogTitle = "Select the file to open"
   dlgOpen.Filter = "All Files (*.*)|*.*"
   dlgOpen.FilterIndex = 1
   dlgOpen.Action = 1


   '_____
   ' Insert menu code here
   frmDynamic.mnuFileList(0).Visible = True
   Load frmDynamic.mnuFileList(nIndex)
   mnuFileList(nIndex).Caption = dlgOpen.FileName
   mnuFileList(nIndex).Visible = True
   mnuFVisible = True
   nIndex = nIndex + 1

   Exit Sub

OpenError:
   On Error GoTo 0
   Exit Sub
End Sub
```

10 Try running the code now. After the form comes into view the only items on the File menu are Open and Save.

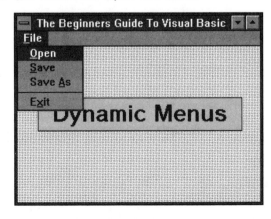

11 Select the <u>O</u>pen menu item from the <u>F</u>ile menu and a common dialog will appear asking you to select a filename.

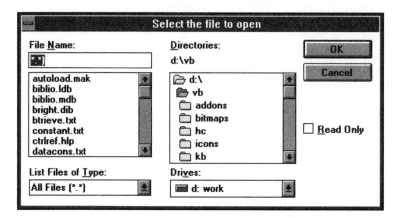

12 Go ahead and select one, then click OK.

13 Now take a look at the <u>F</u>ile menu once more. The separator bar has appeared and our new filename is beneath it.

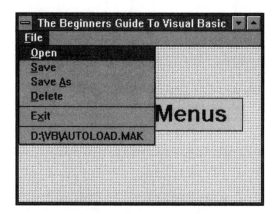

How It Works

Let's take a look at the code behind this. The first thing we have to do when a filename has been selected is to make the separator bar visible. We already know that the index of this in the **mnuFileList** array is 0. You gave it this index in the menu editor. Therefore, the first line just makes the separator bar visible:

```
frmDynamic.mnuFileList(0).Visible = True
```

If it's already visible (perhaps because you've already selected a filename) then *that* code will have no effect.

Next the `Load` command is used to load a new **element** of the control array:

```
Load frmDynamic.mnuFileList(nIndex)
```

This is a complex area of Visual Basic, mainly because of the terms involved like instance, object variable and so on. Each control you put on a form, each menu item you create, and each form itself is referred to as an **instance**. You can create new instances of controls in a control array with the `Load` command, which is what we've done in this example. The `FileList` menu item is set up with an **Index** number of 0 which tells Visual Basic that this is the first item in a menu control array. We can then use `Load` to create copies (new instances) of this menu by telling Visual Basic what the new **Index** number should be.

Don't worry too much about the technicalities. You can just import this code into your own applications as it stands. Chapter 12 - Object Variables, gives a more complete description of this whole area.

The `Load` command creates a new element, or member of the array, and tacks it onto the end. Our global variable **nIndex** not only shows us how many elements are already in the array, it also gives us the number of any new elements we want to create. Therefore, tell Visual Basic to load a new element into the **mnuFileList** array numbered **nIndex**.

The next two lines are straightforward:

```
mnuFileList(nIndex).Caption = dlgOpen.FileName
mnuFileList(nIndex).Visible = True
```

The new menu item is made visible and its caption is set as the filename returned from the common dialog.

Finally, we add **1** to the **nIndex** variable to show that a new element has been added:

```
nIndex = nIndex + 1
```

It makes sense that if you **Load** new elements into a control array, you use **Unload** to get rid of them. We can add code to the **Delete** menu item to do just that.

▶ Bring up the code window for the **Delete** item **Click** event, **mnuFDelete_Click**.

▶ Type in code so that the event looks like this:

```
Sub mnuFDelete_Click()

    If nIndex = 1 Then Exit Sub
    nIndex = nIndex - 1

End Sub
```

A Note on Good Design

Whatever your personal view on Windows (and I'm assuming that you don't actually *hate* it), it's hard to disagree with the notion that keeping the design of the user interface as standard as possible across various applications is a worthwhile objective.

Microsoft themselves have issued guidelines for how Windows applications should look. The best source of this information is the book:

The Windows Interface - An Application Design Guide
Microsoft Press 1992 ISBN 1-55615-439-9

The bottom line on menus is that the more your menus resemble the applications your users are familiar with, the easier they'll find their way around your program.

For example, take a look at the menu bars for three well known Microsoft applications:

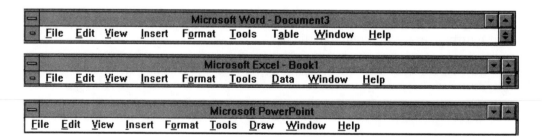

Summary

Menus are very useful tools for both you as a developer and for the users of your applications. In this chapter you learnt how to:

▶ Create new menus from scratch

▶ Nest and sub-nest menus

▶ Change the order of menu items

▶ Add separator bars to the menus

▶ Add code to the menus

▶ Turn a standard menu into a pop-up one

▶ Name menus in a standard way

In the next chapter we'll take a look at dialogs. These are pop-up information windows that perform a variety of functions. Some of them, like the common dialogs we used to save and load files, come up as a result of menu selections.

Chapter Seven

Dialogs

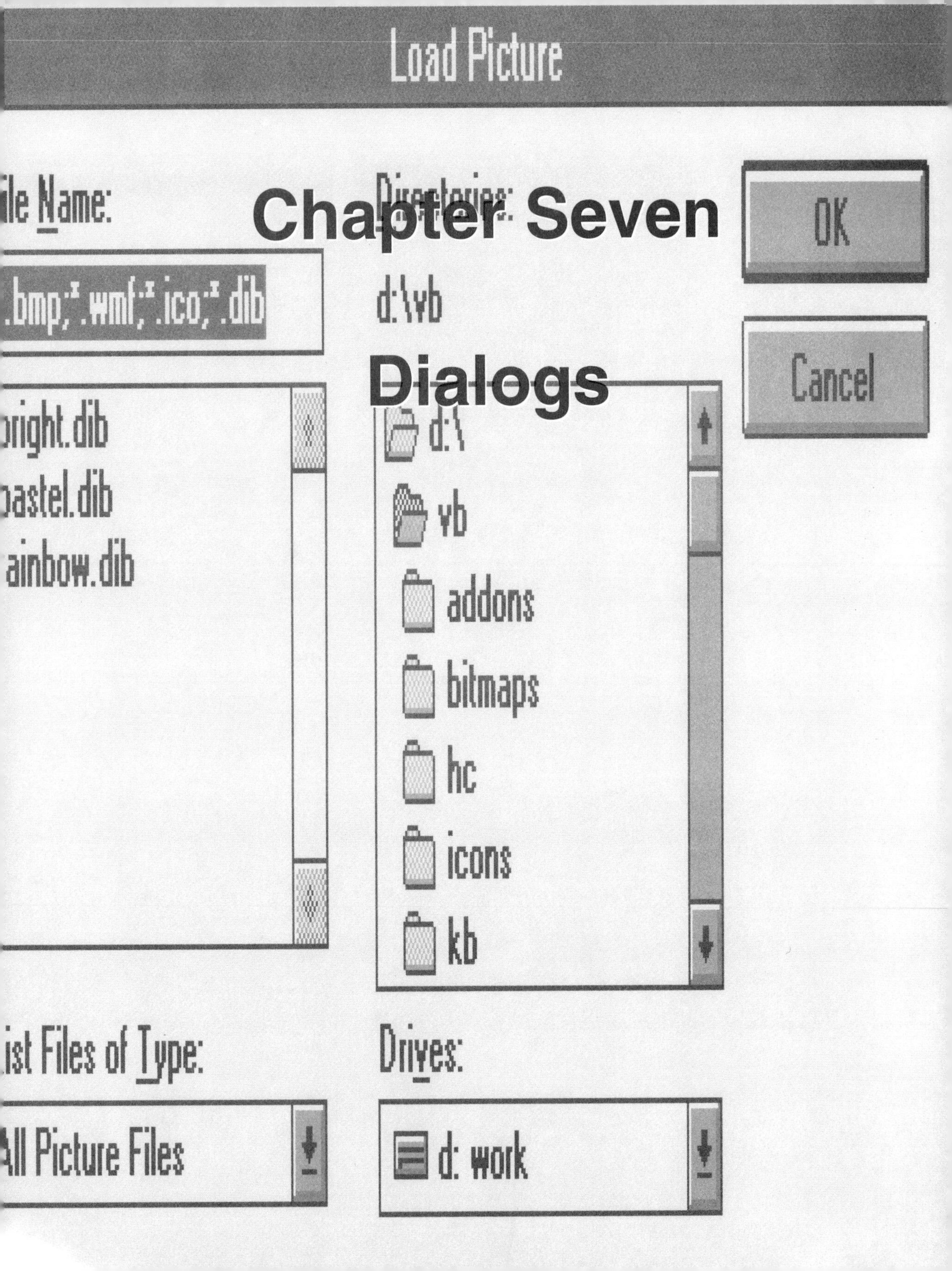

Load Picture

File Name:

.bmp;*.wmf;*.ico;*.dib

bright.dib
pastel.dib
rainbow.dib

List Files of Type:

All Picture Files

Directories:

d:\vb

d:\
vb
addons
bitmaps
hc
icons
kb

Drives:

d: work

OK

Cancel

CHAPTER

7

Dialogs

Dialogs are a useful way of getting specific bits of information to and from your users. They serve to focus the user's attention on the job at hand and are therefore extremely useful in Windows applications.

Dialogs come in a variety of forms, each adapted to a particular purpose. In this chapter we'll look at each of the four main types of dialog, and examine how and when to use them.

In this chapter you'll learn about:

- ▶ What dialog boxes are
- ▶ When to use them
- ▶ Message boxes
- ▶ Modality
- ▶ Input boxes
- ▶ Common dialogs
- ▶ Custom dialogs

Introducing Dialog Boxes

It doesn't take very long in the company of Windows developers (not to mention on every other page of every Windows magazine!) before you start to come across the term **dialog**. Dialog boxes are the small windows that pop up now and again in Visual Basic and Windows to give you an error message, or to ask for further information to complete a certain operation.

For example, if you try and leave Word without having saved your file, you'll see something like this:

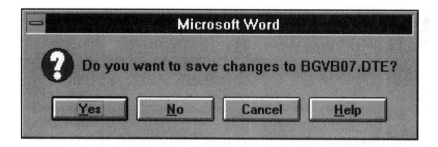

We've used message boxes, input boxes and common dialogs very briefly in earlier chapters. I said I'd explain it all later and sure enough, here I go!

Although dialog boxes are common, their appearance can differ dramatically depending on the type of dialog box being shown. All of them, however, are just variations on four basic types.

Message Boxes

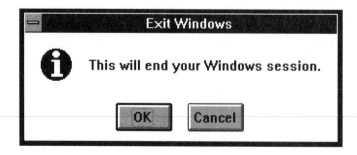

These are invoked by **MsgBox.** As a **statement** they show text with an OK button to acknowledge. As a **function** they pass back the ID of the button the user presses.

Input Boxes

These are invoked by **InputBox.** These are boxes with a message that allows the user to enter a line of text.

Common Dialogs

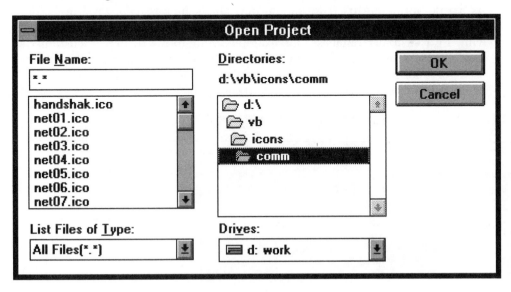

These are invoked by the setting the **Action** property of common dialog control you have added to a form. They present a variety of standard Windows dialogs for system settings.

Custom Dialogs

You assign your own name to these (in this case **frmYourName**). They are standard Visual Basic forms, dedicated to a single message or function, and made to look like a message box.

Over the course of this chapter we'll look at each type of dialog, and learn how to use them in applications.

When to Use Dialog Boxes

Dialogs are important tools in a programmer's toolkit, but they are very different from the forms and windows that you're used to.

As a rule, forms are used to handle data that's fundamental to your application; that is, the data that your program was actually written to deal with. In a customer database, for example, your forms display a customer's details, or get those details from the user. Dialog boxes, on the other hand, are used for information about the operation of the program itself, and not necessarily the data that the program deals with.

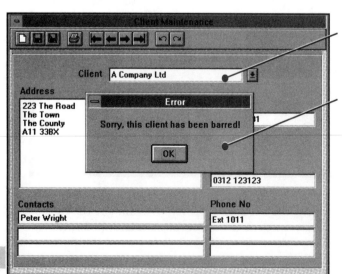

Here's the data that the application is about, on the form.

This is information that deals with how the program executes, on a dialog box.

For example, if your user decided that the font used in your application needed changing, then you'd display a font dialog box. This has no relationship to what your program actually does, but instead controls the way the program itself works.

> Dialog boxes allow you to display and obtain information about what your program is doing, to display error messages, or to warn the user (wake them up) if they do something potentially dangerous. It's bad practice to use them to actually get information about the program data; users expect to see proper forms for that.
>
> There's nothing stopping you using dialogs to obtain data, but the idea behind Windows is to keep everything standard. Therefore, the *very general* rule is: Use dialogs for program and system information, and forms for program data!

Message Boxes

The simplest form of dialog in Visual Basic is called a **message box**.

The Components of a Message Box

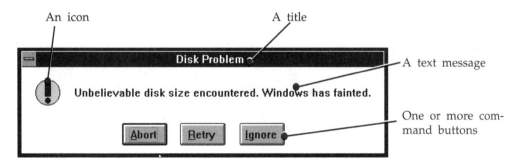

Using the **MsgBox** command all these features of the message box can be set up with just one small line of code.

Message boxes come into their own when you need to give the user a simple message, such as an error message or a warning. When the you close down Windows, a message box appears with an OK and a Cancel button which checks that you really *do* want to exit Windows. Let's copy that message box in an example.

Try It Out - A Simple Message Box

1   Load up Visual Basic and create a new project.

2   We're going to get rid of all the forms in this project, and just use a message box instead. Select Project from the Window menu.

3   Click on the form in the Project window.

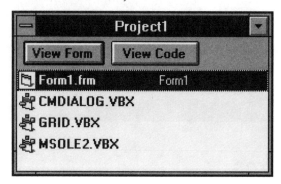

4   Now select Remove File from the File menu in order to delete the form from the project.

5   Create a new module by selecting File then New Module.

6   A code window appears.

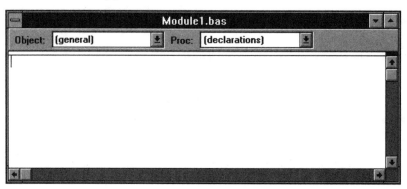

7   Type the following code directly in the window.

```
Sub Main()
MsgBox "This will end your windows session.", 65, "Exit Windows"
End Sub
```

8 Now run the program. A message box appears which is identical to the Windows exit message box.

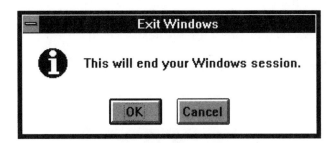

How It Works

The message box you've just created is the simplest possible type: a **MsgBox** subroutine. No data is returned to your program as the user just presses OK when they've read the message.

Let's take a look at the code you just entered. **MsgBox** is the Visual Basic command which displays a message box (no surprises there!). There are actually two **MsgBox** commands in Visual Basic. One is a subroutine (the one we used here) and the other is a function. They look identical, but the difference between them is that the function returns a number which allows you to see which button was pressed. This isn't important for the moment. We'll look at the **MsgBox** function a little later .

Immediately following the **MsgBox** command there is a text string:

```
"This will end your windows session."
```

This is the message we want displayed in the box.

After the message that appears in the box comes the number **65**. This is the value we pass to the **MsgBox** command that dictates what kind of message box we want to use. We'll look at which options we can choose from in a moment.

The final part of the message box command is another text string:

```
"Exit Windows"
```

Take a look at the screenshot again and you'll notice that this piece of text is actually used for the message box title bar.

Message Length in Message Boxes

If you place a big message into a message box, Windows will automatically split it over a number of rows of text. While this is a handy feature, the result can look a real mess. You can split the text in a message box by inserting a **CHR$(10)** character into the message text, like this:

```
MsgBox "This is a multi-line " & chr$(10) & "message."
```

The resulting message box is then:

Earlier in the book we used **CHR$(9)** to tell Visual Basic that we want to embed a *Tab* character into a string. **CHR$(10)** functions in a similar way, as though it's telling Visual Basic to start a new line. In reality **CHR$(10)** is actually called **line feed**, a printer term meaning 'start a new line'.

Selecting the MsgBox Type

Immediately after the message text in the previous example there's a number which tells Visual Basic exactly what kind of message box to display. This number dictates how many buttons to display, what the captions of those buttons should be, and which icon to display to the left of the message.

The number is the sum of two other numbers, one of which determines the buttons on the form, the other the icons. Like other such values in Visual Basic, you can either use the number itself, or load the **CONSTANT.TXT** file into your application and use the constants there instead. Both are shown in the tables.

Message Box Button Options

Value	CONSTANT.TXT	Appearance
0	MB_OK	OK
1	MB_OKCANCEL	OK Cancel
2	MB_ABORTRETRYIGNORE	Abort Retry Ignore
3	MB_YESNOCANCEL	Yes No Cancel
4	MB_YESNO	Yes No
6	MB_RETRYCANCEL	Retry Cancel

Message Box Icon Options

Value	CONSTANT.TXT	
16	MB_ICONSTOP	STOP
32	MB_ICONQUESTION	?
48	MB_ICONEXCLAMATION	!
64	MB_ICONINFORMATION	i

Building the MsgBox Parameter

Firstly, look at the **Buttons** table and decide which you want. In our example we wanted an OK and a Cancel button. The number is therefore **1**. Next, take a look at the **Icons** table and decide which you want. In our case we wanted to use the information icon, which is number **64**. All you do then is add the two numbers together to get **65**. There you have it: a message box with an OK and Cancel button and an Information icon!

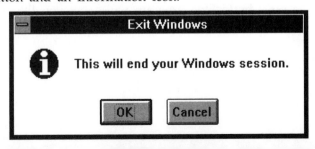

A Program to Show MsgBox Options

The **MSGBOX.MAK** example program shows you how all this fits together. In fact, there's also a compiled **.EXE** version which you can run from Program Manager to help you build your message boxes while you work in Visual Basic.

Either load up the project and run it now from within Visual Basic, or run the executable program using Program Manager.

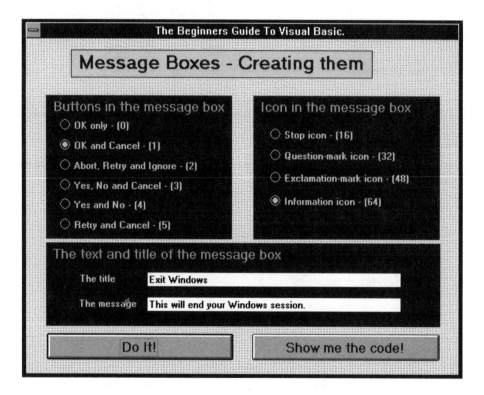

The program is very easy to use and shows you how to figure out these weird numbers and build a message box. Click on the option buttons which correspond to the way you want the message box to look. If you then click the Show me the code! button the program will show you the code which you need for the that particular message box. Clicking Do It! actually shows the message box in question.

Using the CONSTANT.TXT File

If you work out the dialog box parameters by hand, when you program it can be laborious as you'll need to keep flipping between your project and the help system, or between the screen and the reference manual. To make life easier a file is included with Visual Basic called **CONSTANT.TXT.**

If you add this file to your project you can then use constant names such as **MB_YESNOCANCEL** or **MB_ICONINFORMATION** instead of the numbers.

Try It Out - Adding CONSTANT.TXT

This is what you do to add the file to your current project:

1 Press *Ctrl-D* in Visual Basic to bring up the Add File dialog.

2 Locate the **CONSTANT.TXT** file. Make sure you set the file type box to all files. The file will probably be in the **\VB** directory.

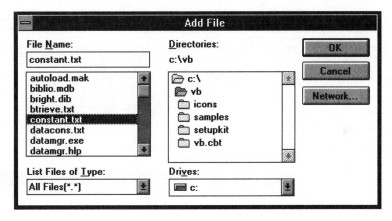

3 Add the file to your project.

Now, instead of entering number combinations to select the right dialog box, you can use the standard text constants. For example, to display Yes and No buttons, with a question mark icon the number you want is **MB_YESNO + MB_ICONQUESTION**.

Our original message box now becomes:

```
Sub Main()
    MsgBox "This will end your windows session.", MB_YESNO +
 MB_ICONQUESTION , "Exit Windows"
End Sub
```

Try It Out - A Better Way of Adding CONSTANT.TXT

There is a problem with doing it this way. The **CONSTANT.TXT** file is big, and to leave the whole thing in your program is an unnecessary waste of space. More seriously, defining lots of unnecessary constants is a drain on machine resources. It's far better to cut and paste the parts of the file you need into your project. I promised I'd show you how to do this in the last chapter, so here we go:

1 Open a new project in Visual Basic.

2 Jump back to program manager and open Windows Write. Open up **CONSTANT.TXT** in Write. Use the new copy of **CONSTANT.TXT** we supplied on the disk. It's with the programs from Chapter 6. When Write asks you if you want to convert the document to Write format, answer No in screentext. This stops Write inserting formatting codes into the file that would upset Visual Basic.

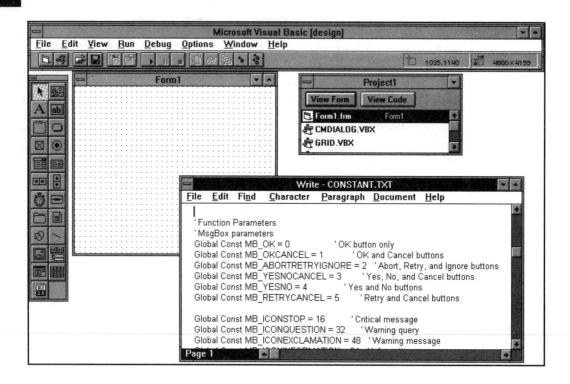

3 Scroll down to the section you want. In our case, it's the Function Parameters section. Highlight this whole section:

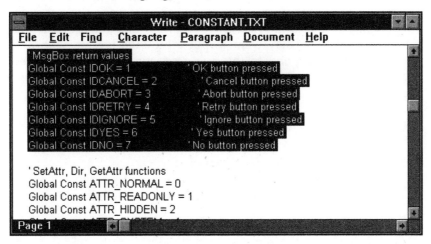

4 Copy this section to the clipboard by pressing *Ctrl-C*. Then switch back to Visual Basic and open up the code window form for the default form. Use the combo boxes to locate the (general) (declarations) section. Click in the code area and press *Ctrl-V* to paste the declarations from the clipboard to the code window.

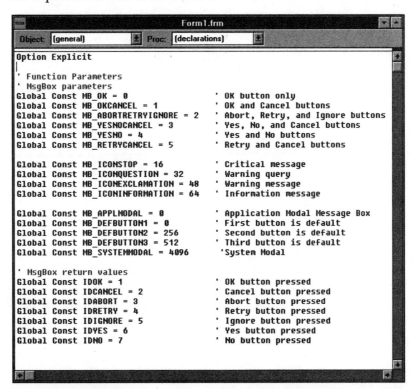

MsgBox as a Function

I mentioned earlier that it's possible to get **MsgBox** to tell us which button was pressed by using the **MsgBox** function. For instance, you could use the message box function in the form **QueryUnload** event. Since this event occurs just before a form unloads, you may want to put a message box up with a Yes and No button, and then respond to the user's selection in the appropriate way. Because it's a function rather than a subroutine, the syntax is slightly different and we now need to place the parameters in brackets.

Try It Out - The MsgBox Function

1 Create a new Visual Basic project.

2 As before, delete the form and create a module instead.

3 Add the **CONSTANT.TXT** file to the project as before by pressing *Ctrl-D*. Then choose the file and in the code window delete everything except the message box declarations section.

4 In the code window that appears for the new module enter this code:

```
Sub Main()
    Dim iResponse As Integer
    iResponse = MsgBox("Hit one of the buttons", MB_ABORTRETRYIGNORE +
MB_ICONINFORMATION, "Hit me")
    MsgBox "You pressed button code " & iResponse
End Sub
```

5 Now run the program. The first message is a function that asks you to press one of the buttons.

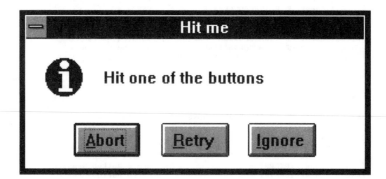

6 The value of the button you press is then assigned to the **iResponse** variable. This is then printed out as part of the **MsgBox** statement at the end.

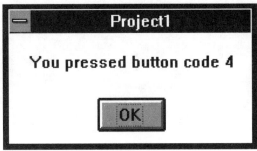

How It Works

The number of the button pressed corresponds to a value in this table:

Value	Name	CONSTANT.TXT
1	OK	**IDOK**
2	Cancel	**IDCANCEL**
3	Abort	**IDABORT**
4	Retry	**IDRETRY**
5	Ignore	**IDIGNORE**
6	Yes	**IDYES**
7	No	**IDNO**

Again these constants are all in the **CONSTANT.TXT**. file.

If you find yourself frequently typing **MsgBox** statements with identical icons and buttons but different text, why not define a global subroutine to deal with them? A common use for this is in a global error routine, like the one shown below:

```
Sub ErrorMessage (ByVal sError as String)
    MsgBox sError, 16, "Error"
End Sub
```

This way, all your error message code is kept in one place, and you don't have to worry about getting the **MsgBox** type number wrong, or about keeping the message box title the same from one message to another. It also makes your code much more maintainable. Changes to the error handler need only be made to one single module rather than to separate error handlers in all the individual modules. If a user then asks you to dump all the error messages to a text file on the disk, you only need to add a couple of lines of code to a single routine, rather than a couple of lines of code to a hundred (or more) routines. You need to put this kind of global routine in its own .BAS module.

Modality

By default, all message boxes are modal. This means that whilst a message box is visible, no other windows in your application can get the focus. The user must respond to the message before they are able do anything else in that application. However, they can still switch to other applications, using *Alt-Tab* and so on. In this instance, the dialog box is application modal.

If you have a very serious message box that you wish to take precedence over everything else (including other Windows programs) then what you really want is a **system modal** dialog box. This is a message box that must be responded to before the user can do anything else, including switching from one application to another.

As with most other control parameters of the message box, system modality is selected by adding a number to the parameter. The number to add is **4096**. This is defined in **CONSTANT.TXT** as **MB_SYSTEMMODAL**.

Try It Out - Creating a System Message Box

1 Start up a new project in Visual Basic.

2 Add **CONSTANT.TXT** as before.

3 Double-click on the default form to display the code window with the form **Load** event displayed.

4 Change the **Load** event so that it looks like this:

```
Sub Form_Load()

  Msgbox "This is a system modal box. Try click and on any other form",
  ⮑MB_SYSTEMMODAL

End Sub
```

Try It Out!

5   Now run the program. Just before the default form appears, a message box pops up. This is a system modal dialog box which means that you can't do anything else anywhere in Windows until you click the OK button. This is great for really serious error messages in your program, since no matter where the user is in Windows, they'll have no choice but to at least acknowledge the dialog box.

Input Boxes

Message boxes are great for relaying information to the user and getting them to press a single button, but what about when you need to get more information from the user? Well, that's where the input box comes into its own.

Input boxes are closely related to message boxes in that they are simple in both appearance and use, and are able to display a message to the user. The difference between the two is that an input box can accept data from the user.

When to Use Input Boxes

Despite their apparent ease of use, both for you and your users, input boxes are very rarely used in state-of-the-art applications. The main reasons for this are simple:

 Input boxes can't be programmed, so there's no way you can validate the data a user enters until *after* they've entered it. For example, if you were using a standard form you could place a text box onto it and add code to either the **KeyPress** or **Change** events to check that the user is behaving. However, with an input box you can't do that.

 The other reason they aren't used too much is that they only allow the user to enter one piece of information. Programmers most often need more than one piece of information and so instead use a custom form.

333

Despite these drawbacks they are a quick and dirty way of getting a single piece of information from your user, so let's take a look.

Try It Out - An Input Box

1 Start a new project in Visual Basic and, as usual, delete the form and create a module.

2 Add **CONSTANT.TXT** as before.

3 Bring up the code window and type this:

```
Sub Main ()
 Dim sReturnString As String
 sReturnString = InputBox$("Enter your name", "Name Please", "Fred")
 MsgBox "Hi there " & sReturnString, MB_OK, "Hello"

End Sub
```

4 Run the program and you should see the input box appear exactly like this:

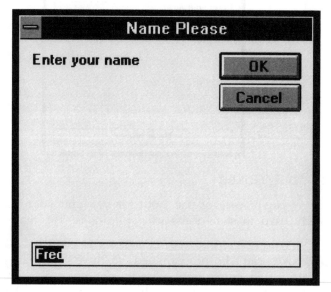

5 The default name Fred is highlighted in the input box. If you don't want to change the name, just press OK and see what happens.

How It Works

Now for the first shock. Although the input box and message box both come from the same family of commands, you can't tell Visual Basic to display an icon, or tell it which buttons to display as it does it all automatically.

The three parameters you can enter are fairly straightforward though. This is the above example:

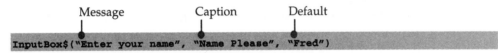

The first block of text is the prompt, in this case **"Enter your name".** In message box speak this is the same as the message. Next comes the caption, which is the same as the title on a message box. Finally, the third parameter is known as default. This is the value that is automatically displayed in the input box when it loads up.

Positioning Your Input Box

There are two other parameters missing from this: X and Y. These are the coordinates at which you want the input box to appear. For the sake of completeness I should say that the X and Y coordinates are measured in Twips, but that is a topic we cover in more detail in the next chapter.

For now, all you need to know is that X is a number beginning at 0, increasing as the coordinates move towards the right hand edge of the screen. The maximum value depends on the resolution of the screen. The Y coordinate begins at 0 for the top of the screen, and increases as it moves towards the bottom.

Try It Out - Placing the Input Box

1 Try adding **0,0** after the third parameter in the input box command above.

```
InputBox$("Enter your name", "Name Please", "Fred"),0,0
```

2 Now re-run the program to see the effect. The input box now appears at the top left corner of the screen.

Data Types and Input Boxes

As with the message box, there are two input box commands, but both are functions; one returns a string value ready to go straight into a string variable, whilst the other returns a variant. As we learnt way back in Chapter 3, Visual Basic deals with variants a lot slower than it deals with explicit data types such as strings or integers.

Whereas **InputBox$** returns a proper string to your code, **InputBox** returns a string type variant. If you needed to get numbers or dates from the user then you would use this function. For instance:

```
Sub Form_Load ()
varValue = InputBox("Please type your age", "Age", "23")
If IsNumeric(varValue) Then
    nAge = Val(varValue)
Else
    MsgBox "No, no, no - enter your age as a number!", , "User Error"

End If

End Sub
```

Common Dialogs

Have you ever noticed how all Windows programs have the same dialog box pop up when you try to load or save something? Have you ever noticed that most of the programs also have identical font, color and printer dialogs too?

The reason for this is the common dialog library. All the functions in Windows which allow programs such as Visual Basic to create windows, move graphics, change colors and so on, are held in files known as Dynamic Link Libraries, or DLLs. One such file, first installed with Windows 3.1, is the common dialog DLL. Visual Basic 3 comes with a special Visual Basic control (VBX), **CMDIALOG.VBX**, which makes using the functions in this DLL easy to master.

A DLL is a collection of functions and procedures, usually written in C, which you can use in your programs to get at features of Windows which aren't normally available.

Actually using DLLs is not entirely straightforward, so Visual Basic encompasses most of the functions of the DLLs in Visual Basic controls (VBXs). **CMDIALOG.VBX** provides you with an easy way to use the functions in the **CMDIALOG.DLL**. Instead of using some weird declaration statements and a lot of code, you can now call the DLL functions simply by changing properties. We'll look at how to use DLLs that don't have their own VBX in Chapter 11 - Interacting With Windows.

Using Common Dialogs

There are five common dialogs: for opening files, for saving files, for printing, for setting colors, and for choosing fonts. The dialogs don't actually do anything to your application or to its data. They simply receive the user's choices and return the values of these choices to your program through the properties of the common dialog control.

Actually programming the common dialogs is a bit of an esoteric exercise. Although there are five manifestations of the common dialog, there is only one common dialog control. There is an action property on the common dialog control which accepts a number telling VB which dialog of the five to show, and makes the control go away and show it. The common dialogs available in the Standard Edition of Visual Basic are:

Value	Name	CONSTANT.TXT
1	**Open File**	**DLG_FILE_OPEN**
2	**Save File**	**DLG_FILE_SAVE**
3	**Color**	**DLG_COLOR**
4	**Font**	**DLG_FONT**
5	**Print**	**DLG_PRINT**

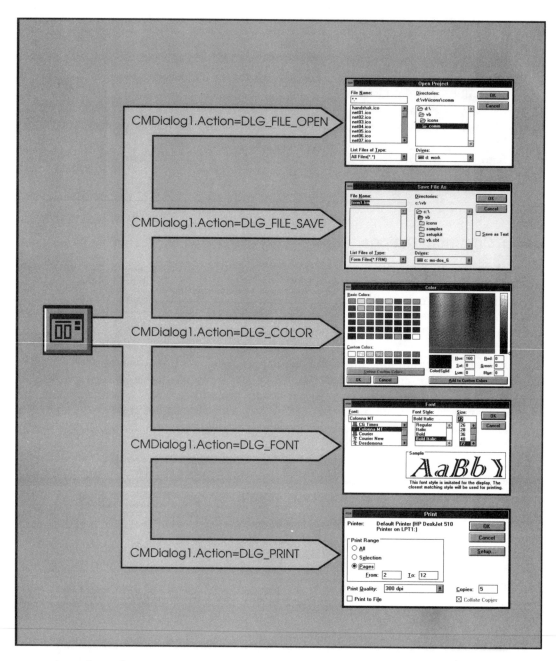

At a first glance a common dialog may appear a little daunting. There are so many controls to think about, surely there must be a lot of code involved? That's the real beauty of common dialogs; they can provide a vast amount of information and functionality to your users but require only a tiny amount of code from you.

The File Open and Save As Dialogs

The file open and save common dialogs both look similar and function in a very similar manner. Both display drive, directory and file lists, and enable the user to move around the hard disk in search of a file name. There's also a text entry area into which the file name selected is displayed, or into which a new file name can be entered. Finally, to the right of the dialog there are OK and Cancel buttons allowing the user to accept or discard his or her choice.

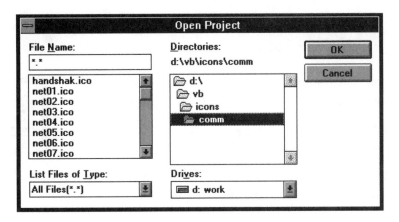

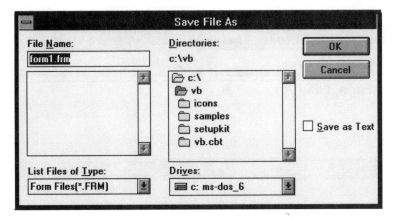

Let's put this into practice with a program that displays an open file dialog box.

Try It Out - An Open File Dialog

1 Create a new project, and add **CONSTANT.TXT** to it as before.

2 Make sure you have **CMDIALOG.VBX** in the project. Check this by looking in the project window. If you don't, then hit *Ctrl-D* and add it to the project. You should find the file in your **WINDOWS\SYSTEM** directory.

> Windows routinely keeps custom controls and DLLs in the **WINDOWS\SYSTEM** directory.

3 Drag the common dialog icon onto the form from the tool palette. This is like the timer control in that it just sits on the form and can't be resized. It also doesn't show on the form at run-time, so it doesn't matter where you place it.

4 Bring up the form's code window by pressing *F7* and find the **Load** event for the form:

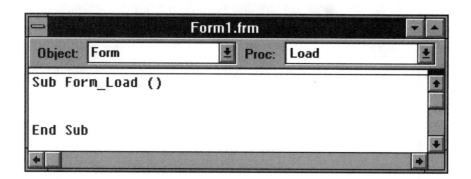

5   Type in code so that your code window looks like this:

```
Sub Form_Load()
    On Error GoTo DialogError

    CMDialog1.CancelError = True
    CMDialog1.Filter = "Executables (*.exe)|*.exe|Com Files
  (*.com)|*.com|Batch Files (*.bat)|*.bat"
    CMDialog1.FilterIndex = 1
    CMDialog1.DialogTitle = "Select a program to open"
    CMDialog1.Action = DLG_FILE_OPEN

    MsgBox "You selected " & CMDialog1.FileName

DialogError:
    On Error GoTo 0
    Exit Sub
End Sub
```

6   If you run the program now, an open file dialog appears asking you to select the name of a file.

7   The drop-down list at the bottom left of the dialog also lets you select the types of files you want to see in the file list.

You can see the same code in the **COMMON.MAK** project. This project has command buttons which display each of the common dialogs.

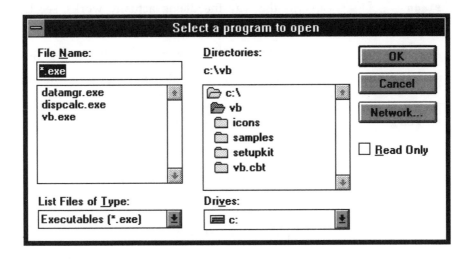

Setting Up the Open File Dialog

The common dialog control is unlike other Visual Basic controls in that it doesn't have any events. Instead, you interact with it by setting various properties. The properties relevant to the open and save file dialogs are as follows:

Property	Description
FileName	The full file name of the selected file, for example, **C:\TEMP\README.DOC**
FileTitle	The file name of the selected file, but without the path, for example, **README.DOC**
Filter	Defines the types of files that the dialog will show. You basically need to enter wildcards into here, with a description of each. For instance, **dlg.Filter = "Text | *.txt | Icons | *.ico"**. This selects which types of files to display in the combo box at the foot of the file dialog.
FilterIndex	Defines the initial filter to use. Earlier we set up two filter values, one for text files and one for icons. If you set **FilterIndex** to 1 before displaying the dialog box it would cause it to display only files matching the first filter, that is, ***.txt** files. Setting it to 2 would display only icons in the file list.
Flags	Governs the way the dialog actually works; see later in this chapter.
InitDir	Specifies the initial directory to list in the dialog.
MaxFileSize	Allows you to tell the dialog the maximum number of characters you want to see displayed for a file name.
Action	1 - Display a file open dialog.
	2 - Display a save as dialog.
	3 - Display a color selection dialog.
	4 - Display font select dialog.
	5 - Display printer dialog.
CancelError	Set this to **True** to trigger a run-time error if the user presses the Cancel button. We can catch this error in our code if we use the **On Error** statement, and then take the necessary action.

You can address each property if you place the name of the common dialog control in front of it. The default name is **CMDialog1**; hence in the example program, we display a file open dialog box using the line:

```
Dialog1.Action  =  DLG_FILE_OPEN
```

Selecting the Correct Files

In our sample program, the open and save dialogs both need to have their **Filter** and **FilterIndex** properties set to control the types of files listed in the dialog. We only want to display files that are able to be executed:

```
    CMDialog1.Filter  =  "Executables  (*.exe)|*.exe|Com  Files
(*.com)|*.com|Batch Files (*.bat)|*.bat"
    CMDialog1.FilterIndex = 1
```

Filter contains a string where each element of the string is separated by a | sign.

> On most keyboards this symbol | is two vertical dashes, one on top of the other.

Firstly, you enter a description for the type of file; for example, **Com Files (*.com).** These descriptions are what appear in the drop-down list box at the bottom of the dialog. After each description you must then enter the wildcard for the files which match that description. In this case it's simply ***.com.** As you select descriptions from the drop-down at the bottom of the dialog, the filename text box changes to the wildcard, and the file list changes to show only those files which match your wildcard.

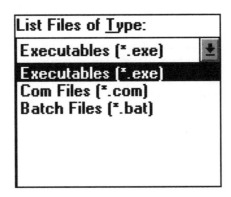

The **FilterIndex** property is a number between **1** and the number of elements in the filter. It defines the default or start-up filter that should be used. In the example I say **FilterIndex = 1**. Therefore, the default filter to use will be the first one, which is **Executable files (*.exe)**.

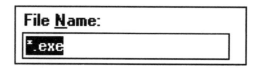

Naming the Dialog

Instead of the normal **Caption** property, common dialogs use the **DialogTitle** property to set the message displayed on the title bar of the common dialog. The following line sets this up:

```
DialogTitle = "Select a program to open"
```

However, if you don't set this property of the dialog, Visual Basic will automatically display an appropriate title of its own, as you'll see later.

Selecting and Launching the Dialog

Finally, loading a number into the **Action** property tells the common dialog control to go away and start work:

```
Dialog1.Action = DLG_FILE_OPEN
```

The number you load in specifies exactly which dialog you want to appear. In our case it is **1** for an open dialog, but it could also have been **2** for a save as dialog. The open and save as dialogs are identical; only the default caption at the head of the dialog is different.

When the user has selected a filename, it's returned in the common dialog **FileName** property.

Error Handling With Common Dialogs

The last line of code in the example is designed to trap errors:

```
DialogError:
      On Error GoTo 0
      Exit Sub
End Sub
```

Why do we need this? Well, when the user presses Cancel on the common dialog an error event is triggered. The **DialogError** code simply takes control out of the main procedure and exits if the Cancel button is pressed.

If you set the **CancelError** property to **True** at the start of the code, clicking Cancel triggers a Visual Basic error:

```
On Error GoTo DialogError

    CMDialog1.CancelError = True
```

This only applies to the Cancel buttons you'll find in the common dialogs. It doesn't apply to the Cancel buttons on message boxes or input boxes.

The Color Dialog

The color dialog is even easier to set up than the file dialogs. Its purpose is to allow the user to select and display colors from the palette, currently available on that particular computer.

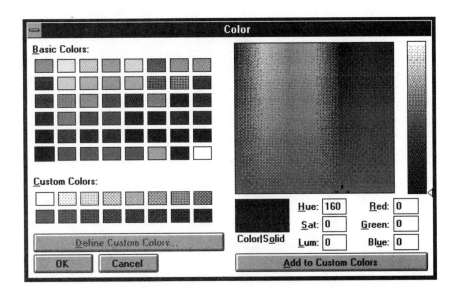

Properties of the Color Dialog

Property	Description
Color	Holds the long integer value of the color the user selected.
Flags	See the section later in this chapter for a run down on the most common flag values.
Action	Set this to 3 to display the Color dialog box.
CancelError	Set CancelError to True to trigger a run-time error if the user clicks on the Cancel button on the dialog box.

The actual color selected is returned in the dialog **Color** property. You can move it directly from there to the color properties of any controls whose color you wish to change.

In terms of functionality, the color dialog is actually a little more powerful than the others. The Add to Custom Colors button, for example, lets you create your own colors and add them to the windows palette. No other common dialog affects windows or your application in this way.

Invoking the Color Dialog in Your Code

To use the color dialog, first place the number **1** into the **Flags** property to initialize it and then place the action code **3**, **DLG_COLOR**, into the **Action** property.

Here is the code for the color dialog from the **COMMON.MAK** project.

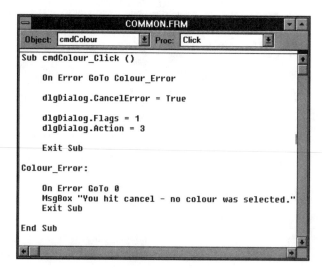

```
Sub cmdColour_Click ()

    On Error GoTo Colour_Error

    dlgDialog.CancelError = True

    dlgDialog.Flags = 1
    dlgDialog.Action = 3

    Exit Sub

Colour_Error:

    On Error GoTo 0
    MsgBox "You hit cancel - no colour was selected."
    Exit Sub

End Sub
```

The color dialog is a way for you to get information from the user. It doesn't actually change the colors in your application. This is the same for all the common dialogs. For example, the font dialog doesn't change the fonts in your program, nor does the print dialog actually print. They all just provide a standard way for you to get information about these subjects from the user.

With the color dialog, for example, when the user has selected a color you should use the color properties of the dialog to update the color properties of your forms and controls.

The Font Dialog

The font dialog actually enables the user to select fonts from the printers font list, from the screen font list, or from both together.

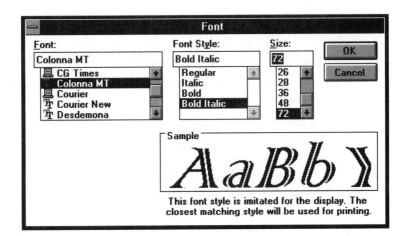

Properties of the Font Dialog

Property	Description
Color	Holds the long integer value of the color selected in the dialog.
FontBold	**True** if the user selected Bold in the dialog, **False** if not.
FontItalic	**True** if the user selected Italic in the dialog.
FontStrikeThru	**True** if the user selected StrikeThru in the dialog.
FontUnderLine	**True** if the user selected Underline in the dialog.
FontName	Use your imagination!
Max	Specifies the size, in points, of the largest fonts to be displayed.
Min	Specifies the size, in points, of the smallest fonts to be displayed.
FontSize	Holds the size of the selected font.
Flags	See the section later in this chapter for some useful values for the flags property.
Action	Set this to **4** to actually display the fonts dialog.
CancelError	Set this to **True** to cause a run-time error whenever the user clicks on the Cancel button in the common dialog. This can trapped in code with the **On Error** statement.

You can set the font list which is visible by loading a number into the **Flags** property in the same way that 1 was loaded in the color dialog to initialize that. The numbers you need to place in the **Flags** property are:

Number	Font
1	Screen fonts
2	Printer fonts
3	Both screen fonts and printer fonts

These are actually defined in the **CONSTANT.TXT** file and are called **CF_SCREENFONTS**, **CF_PRINTERFONTS**, and **CF_BOTH**.

If you don't set the **Flags** property to one of these values before displaying the fonts dialog then you'll get an error - No Fonts Exist.

The font dialog can even be used to select a font color. This is done by adding 256 to the value in the **Flags** property. If you don't do this you won't be able to select colors, only font names, styles and sizes.

The **Action** code to display the font dialog box is **4**. When the user exits out of the dialog, your code can then check the **Color, FontBold, FontItalic, FontStrikethru, FontUnderline, FontName** and **FontSize** properties to find out exactly what the user chose.

The code from **COMMON.MAK** that displays the font dialog looks like this:

```
Sub cmdFont_Click ()
    ' Clicking the Font button causes the Fonts common dialog to appear.
    ' In this example we want to see the fonts for both screen and printer
    ' appear so a value of 3 is loaded into the Flags property.
    ' The Action code of 4 actually displays the dialog.

    ' This line tells VB where to go (in the nicest possible way)
    ' when a trappable error occurs. The CancelError property is
    ' set so that if the user clicks on the Cancel button in the
    ' dialog a trappable error occurs

    On Error GoTo Font_Error
    dlgDialog.CancelError = True

    dlgDialog.Flags = 3
    dlgDialog.Action = 4

    Exit Sub

Font_Error:

    ' Turn off the error trapping
    On Error GoTo 0

    MsgBox "You hit cancel - no font was selected."

    Exit Sub

End Sub
```

The Print Dialog

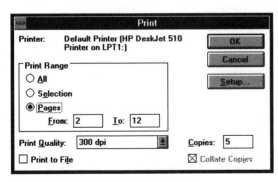

The print dialog allows the user to not only determine how much data he or she wants your application to print, but also to determine how the printer itself should work This includes at which resolution and speed the printer should print, which printer or printer driver to use, and even whether or not to ignore the printer totally and print direct to a disk file. Just to really confuse your application, the dialog even allows the user to specify a number of copies to print and whether these copies should be collated. This last option is only available on some printers.

Properties of the Print Dialog

Property	Description
Copies	Holds both the initial value and the value entered by the user for the number of copies to print.
FromPage	Holds the number of the first page to print. Can be set by code before the dialog is displayed, and can be set by the user keying in a number.
Max	Holds the maximum number of copies the user can select.
Min	Holds the minimum number of copies the user can select.
PrinterDefault	If you set this to **True**, then any changes the user makes in the Printer Setup dialog are saved into the **WIN.INI** file. They will also affect any other programs running which may want to make use of the printer.
ToPage	Holds the number of the last page of the report to print.
Flags	See later for some of the more useful flag values for this property.
Action	Set this to **5** to actually display the printer dialog box.
CancelError	Set this to **True** to cause a run-time error if the user clicks on the Cancel button on the print dialog.

Unlike the color and font dialogs the print dialog box doesn't need to have anything placed into its **Flags** property. The only property you need to set up is the **Action** one, and the number there is **5**.

Three properties are used to return the user's selections to your program; **Copies, FromPage** and **ToPage**. You can set these properties up before displaying the print dialog in order to supply the user with some default values.

Common Dialog Flags

The **Flags** property provides a useful way to control the operation of the common dialogs, and the information they present your users with. In all, there are 48 different values you can use for the **Flags** property, and these can all be combined to give you some really weird custom effects. However, of those 48, only a handful are really common.

The table below shows you which are the most useful flags and their names as defined in the **CONSTANT.TXT** file. I guess you'd call it 'My Favorite Flags'.

Name	Dialog	Description
PD_PRINTSETUP	print	Displays the printer setup dialog instead of the print options dialog.
PD_NOSELECTION	print	Stops your users from choosing to print only the current selection of text. It involves a lot more code to implement this feature and you may not be keen on that.
PD_DISABLEPRINTTOFILE	print	Disables the print to file option on the dialog, for the same reasons as above.
CC_PREVENTFULLOPEN	color	Stops the user from defining his or her own custom colors.
CC_FULLOPEN	color	Starts the dialog up with the custom color window already open.
CF_WYSIWYG	font	Shows only fonts which are available on both the printer and the screen. You also need to add it to **CF_BOTH** and **CF_SCALEABLEONLY**
CF_BOTH	font	Lists all the printer fonts and all the screen fonts.
CF_SCALEABLEONLY	font	Only shows you fonts which can be resized, normally Truetype fonts.
CF_PRINTERFONTS	font	Lists only the printer fonts.
CF_SCREENFONTS	font	Lists only fonts which can be displayed on screen.
OFN_ALLOWMULTISELECT	file	Allows the user to select more than one file from the file dialog boxes.
OFN_FILEMUSTEXIST	file	The user can only type in the name of a file that exists.
OFN_OVERWRITEPROMPT	file	In the save as dialog box, if the user selects a file that already exists, then the dialog will ask the user if they really want to overwrite that file.

Custom Dialogs

The alternative to message boxes, input boxes and common dialogs is the do-it-yourself approach, where you create your dialogs in exactly the same way as you would create any form in your application. This approach has both benefits and drawbacks.

On the benefits side, because you design the form you'll use as a dialog, you can ensure that it keeps the same colors and interface standards as the other forms in your application. Since it is 100% home made you are free to put whatever icons, controls, text or graphics you want on it. The only limit is your imagination.

The drawbacks on the other hand are substantial. Each form in your application uses system resources when your program is running; resources like memory, processor time and so on. It doesn't take that many custom dialogs in your application before something as simple as trying to run the application could cause a lesser-powered machine to grind to a halt.

Try It Out - Creating a Custom Dialog

1 Load up **WROX6.MAK**. This is a simple form with a menu at the top and a couple of toolbars, a ruler and a status bar. It forms part of a major new contender in the wordprocessing stakes: Wrox 6, part of the Messy Office suite!

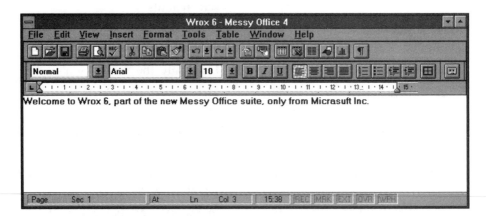

2 Run the program. You can enter text into the text window, cut and paste with the normal keys, in fact most of the stuff you'd expect as the bare minimum for a wordprocessor. Wrox 6 is still in development. The problem is, you're the developer. One of the things your client has asked you for is for an options dialog. I feel a custom dialog coming on.

3 On the disk there's just the dialog box you want, **WROX6.FRM**. If the program is currently running then stop it and select A__d__d File from the F__i__le menu. Then choose **WROX6.FRM** as the file to add.

4 So far so good. We have a new form in the project with a fixed border and no resize buttons, hence a custom dialog. To see it, press Show Form on the project window.

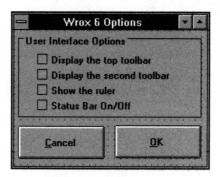

5 All we need to do now is add code to make it work. In design mode, select O__p__tions from the T__o__ols menu on the main form. The code window for that menu click-event pops up. Change it to look like this:

```
Sub mnuOptions_Click ()

  Load frmOptions
  frmOptions.Show 1

End Sub
```

6 This loads up the options form, and **frmOptions.Show 1** causes it to be displayed as a modal form. In other words, a dialog box.

7 One more bit of code to go. Use the project window to select the options form. When it appears, double-click on the OK button. What we want to do here is hide or show the toolbars and so on, based on which check boxes were set. Change the code so that it looks like this:

```
Sub cmdOK_Click ()

  frmMain!picToolbar.Visible = chkToolbar1.Value
  frmMain!picToolbar2.Visible = chkToolbar2.Value
  frmMain!picRuler.Visible = chkRuler.Value
  frmMain!picStatus.Visible = chkStatus.Value

  Unload frmOptions

End Sub
```

8   There you have it! A very simple options window, yet good enough to show your client when they come to look at the product. Run the application and play with the new dialog by selecting Options from the Tools menu to see how it works.

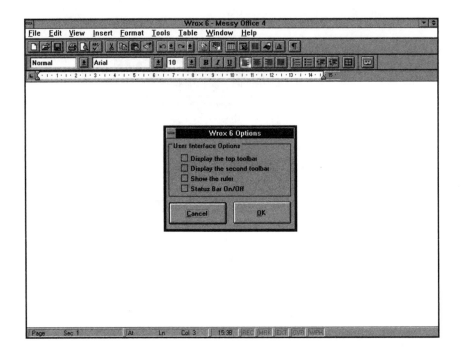

Users appear to your programs like planes do to an Air Traffic controller. If you don't talk to them for a while they tend to wander off on their own and get into all sorts of trouble. Your custom dialogs can ensure that you grab the user's attention and don't let go.

Microsoft approach the problem by displaying animated dialog boxes whilst you install programs, but even these may not be enough to keep the user seated. Imagine the situation where you're copying data from a stack of about 12 disks and need the user to insert the next disk after quite a long pause. You can place a timer event on your custom dialog so that the timer event is triggered 20 seconds after the box appears, and every 2 seconds thereafter. The timer event could simply beep. Users tend to sit up and take notice, or get dragged back to their desks by their co-workers if a computer begins to exhibit this kind of rude behavior. Just what we want! See the section on timer controls back in chapter 2. Also, take a look at **ANNOY.MAK** in the sample code supplied with the book.

That's it for here. Later, in Chapter 13, you'll see how by placing you custom dialogs in separate forms you can build up a library of custom dialogs. There we'll tackle a real world program that puts everything you've learnt about Visual Basic into practice.

Summary

By now you should be well acquainted with dialog boxes. You've learnt how to create your own and how to use the built-in ones in your own applications. We have covered:

▶ Using the **MsgBox** function and procedure to display a message box

▶ Using the **InputBox** and **InputBox$** functions to get user input

▶ Application and system modal dialog boxes

▶ Using common dialogs to add functionality and professionalism to your programs

▶ Creating your own custom dialogs

In the next chapter, we start to bring all the things we've learnt so far into more substantial and challenging programs.

Chapter Eight

Graphics

CHAPTER 8

Graphics

Graphics sell software. Think about what people look for when they buy
computer magazines. Sure, there are reviews of hot new programs, be they for
a spreadsheet or a game. The copy might be interesting, but what are the first
things you look at? The screenshots of course. Graphics catch peoples attention
and make them dig deep for your program, so they are well worth taking
some time over.

In this chapter you'll learn about:

▶ The simple Print command

▶ How Visual Basic handles color

▶ How Visual Basic screen co-ordinates work

▶ The four Visual Basic graphics controls

▶ The graphics methods and when to use them

▶ An overview of how to create really great graphics

What You Need to Know About Graphics

Visual Basic allows you to create graphics in two ways:

▶ Using the graphics **controls.** These are pre-defined shapes and symbols drawn on the form in the same way as any other control.

▶ Creating graphics on the fly, using the built-in graphics **methods**.

We're going to discover both of these processes in this chapter. In addition you'll find out about the different co-ordinate methods that Visual Basic uses. We'll also look at some technical stuff like how to create your own colors, what a brush is in Windows speak, and how to fling objects around the screen faster than a speeding bullet. OK, maybe not that fast. But you'll be impressed! Graphics is a big area, and Visual Basic provides lots of graphics facilities. However, we're only going to look briefly at each of the sections. There are two reasons for this:

▶ Graphics in Visual Basic are fairly straightforward and intuitive. Once you understand the basic concepts and the tools at your disposal, the best way to learn will be to experiment. Apart from a few simple ground rules, there are no right or wrong ways to do things; what matters is the effect you want to create.

▶ Visual Basic isn't really a graphics tool. It's not the world's fastest graphics environment (so much for the speeding bullet!), and at the time of writing you can't develop decent animated games with it. Microsoft is taking Visual Basic further into the corporate development arena by adding features such as the Access database engine. Much as we all love graphics, most of us have our wages paid for developing serious text and number corporate applications, so that's what we should spend most of our time covering.

Of course, even the most straight-laced application can benefit from a bit of flair and excitement, so let's get to it.

Printing on the Screen

If your experience with BASIC harks back to the heady days of the TRS-80 and Commodore's ubiquitous PET, then you'll be familiar with the good old Print command. For the less wizened among you, Print was (and still is) a simple command which can be used to display a string of text directly onto the screen. For many newcomers to BASIC, Print was the first command they ever learnt.

Not only have Microsoft kept the Print command in Visual Basic, they've also extended its usefulness somewhat. Older micros displayed information in two modes: text and graphics. It was rare if you found a BASIC system that could Print in graphics mode, or draw in text mode.

With Visual Basic you are always working in what would traditionally be called graphics mode. This in turn means that the usefulness of the Print command has been extended. You can now animate by doing nothing more than changing some properties and then printing some text. Text can also be printed in a variety of fonts, font styles, colors and font sizes, again just by changing or setting some properties and then printing. The Print command can also be used within Visual Basic as an aid to debugging, as we'll see later!

Let's write some code to see how Print works.

Try It Out - Using the Print Method

Let's create a simple program that prints directly onto the form.

1 Start up a new Visual Basic project.

2 When the form appears double-click on it to bring up the code window with the form **Load** event.

3 Type in code so that your code window looks like this:

```
Sub Form_Load ()
    Dim nLineNumber as Integer
    Form1.Show
    For nLineNumber = 1 to 10
    Form1.Print "This is line " & nLineNumber
    Next
End Sub
```

4 Now go to the form properties windows and change the AutoRedraw property to **True**. This makes Visual Basic recreate the window if it goes out of view. Try switching between applications when this property is off and the text is in the window. When you come back, the form is still there but the text has gone. We'll cover this phenomenon, known as **persistence,** later in the chapter.

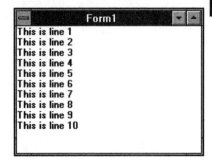

5 Run the program.

How It Works

The program runs a `For...Next` loop 10 times, each time using the `Print` command to display. This line is followed by the line number. Notice how each line of text automatically appears beneath the previous one. This is something that `Print` does for you automatically, but you *can* stop it happening, as you'll see in a moment.

The `Print` method can only be used with forms and picture boxes, and not with any other controls. For example, add a picture box to your form, and change the line on the code to read:

```
Picture1.Print "This is line " & nLineNumber
```

The form now looks like this:

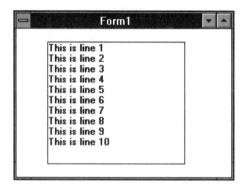

Introducing AutoRedraw

The text you print is drawn direct onto the form itself. Printing to a form won't overwrite any controls you may have on the form. Also, because the text is drawn, Visual Basic has no real way of keeping track of it should the form get hidden or overlaid with another form. If this happens, the text printed will vanish from the covered area.

> To get around disappearing text you need to set the form's AutoRedraw property to `True`. Unfortunately, this slows printing down substantially. This is because if you set AutoRedraw to `True` Visual Basic is told to keep a copy of the form in memory at all times. Anytime something happens or changes on the form, Visual Basic updates its own copy, as well as the one on the screen. You end up drawing everything twice. Then, when the form gets covered and uncovered, Visual Basic uses its own copy of the form to fill in the parts of the form that need it.

> The Paint event is triggered by a form being redrawn by Visual Basic.

Printing Fonts

The way in which text appears is controlled by the Font properties of the object you print, and by the ForeColor and BackColor properties which determine the text's colors. In the next example we'll change the FontSize and ForeColor properties of a form to demonstrate the way you can alter a text's appearance.

Try It Out - Changing the Font and Color Properties

1 If the last program is still running, stop it.

2 Bring up the code window again to view the **Form_Load()** event that you've just coded.

3 Change the **For..Next** loop so it reads:

```
For nLineNumber = 1 To 10
    Form1.FontSize = Form1.FontSize + nLineNumber
    Form1.ForeColor = QBColor(nLineNumber)
    Print nLineNumber;
Next
```

Notice the semicolon at the end of the penultimate line.

4 Run the program again.

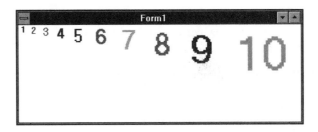

How It Works

This time there are three major differences from the previous example:

▶ The numbers are printed side by side, instead of on separate lines. The semi-colon you placed at the end of the **Print** command tells Visual Basic that the next time you print the text, it should be displayed on the same line as before.

Try It Out!

▶ The text gets bigger with each successive number. The first line of the **For...Next** loop adds the value of the **nLineNumber** variable to the current FontSize property value. The result is larger text.

▶ The color of each number is also changed. Visual Basic gives you a number of ways to select and change colors for graphics, controls and printed text. In our example, the **QBColor** function is used to load a color value into the ForeColor property of the form. The ForeColor property (same as the BackColor property) accepts a hexadecimal value to specify the color. You normally don't have to do this by hand; simply double-click the appropriate entry in the properties box and the Visual Basic color palette appears.

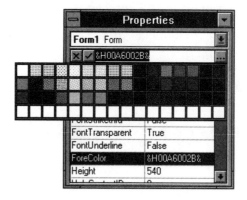

Specifying Screen Colors

Visual Basic assigns a number to each of the colors it can display and lets you choose and specify the color number for objects like forms and text in four different ways.

▶ You can assign the number directly, or you can choose the color from the palette on the properties menu. The problem here is that the color numbers are all hexadecimal (base 16, known as **hex**) so keying them by hand takes some doing. Visual Basic provides some simpler methods.

▶ The **QBColor** function selects one of 16 colors which were supported by earlier editions of Basic.

▶ The **RGB** function produces a color by mixing red, green and blue.

▶ A hex value can be assigned as a constant from the **CONSTANT.TXT** file for the color you want.

Before we dive into hexadecimal, let's first look at an easier method.

The QBColor Function

This function is primarily for those Basic programmers who have come to Visual Basic from Microsoft's venerable QBasic environment. In QBasic you specify colors as single digit numbers; thus, color number 1 would be blue, 2 green, 3 cyan, and so on. The **QBColor** function allows you to use these QBasic color codes without having to worry about converting them into long integers by hand. You simply use:

```
Form.ForeColor = QBColor(<Color number>)
```

Value	Color	Value	Color
0	Black	8	Gray
1	Blue	9	Light Blue
2	Green	10	Light Green
3	Cyan	11	Light Cyan
4	Red	12	Light Red
5	Magenta	13	Light Magenta
6	Yellow	14	Light Yellow
7	White	15	Bright White

Try It Out - The QBColor Selection

We can adapt our last program to show the full range of colors for this function.

1   Load up the last program. If you don't still have it, it's on the disk as **PRINTFUN.MAK**.

2   Change the **For...Next** loop to run through all the colors from 0 to 15.

```
For nLineNumber = 0 To 15
    Form1.ForeColor = QBColor(nLineNumber)
Print nLineNumber;
Next
```

Try It Out!

3 Change the FontSize property in the form property box to 24 point.

4 Run the program.

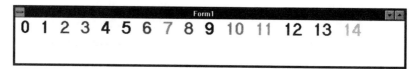

Hexadecimal Notation

A few lines back I confused the hell out of you by mentioning **Hexadecimal Notation**. You need to know hexadecimal to be able to specify color values in Visual Basic directly. It's not that difficult really, so let me explain.

We in the western world use decimal notation as our number system. In decimal notation there are ten digits used to form our numbers, the digits 0 through 9.

In the hexadecimal system there are 16 digits (if you studied Latin in school you'll probably know that already!). Not only are there the numbers 0 through 9, but also the letters A - F.

Decimal	0	1	2	3	4	5	6	7	8	9	10	11	12	13	14	15
Hexa-decimal	0	1	2	3	4	5	6	7	8	9	A	B	C	D	E	F

Our decimal numbers can be broken down into columns. The right-most column is units, the next is tens, the next one hundreds, and so on. Therefore the number 4524 is 4 thousands, plus 5 hundreds, plus 2 tens, plus 4 which equals four thousand, five hundred and twenty four.

Hex works in a similar way. The columns from right to left are units, sixteens, two hundred and fifty sixes, and so on. Therefore, the number 9CD is in reality (9 x 256) + (12 x 16) + 13, which equals 2509!

Why Put This Hex on Me?

The maximum number you can store in a long integer is FFFFFFFF written in hex, which is a lot more readable than its decimal equivalent. I said earlier that color values are held in long integers. Three separate numbers are actually combined into one, these three numbers being exactly how much red is in the color you want (between 0 and 255), how much green (same again) and how much blue!

Because each of these settings can be between 0 and 255, or between 0 and FF in hex, it's fairly easy in hex to invent your own colors. White, for example, has the maximum amount of red, green and blue, so the color value is hex **FFFFFF**. This is written in Visual Basic as **&HFFFFFF&**. The **&H** tells Visual Basic that we're now giving it hex numbers, the **&** at the end shows that the value is stored in a long integer. Therefore, blue would be the value **&HFF0000&**, green is **&HFF00** and red is **&HFF**. A bright red form would therefore be:

```
Form1.BackColor = &HFF
```

The RGB Function

However, you might not like the idea of hex; all those weird symbols and & signs everywhere - nasty business! Fear not, at the expense of a little speed at run-time there's a function called **RGB** you can use to produce your hex number for you.

Try It Out - Hassle-Free Hex Using RGB

1 Load up the **RGB.MAK** project from the samples provided with the book.

2 Run the project.

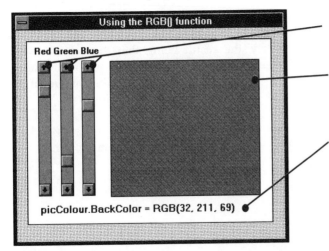

These vertical sliders produce the color mix.

This picture box shows you the color so far.

This label shows you the **RGB** function code you need to create the chosen color through your own Visual Basic code.

Try It Out!

How It Works

We covered sliders and scroll bars back in Chapter 3 - Advanced Controls, so you should feel comfortable with how they work.

Since each element of a color, red, green or blue, can be a number between 0 and 255, the sliders are all set up with a minimum value of 0 and a maximum of 255. All three sliders are also in a control array, which means that they all share the same event code. All these are set up in the properties window.

The **Change** event in this program does all the work. It redraws the picture box with its new color and displays the Visual Basic code line at the bottom of the frame. Because they are in a control array, there's only one handler for all three scroll bars:

```
Sub vscrColors_Change (Index As Integer)
    Dim sCode As String
    picColor.BackColor = RGB(vscrColors(0).Value, vscrColors(1).Value,
      vscrColors(2).Value)
    sCode = "picColor.BackColor = RGB(" & vscrColors(0).Value & ", "
    sCode = sCode & vscrColors(1).Value & ", " & vscrColors(2).Value & ")"
    lblCode.Caption = sCode
End Sub
```

If you pass the values of the three scrollbars to the **RGB** function the picture box color is built up. The value returned by the function is placed into the picture box **picColor**'s BackColor property, the result being that the color changes to reflect the new color selected by the user. Each color has a unique identifying hex value. The **RGB** function calculates the composite hex value of a new color depending upon the amount of each required base color.

For certain values, the color in the box is not homogeneous, but appears to be made up of blobs of other colors. This effect is known as **color mapping**.

Color Mapping

Depending on your screen resolution, the actual color you see can vary slightly. Most Video Graphics Adapter (VGA) systems can display a maximum of 256 colors on screen at once. This is owing to a design limitation, although some would call it a feature! However, a little math will soon show you that the **RGB** function is capable of returning a value representing any one of 16,777,216 colors.

To be able to accommodate this, Windows does a thing called **color mapping.** The color you want to display is matched against the colors available. If an exact match is found then the color is displayed. However, more often that not Windows will combine two or more colors to create what is called a **custom** color. On screen this appears as a dotty color, with dots of different hues and tints placed next to each other to give the illusion that you have a new color on screen. It's rather like a painting by Seurat, though it won't fetch half a million at auction!

You need to be aware of the differences between screens if you plan to distribute your Visual Basic applications to other users and computers. You may have designed the application using a state of the art VGA display. Your users, however, may only be using systems that can display 16 colors at a time. The way your forms and colors appear on your screen can differ dramatically from their screen.

Choosing Color Values From CONSTANT.TXT

One final option is to select the color you want as a constant from the **CONSTANT.TXT** file. You can copy and paste just the relevant part into the (general) (declarations) section of your form. The part you want looks like this:

```
' Colors
Global Const BLACK = &H0&
Global Const RED = &HFF&
Global Const GREEN = &HFF00&
Global Const YELLOW = &HFFFF&
Global Const BLUE = &HFF0000
Global Const MAGENTA = &HFF00FF
Global Const CYAN = &HFFFF00
Global Const WHITE = &HFFFFFF
```

Having declared these values as constants, you can then use them as words in your code, for example:

```
Form1.ForeColor = BLUE
```

Coordinate Systems

The screen, and the form you display on it, is divided up into tiny dots. When you start drawing things on your forms you need to be able to specify at precisely which dot on the form or screen you want something to appear. This is where co-ordinates come in.

The top of the screen is co-ordinate 0,0. Here X = 0 and Y = 0. As you move across the screen the number of the X co-ordinate increases. As you move down the screen the number of the Y co-ordinate increases.

I frequently mention screens, but in Visual Basic you can only draw on forms and picture boxes. Each has its own co-ordinate system, therefore (0,0) on a form is very different from (0,0) on the screen. Whenever you draw on an object always use a co-ordinate system that relates to the top left corner of the object you are drawing on.

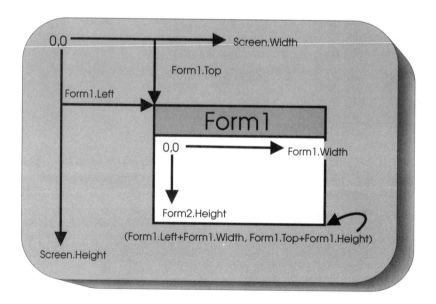

There are parts of an object you can't draw on; for example, the title bar and borders of a form are strictly off-limits. Visual Basic only lets you draw in a form's **client** area. So how do you find out where the client area starts and ends? Objects you draw on have two properties; ScaleHeight and Scalewidth. These tell you the maximum height and width of the object's client area.

Try It Out - Placing a Letter in the Center of a Form

1 Start a new project in Visual Basic and bring up the code window.

2 In the code window, select the form **Resize** event.

3 Type code so that your code window looks like this.

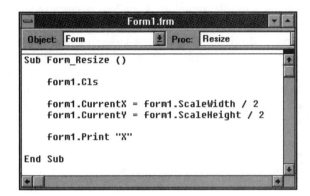

4 Run the program, and see how the letter stays in the center of the form, even when you resize it.

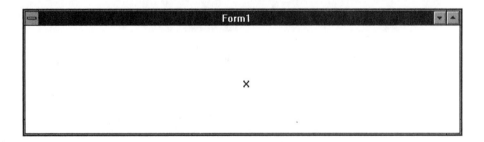

How It Works

Let's take a look at how the code works. The first line of real code uses the **Cls** method to clear **form1**:

```
form1.Cls
```

Attached to each form is an invisible object known as a **cursor**. This is the point on the form at which subsequent **Print** statements will display text. Therefore, if you set the form's CurrentX and CurrentY properties the cursor moves to the point you specify.

We've already seen that ScaleWidth and ScaleHeight give us the dimensions of the client area. Therefore if you set CurrentX and CurrentY to half the client area width and height this has the effect of moving the cursor to the center of the screen.

Twips, Pixels, Inches and Centimeters

The actual co-ordinate system used on a form is by default called **twips**. In twips each point is roughly equal to 1/567 of a centimeter. So if you drew a line on your form that was 567 units long, it would appear a centimeter long. This is known as **a device independent** co-ordinate system; it doesn't matter whether you are drawing a line on a standard VGA display, on a printer, or on the latest state-of-the-art high-res screen. The resulting line will still appear about a centimeter long. Twips are great if you're producing **what you see is what you get** applications, such as a desktop publishing package or a wordprocessor.

In reality, however, a much more useful co-ordinate system is called **Pixel**. Here each unit on the X or Y co-ordinates of the screen equals exactly one dot, or pixel.

In addition, using the Pixel co-ordinate system you can draw your graphics more speedily on screen. Windows knows that one pixel equals to one dot and doesn't have to worry about converting your co-ordinates into something that can actually be drawn.

You can change the co-ordinate system of a form if you bring up the properties window of the form and double-click on the ScaleMode property to cycle through all the available choices.

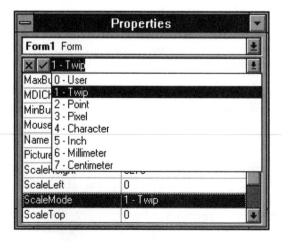

Changing the scale mode doesn't have any immediate visible effects on your application, but it is something that you need to take into account when dealing with co-ordinates in your code. A line that was previously drawn 100 twips long may actually be only 20 pixels long, therefore having a completely different effect.

Changing the coordinate system on a form only affects any subsequent changes to the form - it doesn't resize or redraw the controls and images already on the form. To accomplish that little feat you need to write some heavyweight code, which is beyond the scope of our brief look at graphics.

The Graphical Controls

Having understood some of the background to graphics in Visual Basic, we can now start putting graphics onto our form. There are two alternative ways to do this in Visual Basic:

> **Graphics Controls** are like ordinary Visual Basic controls which are placed on your form and can be laid out interactively at design-time. Two of the controls, **image** box and **picture** box, allow you to work with various image files, while the **Line** and **Shape** controls lines and shapes on your form (what a surprise!).

> **Graphics Methods** are commands that enable you to draw directly onto your form at run-time. The commands available for this in Visual Basic are **Cls, Pset, Point, Line** and **Circle.**

For some jobs, controls and methods are interchangeable. We'll cover the pros and cons of each later, but first we'll take a look at the graphics controls.

Image and Picture Boxes

The most common graphical controls are the picture and image box controls. These both let you load up images from the disk and display them on screen, either in design-mode, or at run-time through your code.

We came across these controls in Chapter 5 - Common Controls, in our sample program **CONTROL.MAK.** In that chapter you learnt about the increased functionality of the Picture control compared to the Image control, and we also looked briefly at how to load images into these controls at run-time. In this section, we'll look at the special features of each of these controls in more detail.

Loading Graphics at Design-Time

To load graphics into a picture box, image box or form at design-time you simply type the filename of the graphic into the Picture property of the appropriate object.

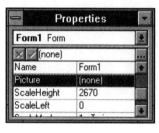 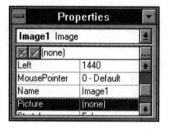 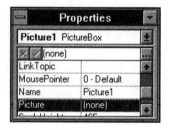

The action is fairly similar for each object, so let's look at one in particular. The image control is a good choice because it has some extra functionality: the ability to stretch the image.

Try It Out - Loading and Resizing an Image Box

1 Start a new project and double-click the image control icon in the toolbox to draw an image control on the form.

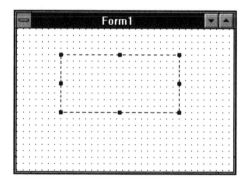

2 Select the image control, and bring up its properties window using *F4*. Find the Stretch property and make sure it is set to **True**. The easiest way to do this is by double-clicking on it.

Try It Out!

3   Now find the Picture property and double-click on it. A file dialog box appears asking you to select a graphic file. Click on the **WROX.BMP** file and then click OK.

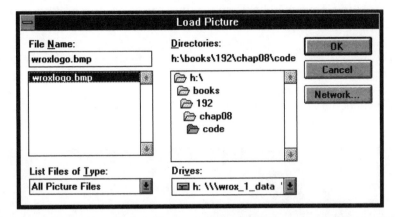

4   The Wrox Press logo appears on the form, inside the image control.

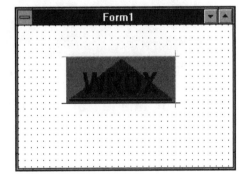

5   Resize the control by dragging its resize handles. Notice how the picture inside also changes.

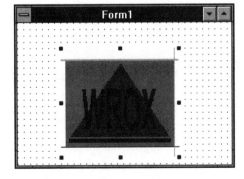

6   If you now run the program though, the size remains fixed.

Loading Images at Run-Time

You'd be forgiven for thinking that adding the image to the object at run-time must be as easy as assigning the right path and filename to the Picture property. Unfortunately it isn't quite that easy: at run-time you have to use the **LoadPicture** function.

The reason for this is that the Picture property doesn't really contain the filename of the graphic you want to display; it contains the graphic itself. At design-time, to simplify the properties window, Visual Basic merely shows you the filename. The actual binary file information is stored inside your project when you save it.

The good thing about assigning your images to the file at design-time is that they don't get lost. The alternative (pointing the control towards an external image file) is that you must make sure that all these files get distributed along with your application. The downside is clear: your program files are much larger.

My advice is to include your images with your code at compile-time if you intend to distribute the application. If you're only going to keep it on your own machine, then load the images at run-time.

Finding Your Images at Run-Time

One of the problems of loading images in run-time is that you have to make sure that the files you want are where your program expects them to be. When you install your application it's easiest to store your image files in a subdirectory off the main directory (in the place where the executable file is). Remember that the user may install your application anywhere he wants, not necessarily in exactly the same drive and directory that you used to create the program. If you store the graphics in a subdirectory away from where the executable is you can then say this at run-time:

```
Image1.Picture = LoadPicture (App.Path & "\graphics\<imagename>")
```

Here **<imagename>** is the name of the graphic file you want to load. The **App.Path** part returns to your code the path along which the executable file is located. This function is always available anywhere in your program.

Try It Out - Loading the Image at Run-Time

1 Start a new project and put a picture control onto your form.

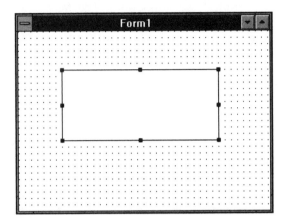

2 To load the **WroxLogo.Bmp** graphic into a picture box at run-time add the following code to your **Form_Load()** event:

```
Sub Form_Load ()
Picture1.Picture = LoadPicture("WROXLOGO.BMP")
End Sub
```

3 In this example, the **WROXLOGO.BMP** file has to be located in your default directory (in my case this is **C:\VB**). If you put the file elsewhere, then you must provide the complete path name.

4 Alternatively you can change the current directory to the one that contains the right files from within Visual Basic by adding a line of code:

```
CHDir C:\IMAGES
```

5 Replace the **IMAGES** directory with whichever is correct.

6 Run the program. There's the graphic.

> There was another example of how the **LoadPicture** function works back in Chapter 2 when you were first introduced to picture boxes and image controls. Load the **CONTROL.MAK** project to get a reminder.

Changing Images at Run-Time

There are situations where you may want to change the image in a control at run-time. This is a useful process if you want to swap images on screen quickly (helpful in things like animation). The fastest way to do this is to assign all the images to controls on the form at design-time. Then have only one control visible on the form, and copy the images to this control as and when you need them. You can copy images like this:

```
Image1.Picture = Image2.Picture
```

Loading Images Into a Form

As well as using the image and picture controls to display images, you can use a whole form to do it as well. This is used a lot in commercial packages to display what is called a **splash screen**. This is an introductory screen that loads up before any other part of your program. It makes your programs look great, and also takes your users minds off the time it takes to load the rest of your program.

Try It Out - Creating and Adding a Splash Screen

Most splash screens are simply forms with their **Picture** property set to display an image. That image might have been created in something like Windows Paintbrush. Since you just have one form and no controls, the form displays very quickly indeed.

1 Go to program manager and load up Paintbrush. It's usually in the program manager group called Accessories.

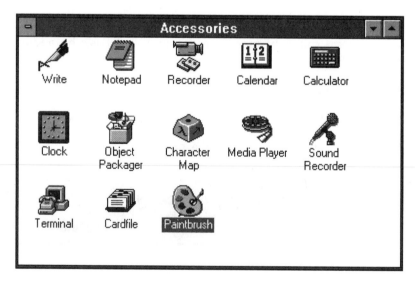

2 When Paintbrush loads up, it lets you create a screen size drawing by default. However, our real aim is to create a form-sized image, something small but eye-catching. On the options menu in Paintbrush there is a menu item called Image Attributes. Select it now.

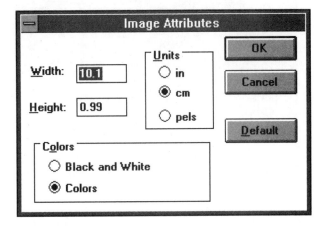

3 The Image Attributes dialog allows you to change the maximum size of image allowed by Paintbrush. Change the Width to 10 and the height to 2 and press OK.

4 Paintbrush draws a white rectangle on the screen to represent the size of the image. Play around with the image attributes until the rectangle is a size you think would be good for a splash screen.

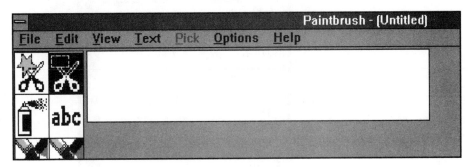

This is a book about Visual Basic, so getting you to draw a splash screen yourselves with Paintbrush is a bit out of our way. Luckily, I've already done the hard work.

5 From the File menu in Paintbrush, select Open and then load up the **SPLASH.BMP** image from the disk.

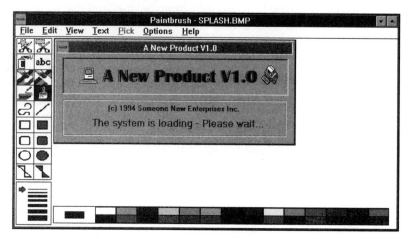

6 Let's see how to get the image onto a form in Visual Basic to create your splash screen. Splash form is a probably a more apt description.

7 Create a new project in Visual Basic.

8 When the default form appears click on it once to select it, then press F4 to bring up the Properties window.

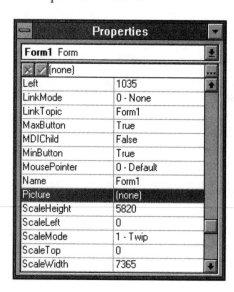

9 Find the Picture property and double-click it. The file load dialog appears.

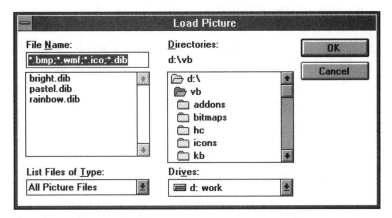

10 Find the **SPLASH.BMP** file included with the samples, and double-click to load it. Since the image is actually a direct copy of a form, you need to make some changes to the form itself to get the desired effect.

11 In the properties window, find the BorderStyle property of the form and set it to 0 - No Border. Resize the form so the image fits neatly inside it.

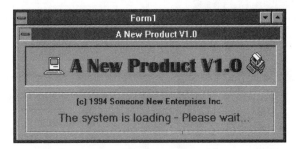

12 Now run the program and the splash form will appear very flash indeed, and in very little time. Since the form has no real border, the only way to stop the program is to select End from the Run menu.

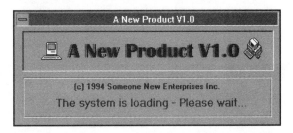

Comparing Image and Picture Controls

Having now used these two controls, in both Chapter 2 and here, you should have an idea of their relative strengths and weaknesses. Let's just summarize them:

▶ Image controls stretch the image they contain as they change shape. Picture boxes and forms don't do this.

▶ Picture controls, on the other hand, can be used as container objects. I'll explain exactly what this means in a moment.

▶ Image controls are **lightweight** controls - an image control consumes less of your PC's memory and is faster to deal with than a heavyweight control such as a picture box. We look at lightweight controls in more detail in Chapter 14 - Interacting With Windows.

▶ The image control is a **bound** control. This means it can be bound to certain data fields in a database. We'll examine databases and bound controls later in the book, but suffice to say it's an important feature.

▶ It all looks a bit one-sided, but the real advantage of the picture box is flexibility. Just compare the properties that are available for each of the two controls.

Image   **Picture**

Picture Boxes as Containers

Unlike the image control, the picture box is a **container** control. A container control allows other controls to be drawn inside it. Anything you then do to the picture box also affects the controls contained within it. For example, if you make the picture box invisible its controls also become invisible; if you move the picture box within the form, the controls go with it.

This is an extremely useful feature. When we looked at option buttons in Chapter 2, I said that all the option buttons on a frame or form were linked together. Clicking one would affect all the others by making them **unclick**. This is where picture boxes come in handy. By placing a picture box on a frame or form, and then placing controls inside the picture box, you can begin to break a large group of functions down into related chunks.

You could, for example, place a group of option buttons together in a picture box. If you change the BorderStyle property of the picture box to 0 - None you can make the picture box seem to disappear. The option buttons will still be in view. They'll still be grouped in the picture box separate from others on the form.

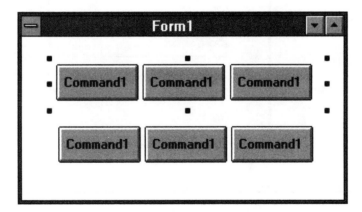

Picture boxes used in this way provide a way of removing a group of option buttons from view. If you change the Visible property to **False** the picture box vanishes completely taking everything drawn on it out of sight too.

Try It Out - Picture Boxes as Container Controls

1 Start a new Visual Basic project, then double-click the picture box icon.

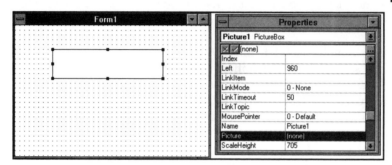

2 Now select the command button icon from the toolbox and draw it inside the picture box.

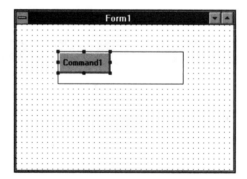

3 Select the picture box and move to a different place on the form. Watch how the command button goes with it.

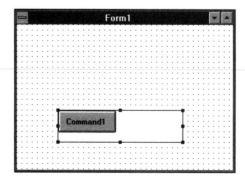

4 Select the command button and try to drag it off the picture box. Visual Basic won't let you do it as the command button belongs to the picture box.

5 Double-click the form to bring up the **Form_Load** code window. Type this code into the window:

```
Sub Form_Load()
    Picture1.Visible = False
End Sub
```

6 Now run the program. When the form appears you'll see that both the picture box and the command button you drew in it have gone. Making the picture box invisible removes from sight any objects contained within it.

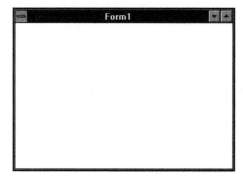

7 Stop the program running, and change the **Load** event so that it sets the Picture boxes Enabled property to **False**, removing the reference to the Visible property.

```
Sub Form_Load()
    Picture1.Enabled = False
End Sub
```

8 Run the program again.

9 This time, both the picture box and command button are visible, but neither can be selected. Try clicking the command button: nothing happens!

Using picture boxes in this way can save you a lot of time and effort. If you need to hide a large number of controls, or make the controls pop up in response to the user doing something, just place those controls inside a picture box and flip the picture box **Visible** property.

Frames

Like the picture box, **Frames** belong to the group of controls known as container objects. They behave very much like mini-forms; controls can be drawn onto them and as the frame moves, so do all the controls sitting on them. Equally, if the frame is made invisible by setting its Visible property to **False**, then it will vanish, taking all the controls inside it with it.

Frames in Action

You can see these effects in the **CONTROL.MAK** program, which we first came across in Chapter 2. Load up the project, and try moving one of the two large rectangles in the top half of the form. These are both frames. As they move so do all the controls inside them.

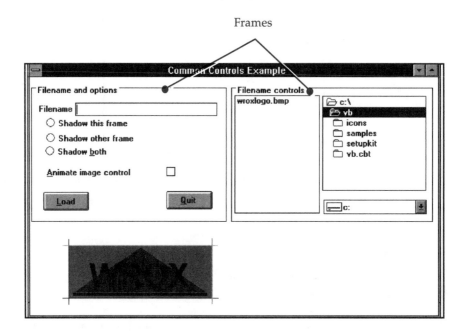

Frames

If you set one of the frames to invisible by changing its Visible property and then run the program, everything on that frame disappears at run-time. The controls on the frame are still there as far as Visual Basic is concerned but because their container is out of sight you can't see them.

Properties

Frames have no new or weird properties that we haven't already seen in other controls. However, some of the properties do work in rather strange ways.

Properties	
Frame1 Frame	
Frame1	
BackColor	&H80000005&
Caption	Frame1
ClipControls	True
DragIcon	(none)
DragMode	0 - Manual
Enabled	True
FontBold	True
FontItalic	False
FontName	MS Sans Serif
FontSize	8.25
FontStrikethru	False
FontUnderline	False
ForeColor	&H80000008&
Height	6090
HelpContextID	0
Index	
Left	150
MousePointer	0 - Default
Name	Frame1
TabIndex	0
Tag	
Top	120
Visible	True
Width	5175

Firstly, let's look at font properties. Thanks to the frame's single line border, many newcomers fall into the trap of thinking of the frame as nothing more than a large label or text box. However, it's actually a container object, that is, a way of breaking up the controls on your form into logical groups. The only text that the font properties applies to on the frame is the frame caption. If you change the font name, colors sizes and styles, it only affects the text that is drawn into the top left hand corner of the frame.

The caption also affects the Backcolor property as well. The actual area of the form that the frame takes up extends from the bottom line of the frame to the top of the highest possible letter in the caption. For this reason, if you change the backcolor it causes the new color to spill out of the top of the frame a little.

I tend to use picture boxes instead of frames wherever possible. If you change the backcolor of a picture box it only affects the color within the border of the picture box.

Normally, a frame has a caption which breaks up the top bar of the border. However, if you delete the caption Visual Basic automatically draws a border line where the caption previously stood. You can see this effect in the previous screen shot, in the frame on the right.

Events

Frames have very few events you can respond to. The most useful of the events you *can* respond to are the click and double-click events, which work in the same way as they do on any other control.

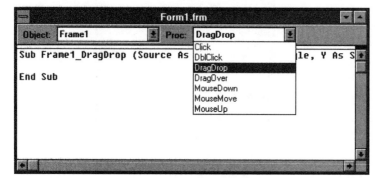

Problems With Frames

While frames can be very useful in breaking down the controls in a form into small neat groups, they can cause some annoying problems. If you start a new project, draw a command button on the form, and then draw a frame on the form. You'll find you can now no longer move the command button onto the frame.

Try It Out - Frames

1   Start a new project in Visual Basic.

2   When the default form appears, select the frame icon from the toolbox and draw a frame on the form.

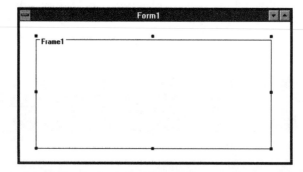

3 Draw a command button onto the frame.

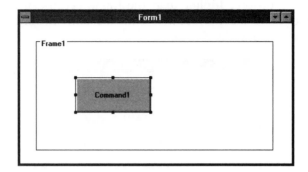

4 Click on the frame and move it. The command button follows it, and stays in exactly the same position in the frame, but moves relative to the form.

5 Try clicking on the command button and dragging it off the frame. Visual Basic won't let you.

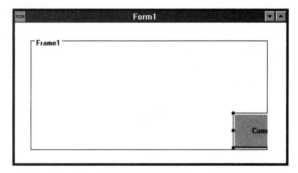

6 Now draw a new command button beneath the frame. If you have resized the form in the way that I have, then you'll probably find it easier to enlarge the form as well.

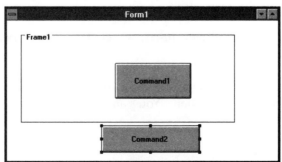

7 Although you've just drawn the button directly onto the form, it's actually floating **higher** than the frame because it was drawn **after** the frame. Drag the new button onto the bottom border of the frame. Now it floats above the frame.

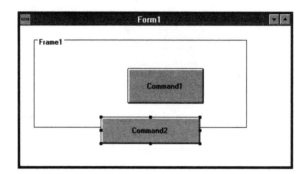

8 Finally, drag the new button into the frame, then move the frame. The new button stays locked to the point where you last moved it. It doesn't follow the frame around.

9 It doesn't follow the frame around because the button is still attached to the form and is floating above the frame. To put the button into the frame itself you'd need to cut and paste it from the form into the frame, in the same way that you would to get the original button out of the frame and onto the form.

Try It Out - Moving Controls Out of a Frame

Visual Basic provides an Edit menu to help you get around these problems. The correct way to move a control from a frame to a form is as follows:

1 Select the control you want to move.

2 Either press the *Delete* button, or select Cut from the Edit menu.

3 Click on the form itself.

4 Either press *Shift* and *Insert*, or select the Paste item from the Edit menu.

The control you just deleted will now appear on the form, allowing you to move it to the correct position. You can use the same cut and paste technique to move all controls.

Copying Controls

The option buttons in the example program were made by placing one control down on the frame, then selecting Copy from the Edit menu, then Paste. Visual Basic creates an exact copy of the control and asks you if you wish to create a control array. In the case of the option buttons a control array was exactly what we wanted, but by selecting No, Visual Basic will assign the new control an entirely different name, rather than the same name and a new Index number.

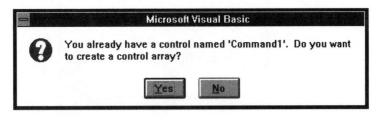

The Shape Control

The shape control allows you to draw a simple geometric shape, such as a line, box or circle, onto the form at design-time. To use the shape control you select the control from the palette and then drag a rectangle on the form in the same way as if you were drawing any other type of control.

Try It Out - Using the Shape Control

1 Start a new Visual Basic project.

2 Double-click the shape control on the palette to place it onto the default form.

3 Try resizing the shape by clicking and dragging the resize handles in the usual manner.

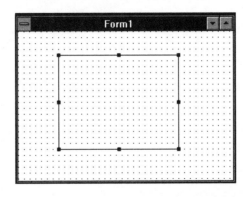

4 Bring up the properties window and find the Shape property. This allows you to change the shape that will be displayed. Double-click the Shape property to cycle through the available shapes.

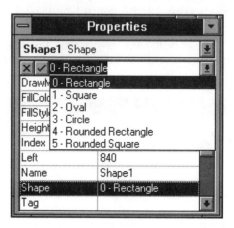

5 You can change the style of the border around the shape between a solid line and various types of dashed line using the Borderstyle property. Find it in the properties list and double-click it to cycle through all the available shapes.

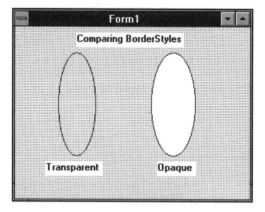

6 You can change the thickness of the border of the shape using the BorderWidth property. Find that property in the properties window and enter the number 10. The style of the border changes dramatically.

> To be honest with you I never use the shape control; it's too limited to build up complex images at design-time. If I need graphics at run-time then I use the graphics methods to create them.
>
> However, many people *do* use them for placing borders around items on forms, without the memory overhead that comes with a frame or a picture box.

The Line Control

The line control is slightly simpler to use than the shape control. This allows you to draw a straight line on your form. It's great for breaking up the controls on a form, or for underlining a particular area. It's something that interface designers call a feature, but everyone else calls it decoration.

Try It Out - Drawing a Line on a Form

1 Double-click the line control on the toolbox to place a line on the form.

2 The line control has two resize handles, one at each end, which you can drag around to change the size and slope of the line.

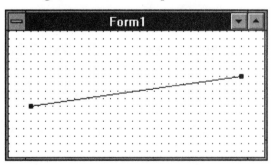

3 Just as with the shape control, you can change the thickness and type of line drawn using the BorderStyle and BorderWidth properties. Bring up the properties window and try double-clicking the BorderStyle property to cycle through the available line types. Otherwise enter a number into the BorderWidth property to change the thickness of the line.

The Graphics Methods

The graphics methods in Visual Basic provide a lot more flexibility when dealing with graphics. Unlike the controls (all of which need to be drawn onto a form at design-time) the graphics methods allow you to create graphics on the fly. This includes drawing lines and shapes, setting individual pixels on the form, and so on. With a little thought these methods can be taken beyond their obvious uses (as tools for creating static charts) into the realms of games and animation programs. In fact, surprisingly little coding experience is needed to create some quite stunning effects, as you'll find out.

Pixel Plotting With Pset

The first method we'll look at is **Pset**. **Pset** actually means **Point Set** and allows you to set individual pixels (points) on the form. For instance, you could cover a form in multi-colored dots to simulate splatter painting, or move dots around the screen in an orderly fashion to explore far off galaxies, to boldly go... (you know the rest!).

Try It Out - Splatter Painting

1   Firstly, splatter painting. The principles behind this are really simple, but the effect could be quite well used as a background for a title form in an application. Load up the **SPLATTER.MAK** project and run it.

2   When the program has finished drawing, end the program in the usual way. Either select End from the Run menu, press *Alt-F4*, or double-click the form control box.

3   Double-click the form to take a look at the code.

```
Randomize

For nIndex = 1 To 2000
    nXCoord = Int(Rnd(1) * frmMain.ScaleWidth)
    nYCoord = Int(Rnd(1) * frmMain.ScaleHeight)
    nRed = Int(Rnd(1) * 255)
    nGreen = Int(Rnd(1) * 255)
    nBlue = Int(Rnd(1) * 255)
    PSet (nXCoord, nYCoord), RGB(nRed, nGreen, nBlue)
Next
```

If you take a look at the code window you'll see that there is a little more code than I've shown here, but the rest just shows the form on the screen and displays a message box when the program has done its stuff. It's the code above that is of most interest to us.

How It Works

First an overview. The **For..Next** loop runs 2000 times, each time deciding on some random co-ordinates at which to display a dot on the screen. This is what the **Rnd()** command does.

> Visual Basic doesn't generate random numbers in the true sense. For example, you're not being asked to close your eyes and hit a key on the numeric keypad. Rather, it generates a sequence of seemingly random numbers which it stores in memory. That's the purpose of the **Randomize** command at the head of the code; **Randomize** generates that sequence of numbers ready for you to pull them out with the **Rnd()** command.

If we use **Rnd(1)** we tell Visual Basic to give us the next number in the random number sequence. The actual number we get is a decimal number somewhere between 0 and 1. Therefore, the line:

```
Rnd(1) * frmMain.ScaleWidth
```

gives us a random number between 0 and the width of the form client area. The client area of a form is the part of the form on which you can draw or place controls. It's the big white bit in the middle, not including the borders and caption bar area.

So far so good! There's still some work to do on this random number before it can be used. Let's say the form width is something like 2437, and the random number that **Rnd(1)** gives us is 0.5412. Multiplying these two numbers together we get 1318.9044. Obviously that can't be used as the X co-ordinate. Visual Basic needs a whole integer number, not a decimal.

As you saw back in Chapter 4 - Making Data Work For You, the **Int** statement converts a number to an integer value. In our example it would convert 1318.9044 into 1318 by just cutting the decimal bits off. Now this is a number we can use. The same technique is applied to get the dot's Y co-ordinate, and the values of red, green and blue which will be used to produce our dot's color. Finally, **PSet** is called to actually draw the dot. The format for the **PSet** method is:

```
Pset ( <X co-ordinate>, <Y Co-ordinate>), <Color value>
```

Since our program has already decided on some co-ordinates for the dot, as well as the random values needed to use the **RGB** function, we have all the components we need to draw a dot somewhere on the screen, in a random color. If you run this 2000 times lots of random multi-colored dots appear, as in the example.

Animation With PSet

Now let's look at some animation. Animation on a computer is really a question of programming the users' eyes, or rather **confusing** them. If you flash an image onto the screen first in one position, then in another, it appears that the image is jumping between the two positions. If you draw an image in one position, then copy it to another position, then another and another, the user thinks the image is being dragged around the screen leaving a trail.

If you want to animate a dot with **PSet** the principles are very similar. Firstly, draw the dot in one position and call it A. Then draw the dot in the next position, and call it position B. Finally, draw another dot at position A, but in the same color as the form's background. The computer can do this so quickly that the user thinks he's watching a dot with a life of its own moving around the screen.

Try It Out - Through the Starfield

Imagine 50 dots, all appearing to move, but at different speeds and in different directions! Remind you of anything? The stars you might see looking off the bridge of the Starship Enterprise, for example?

1 Load up **WARP.MAK** and run it. Wow - stars!

2 As before **PSet** is used to actually plot the points which represent the stars on the screen. Take a look at the declarations section of the program:

```
Option Explicit
Dim nXCoord(50) As Integer
Dim nYCoord(50) As Integer
Dim nXSpeed(50) As Integer
Dim nYSpeed(50) As Integer
```

How It Works

Four integer arrays are used to hold information about each star; information such as the star's current X and Y co-ordinates, as well as two-speed variables. Because the arrays are each set up to hold 50 values, it should make some sense when I tell you that the maximum number of stars the program can kick around the screen at any one time is 50. Each current star will have its own set of values, identified by a common index of each array.

If you take a look at the form itself you'll see that there's a timer control drawn on it.

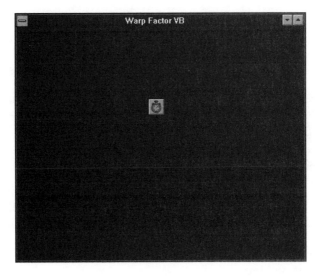

In the timer event, the values held in these X and Y speed variables are added to the stars current X and Y co-ordinates to give the impression that the star is moving. Close the code window down, then double-click on the timer control itself to view the timer event code.

```
Sub Timer1_Timer ()
    Dim nIndex As Integer
    Const BLACK = &H0&
    Const WHITE = &HFFFFFF&
    For nIndex = 0 To 49
        PSet (nXCoord(nIndex), nYCoord(nIndex)), BLACK
        If nXCoord(nIndex) < 0 Or nXCoord(nIndex) > frmMain.ScaleWidth Or
⤷nYCoord(nIndex) < 0 Or nYCoord(nIndex) > frmMain.ScaleHeight Then
            nXCoord(nIndex) = frmMain.ScaleWidth \ 2
            nYCoord(nIndex) = frmMain.ScaleHeight \ 2
            nXSpeed(nIndex) = Int(Rnd(1) * 200) - 100
            nYSpeed(nIndex) = Int(Rnd(1) * 200) - 100
        End If
        nXCoord(nIndex) = nXCoord(nIndex) + nXSpeed(nIndex)
        nYCoord(nIndex) = nYCoord(nIndex) + nYSpeed(nIndex)
        PSet (nXCoord(nIndex), nYCoord(nIndex)), WHITE
    Next
End Sub
```

It looks a little daunting doesn't it! Don't panic. Each time the timer event occurs, a **For...Next** loop is used to update the positions of each of the 50 stars on the screen. The first **PSet** in the loop erases the star at its last known position by redrawing it in black, the same color as the form's background color. Next, a check is made to see if the current star determined by the **nIndex** variable has moved off the screen.

The co-ordinates of the star are checked to see if either of them has gone off any edge of the form. If one has, the co-ordinates are reset to the center of the form and some speed values are decided at random. These speed values then become that particular star's new speed until it vanishes off screen again.

```
If nXCoord(nIndex) < 0 Or nXCoord(nIndex) > frmMain.ScaleWidth Or
⤷nYCoord(nIndex) < 0 Or nYCoord(nIndex) > frmMain.ScaleHeight Then
    nXCoord(nIndex) = frmMain.ScaleWidth \ 2
    nYCoord(nIndex) = frmMain.ScaleHeight \ 2
    nXSpeed(nIndex) = Int(Rnd(1) * 200) - 100
    nYSpeed(nIndex) = Int(Rnd(1) * 200) - 100
End If
```

Finally, the values of the speed variables are added to the star's current X and Y co-ordinates to get its next position on screen. Remember, the star has already been erased at the start of the loop, so if you calculate a new position for it and draw it in that position it gives the user the impression that the star is actually moving.

```
nXCoord(nIndex) = nXCoord(nIndex) + nXSpeed(nIndex)
nYCoord(nIndex) = nYCoord(nIndex) + nYSpeed(nIndex)
```

Unless you're running the program on a very powerful PC, you'll have noticed that moving images are not one of Visual Basic's strong points. Windows is slow anyway, and on top of that Visual Basic doesn't produce the fastest possible programs. The result is that animation and Visual Basic don't really mix yet.

You can get around the speed limitations by delving into the murky depths of something called the Application Programming Interface (API). We cover some uses of the API a little later in this book, but graphics and API is well beyond our scope I'm afraid.

Drawing Lines

Dots are fine for learning about how graphics are drawn and about Visual Basic's rather eccentric co-ordinate system. However, for graphs and really impressive graphics you need to start thinking about drawing lines. Though this might be taken for granted, the ability to draw lines in your code opens up an infinite number of programming possibilities.

If you can draw lines then you can also draw graphs, three dimensional graphics and explore virtual reality. You could even simply mellow out with the computer equivalent of a psychedelic laser show!

Visual Basic has an extremely versatile command for drawing lines called the **Line** command. In its most basic form, you give the **Line** command two sets of co-ordinates, one stating where the line starts, the other where the line ends. You can also supply a color value just as you can with **Pset**. Visual Basic will then happily wander off for a few fractions of a second and draw the line for you.

Try It Out - Drawing Lines

1 Start a new project in Visual Basic and run it.

2 When the project is running either press *Ctrl-Break* to pause the program, or click the pause icon on the Visual Basic toolbar.

3 Now the program is paused, press *Ctrl-B* to bring up the debug window. The debug window allows you to enter most of the commands that you would normally type into the code window. The difference between the two types of window is that as soon as you hit *Enter* in the debug window the command is run.

4 Arrange the form and the debug window so you can see them both on the screen, like I've done here:

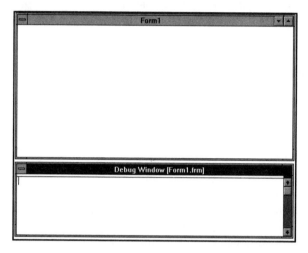

5 Let's draw some lines. Type **Line (0,0)-(1500,1500)** in the debug window and press *Enter*. Instantly a line appears on the form.

6 Unless you specify otherwise, Visual Basic draws a line in the color:

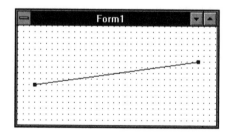

specified in the form ForeColor property. You can also specify a color in the **Line** command itself. Type this into the debug window and press *Enter*.

```
Line (0,0) - (2000,900), &HFF00FF&
```

7 This time the line is drawn in pink.

8 You can also tell Visual Basic to draw a line from the point at which the previous line ended. Type these two commands in and press *Enter* after each.

```
Line -(3000,3000)
Line -(0,0)
```

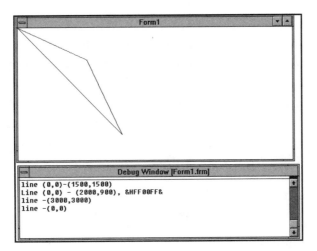

9 Finally, the line command can also be used without specifying exact co-ordinates, by instead using **offsets**. Try typing these lines in:

```
Line (0,0)-Step(1000,400)
Line Step(2000,1000)-Step(500,500)
Line -Step(2000,-800)
```

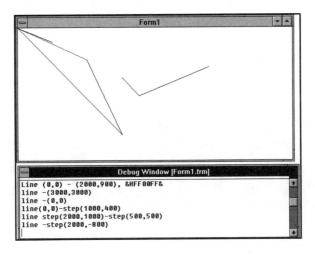

10 You get some pretty weird results with these. The **Step** keyword tells Visual Basic that the co-ordinates after the word **Step** should be added on to the last co-ordinates drawn. So **Line(0,0)-Step(1000,400)** starts the line at **0,0** and ends it at **(0+1000, 0+400)**.

In this project, you used the debug window to pass commands to Visual Basic in the middle of execution. This isn't really intended as a design tool in the way we've used it, but rather as a way to **debug** your code to find hidden errors. If you send commands you can often root out the offending piece of code by seeing how the system reacts to different things. We'll learn how to use debug in anger in Chapter 10 - Writing Programs That Work.

Try It Out - Animation Using Lines

1 Now you're up to speed with the **Line** command, let's try something impressive. Load up the **WOW.MAK** project.

2 Run the project.

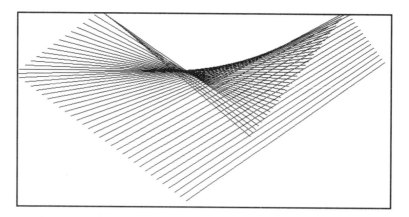

Programs like this are an excellent demonstration of the power of Visual Basic, as well as an example of a computer's ability to fool the sharpest of minds. If the program is still running watch it for a while. It looks like the computer is drawing about 50 lines on the screen and animating them, doesn't it? Wrong! It also looks like the code is doing some pretty complex rotations to get the curve effects right? Wrong!

How It Works

The program is based around four bouncing balls. Two of the bouncing balls, which are really just dots, are joined by a blue line. The other two follow in exactly the same path as the first two balls, but 50 steps behind. These latter points are joined by a black line.

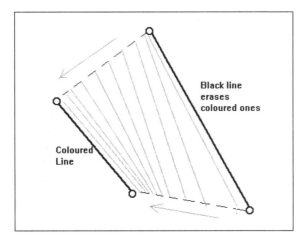

The program draws 50 lines on the screen before the black line erases each of those 50 lines one by one.

The animation itself is easy. Just as with our stars program, the end of each line has a set of co-ordinates and an X and Y speed. If any point hits the edge of the screen then the appropriate speed is reversed. Let's say, for instance, that one of the points is having 50 added to its X co-ordinate and 25 to its Y co-ordinate on every timer event. If that point hits the bottom of the form the code changes the Y co-ordinate to -25. Likewise, if the point hits the right or left edges of the form the X speed is reversed. There are no complex curves here, just plain old fashioned straight lines and bouncing dots. What's more, since Visual Basic is only ever drawing two lines on the screen the program is quite rapid.

If you want to find out more, then by all means take a peek at the timer event code, which is heavily commented to lead you through what it does.

Circles, Curves, Arcs and Bendy Bits

An extremely complex area of computer graphics has always been that of drawing curves and circles. Thankfully, Visual Basic simplifies the process greatly with its **Circle** command. Despite its rather misleading name, the **Circle** method can draw curves, circles, ellipses and segments of circles which is excellent for pie-charts!

Let's take a look at normal circles first.

Try It Out - Drawing Circles

1   Start a new project in Visual Basic, run it, then pause the program by using *Ctrl-Break*. Bring up the debug window with *Ctrl-B*. Catch your breath and pat yourself on the back for getting this far with no hassle.

2   Arrange the two windows as before and in the debug window type this (don't forget to press *Enter* at the end of the command).

```
Circle (2000,2000), 1000
```

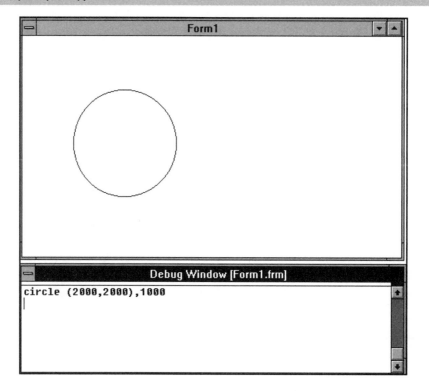

3   A circle appears. The co-ordinates which you specify in the brackets are the center of the circle, in this case 2000,2000. The number outside the brackets is the radius of the circle, here 1000.

4   You can see this even better if we draw two lines over the circle to show the center and the radius.

```
Line (2000,2000)-Step(0,1000)
Line (2000,2000)-Step(1000,0)
```

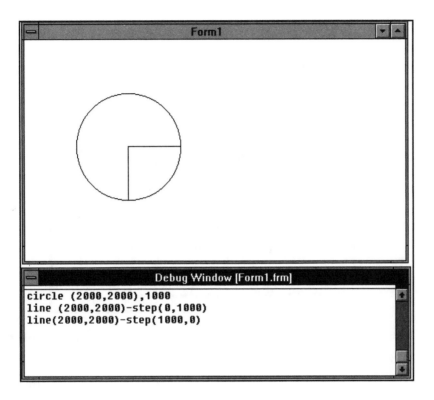

Drawing Arcs

Arcs require a little more effort. The **Circle** method you've used so far is a cut down version of what it can actually do. The actual syntax for **Circle** is:

```
Circle (x,y), <radius>, <color>, <start angle>, <end angle>, <aspect>
```

Just to be awkward, most computers calculate angles and related stuff in terms of radians rather than degrees. I won't go into the logic of it all, nor give an explanation of what radians are - you don't need to know, and I failed pure math in college!

All you *do* need to know is that to convert a number in degrees to its equivalent in radians you multiply the angle by Pi (3.142 roughly) and divide the result by 180. If you're confused there's a **.BAS** called **RADIANS** on the examples disk which contains a function to do just that. We'll use it in a moment.

Try It Out - Drawing Arcs and Slices

1 Create a new project in Visual Basic.

2 From the File menu, select Add File (alternatively press *Ctrl-D*). When the file requester appears, add the **RADIANS.BAS** file from the samples disk to the project.

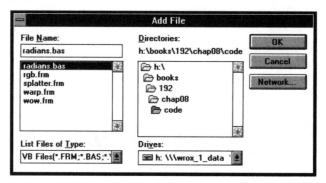

3 Run the program, then pause it in the normal way. Hit *Ctrl-B* to bring up the Debug window.

4 We'll now draw an arc which goes from 45 degrees of a circle to 230 degrees.

```
Circle (2000,2000), 1000,  , Rads(45), Rads(230)
```

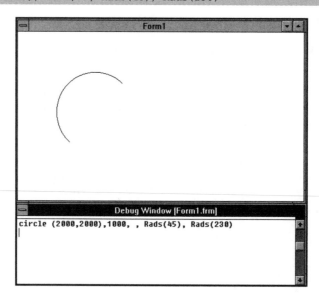

5 We said to draw the part of a circle (center at 2000,2000, radius 1000) that goes from 45 degrees round to 230. The **Rads** function is the code included in the **RADIANS.BAS** module you added to the project. This converts the degrees figure (given as a parameter) to radians.

6 Previously we drew lines onto the circle with the **Line** command to mark out the radius and center. **Circle** can do that for you itself. Type in the following:

```
Cls
FillStyle = 0
FillColor = QbColor(14)
Circle (2000,2000),1000, , -Rads(90), -Rads(45)
FillColor = QbColor(1)
Circle (2050,1900),1000, , -Rads(45), -Rads(90)
FillStyle = 1
```

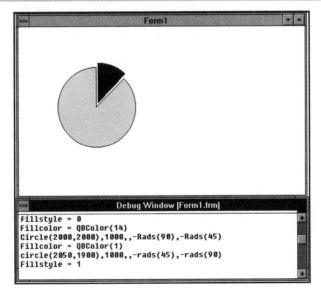

How It Works

There are some other interesting lines of code in what you've just typed. The **Cls** method actually stands for clear screen, but in Visual Basic it merely clears the form. After clearing the form with the **Cls** command, we set the form FillStyle to property **0**. This tells Visual Basic to fill in any graphics it draws with the color in the FillColor property of the form. The next line sets the color to **14** (yellow) with the **QBColor** method.

In the two circle commands, we pass negative start and end angles. This tells the **Circle** command to draw connecting lines from the start and end to the center of the circle. The last FillStyle line turns off the auto filling.

The **RADIANS.BAS** module contains this code:

```
Function Rads (ByVal nDegrees As Single) As Single
   Const Pi = 22 / 7
   Rads = (nDegrees * Pi) / 180
End Function
```

Even assuming your math is as basic as mine, this is fairly easy to follow.

Drawing Ellipses

The final use of the **Circle** command is to draw ellipses. To draw an ellipse, all you need do is draw a circle in the normal way, then give Visual Basic a number for its **Aspect** parameter.

Before we go any further I'd better explain what **Aspect** is. The aspect is the relationship between the horizontal radius and the vertical radius. For instance, an aspect of **2** would mean that the horizontal radius is twice as large as the vertical radius. Conversely, an aspect of **0.5** would put the circle on screen which is twice as high as it is wide.

Try It Out - Ellipses.

1 Start a new project in Visual Basic, run it, pause it (*Ctrl-Break*) and bring up the debug window (*Ctrl-B*).

2 In the debug window, type in the following, and press *Enter.*

```
circle(2000,2000),1000,,,,3
circle(2000,2000),1000,,,,.5
circle(2000,2000),1000,,,,2
```

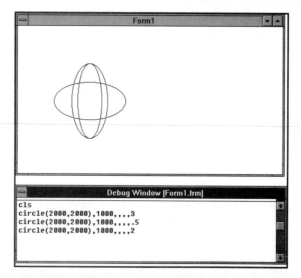

Even though I've called them commands and statements, and we've used them interactively in the debug environment, you must remember that these are graphics methods. When used in code, they **must** apply to an object, which often defaults to the current form.

Drawing Properties - Weird and Wonderful Effects

There are many different properties of graphics objects which you can use to create various effects.

The FillStyle Property

We saw that setting the FillStyle property of a form to **0** fills the circle with a solid color. Setting it to **1** (the default) leaves the circle's contents transparent. FillStyle actually has a number of settings, each of which does different things to the shape you're drawing. The table below lists these settings and their effects on your works of art.

Setting	Effect
0	Solid fills the object
1	Transparent - doesn't fill the object with anything
2	Fills the object with horizontal lines
3	Fills the object with vertical lines
4	Fills the object with left bottom to right top diagonal lines
5	Fills with diagonal lines from left top to right bottom
6	Draws a cross hatch pattern over the object
7	Draws a diagonal crosshatch pattern over the object.

You can try out all these settings to your heart's content using the debug window as we've done for the other examples. Just run your project, pause it, go to the debug window, set the Fillstyle property and draw away.

The DrawWidth Property

Another interesting form property is DrawWidth. This specifies the thickness of the lines that your objects are drawn in, be they lines, boxes, circles, arcs, ellipses or whatever. If you make this number larger, the thickness of the objects increases as you draw with the Visual Basic graphics methods. Similarly, if you decrease it, the lines you form are that much thinner, down to a maximum of one pixel thick.

409

The DrawStyle Property

Another good one to play with is the DrawStyle property. This lets you flip between drawing solid lines to dashed ones of varying types, such as .... style lines, or . -- . -- . -- .— lines and so on. The best way to learn about these styles is to play with them using the debug window.

The DrawMode Property

By far the most interesting property is the DrawMode property. This has 4 possible settings which govern how Visual Basic goes about drawing things:

Setting	Effect
4	Inverts the current pattern you have when drawing. The pattern is from FillStyle property.
7	XOR Pen. Lets you draw an object, then when you redraw it, restores what was previously drawn.
11	Does nothing. It's like saying don't draw anything.
13	Copy pen. This is the default DrawMode that we've so far been using.

The **XOR** mode needs a bit more explanation. It's mainly used for games and such. You may want to have a background graphic drawn on a form, and then move objects over the top of it. **XOR** mode lets you do this. When you first draw something onto the form it appears exactly as you'd expect. However, if you redraw the same object, in the same place, it vanishes, and the background that was there previously comes into view once again.

Repainting Forms Efficiently

I love Visual Basic. It's without doubt the best thing to happen to Windows programming. But even I have to admit that Visual Basic is a bit of a slouch when it comes to complex graphics. The problem is partly Visual Basic, and partly Windows, but whatever the cause, there are some things you *can* do to make your Visual Basic graphics programs slicker and more efficient.

ClipControls

Let's start with ClipControls. Whenever you draw something on a window, or move an icon or the mouse across it, Visual Basic and Windows decide which areas of the form need to be repainted. For example, you wouldn't want to see the mouse trail left on the form indefinitely.

This is what ClipControls does. With the AutoRedraw property set to **False**, your program will receive paint events whenever part of the form needs to be redrawn. The ClipControls property governs where you can draw. When it is set to **True**, you can redraw any part of the form you want to in the paint event. Something called a **clipping region** is created around the controls on the form to make sure you don't draw over them.

With ClipControls set to **False**, no matter where you try to draw on a form, Visual Basic will only change the areas of the form it thinks need repainting. ClipControls also affect the way Visual Basic handles redrawing when the AutoRedraw property is set to **True**. When AutoRedraw is set to **True**, Visual Basic handles the redrawing of the graphics on the form, should the form get resized, moved or overlaid with another. The setting of ClipControls tells Visual Basic whether or not it needs to redraw the whole form, or just the affected parts of it.

To get your forms displaying and redrawing quickly you need to have ClipControls set to **False**. This way only the affected areas of the form are redrawn and Visual Basic and Windows don't have so much graphical data to deal with. You should only have ClipControls set to **True** if you're changing all the graphics on a form every time you redraw, such as in an action game where you might need to redraw the whole playing area a number of times every second.

AutoRedraw

Much more useful is the AutoRedraw property itself. By default this is set to **False**. This means that if another window appears on top of the one you're drawing, Visual Basic thinks you'll have to redraw the first. The net result of this is that because Visual Basic assumes you can redraw your own graphics, everything runs that much faster.

Setting the property to **True** however, tells Visual Basic that it should take care of your graphics for you. Each time you draw something, Visual Basic makes a mental note of what you did. Should parts of the form get covered by another object, Visual Basic automatically knows what to do to redisplay your graphics. This also works if your user switches to another application. When your form comes back into view, it's restored to its former glory. The downside is that your graphics run quite a lot slower.

If you want fast graphics, set AutoRedraw to **False**. If you don't want the hassle of the users mucking up your displays by dragging windows around indiscriminately, then you'd better set AutoRedraw to **True**, and live with the consequences.

Summary

This has been a lightning tour of graphics with Visual Basic. I don't claim to have told you everything, but as we said at the beginning, graphics are nice but they're often the icing on the cake. However, we did get a quick tour of the highlights, namely:

- How color works in Visual Basic
- The co-ordinate system
- Graphics controls, with image and picture boxes, and the shape and line controls
- Graphics methods

Along the way you learnt how to choose between the image and picture controls, and the difference between graphics controls and methods. You learnt how to create simple animation, and finally how to get the best performance from Visual Basic.

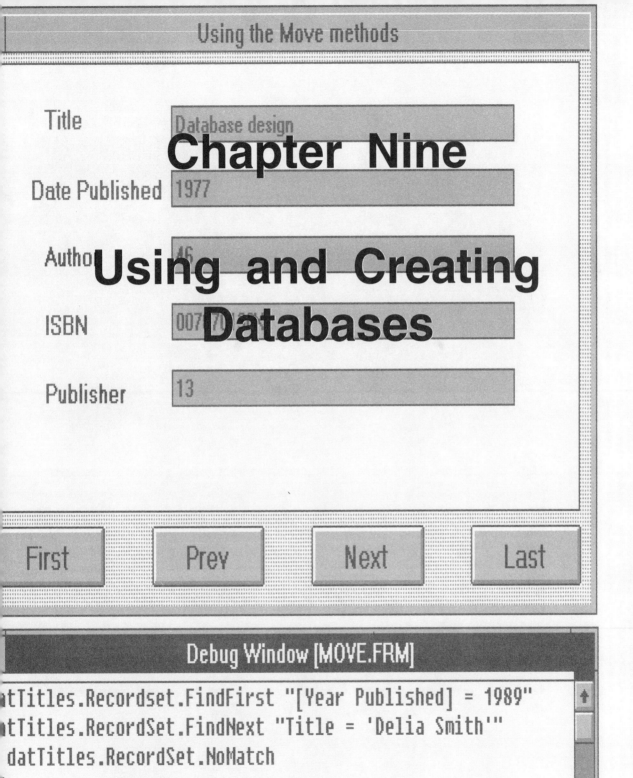

Using the Move methods

Title Database design

Chapter Nine

Date Published 1977

Autho **Using and Creating**

ISBN 007 **Databases**

Publisher 13

First   Prev   Next   Last

Debug Window [MOVE.FRM]

```
atTitles.Recordset.FindFirst "[Year Published] = 1989"
atTitles.RecordSet.FindNext "Title = 'Delia Smith'"
 datTitles.RecordSet.NoMatch

atTitles.Recordset.MoveFirst
atTitles.Recordset.FindNext "Title like '*Design*' "
```

CHAPTER 9

Using And Creating Databases

Welcome to the information revolution! By far the most popular application for computers in the 90s is the management of information: customer lists, accounts records, stock records in a warehouse, personnel information, and so on. The ideal tool to manage all this information is a good database system. Visual Basic has recently taken the database development market by storm because of its power, flexibility and ease of use.

In this chapter you'll learn:

- How databases work
- Why Visual Basic is a good choice for database developers
- How to access existing databases using controls and properties
- How to access existing databases using code
- How to create your own databases

What is a Database?

The easiest way to understand how databases work on a computer is to consider how people organize their information in real-life. The objective of any database is to make life easier. This implies you know exactly what the information you have to organize is, and what people want to use it for. This sounds trivial, but it's at this stage that most databases start to go wrong. Only through careful planning and design will your database actually be usable.

Like all things to do with computers, there's a lot of terminology associated with databases. Some of this is especially confusing because it describes abstract concepts. Because databases are general tools, we tend to talk about **fields**, rather than **the place where the street name goes**, and so on.

We'll start at the very beginning, by seeing how computer databases are a logical evolution of the ways we organize information in real-life. In the process, you'll be able to anchor the fundamental concepts in your own experience, so that when we start to actually use and build our own Visual Basic databases, you won't get swamped by a wave of alien jargon.

A Living Database

Imagine a filing cabinet with three drawers.

▶ The top draw contains customer information such as a customer's name and address.

▶ The second draw holds information about all the stock of the business, perhaps the goods it sells, or the raw materials it holds in order to produce goods in the first place.

▶ The third drawer contains invoices that the business has sent out to its customers.

A Filing Cabinet

The filing cabinet is a simple database. Each drawer in database terms is called a **table**.

Inside each drawer there are folders containing information about one specific subject. There may be folders in the customers drawer, for instance, holding details on J. Smith Industries Inc., or F. Bloggs Manufacturing Co. Each of these folders is called a **record** in Visual Basic.

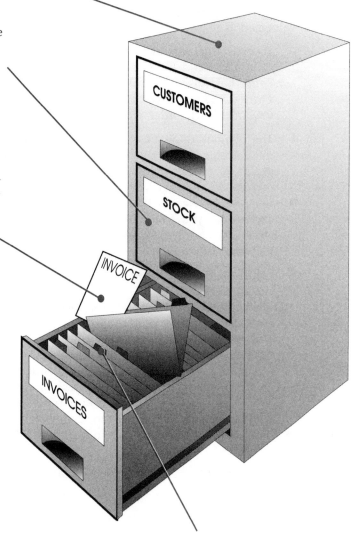

The invoice drawer is organized by invoice number order. In this drawer each invoice is itself a **record**. It is a self-contained item. On each invoice there are a number of different pieces of information, such as the date, the customer's name, and a list of the parts they ordered. Each one of these individual bits of information is a **field**.

Obviously as each of the drawers gets filled with more and more information there needs to be some method of locating that information quickly. A customer may call up asking to place an order for Gizmos and Widgets. The poor old clerk on the end of the phone needs to be able to quickly find the stock information for Gizmos and Widgets to tell the customer when the order will be completed. So, each drawer has tabs inside which splits the records down into alphabetical order. In Visual Basic this is called an **Index**. The index may specify that the customer records are stored alphabetically based on the customer's name. The customers name is then the **key** to the index.

Getting Information Out of a Real Database

Continuing the example, let's say that a few days after placing his order for Gizmos, the customer still hasn't received his delivery. So he phones you, the clerk at J. Smith Inc., and asks when the order was dispatched. This sounds like a simple request, but think about it. It's actually quite tricky. Think about the information that each of the three drawers contains:

> ▶ The **customer drawer** has a separate file for each customer that contains their name and address details, and a list of all the invoices that J. Smith has raised for this customer. Take a look at that customer's file. There's a list of invoice numbers and amounts, but that's it. How can you tell which order was for the Gizmos?

> ▶ The obvious thing to do is to make a note of the invoice number from the customer's file, and look in the **invoices drawer**. This drawer is placed in invoice number order; in database-speak it is **indexed** on invoice number. So, you can now pull out the invoice you want. There it is, the invoice to the customer who called in. Bad news! The invoice shows that you back-ordered the Gizmos because you were out of stock. Oh no - angry customer! You therefore decide to take a look in the stock drawer and see when a new delivery is due to come in.

> ▶ Luckily the **stock drawer** is also indexed in alphabetical order like the customer drawer, so it's easy to pull out the Gizmos file and look at when the next delivery is due to arrive - next Friday. You call up the customer and he's cool about it.

You've probably done something like this yourself many times. In fact, what you've just done is a **multi-table relational query**. It's **multi-table** because you had to use three filing drawers (or **tables**) to get all the information you need. It's **relational** because you had to find a piece of information from one table (the invoice number from the customer drawer) and relate it to another table (the invoice drawer) in order to find the right file.

Relational Databases

Databases on computers are broken down into two camps; **flat-file** databases and **relational** databases.

With flat-file databases you tend to have a separate file on the disk for each table, and separate files for each index to a table. Actually relating information from one table to another can be a tricky affair with flat-file databases since each table is really a totally independent entity to the rest of them.

Relational databases are a more elegant solution. With a relational database most of the tables that hold the data are held in one large central database file, just as our filing drawers are all in the same cabinet. Organizing and accessing the information in these tables is usually done for you by something called a **database engine.** The clerk who searches through the files at J. Smith Inc. is in fact a database engine.

What the Database Engine Does

Not only does the database engine manage access to the database, it also does a lot of house-keeping to keep the relational database nice and tidy. The clerk at J. Smith Inc. not only gets information out of the database, but also has to file new invoices in the right place, and keep the stock and customer files up to date.

He also has to check that what's going into the database is not rubbish. To do that he has some simple rules. For example, if the clerk gets an invoice through with a customer name that isn't already in his customer drawer, then he won't file it away until that customer is set up properly. Otherwise the invoice would disappear into the drawer and not be related to anything. As invoice numbers don't mean anything on their own, it will probably just sink without trace. A database engine does this kind of checking in a computer database.

Relational databases are also rather special in that the information held within the tables of the database is rarely duplicated. The database engine makes it easy to pull information out of more than one table at once, so duplication of information can be kept to a minimum.

In our customer and invoice example for instance, when the time comes to print the invoice, your application would need to get the customer's name and address from somewhere to print on the invoice. All you'd need to store on each invoice record is some kind of unique customer identification number, like an account number, so you could tell the engine to get the name and address of the customer from the customer table for you automatically. From a maintenance point of view this is great; if a customer rings you up to change their address you don't need to trot through the database changing hundreds of old invoices. You only need to change the relevant records in the customer file since that will be the only place where this information is held.

In this example, the customer account number that is used to find the right file in both the customer file and the invoice file is called the **primary key.** This is the item that **relates** the two tables together.

The Important Jargon

Now you have an idea about what databases really are, let's review the words that cropped up:

> **Tables** are collections of information that have some logical reason to fit together, like all the names and addresses of customers. In our example this is a drawer in the filing cabinet.

> **Records** are the individual entries in a table, like all the details for one particular customer.

> **Fields** are the items that make up a complete record, like the street name of the customer's address.

> An **index** is a field that is used to sort the contents of a table into a logical order. In the customer table, the best choice is the customer's name. That way the table is in alphabetical order.

> A **primary key** is a field in a table that identifies each record uniquely. The same field then also appears in another table, so allowing the data in each to be **related** together. In our example, the customer account number appears in both the customer table and on all the invoices. Often the index field and the primary key are the same thing.

> The **database engine** is the person, or as we shall see the program, that files, organizes and retrieves all the data from our tables. The great strength of relational databases is that the database manager is separate from the data itself. That means we can use Visual Basic to read Paradox data, and so on.

> A **query** is the process of sending the database manager away to find the information we want from the database.

One way to think about a relational database is as a collection of components that work together. Your job is to define what those components are and how they fit together. You can dice the data in any number of different ways; there is no real right or wrong way. What matters is that it's easy to understand, safe and efficient. Database design is an art, and we can't hope to cover such a massive and open-ended subject here. However, if you stick to simple rules, and always try and relate it back to a clerk sorting through a filing cabinet, you'll be fine.

Databases and Visual Basic

Both the Professional and Standard Editions of Visual Basic come with the **Jet** database engine built in. This is one of Visual Basic 3's main selling points. Jet is the set of control software used in Microsoft's **Access** database system.

The Jet engine can create and manage information in a wide variety of database formats. Using Jet you can deal with Access databases, Foxpro, DBase, Paradox, Oracle, SQL Server and Btrieve databases right from the word go. These databases comprise the best selling databases available for PCs today. Being able to connect to them and read and write the information they hold can make you a very valuable commodity to many businesses. This has made Visual Basic the leading tool for Windows database development.

In the Standard Edition, you access and manipulate databases mainly through the **Data Control**. The data control lets you view and modify records in a database with no code at all. With only a little code you can let your users add and delete information.

Building Visual Basic Databases

What is slightly harder in Visual Basic is to build databases from scratch. You can create your own database using an add-on program supplied with Visual Basic called **Data Manager**. This does have limitations and is not very easy to use. The Standard Edition of Visual Basic won't let you define or amend the structure of a database from within your code. You can only do that at design-time. This means you couldn't have an option in your program to add new fields to the database should you need them. You can only do this by stopping the program and redefining the database at design-time.

The best way to build databases is to use either Access itself, or the Professional Edition of Visual Basic. You can, however, still do a hell of a lot with the Standard Edition as it stands.

How This Chapter is Organized

We're going to cover things seemingly back to front here, but there is method in my madness. First, we're going to look at how to build a program that works with an already completed database. After that I'll show you how to create a database of your own. At the start of the chapter I said that unless you know what it is you want to get out of the database, it's a bad idea to rush into designing it. In real life the kinds of reports and queries that your users will want to produce determine the underlying structure of tables and records you end up with.

Using the Data Control

The data control is one of the most powerful controls in the Standard Edition of Visual Basic. With it you can create an application to browse records in a database with absolutely no code. The data control goes beyond this. Through its properties and methods you have complete access to the facilities of the underlying Jet database engine. This allows you to write code to search for individual records, to add new records and delete existing ones.

The Data Control Itself

On its own, the data control is pretty useless. On the screen it looks like this:

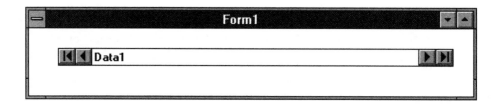

It provides you with a set of buttons looking very much like a VCR. These buttons move through the records in your database, but the data control itself provides no way of actually viewing the data in the current record. What the data control provides is the glue that connects the database itself to other controls on the form that you can use to display the data you want.

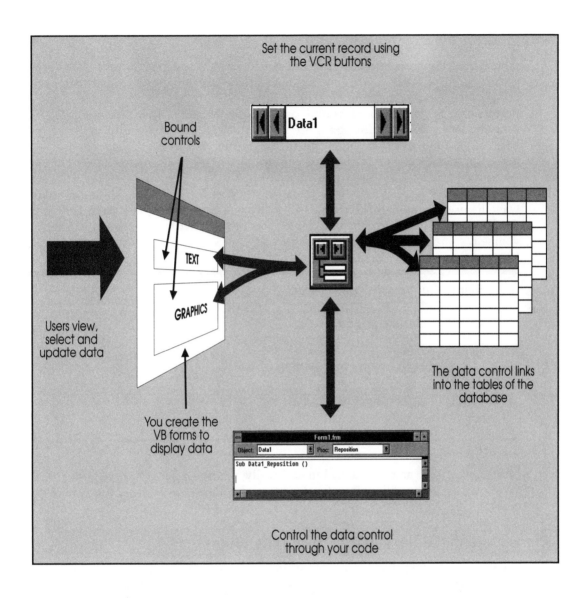

Set the current record using
the VCR buttons

Bound
controls

Users view,
select and
update data

You create the
VB forms to
display data

The data control links
into the tables of the
database

Control the data control
through your code

The VCR button control is great, but it has limited capabilities. To do anything really useful with the data control, you'll have to write some code for some of its events. Also, you'll probably have to write some code to display the information you want, as not all controls have the ability to **see** data from a database. This ability is only possessed by **bound** controls.

Bound Controls

Bound controls are controls which can be **linked** at design-time to a data control, and be made to display the data in the current record. All these complicated terms can be more than a little daunting at first, but don't panic - you've already used bound controls! Text boxes, check boxes, image controls, labels and picture boxes are all bound controls. They're all able to take information from certain fields in the current record of the current database, and display that data on a form.

Bound controls have the code to make this connection built into them. If you want to use a non-bound control, like a list box, to display data from a database, which is perfectly reasonable, you have to write the code to do it yourself.

Bound Controls in Visual Basic 3
Labels
Images
Text Boxes
Check Boxes
Picture Boxes

The controls that aren't bound, but are really worth knowing how to bind with your own code, are all types of list and combo boxes, as well as the grid control.

Connecting the Data Control to a Data Source

On the sample disk included with Visual Basic is a Microsoft Access database called **BIBLIO.MDB**. The **.MDB** extension is standard for all Access databases. Before you can start to display information and use the data control to walk through the records in a database, you need to connect it to the database in question. This is as simple as placing the name of the database in the data control's DatabaseName property.

Try It Out - Connecting to a Database

1 Start a new project in Visual Basic. Draw a data control on the form so that it looks like this.

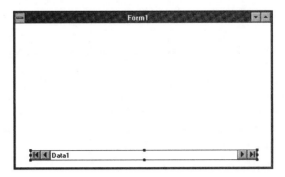

2 Bring up the properties window of the data control by pressing *F4*. When the properties window appears, find the DatabaseName property and double-click it.

3 A dialog box appears. Use the dialog box to find the **BIBLIO.MDB** database. This will have been installed in the directory for examples from Chapter 9 of the book. When you have found the database, double-click it to select it.

You must make sure that the pathname in the DatabaseName property is right. All the programs in this chapter assume that **BIBLIO.MDB** is in the Chapter 9 directory. If your pathname is different, then make sure you change the DatabaseName property in each of the projects.

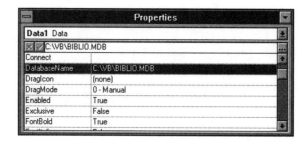

By selecting a database and putting its name and path into the DatabaseName property you are actually telling Visual Basic which database to use for this data control. Each data control on your application can connect to one database only. Obviously if you have three data controls on a form you can connect to three databases at once. In all the examples you will see here though, we only ever connect to one database at a time.

At the moment not much has happened to our form. The next step is to select a table from the database whose records we want to look at. This involves setting the RecordSource property of the data control.

Choosing Tables From the Database

We saw in our introduction how a database can be made up of different tables. The tables correspond to the drawers in our filing cabinet. When deciding which tables you need, think about what information you want to display. In this project, we want to produce a single form that shows the details about an individual book title.

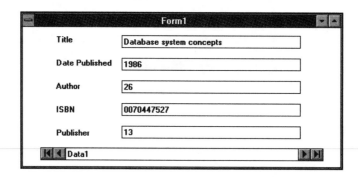

So that's where we're going. Now, how do we get there?

Try It Out - Selecting Tables From the Database

1 In the data control properties window, find the RecordSource property.

2 If you double-click on the RecordSource property itself you can cycle
through each of the tables in the database. Alternatively you can click
on the down arrow to the right of the property to drop down a list of
options.

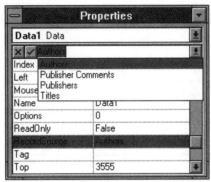

3 Select the Titles table.

That's all there is to it. You have now selected a database and a table from
that database. The next stage is to start using the bound controls to actually
view the data in the table.

Using Bound Controls

The check box, image, label, picture box and text box controls are all data-
aware. This means they can be linked to a data control, and display data from
the control automatically.

Having drawn a data control onto a form, connected it to a database and
selected a RecordSource, the bound controls can be linked to the data control
via their DataSource property, and to a specific field from the data control with
the DataField property. Let's add some more controls to our form to see how
this all works.

Try It Out - Binding Controls to the Data Control

There are five fields in the Titles table in the **BIBLIO.MDB** database. We'll draw text boxes and labels on the form to allow us to see the contents of these fields. By the end of the example you'll be able to move through all the records in the Titles table, still without any code at all.

1   Draw five labels onto the form and set their caption properties so that the form now looks like this:

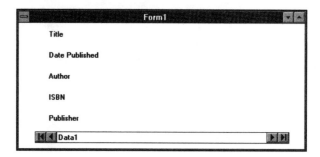

2   Draw the five text boxes that will actually hold the data from the database onto the form to the right of the labels.

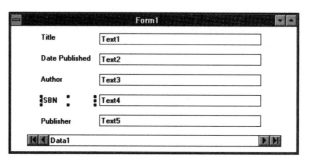

3   Clear the text property of all the text boxes. The easiest way to do this is to click on one of the text boxes, then click on the others while holding down the *Ctrl* key. All the text boxes will highlight.

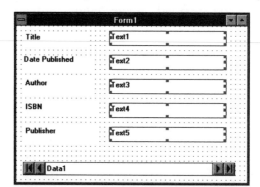

4 Now press *F4* to bring up the properties window. When it appears find the Text property and clear whatever is in it. As soon as you press *Enter*, the text in all the text boxes will vanish.

5 With the text boxes still selected, and the properties window still visible, find the DataSource property. Double-click the property and the name of the data control on the form will appear at the top of the properties window. Although the word Data1 doesn't appear alongside the DataSource property, you have now bound all the text boxes to the data control.

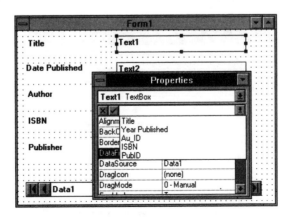

6 Click anywhere on the form to deselect all the text boxes. Select each text box in turn, and with the properties window set the DataField property to the values shown below. Again, you can double-click this property to cycle through the available fields, or use the drop-down settings box.

Set the DataField property for each of the Text boxes to the following fields:

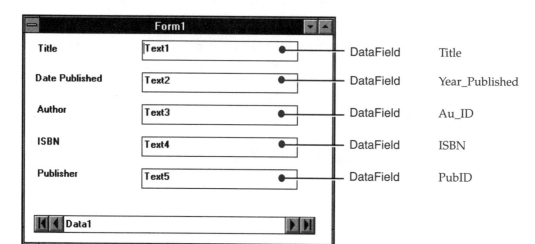

The field names we've used here have all been set up when **BIBLIO.MDB** was created.

This project is on the companion disk and is called **BIB_VIEW.MAK**.

How It Works

You have now bound all the text boxes to the data control, and using the DataField property you have told Visual Basic which fields to display in which text boxes. Try running the program now.

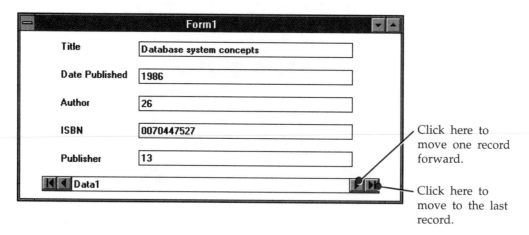

Click here to move one record forward.

Click here to move to the last record.

By just setting properties on the data control and the text boxes you now have a complete database application. You can move through the records of the table by clicking on the data control arrows. You can even change the records displayed just by clicking in the text boxes and then typing in the new information.

When you've typed what you want in, click on the data control icons again to move to a new record. Visual Basic automatically writes the changed records to the database. From now on, every time you run the program, or look at the Titles table with any other database browser, the changes you made will be there for all to see.

You can also bind labels to the database to display the contents of a field. This is great for displaying fields on the screen which you don't want the user to be able to change. In this example though, we'll use text boxes to display the data and let the user change it. Labels can be very useful for displaying read-only information from a database - information which you don't want your users to change. Just because the control in question is a label control, don't expect the label to display the field names; it will only ever display the contents of a field, the same as any bound control.

Once you bind controls to a database you are no longer dealing with those controls in the traditional way. Normally, if you make a change to the contents of a text box it doesn't matter unless you have code which stores that value somewhere. If you make changes to a bound control though, you are directly changing the data in the database.

Taking Data From Multiple Tables

So far you have seen how to use bound controls to display information from just one table. The Access database is a relational database and lets you take information from more than one table as easily as from one.

Relational databases reduce the actual information in a database by relating tables to each other. Take the Titles table from the above example. Titles has an Au_Id field and a PubID field, both of which contain numbers. It could hold data on many books written by the same author, or many books published by the same publisher. As a user of the program you wouldn't want to have to key in the author and publisher over again each time you add a new title.

Instead the full author and publisher names are held in separate tables, and each is given a unique number. These numbers are stored in the Titles table to **relate** the records in that table to the author and publisher tables.

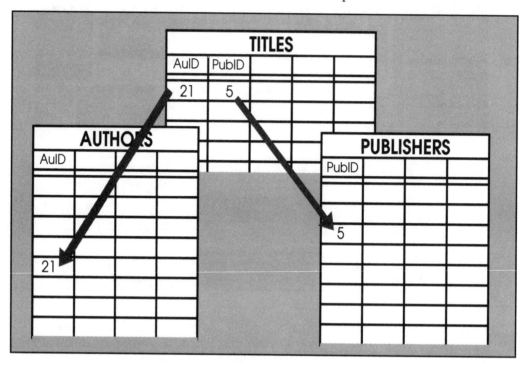

You can actually tell the data control to take these links into account when you use it. For example in the previous **Try It Out**, what would be really nice is to display the publisher's name and the author's name from the Publisher and Author tables. You can do this using the **Select** command.

Selecting From Multiple Tables

With **Select** you tell the data control which fields you want to display and from which tables these fields come. In our case, we'd use it like this:

```
Select [title], [Year Published], [ISBN], [Author], [Name] from Titles,
Authors, Publishers
```

This is actually the shorthand way of doing it. All the above field names are unique. For instance you can't find an **ISBN** field in the Publishers table. If that wasn't the case we'd have to specify the tables and the fields together like this:

```
Select Titles.[Title], Titles.[Year Published], Titles.[ISBN],
Authors.[Author], Publishers.[Name] from Titles, Authors, Publishers
```

This way there's no doubt as to where each field comes from. Each field is prefixed by the actual table name in the same way you'd prefix a property name with the name of its control. Notice also how the field names are enclosed in square brackets.

Even now, Visual Basic has no way of knowing how to relate records in the **Authors** table to records in the **Titles** table for example. To do this we need to add a **Where** command to the end of the **Select** statement, like this:

```
Select Titles.[Title], Titles.[Year Published], Titles.[ISBN],
↳Authors.[Author], Publishers.[Name] from Titles, Authors, Publishers
↳Where Authors.[Au_Id] = Titles.[Au_Id] and Publishers.[PubID] =
↳Titles.[PubId]
```

In this case the **Where** clause tells Visual Basic to pull values from the **Publishers** and **Authors** tables where the **Au_Id** in the **Titles** and **Authors** tables match, and where the **PubId** field in the **Publishers** table matches that field in the **Titles** table.

Unlike other commands in Visual Basic the **Select** command can only be used in the **RecordSource** property of the **DataControl** (it isn't something you can type direct into the code window). Let's try it out, and add a bit of polish to the previous example.

Try It Out - Selecting Information From Related Tables

1 Load up the **BIB_VIEW.MAK** project. This is the same code you entered in the previous **Try It Out**.

2 Bring up the window with the bound controls on it, and select the Data control by clicking it once. Display the properties window for the Data control and find the RecordSource property.

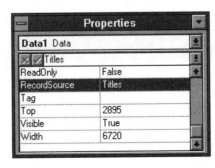

3 Type this **Select** statement into the RecordSource property. There's a lot of it so be very careful. Visual Basic doesn't check what you key into the RecordSource property until you run the program, unlike the code you might key into a code window.

```
Select  Titles.[Title],  Titles.[Year  Published],  Titles.[ISBN],
↳Authors.[Author], Publishers.[Name] from Titles, Authors, Publishers
↳Where Authors.[Au_Id] = Titles.[Au_Id] and Publishers.[PubID] =
↳Titles.[PubId]
```

4 Press *Enter* after keying in the new RecordSource to accept it.

5 Select the text box set up to display the publisher information. Again, bring up its properties window. Set the DataField property for this text box to Publishers.[Name] and press *Enter*.

6 Find the textbox you're using to display the author. Change its DataField property to Authors.[Author] and press *Enter*.

7 Run the program now. Instead of meaningless ID numbers for the author and publisher, you now see both their full names.

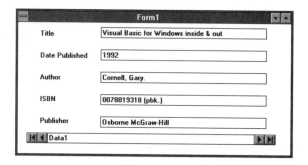

Select is actually a statement from SQL (Structured Query Language). We'll look at this again in Chapter 13.

Programming the Data Control

The Data control is very good at taking control of things on its own as they happen, such as writing updates out to the original database when it thinks they should be done. However, to many companies their databases are one of their most valuable assets. For this reason it's sometimes necessary to take control yourself to prevent the Data control from doing things of its own accord, or to simply keep a record of what goes on.

The Validate Event

The most useful event available to monitor the activity of the data control is the **Validate** event. As far as events go, **Validate** is a very flexible tool. Everything that happens to the data control, and more importantly the data it provides access to, can be caught, monitored and even canceled through the **Validate** event. In fact, you can even use the **Validate** event to tell the data control to do something totally different to what it was originally hoping to do. Before we start to look at some code you need to know a little more about how bound controls work.

How Bound Controls Work

Database information is held in three places while your program is running:

▶ The data you see on screen in the bound control is held in a part of memory specifically reserved for this purpose. Once a bound control has pulled data from the database, it stores its own copy of this information somewhere in memory.

▶ The database itself has a copy buffer in memory. This is where information that has just been read from, or is about to be written back to the database is held. As you change information in the bound controls, Visual Basic copies the new data from the control to the copy buffer.

▶ Then when all the changes have been made the **Update** method updates the actual database record with information from the copy buffer.

The **Validate** event is the last stop for everything that affects the data control. Everything you can do to the records in a data control triggers the **Validate** event: moving to a new record, moving to the first or last records, writing a record to the database and so on. You can use the **Action** parameter that is passed to the **Validate** event to find out exactly what is about to happen; the **Validate** event always occurs before something happens, not after it. This makes the **Validate** event the ideal place to catch changes to the data and prevent them from happening.

One of the most common uses of the data control **Validate** event is to catch the times when the data control is about to move information from the copy buffer to the data buffer. If you don't want the update to take place, or you only want part of the data to move from the copy buffer to the data buffer, then you can use code in the **Validate** event to handle it.

Using the Validate Event to Prevent Changes to Data

Let's add some code to the **Validate** event so that updates to the **Titles** table can't take place under any circumstances.

Try It Out - Coding the Validate Event

1 If you don't still have the last project open, then find it on the companion disk under the name **BIB_VIEW.MAK**, and open it up.

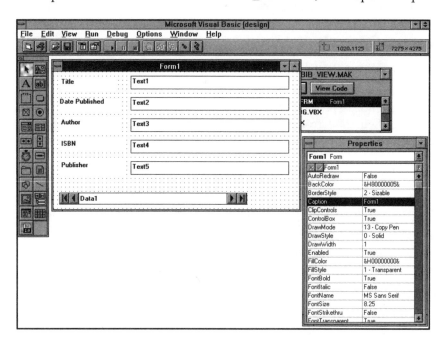

2 Double-click on the Data control to bring up its code window, with the **Validate** event ready to go.

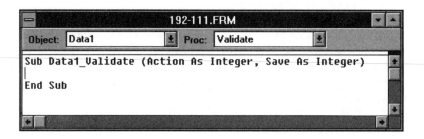

3   Type in code so that the event looks like this:

```
Sub Data1_Validate (Action As Integer, Save As Integer)

    If Save = True Then
        MsgBox "You cannot edit data in this database." & Chr$(10) &
  "Changes have been abandoned"
        Save = False
    End If

End Sub
```

4   Try running the program now and changing the data you see on screen.

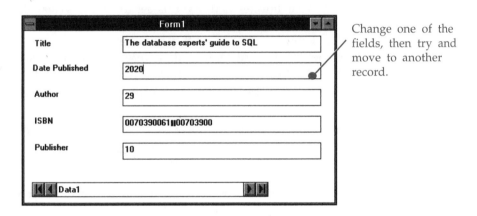

Change one of the
fields, then try and
move to another
record.

5   As soon as you try to move to a different record, a message box
appears and the information you changed is reset to its previous value.

How It Works

The **Validate** event gets two parameters which we can use at run-time to check what's going on.

```
Sub Data1_Validate (Action As Integer, Save As Integer)
```

Here, the **Save** parameter is the most important of the two. **Save** is actually a logical value, either **True** or **False**. It does nothing to your event code, but has an effect when the event exits. **Save** tells your code whether or not any of the information in the bound controls has been changed since it was loaded in. The results of **Save** being either **True** or **False** are:

> ▶ If the **Validate** event finishes and **Save** is set to **True**, Visual Basic automatically fires off the **Edit** method to tell the database that it is going to change some information. After this, Visual Basic runs the **UpdateRecord** method to write information from the bound controls to the copy buffer, and then finally out to the current record of the database. We'll look at these two methods in a little while, for now just take my word for it.

> ▶ If the **Validate** event finishes and **Save** is set to **False**, then the changes made to the bound controls on screen are lost forever and aren't copied back into the database table itself.

You saw two new methods there; the **Edit** method and the **UpdateRecord** method. Before you can make changes to the records in a table you must use the **Edit** method to **lock** the record and prevent other users from making changes at the same time. The **Validate** event will do this automatically for you if the bound controls have been changed on screen and you attempt to move to a new record.

The **UpdateRecord** method does just what it says. After the **Edit** method has been used, the **UpdateRecord** method copies the contents of all the bound controls relating to this data control back into the database. We'll look at the **Edit** and **Update** methods in a lot more detail in a little while.

The **Action** parameter can be used to check exactly what is going to happen when the validate event finishes. The **Validate** event always occurs immediately before something happens, that something is held in the **Action** parameter.

The Action Parameter

In the **CONSTANT.TXT** file supplied with Visual Basic there are a set of constants defined which you can use in your code to check the **Action** parameter.

CONSTANT.TXT	Action to be Performed
DATA_ACTIONCANCEL	Cancels any operation that is about to happen.
DATA_ACTIONMOVEFIRST	The **MoveFirst** method was called.
DATA_ACTIONMOVEPREVIOUS	Moving to the previous record.
DATA_ACTIONMOVENEXT	Moving to the next record.
DATA_ACTIONMOVELAST	The **MoveLast** record was called.
DATA_ACTIONADDNEW	A new record is about to be added.
DATA_ACTIONUPDATE	The copy buffer (not the bound control) is about to be written to the database.
DATA_ACTIONDELETE	The current record is about to be deleted.
DATA_ACTIONFIND	The **Find** method was called to find a record.
DATA_ACTIONBOOKMARK	The **BookMark** property was set.
DATA_ACTIONCLOSE	The data control is about to disconnect from the database.
DATA_ACTIONUNLOAD	The form is about to **Unload**.

Many of these terms, such as **AddNew, MovePrevious, Bookmark**, will be unfamiliar to you. Don't panic just yet though, over the course of the next few sections all will be revealed.

You can check the **Action** parameter against any of these values to try to determine what's about to happen. To stop anything from happening just set the **Action** parameter to **DATA_ACTIONCANCEL**. For example, if the user has clicked the icon on the data control to move to the next record, you can stop them moving by setting **Action** to **0 (DATA_ACTIONCANCEL)** whenever the event occurs with **Action** set to **3 (DATA_ACTIONMOVENEXT)**.

Be careful though! Just because you're canceling the current action it doesn't mean that you'll cancel any updating of the records that may take place out of sight. If the **Save** property is **True** when the event finishes, the data in the bound controls will be written to the database, regardless of what you did to the **Action** parameter.

The Update Methods

Visual Basic provides you with three ways of updating information both in your tables and on screen, known as **Update** methods.

Update

The first and simplest is **Update** on its own. For example, if you directly change the value of fields in code to change the **Au_ID** field selected from a data control named **Data1**, you can write this change out to the database using the **Update** method.

```
Data1.Recordset.Fields(Au_ID) = 12
Data1.Recordset.Update
```

Beware though. To use **Update** you must first use **Edit** or **Add New**. The **Edit** method tells Visual Basic that we are about to make changes to the fields in a database, then **Update** tells it to actually save those changes.

```
Data1.Recordset.Edit
Data1.Recordset.Fields("Au_ID") = 12
Data1.Recordset.Fields("Title")  = "The Beginners Guide to Visual Basic"
Data1.Recordset.Update
```

Normally the data control does all this for you. If you change the values in a bound control, such as text box, at run-time, and then move to a new record,Visual Basic automatically does an **Edit**, changes the fields in the appropriate tables and then does an **Update**.

UpdateRecord

To do what the data control does yourself could require a lot of code. If you have a form with fifteen bound controls on it, to copy the contents of these controls to the fields one by one and then do an **Update** can take a lot of typing. The **UpdateRecord** method provides an easy way around this:

```
Data1.UpdateRecord
```

This does the **Edit** for you, copies the bound control contents to the database, then does an **Update** all in one swoop.

UpdateControls

The inverse of this is the **UpdateControls** method, which copies the data from the table to the bound controls. For example, if your users change data in the bound controls and then decide they want to cancel the operation, you can use **UpdateControls** to restore the values that were in the controls before the user confused the issue:

```
Data1.UpdateControls
```

We won't go into any more detail than that about the **Update** methods here. The **BUGTRAK.MAK** application in Chapter 13 - Putting It All Together, shows you how these methods can be used in a real world application.

Method	Description
Update	Used after an **Edit**, and after you change the fields in the data control by hand with code. **Update** saves the changes you make to the fields into the database permanently.
UpdateRecord	Stores the values of the bound controls into the underlying tables.
UpdateControls	Copies information from the fields selected with the data control, into the bound controls. Great for canceling changes that the user has made and restoring the bound controls to their initial value.

The Reposition Event

Sometimes you may want to do something to the display, or to the database, after a new record has been found. The **Validate** event is obviously useless for this, as it only occurs **before** something happens, not **after**.

The **Reposition** event on the other hand is much more useful. The **Reposition** event occurs whenever the data control moves to a new record. That's all there is to it really. As soon as the event occurs your new record is waiting in the data control, the bound controls have been updated and you are generally ready to play ball.

Creating Records

Databases would be pretty useless if you could only update the information they currently hold. You need to be able to create new records in order to let your databases grow to keep in tune with your business and personal needs. The **AddNew** method serves just this purpose. It allows you to create new records to your heart's content.

Each data control in your application has a **RecordSet** property. This is very different to the **RecordSource** property you set to tell the data control where to look for its information. The **RecordSet** property actually provides a way for you to get at the information in a record with your code.

The RecordSet Object

Earlier on we used the data control to select groups of records from single tables and multiple related tables. The **RecordSet** object, often called the **RecordSet** property of a data control, lets you access the selected records as if they were all in one table. It creates a temporary collection of the records you want for the time that your program is running.

For example, you may have a **Select** statement in a data control which pulls information from three tables. Rather than having to worry about all three tables in your code, you can deal with the **RecordSet** object instead, which brings the contents of all three tables together.

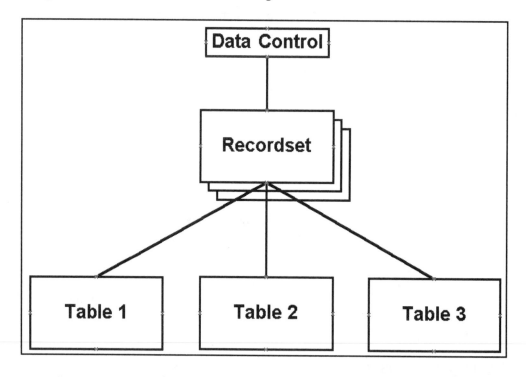

The RecordSet is also called a Dynaset. It's a table that exists only while the program is running, and which can consist of fields from a number of different tables. It's a dynamic set of records.

The `RecordSet` has a number of properties of its own. Two of the most useful are the `BOF` and `EOF` properties. These mark the beginning of the `RecordSet` (`BOF`) or end of the recordset (`EOF`). If both these properties are set to `True` then you are at the beginning and end of the `RecordSet` - the `RecordSet` is empty.

We'll take a look at these properties in more detail later, but for now, here's a quick run down of the most useful `RecordSet` properties.

Property	Description
BOF	`True` if you are at the beginning of the `RecordSet`, before the first record.
EOF	`True` if you are positioned after the end of the `RecordSet`.
BookMark	Reading this gives you the unique ID of the current record. Writing to this property jumps you immediately to the record with the same `BookMark` as the value you write.
LastModified	The `BookMark` of the last changed record.
LastUpdated	The `BookMark` of the last updated record.
NoMatch	Used when searching for records using the `Find` events you will see later. If this property is true then no match could be made, no record could be found.

Adding New Records

You can add new records with the `AddNew` method on the `RecordSet` object:

```
DataControl.RecordSet.AddNew
```

Once you see this format, you can understand why `RecordSet` is an object rather than a property. It can have properties of its own.

This line tells the database to find a space in the current table where it can add a new record. The database dutifully does this, clears out all the fields for you and blanks out all of your bound controls. You can then set about putting values into the fields of the table, either by editing the bound controls or the fields directly with code.

Once you have all the data you want in the new record you can call either the **UpdateRecord** event to copy the bound controls to the record, or the **Update** event to move the copy buffer to the record. If you do another **AddNew** then the current **AddNew** is canceled.

Try It Out - An Improved Database Viewer

On the companion disk there is an improved viewer that works with the Biblio database.

1 Load up the **BIBLIO.MAK** project to see how all this fits together.

```
┌─────────────────────────────────────────────────┐
│ ─           Updating with the data control      ▲▼│
├─────────────────────────────────────────────────┤
│                                                   │
│   Title           Database system concepts        │
│                                                   │
│   Year Published  1986                            │
│                                                   │
│   ISBN            0070447527                       │
│                                                   │
│   Author          Korth, Henry F.               ▼ │
│                                                   │
│   Publisher       McGraw-Hill                   ▼ │
│                                                   │
│   │◄│◄ Use the arrows to scroll through the titles in the database ►│►│ │
│                                                   │
│   Add new record      Delete Record     Cancel changes │
└─────────────────────────────────────────────────┘
```

As with the **Try It Outs** you have been working on, this program connects to the Biblio database. However, this one provides you with combo boxes for the author and publisher, instead of confusing numbers, and also lets you add and delete records.

2 In design mode double-click the **Add** command button to see its event code. When the Add button is clicked, the bound controls are all cleared out and a new record is added to the database using the **AddNew** method:

```
Sub cmdAdd_Click ()

    If miAdding Then Exit Sub
    sPreviousRecord = datTitles.Recordset.Bookmark
    datTitles.Recordset.AddNew
    miAdding = True

End Sub
```

The **miAdding** variable is a module level integer variable which is used to hold the details of the current operation. This is checked by the Cancel button to see whether we are currently adding a new record or not.

The code in the actual program is commented for more explanation.

3   Still in design mode double-click the Cancel button.

```
Sub cmdCancel_Click ()

    If miAdding Then
        miCancel = True
        datTitles.Recordset.Bookmark = sPreviousRecord
        miAdding = False
    Else
        datTitles.UpdateControls
    End If

End Sub
```

The Cancel button code checks the value of **miAdding** to see if we are currently adding a new record. If we are, then a second module level variable, **miCancel**, is set to True.

4   Take a look at the **Validate** code. When the **Validate** event occurs to save the information, it checks this variable and cancels the save operation if **miCancel** is **True**.

```
Sub datTitles_Validate (action As Integer, Save As Integer)

    If Save And miCancel Then Save = False

End Sub
```

When the **Validate** event kicks in it passes a parameter called **Save**. If this is set to **True** then it means that the data control is about to save information out to the database. We can reset this to **False** if necessary and stop the save taking place. That's exactly what happens here. If **Save** is **True** and **miCancel** is **True**, meaning that the data control wants to save the data but we don't, then **Save** is reset to **False**.

How It Works

Let's take a closer look at the Cancel button click event:

```
Sub cmdCancel_Click ()

    If miAdding Then
        miCancel = True
        datTitles.Recordset.Bookmark = sPreviousRecord
        miAdding = False
    Else
        datTitles.UpdateControls
    End If

End Sub
```

Bookmarks allow us to jump around the records in a data control very quickly. If the user cancels an **Add** record operation, then this line jumps back to the record that was on display before the user hit Add. We'll look at exactly what this all means a little later.

The **datTitles.UpdateControls** line updates the bound controls with the data from the current record. This means the controls are reset to their former values. In the case of **AddNew**, the previous record loaded before the first **AddNew** is relocated and its data is loaded in. If you're just editing data which is already on the screen, then it's reset.

The program uses combo boxes to display and enter publishers and authors by name, rather than by number. Combo boxes are not bound controls, so how does this work? Take a look at the form in design mode:

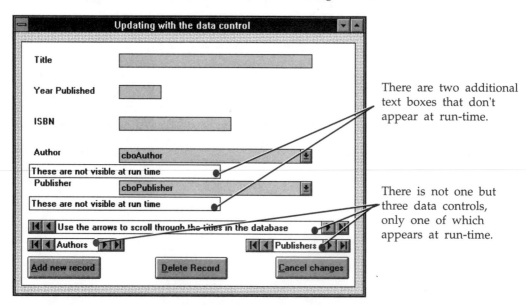

There are two additional text boxes that don't appear at run-time.

There is not one but three data controls, only one of which appears at run-time.

The two new data controls look up records in the publishers and authors tables, as the captions on them suggest. The two text boxes are bound to the Titles table, and hold the author and publisher ID records. There is code in the **Change** events of both these text boxes so that when a new record is loaded up, the full name of the author and publisher is displayed in the combo boxes.

```
Sub txtPublisher_Change ()

    Call Display_Publisher

End Sub
Sub txtAuthor_Change ()

    Call Display_Author

End Sub
```

The **Display_Author** and **Display_Publisher** routines take the values in the two text boxes, find a matching record in either the Publishers or Authors tables and display the full name.

The reverse happens if you select a name from either combo box. The **ItemData** property of each item in the list is used to store the ID of the record. So in the Authors combo box the **ItemData** property holds the **AuID** field of each author, and in the Publishers combo box, the **ItemData** property holds the **PubId** of each publisher.

When you select a new publisher or author from the list then these ID numbers are placed into their respective text boxes. Since the text boxes are bound, Visual Basic automatically handles copying them out to the underlying database.

We'll look at making non bound controls behave as though they are bound in some detail in Chapter 13 - Putting It All Together. Understanding how the combo boxes work right now is not crucial. If you have a mad craving to learn more then take a look at the code, and also the code in the **Form_Load** event which actually builds up the combo box lists.

Editing Records

You can edit records directly using bound controls by typing new values into these controls. However, you can also edit records through code using the **Edit** method. You can even obtain and change the value of fields in the data control through code, as you'll see shortly.

The **Edit** method works in exactly the same way as the **AddNew** method; you simply place the word **Edit** after the data control **RecordSet**:

```
Datacontrol.Recordset.Edit
```

Just like the **Addnew** method, if you do another **Edit** without saving the data using **UpdateRecord**, then the second **Edit** cancels the first. You need to be careful though, once you start an **Edit** or **Addnew** operation and actually change some fields you can't normally cancel the operation. Instead you have to catch when the data control tries to update the database and stop it there.

You saw how this is handled in **BIBLIO.MAK** where we changed the **Save** parameter in the **Validate** event to cancel the update.

Deleting Records

The **Delete** method can be used with a **DataControl** to delete the current record it points to. Just as with **AddNew** and **Edit**, the way you do this is fairly straightforward:

```
DataControl.Recordset.Delete
```

Load up the **BIBLIO.MAK** project again, if it isn't already loaded. In design mode, double-click the Delete command button to see its code:

```
Sub cmdDelete_Click ()

    Dim nResponse

    If miAdding Then
        cmdCancel_Click
    Else

        If datTitles.Recordset.EOF Or datTitles.Recordset.BOF Then Exit Sub

        nResponse = MsgBox("Do you really want to delete this record?",
    20, "Delete Record")
        If nResponse = 6 Then

            datTitles.Recordset.Delete
            datTitles.Recordset.MoveFirst

        End If

    End If

End Sub
```

Once you delete a record there is no going back. The message box line in the above code is a common way around this. It assumes that most humans can make mistakes and checks with the user that they really want to delete a record before going ahead and doing it. If the user clicks the Yes button (value 6, or **IDYes**) then the record is deleted.

When the user clicks on the Delete button we need to make sure that there is actually a record on screen they can delete. This is done by the following line:

```
If datTitles.Recordset.EOF Or DatTitles.Recordset.BOF Then Exit Sub
```

If the **BOF** property is true then that means that the data control is currently looking at the record in front of the very first one in a **RecordSet**. Think of the **RecordSet** as a book. All the interesting information is contained on the pages of the book, not on the front or back covers. **BOF** essentially tells you that the data control is looking at the cover of the book, rather than at a meaningful page of information within it.

EOF does a similar function, telling you when the data control has moved beyond the end of the **RecordSet**, in other words looking at the back cover of the book. If either of these properties are set there is currently no valid record; if the user tries to do a delete in either of these cases then an error will occur. If both **EOF** and **BOF** are true then that tells us that there are no records in the **RecordSet** at all.

In the code, if either of these properties are set then the subroutine is exited using **Exit Sub**, preventing the delete from taking place, and preventing embarrassing run-time errors from occurring.

Moving Around in the Database

Simply using the data control to display records from a table in the existing order is rather limiting. One of the real powers of database applications is their ability to find individual pieces of data for you quickly and easily. In order to do anything more sophisticated we need to first understand how the data control moves through the records.

In this section we look at the **Move** methods which the data control actually calls with its VCR buttons, as well as the **Find** methods which you can use to locate individual records.

In Chapter 13 - Putting it All Together, you'll see how the **BugTrak** application uses a third way of finding records called the **Select** statement to locate whole groups of records from a table.

Using the Move Methods

Visual Basic has four move methods to let you move around a table record by record regardless of its contents. These are:

Move Method	Action
MoveFirst	Moves to the first record in a table.
MoveLast	Moves to the last record in a table.
MoveNext	Moves to the next record in a table.
MovePrevious	Moves back one record, to the previous one.

The four methods all relate to the four icons you see on a data control when you draw it on a form.

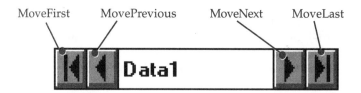

Try It Out - Moving Around the Database

1   Load up the **MOVE.MAK** project.

2 The program looks very similar to the one you built using the **Try It Outs**. However this time, in addition to the data control, there are four command buttons at the base of the form which allow you to move through the records using the **Move** methods.

3 Try running the program to get a feel for how it works.

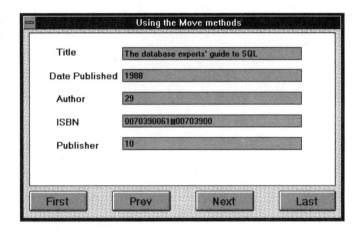

4 The **Visible** property of the data control is set to **False** so that while it appears in design mode, it isn't visible at run-time.

How It Works

Return to design mode and double-click the First command button to see the code:

```
sub cmdFirst_Click()

    datTitles.Recordset.MoveFirst

End Sub
```

This one line moves to the first record of the Titles table, using the invisible data control. The bound controls change as soon as the data control arrives at the new record.

Moving to Previous and Next Records

The Last command button works in a similar way to the First, but uses the **MoveLast** method instead of **MoveFirst**. The Prev and Next buttons are a little more complex.

There are only ever a finite number of records in a database. The **EOF** and **BOF** properties check whether or not the user has reached the beginning or end of the file:

```
Sub cmdNext_Click()

    if not datTitles.Recordset.EOF then datTitles.Recordset.MoveNext

End Sub

Sub cmdPrev_Click()

    if not datTitles.Recordset.BOF then datTitles.Recordset.MovePrev

End Sub
```

Bookmarks

Bookmarks, like a bookmark inserted into a book, allow you to locate a record very quickly indeed. Each record in the database has a unique bookmark which you can read and store in a string variable for later use. Setting the bookmark property of a data control actually jumps you to the record with the matching bookmark straight away.

Try It Out - Setting and Using Bookmarks

The **BIBLIO.MAK** project uses bookmarks to jump back to the previous record if you cancel an **AddNew** operation. Load up the project now to see how it works.

1   When the project has loaded, bring up the main form and press *F7* to display the code window. Using the Object: combo box to find the (general) section of the code, and display the declarations section:

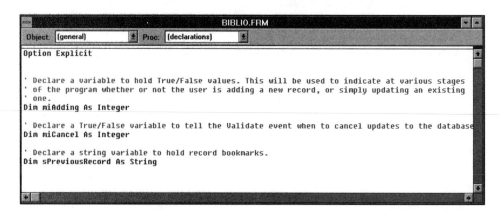

The **sPreviousRecord** is declared as a string. Bookmarks are string values so to store a bookmark in a variable you need to declare it as a string.

2   Press *F2* to bring up the procedures list, and select the **cmdAdd_Click** event:

```
Sub cmdAdd_Click ()

    If miAdding Then Exit Sub
    sPreviousRecord = datTitles.Recordset.Bookmark
    datTitles.Recordset.AddNew
    miAdding = True

End Sub
```

Before the **AddNew** is actually done the bookmark of the current record is copied into the **sPreviousRecord** variable. After the **AddNew** happens, the data control creates a blank record at the end of the table and moves there. It's helpful to know how to get back to where we were originally if everything goes wrong.

3   Take a look at the **cmdCancel_Click** code:

```
Sub cmdCancel_Click ()

    If miAdding Then

        miCancel = True
        datTitles.Recordset.Bookmark = sPreviousRecord
        miAdding = False

    Else

        datTitles.UpdateControls

    End If

End Sub
```

If we are currently adding a new record when the user hits Cancel (indicated by the **miAdding** variable) then we copy the bookmark we saved earlier back into the data control. This has the effect of jumping instantly to the record we were looking at before.

Many other applications use bookmarks as a way of allowing the user to set *bookmarks* of their own which they can jump to whenever they want. You may have a client table which the user is working on when the phone goes. You could allow the user to store the bookmark of the current record in order to return to it later.

Be careful! You can only store bookmarks in variables. There is little point in saving them in files or even in the database since they can change each time the database is used. You can only set a bookmark for as long as your data control is active.

Finding Records

The **Find** methods provide the most powerful and versatile way of locating records in your data. Let's explore these methods interactively - it's a much easier way to get a feel for how they work.

Try It Out - Finding Records

1   Start up the **MOVE.MAK** project again.

2   When the program is running press *Ctrl-Break* to pause it, then *Ctrl-B* to bring up the debug window. You can use the debug window to enter commands like we did in Chapter 8 - Graphics. In the debug window type this, and press *Enter*.

```
datTitles.Recordset.FindFirst "[Year Published] = 1989"
```

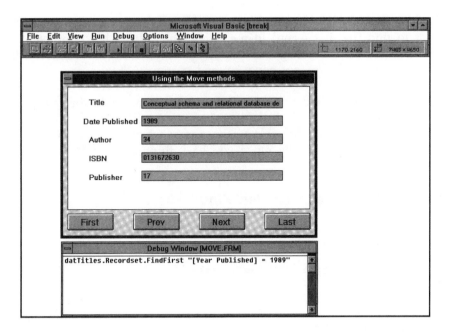

This finds the first record in the titles file where the year in which it was published is 1989. The syntax of all the **Find** commands is the same; after specifying which **Find** method you want to use, **FindFirst, FindNext, FindPrev**, or **FindLast**, you put the criteria that you want to match to inside quote marks.

How It Works

In the example above, the field we want to match is called **Year Published**. We'll look at how to find out what fieldnames are available to match later.

Since this field name actually contains a space I've put square brackets **[]** around the name. It's good practice to do this all the time to prevent confusion between field names and the values you are searching for.

Straight after the field name the phrase `=  1989` tells Visual Basic that we want to find the first record in the Titles table where the `Year   Published` field is equal to `1989`. You could equally well have put `>` for greater than, `<` for less than or `<>` for not equal to, and so on.

The `FindFirst` method finds the first matching record in the table, regardless of which record you were looking at before you did the find. You could have had the last record in the table up on screen when you did the find and Visual Basic would actually move you back through the table to the matching one.

Try It Out - More Ways to Use Find

1   In the debug window type in:

```
datTitles.RecordSet.FindNext "Title = 'Delia Smith'"
```

This attempts to find the next record in the table where the `Title` field `=` `'Delia  Smith'`. The text you are searching for is placed inside single quotes, then inside the double quotes.

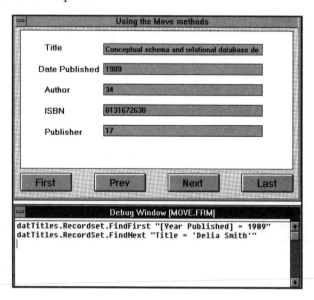

2   This time, when you press *Enter* nothing happens. The current record doesn't appear to change. Why? Type this in to find out:

```
? datTitles.RecordSet.NoMatch
```

```
Debug Window [MOVE.FRM]
datTitles.Recordset.FindFirst "[Year Published] = 1989"
datTitles.RecordSet.FindNext "Title = 'Delia Smith'"
? datTitles.RecordSet.NoMatch
-1
```

Visual Basic responds with a **-1**, the value for **True**. The **NoMatch** property is set to **True** whenever the **Find** method resulted in no match being found. You'll see how to use this in your code in the final chapter - Tying It All Together.

3 You can also use the **Find** methods with wildcards, and the words **And** and **Or** that you would use in a normal Visual Basic **If** command. Type this into the debug window:

```
datTitles.Recordset.MoveFirst
datTitles.Recordset.FindNext "Title like '*Design*' "
```

```
Using the Move methods

Title            Database design

Date Published   1977

Author           46

ISBN             007070130X

Publisher        13

   First        Prev        Next        Last

Debug Window [MOVE.FRM]
datTitles.Recordset.FindFirst "[Year Published] = 1989"
datTitles.RecordSet.FindNext "Title = 'Delia Smith'"
? datTitles.RecordSet.NoMatch
-1
datTitles.Recordset.MoveFirst
datTitles.Recordset.FindNext "Title like '*Design*' "
```

The first line moves you to the very first record in the table. The next line then finds the first record where the title field contains the word **Design**. The **like** keyword lets you find matches of string fields based on only a small amount of data. The ***** signs mean **anything**. So the **FindNext** line actually reads: **Find the next record where the title begins with anything, has design somewhere in it, and ends in anything.**

You can keep moving the cursor up to the **FindNext** line and pressing *Enter* and Visual Basic will step through all the records in the database that have the word **Design** in their title.

What you've learnt so far in this chapter covers the basics of using databases in Visual Basic. Chapter 13 - Putting It All Together, walks you through a complete database program called **BugTrak**, showing you how to pass records between data controls on different forms, and how to make the non bound controls like list boxes, combo boxes, and grids act as if they really are bound. Take a look at that chapter to see how the whole area of databases and Visual Basic comes together in the real world.

For now, we'll take a short look at how you can create your own database in Visual Basic.

Creating Your Own Database

Getting data out of and back into a database is fine, so long as you actually have a database to start with. How do you get one in the first place? In the true spirit of free enterprise, Microsoft heartily recommend that anyone serious about getting into databases and Visual Basic should invest in the full blown Access database product.

However, for those on a slightly smaller budget, and who don't need a fully featured database package, Visual Basic comes with a program called **Data Manager** which you can use to create, examine and modify databases.

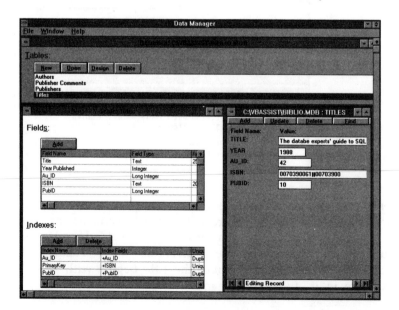

What is Data Manager?

So far we've used code to load new data into established database structures. What we haven't done is set up that original database structure itself. The Professional Edition of Visual Basic supports database methods that are not present in the Standard Edition to do just that. These additional methods can be used to create databases, tables in those databases, fields in those and indexes based on the fields. However, all is not lost for Standard Edition users.

Both versions of Visual Basic come with a stand-alone program called Data Manager that provides you with all the tools you need to:

▶ Create new Access format databases.

▶ Add tables, fields and indexes to those databases.

▶ Browse the data currently in the fields of a database.

▶ Add, update and delete information held in a database.

▶ Open and browse formats of databases other than Access.

Data Manager provides you with the bare essentials necessary to make yourself self-sufficient, without having to dig still deeper to buy the full blown Access package.

Let's see how Data Manager works, and the features it provides you with.

Try It Out - Using Data Manager

1   To run Data Manager, pull down the Window menu in Visual Basic and select Data Manager.

```
┌─────────────────────────────┐
│ Window   Help               │
├─────────────────────────────┤
│ Color Palette               │
│ Debug            Ctrl+B     │
│ Menu Design      Ctrl+M     │
│ Procedures       F2         │
│ Project                     │
│ Properties       F4         │
│ Toolbox                     │
├─────────────────────────────┤
│ Data Manager                │
└─────────────────────────────┘
```

459

2 After a short pause Data Manager will load up.

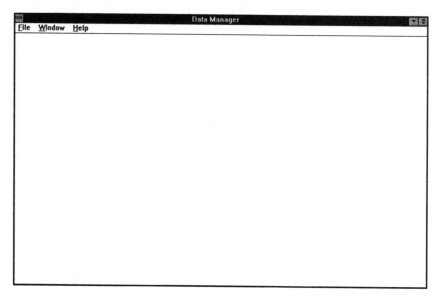

3 When Data Manager has loaded select File then Open. A list of available database formats will appear.

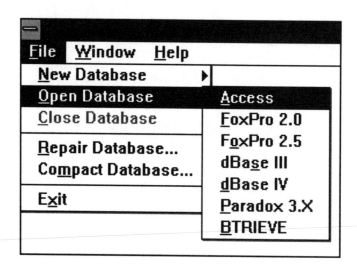

Unless you absolutely must connect to a Fox, Btrieve or any other exotic format of database, then leave those options well alone and stick to Access. If you start to use database formats other than Access then there is a fair amount of setting up work involved in getting Visual Basic to deal with them.

4   For the time being select Access. When the File dialog box opens up, find the **BIBLIO.MDB** database and click it.

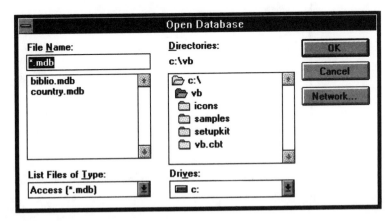

5   A list of all the tables in the database will appear.

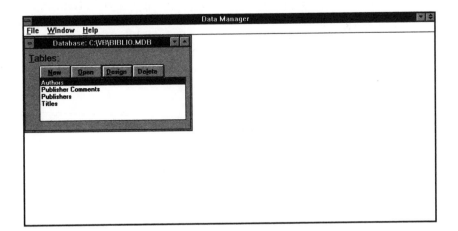

6 From here you can click on <u>D</u>esign to start designing the table's fields and indexes, click De<u>l</u>ete to delete a table, <u>O</u>pen to view the data in a table or <u>N</u>ew to create a new table. For now though, select the Titles table by clicking it once, then press the <u>D</u>esign button.

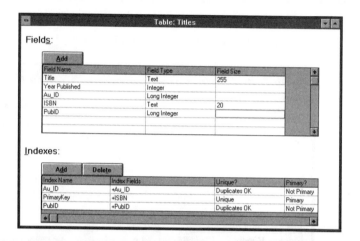

This is also another way to find out the names of the fields in a table.

This is the same form that you can use to actually add new fields and indexes to your own databases. You simply click on the <u>A</u>dd button at the top of the Field list to add a new field, or the A<u>d</u>d button at the top of the Index list to add a new index. Rather than mess up the Biblio database, let's create a simple database and table of our own.

Try It Out - Creating a Database

1 Close down all the Windows you might still have open in Data Manager, and start afresh.

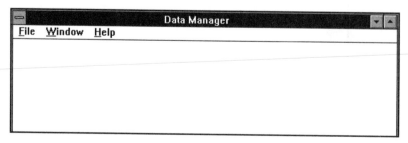

Try It Out!

2   From the File menu in Data Manager select New Database. Another menu will appear asking you if the database should be Access 1.0 or 1.1 format. Access 1.1 format is faster and is the one you should use, so select it.

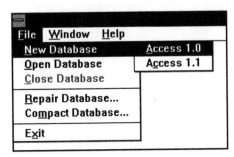

3   A file dialog will now appear asking you for a name for your new database. Use the dialog to select the directory where you want to store the database and type in Test as the name, then click OK.

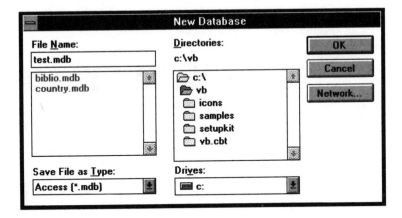

4   When the tables window appears, it will be blank. This is a new database after all and has no tables in it.

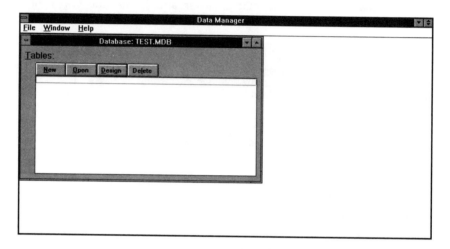

5   Click on the New button to create a new table. We're going to create a little table to hold phone numbers, so when the Table Name dialog appears, type in Phones for the table name.

6   The field and index editor will now pop up.

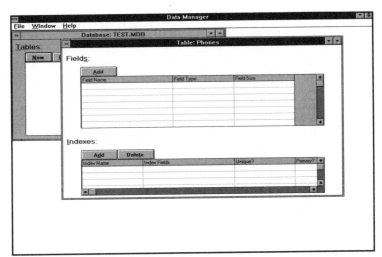

7   We're going to add two fields to the database: one for the person's name, the other for their phone number. Click on the Add button on top of the Fields list to add a new field. You'll now be asked to enter the field name, type and size. For the name enter Name, for the type use the combo box to select Text, and for the length enter 50, meaning that our Name field can hold a piece of text up to 50 characters long.

8   The Name field appears in the window.

Add		
Field Name	Field Type	Field Size
Name	Text	50

9 Do the same again, but this time create a field called Number which is a text field of only 20 characters long.

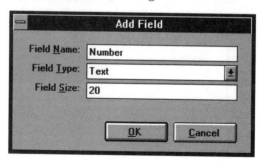

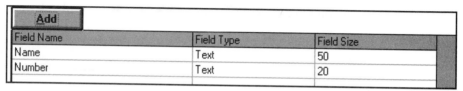

We have used simple text fields alone in this example. You can use fields of a number of different types, all of which are listed in the drop-down combo box attached to the Field Type in the Add Field dialog. For example using the binary field type you can place images in your database.

10 Now that we have all the fields entered, we need to create some indexes in order to be able to get at that data quickly and easily. In the Standard Edition you never actually use indexes in your code, but Visual Basic uses them itself to make searches quick and efficient. Click on the Add button on top of the Index list to add a new index.

You'll now be asked to enter an Index Name, call it Primary.

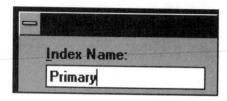

11 The Primary Index is the main index of a table; it can only contain unique values and will be the most common index that Visual Basic uses to get at your data. The most common way we'll want to get at our data is through a persons name, so select **Name** from the list of fields and then click the Add (asc) button to add it to the index.

12 Finally, click the Unique and Primary checkboxes at the bottom of the window to tell Visual Basic that we've now created a unique primary index.

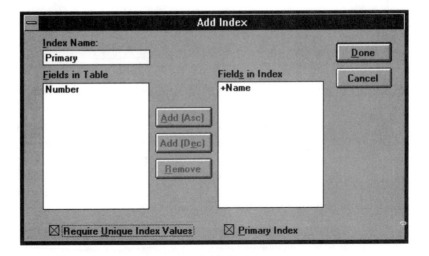

13 All that remains now is to click Done to save the Index to the database.

What we have now is an empty database structure. There are two ways to place data into it. One is to create a browsing tool like we did at the start of the chapter, and then enter each record as you move through the database. The other is to use Data Manager.

Try It Out - Adding Data Using Data Manager

1 Close the design window if it's still open by double-clicking on the control box in the top left, and return to the opening screen.

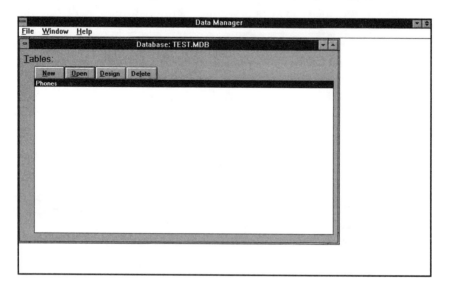

2 Click the Open button to display the table access window. This works like a ready made viewer of the type you created yourself in this chapter. Click the Add button to open a new record. All we do now is to enter the data into each record, which is then written to the database by using the data control buttons or the buttons at the top of the screen to move to the next record.

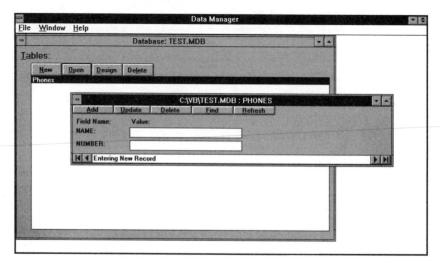

3 Go ahead and enter a few made up names in the database. After each record, press Update and then confirm that you want to commit the entry to the table.

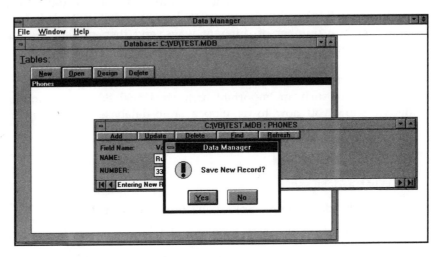

If you exit before committing a record, Data Manager does it for you automatically.

4 When you've finished inputting all the records you want, close the table access window and then select Close Database from the File menu. You now have a finished **TEXT.MBD** database.

Summary

A big part of Visual Basic's popularity rests on its ability to handle databases. The Standard Edition of Visual Basic does not have all the database power of the Professional Edition, but it is nonetheless an excellent tool. It can browse through data in a number of different ways, and then present the data easily to the user using bound controls.

We've covered a lot in this chapter, and introduced you to a few new concepts. As databases are such an important area for Visual Basic programmers I've decided to show you how to develop a large database application in Chapter 13 - Putting It All Together.

In this chapter we covered:

▶ What a database is

▶ How the data control links your program to a database

▶ How to set up the data control and bound controls interactively

▶ How to program the data control and its objects like **RecordSet**

▶ How to build your own databases using Data Manager

Message Boxes - Creating them

Chapter Ten

Buttons in the message box

Icon in the message box

○ OK only - (0)

○ OK and Cancel - (1)

○ Abort, Retry and Ign

○ Yes, No and Cancel

○ Yes and No - (4)

○ Retry and Cancel - (5)

Writing Programs that Work

Wrox waz ere!

Wow - a working message box.

48)

OK

Debug Window [MSGBOX.FRM]

```
conCode = 48
---------------------------------
nt mnButtonCode

GO_Click
---------------------------------
Button Click Event
uttonCode = 0
conCode = 16
---------------------------------
```

he code!

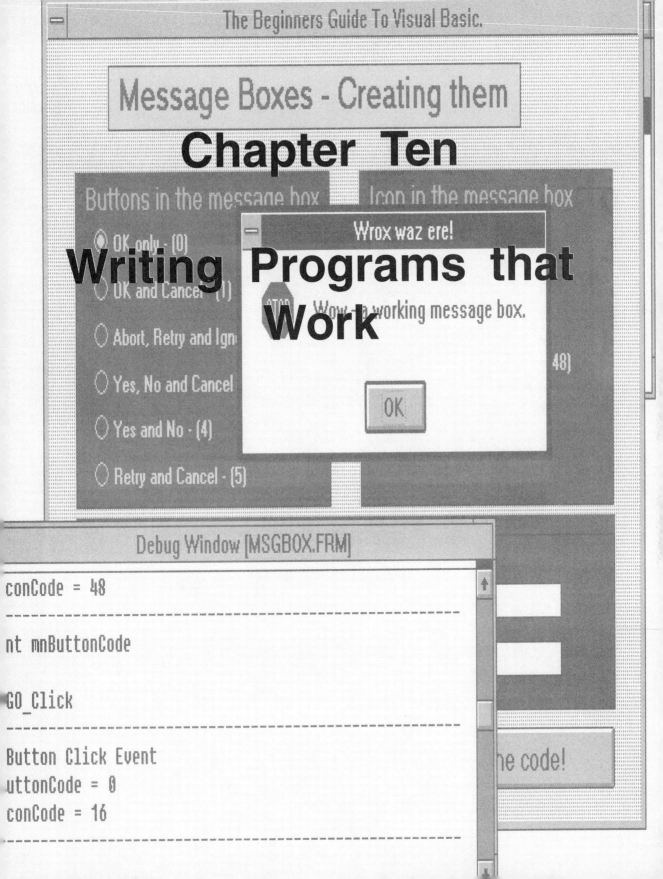

Writing Programs That Work

This chapter is about the reality of programming in an unpredictable world. So far we've made some unsustainable assumptions about Visual Basic programming: you will never make mistakes in your code, users behave impeccably, you have all the time in the world. It's time to get out of the play-pen and see what we can do to increase our chances of actually getting working programs out in time in real life.

This chapter covers:

- How to organize your code into small *re-usable* blocks of code to reduce the chance of errors and increase your efficiency

- How to write maintenance-friendly code (code that is easy to change when you come back to it later)

- How to handle events that you didn't really expect at run-time without crashing your program

- How to debug programs that don't work

Writing Programs That Work

To write code that works, you have to first have a good plan. Then you have to write your code in such a way that the errors are minimized and easy to find. Then you have to be able to find them and remove them, or else be prepared to deal with them at run-time.

Designing Safe Programs

I have already said that the bigger the program becomes, the more likely it is that you will introduce bugs into it. Think about this - if you write a three-line program that takes a number from the user, checks to see that it is a number and then displays the number on screen, it should be pretty easy to test it. You could even go so far as to tell the users that the system is totally bug free - it's only got three lines of code so that's not too difficult to do.

Now think about this - you have just spent the past 9 hours sitting at a keyboard and typed in roughly 900 lines of code. The code takes a number from the user, checks a database to find a match, loads up some records to do some calculations, multiplies the original number by the number of records you have found, adds in your age in minutes and displays the number on screen whilst playing the Star Spangled Banner! Easy to guarantee no bugs in that little lot? No, not really!

You could test it by running it over and over and over again. You could hand it to other people to test, who, like you, would run it for days and days and still find no problems. Then the fateful day comes - you give the system to a paying customer who inadvertently enters a decimal number where everyone else had assumed that whole numbers would be used. Result, the program crashes in a heap and you have one very upset customer on your hands - and no pay check.

So where did we go wrong? If you can guarantee that 3 lines of code will work with no problems, why not 6, 12, 24, 58 or even 900? The reason for this is something called **cohesion**. The first example has 3 lines of code and performs one specific function: it checks a number to see if it is OK, displaying it if the check went without a hitch. The second example performs a number of totally different functions: it gets a number, finds some records, does some sums, and plays music.

The first routine has very strong cohesion. It is a very small program consisting of one routine that performs one and only one function. The second example has very weak cohesion. The whole program is dependent on the operation of a single part. Imagine if your whole house was on one electrical circuit, with a single fuse for all the outlets. Every time one outlet blew, the whole place would go down. Instead, each area has its own circuit. When a single circuit goes down, not only can the rest of the house carry on, but the repair man only has to check a small number of outlets to find the fault.

To increase your chances of success, it's better to write programs that consist of smaller blocks of code, each of which has strong cohesion. Each small block of your program should do just one thing, and do it well. If the 900-line program had been written so that it consisted of eighteen 50-line routines, then it would be much easier. You could check and debug each of the eighteen routines rather than the one big program!

Visual Basic programs can be broken down into separate modules called procedures and functions to achieve this.

Designing Efficient Programs

Using modules to create libraries of useful routines has great benefits in terms of programming efficiency as well as safety. Placing code that you use repeatedly into separate modules can ultimately save you hours of typing and design. This operates both within a single project, and across all the projects you work on.

If, for example, you have a very data intensive application that has a lot of fields in which the user has to type in information, you may want to verify the input to each field as it is entered. It makes sense to place a routine that verifies this input into a single central routine, rather than rewriting it over and over again in the event handler for each individual control.

Once you have written this input verification routine, you could then attach it to other projects that require input checking, without writing it over again.

Planning for the Unpredictable

No matter how well you design and structure your program, things will happen that you didn't expect, or that happen so rarely that you can't consider them a normal event for your program to deal with. As football coaches love to say, "It's all out there waiting to go wrong". Users press infeasible key combinations, disk drives crash for no reason (try putting a disk in - it helps...), networks go down mysteriously. The list of possibilities is endless. The only thing you know for sure is that it's your fault when your program crashes, even if the file-server got hit by a meteorite in mid-flow.

Therefore it's a good idea to build in some code that makes an attempt to deal with unforeseen events. Visual Basic provides some help by giving you the chance to deal with run-time errors in your own way, rather than just throwing up its hands immediately and crashing your program.

Making Your Code Work

"Its a bug in the system, sorry ...... the computer's are down, we can't find your records until Monday ..... no, no - its a computer fault, can't be helped, we'll fix it as soon as we can!" Sound familiar? They are all common excuses that everyone comes up against when dealing with companies that use computers. Banks overcharging blame computer errors, mail order companies blame the computer when your order goes astray, employers blame payroll systems when excess tax is deducted, or too little is deducted and the tax man finds out.

There are very rarely any true **computer errors**. Computers always do exactly as they are told. If, in an invoicing system, you tell the computer that the total amount your customers should pay is the bill **minus** sales tax, it's not the computer that gets it wrong, it's you! So, how can we cut the bugs (as they are known) out of the applications we write?

The answer to this question is that you can't. The more controls you add to your Visual Basic applications, and the more code you write to respond to events, the higher the likelihood that you have written bugs into your system. You can be sure that these bugs will do their best to remain hidden until:

- You need the program to do something urgently.

- You demonstrate the program to someone who may want to buy it.

- You let someone else use it.

However, the tricks and tips you will come across can never guarantee that you will never send a system out with bugs. Debugging and structured programming aren't safety nets for programmers, they are damage limitation techniques. If you are an employed programmer then think yourself lucky that you are in one of the few professions where you **can** make mistakes and get away with it. Thankfully, the same isn't true about doctors. Do it too often though and your employers will soon start to think again about your pay check!

Putting Code in Modules

Ultimately, the best way to reduce bugs in a system is to design it properly. However, this is a book on programming. All programmers, including me, detest writing thousands of flowcharts and reams of text explaining what a system should do, preferring instead to get stuck in and write the system. So what we will concentrate on here is how to reduce the bugs and write **nice** code, rather than how to design the perfect system - there are some excellent books on system design. For the time being leave the analysis to the analysts, and the fun to us!

Breaking code into modules has two benefits:

◆ Readability and discipline. In Chapter 3 - Writing Code, you learnt how to create small subprocedures that could be used to perform specific jobs in response to certain conditions.

```
If nChoice = 1 Then
     DoThis
Else
     DoThat
EndIf
```

In this example, **DoThis** and **DoThat** are subprocedures that are called when **nChoice** is the right value. This is called **structured programming**, and makes your code easy to follow and to control.

◆ By placing code inside modules you can build up libraries of useful routines. In the introduction to this chapter, we discussed a global input validation module. When the time comes to do some validation in a new project, simply include the validation module in your new project and save re-inventing the wheel. Ultimately, this strategy reduces bugs, since you know that the previously tested code in the global module is bug free, and you spend less time typing away introducing new bugs.

Let's remind ourselves how to create a useful procedure.

Try It Out - Creating a Procedure to Center a Form

To see how modules are created and used, let's create a routine in a module which centers forms on the screen.

1 Load up Visual Basic and start a new project.

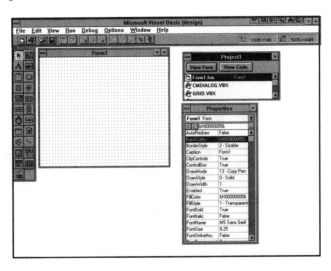

2   Select the New Module item on the File menu.

Alternatively click on the new module icon on the toolbar.

New module icon

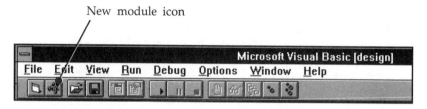

3   A code window will appear looking like this:

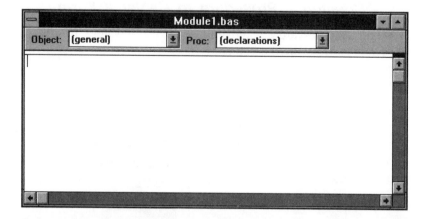

Visual Basic automatically names the module Module1.bas, in the same way that forms are automatically numbered Form1 and so on. There is no form attached to the module - modules consist of nothing but code.

4 Let's put some code into the module. Type this into the code window, exactly as shown.

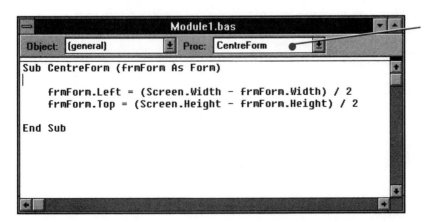

Visual Basic reads your procedure name and puts it in the window.

This procedure, called **CentreForm,** can now be used like a built-in Visual Basic method. You can use it from any event code, or any other subroutine or function anywhere else in the current project. Let's try calling our new procedure from the **Form_Load** event, so our form starts off in the middle of the screen.

5 First of all we need to get to the **Form_Load** event for our main form. Try looking at the Object: list in the code window.

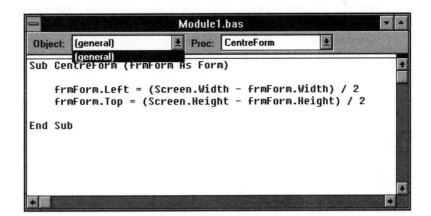

6 Not even the main form is shown. That's because we are in a different module.

7 Double-click on your form, which is probably behind the Module1.bas code window, to bring up the code window for the main form.

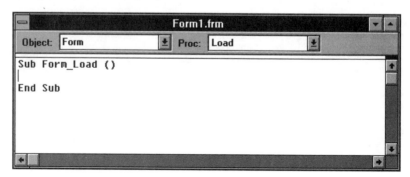

8 We'll enter some code now that uses the procedure in the module we just created. Type in this code:

```
Sub Form_Load ()

    CentreForm Form1

End Sub
```

9 Now, run the program. The form will load up centered in the middle of the screen.

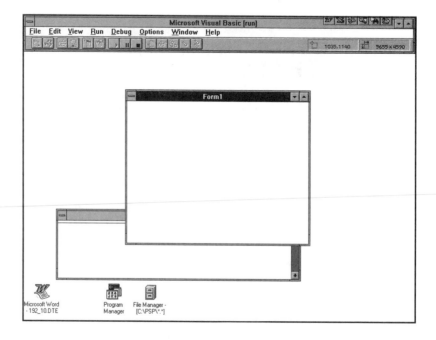

10 To view the code in Module1.bas again, stop the program.

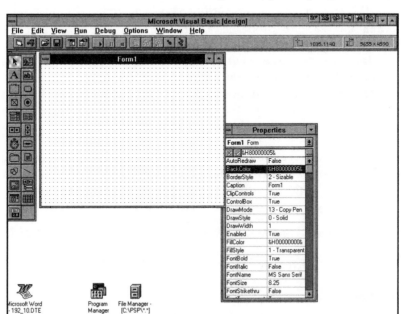

11 Bring up the project window by selecting Project from the Window menu.

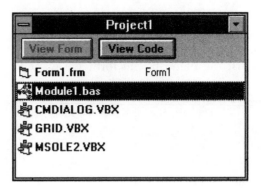

12 Select Module1.bas and click the View Code button. Up comes the code for Module1.bas.

How It Works

The functional part of the procedure **CentreForm** is straightforward. We used the **Width** and **Height** properties of the **Screen** object to center a form before. However, when we used this technique before, the code was contained within **frmForm** itself. Therefore, all the properties of that form, **Left**, **Right**, **Width** and **Height** were readily available. This time, the code is floating about in its own module, with no connection to the main form. In order for it to be able to work, we have to pass the form, along with all its properties, to the procedure to let it do its work.

The first line of **CentreForm** tells Visual Basic that this is a **Sub**procedure called **CentreForm**, and then **declares** to Visual Basic that it will place the form that needs to be centered into an object variable called **frmForm**.

```
Sub CentreForm (frmForm As Form)
frmForm.Left = (Screen.Width - frmForm.Width) / 2
```

The **As Form** part of the declaration notifies Visual Basic that this is the form type of **object variable**. The object **frmForm** is known as the **parameter** for **CentreForm**.

Having set up **CentreForm** to accept a form as its parameter, we have to name the form we want to send to it in our calling program. Here, we send our main form, **Form1**, to be centered:

```
CentreForm Form1
```

Although we chose to name the form **frmForm** *inside* the procedure **CentreForm**, this doesn't affect anything we do *outside* it. The name we pass to it is always just the name of the form we want to change.

> I've been a bit naughty and introduced a new idea here through the back door - that of object variables. One of the strengths of Visual Basic is that it lets you treat almost anything as a variable, including controls and forms. We'll explain just how powerful this can be in Chapter 12 - Using Object Variables.

Functions

Functions work in a very similar way to procedures. The only real difference is that a function returns a value to the code that called it. The **CentreForm** subprocedure, for example, doesn't return anything to the code that calls it - it has a job to do and goes away and does it. Functions are used when you need to get something back - the result of a calculation, for instance, or the name of an employee from an employee record in a database.

> A function has to be assigned to something on its return, and it also has to have braces after it. Otherwise it's a procedure.

Built-in Functions

A good way to understand functions is to look at one of the many that are part of Visual Basic itself. In Chapter 8 - Graphics, you used the built-in **RGB** function to work out proper color values for you. The function accepts as parameters the amount of red, green and blue you want in the color mix, and the function returns a color value to you which you can then use to set the color property of various objects.

You can assign the return value of the function to a variable quite easily:

```
nMyColor = RGB(255,255,255)
MsgBox "The color is " & nMyColor
```

Also, since functions return data to your code, you can even use them in conditional statements and calculations - in fact anywhere you can use a variable. The only place you can't use them like a variable is on the receiving end of an = sign - you can't assign a value to a function. Visual Basic won't let you say:

```
RGB(255,255,255) = "Peter"
```

Although you can say:

```
If RGB(255,255,255) = 12 then MsgBox "Something's wrong, it should have
⤷been  much  higher"
```

or

```
Msgbox "The color is " & RGB(255,255,255)
```

483

Passing Parameters to Procedures and Functions

Procedures and functions do not have to accept parameters. A procedure that clears all the cells in a grid control need not be told anything other than Do It! Likewise, a function that gets the current date and time returns a value without any parameter being needed. However, most useful procedures and functions that are at all flexible will accept a variety of parameters.

In our initial example of the procedure to center a form on the screen, we defined a form object variable and passed it to the procedure:

```
Sub CentreForm (frmForm As Form)
```

Often you may need to pass a subprocedure many parameters. For example, you may need to write a procedure yourself which writes some data out to a database. In that particular case, it could be helpful to pass each element of data that you want written out as a parameter:

```
Sub WriteEmployeeData ( sEmployeeName as String, sDepartmentID as
 Integer,  sAge  as  Integer)
    :

    :
End Sub
```

There are two ways in which parameters can be passed to functions and subprocedures. The easiest method is the one we have seen in the examples so far, **passing by reference**. The other method is called **passing by value**, and has some benefits in terms of protecting your data, although it is a little more complex.

Passing Parameters By Reference

This is the method we have used so far. You just declare the parameter in brackets following the subprocedure or function name:

```
Sub DisplayEmployee (nEmployeeID As Integer)
```

Here, the **nEmployeeID** parameter is passed by reference. What this actually means is that if we have code in the subroutine which changes the parameter, for example by saying **nEmployeeID = 100**, then the original value of the parameter that's passed to **DisplayEmployee** will itself be changed. This can be useful, but it can be a real pain if you forget about it. Let's see what I mean in some real code.

Try It Out - Problems With Passing By Reference

1   Create a new project in Visual Basic. Select the default form that appears and then remove it from the project by selecting Remove File from the File menu.

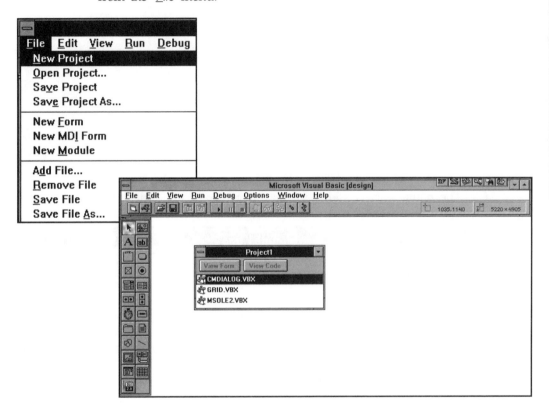

2   Create a new code module by pressing the new module button from the tool bar.

3   When the code window appears, type in this subprocedure:

```
Sub SubProc( nNumber as Integer)

    nNumber = 9999

End Sub
```

4 This sets up a subprocedure called **SubProc** which sets the parameter it receives to the value 9999.

5 Move the cursor to the line following the **End Sub** statement. We are going to insert a main procedure.

6 Create a **Main()** subprocedure by typing this into the code window:

```
Sub Main()

    Dim nAge As Integer
    nAge = 24
    MsgBox "The age is currently " & nAge
    SubProc nAge
    MsgBox "Age is now " & nAge

End Sub
```

7 The name Main is added to the Proc: box in the code window.

8 When you have typed everything in, run the program.

9 A message box appears showing you that the current value of the **nAge** variable is 24.

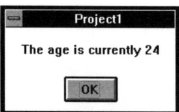

10 When you click OK in the message box, the next line of code calls the **SubProc** procedure.

11 A message box then appears showing you that **nAge** has been changed to 9999.

This highlights the problem of passing by reference. The procedure or function has access to the original parameter, so any changes made to the parameter also affect the variable that was passed in the first place.

Sometimes this can be useful; it's a convenient way of getting a subprocedure or function to return a number of values to the code that called it. However, there is an overhead in passing variables by reference. Visual Basic needs to use more conventional memory for these variables than it does for passing them by value.

Try It Out - Passing Variables By Value

Let's change our last example to pass variables by value rather than by reference.

1 Stop the program running. If you don't have the last example still loaded, then it's on your examples disk called **PARAM.MAK.**

2 In the code window, find the **SubProc** procedure that you just typed in.

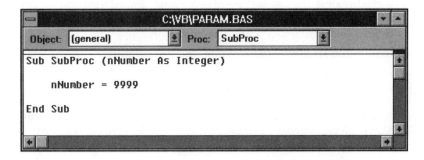

```
Sub SubProc (nNumber As Integer)

    nNumber = 9999

End Sub
```

3 Change the **Sub SubProc** line at the top to look like this:

```
Sub SubProc( ByVal nNumber as Integer)
```

Try It Out!

4 Run the program again.

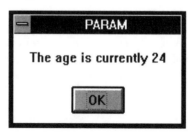

Now the message box pops up the same value of the **nAge** variable both times. Passing a parameter by value does just that - it passes the value of the parameter, not the original variable itself.

Passing By Value Reduces Bugs

Aside from the small memory overhead incurred when passing by reference, another reason to use **ByVal** wherever possible is that it can reduce the likelihood of bugs. It only takes a small lapse in concentration as you write the code to assign a value to a parameter passed by reference, when in fact you didn't really mean to. This can have a domino effect as the value is passed back to the code that called the subprocedure (and possibly on even further), or it may be passed to other subprocedures and so on.

You will also find the **ByVal** keyword being forced on you when you come to deal with **API** calls later in the book. When you deal with API calls, passing a parameter by value when you meant by reference, or vice versa, can crash your computer, or more likely your client's computer.

Changing the Scope of Procedures

By default, any functions of subprocedures you define in a module are **global**. Just like a global variable, these blocks of code can be used by any other function, subprocedure or event routine anywhere else in the program. Using the **Private** keyword you can tell Visual Basic that a certain function or subprocedure is **Private** to the module it is contained in. Then only other functions and subprocedures in the same module can use the routine.

You can declare a private function or subprocedure by simply typing the word **Private**, in front of the declaration:

```
Private Function Square (nNumber as Integer)
Private Sub CentreForm (frmForm as Form)
```

Private functions and subprocedures are the same as the event handlers you type into a form, which are all private as well. You can't call a form load event from another form. The load event, in fact any code in a form, is private and can only be used by code also in that form.

What's the point of a private function or subprocedure? Well, it's all to do with something called resources. Every global variable, constant function or subprocedure has its name stored in something called the **User Heap**. This is very small, only 64K (64,000 characters) and is shared by all the programs running under Windows. Obviously, if you can reduce the amount of stuff that Visual Basic stores in this heap not only will your programs leave more space for other Windows applications, but they will also stand less risk of crashing.

Accessing Data Across Modules

Let's take a few steps backwards and look at scope again. Variables declared in functions and subprocedures are local to that block of code - they can't be used outside that single routine. These local variables are normally created as soon as the routine they are declared in is run, and destroyed as soon as an **End Sub** or **End Function** statement is encountered.

You will probably recall that the exception to the rule is the **Static** variable. This is similar to a local variable in that it can only be used by the routine that declared it. However, unlike local variables, a **Static** variable is not destroyed when the **End Sub** or **End Function** statement is met. Its value is saved in a safe place in memory. The other routines in the application are still unable to use the variable, but the next time this routine is called, the variable still has the same value in it that it had last time.

There are two other types of variables, module level and global ones. Both are declared in the declarations section of a module:

```
Object: (general)        ±  Proc: (declarations)      ±
Option Explicit
```

One is declared using the **DIM** keyword, the other using the **Global** keyword:

```
' A module level variable if typed into the declarations section
Dim mnAge As Integer

' A global variable
Global gnAge as Integer
```

Module level variables are like private subprocedures and functions; they can only be accessed by code in the same module as the variable. Global variables on the other hand can be examined and changed by code anywhere in the application.

Many beginners use global variables to pass information between forms and modules because of their ease of use. Be careful! Like global subprocedures and functions, global variables take a large chunk out of the available user resources. When the user resources bottom out, the application will crash.

Using Parameters

A much better way is to pass information around using parameters. Imagine a program with two forms: the first where the user selects an employee from a list, the second where the details of the selected employee are displayed on the screen and the user is able to update them.

The bad way to implement this would be to store the selected employee in a global variable, then load the second form. Code in that form load event would then check the global variable and display the appropriate details on screen. Using a subprocedure stored in a module, you could write this:

```
Display_Employee_Details  (lstEmployee.Text)
```

The code in the subprocedure would then look like this:

```
Sub Display_Employee_Details (sEmployeeName As String)

    Load frmDetails
    frmDetails.Show

    frmDetails!txtEmployee = sEmployeeName


    :
    :        Further code to display the rest of the details.
    :

End Sub
```

This approach has other advantages, mainly that the code is a lot easier to read and maintain. There is nothing worse than going back to one of your own programs a couple of months after it was written and trying to figure out what **sEmployeeName** means, because it is actually declared as a global variable in a totally different module.

The other benefits of using parameters are:

- Reducing resource usage

- Improving the readability of the code

- Keeping all the variable declarations relating to a routine in one place

- Being able to change the way the routine works without having a knock-on effect to too many other routines

Building a Procedure Library

One of the most useful aspects of modules is the ability to create code libraries. Procedures, including both subprocedures and functions, can be written in such a way that they are re-usable. A textbox validation routine, for example, could be written in such a way that it doesn't need to assume anything about form or control names it works with, thus enabling it to work anywhere.

These **generic** procedures can form the basis of a code library. This is a collection of modules all containing useful routines which can just be bolted on to new applications as and when required. Theoretically the code would have been tested when it was first written, so bolting on code like this can reduce not only your coding time, but also the potential number of bugs in your system.

To build up a code library effectively you need to ask yourself a number of questions whenever you write code in modules:

- Can you envisage a use for this procedure in other applications?

- Does the code assume anything? For instance, does it rely on global variables, forms or controls with specific names? If it does then change it!

- How can we make the procedure as crash-proof as possible? Add error checking, add code to check the parameters, add code to deal with these errors, or call an error handling routine in another of your libraries.

Included on the examples disk is a collection of .BAS modules which are taken from my own code libraries. Let's see how these can be added to and used in projects of your own.

Try It Out - Loading a Module into a Project

1   Load up the **MSGBOX.MAK** project from the samples provided.

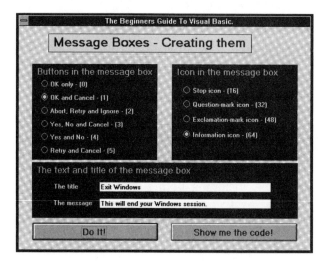

2   This is the same **MSGBOX.MAK** project that you saw a while back when we delved into the world of dialogs. This time around we are going to add a module to the project to make the message boxes 3D. Wow!

3   From the File menu, select Add File, or alternatively press *Ctrl-D* together. A file requester will appear:

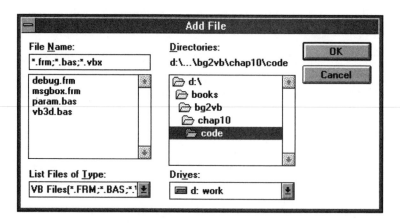

4   Select the file title **VB3D.BAS** and then hit OK.

5   The **VB3D.BAS** module is explained a little later, but basically it includes two subprocedures which you need to call to turn the dialogs in your application into 3D ones.

6   From the <u>W</u>indow menu, select <u>P</u>roject to make the project dialog box appear.

7   **VB3D.BAS** is now in the project list. Double-click on the MSGBOX.FRM entry to display the message box form.

8   We need to add a line of code to the form **Load** and **Unload** events, first to turn on the 3D effects, and then to turn them off.

9   Press *F7* to bring up the code window, or double-click on the form.

10   When the code window appears make sure that the event shown is the form **Load** event:

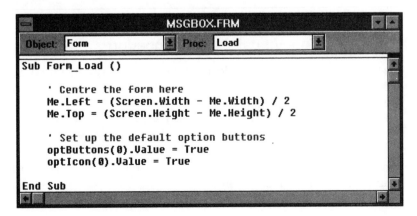

11 Add code to the event so that the top three lines look like this:

```
Sub Form_Load ()
    Call Start3D
    ' Centre the form here
```

12 **Start3D** is a subprocedure in the module we just added which turns on the 3D effects. Now use the Proc: combo box at the top of the code window to find the form **Unload** event.

13 Add a second call to this event so that it looks like this:

```
Sub Form_Unload()

    Call End3D

End Sub
```

14 Again, **End3D** is a subprocedure in the module.

If you now run the program and click on the Do It! button you will see the dialog appear in all its three dimensional glory, courtesy of the **VB3D.BAS** module that you added:

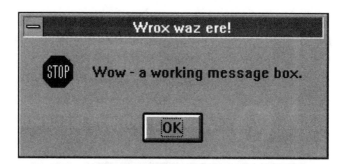

Peter Wright's Top Visual Basic Procedures

VB3D.BAS is one of four code modules that I have included on the examples disk for you. As you spend more and more time working with Visual Basic you will come to build up a list of your own favorite and most useful routines. These will be routines which generally either save you a lot of coding time, or which can't be done with an off-the-shelf VBX.

The following four are the most common ones I use when dealing with the Standard Edition Visual Basic.

Procedure	Description
VB3D.BAS	This module consists of two subprocedures: **Start3d** and **End3d**. These turn all the system dialogs (like message boxes, input boxes and common dialogs) into 3D style boxes. These are just like the ones you will see in recent Microsoft applications such as Excel 5 or Word 6. To use the module call **Start3d** at the very start of your program (the first form **Load** event is a good place). Choose **End3D** at the very end of your program.
VALIDATE.BAS	This contains two subprocedures which can prove very useful when dealing with text boxes. The first, **GotFocus**, selects the text in a text box as soon as it gets focus. You have to call the routine from each text box **GotFocus** event. The second, **KeyCheck**, can be called from the **KeyPress** event of each text box. It checks the key pressed against the required data format for this text box. The format is entered into the text box Tag property. For more details of how to call these subprocedures, check out the code in the module itself.
MSGBEEP.BAS	Windows 3.1 and later allow you to link sampled sounds to certain Windows events, and to certain styles of message box icon. There are two routines in this module called **MsgBoxF** and **MsgBoxS.** They work in exactly the same way as the **MsgBox** function and subprocedures in Visual Basic. The difference is that these play the associated sound when the message box appears.
SOUNDER.BAS	**SOUNDER** consists of just one function, **PlayIt**. By passing the name of either a Midi file (**.MID**) or a wave file (**.WAV**) to the function, the code will then play the sound. This assumes of course that you have a suitable sound card. This is great for playing short bursts of music over title screens, or for providing proper audible help to users of your programs. Again, see the code for a complete run down of the parameters required.

Handling Errors at Run-Time

Applications, and more importantly users, are never perfect. In any large program you write there will always be logic errors which can crash the system, or events like key-combinations from the users that you had never imagined could happen.

Thankfully, Visual Basic incorporates a very powerful way for you to trap errors. There are literally hundreds of possible errors that Visual Basic can catch and deal with. Describing them all in detail here would take a long time. What we will do here is look at the generic methods involved in trapping these errors and dealing with them.

Responding to Errors Using On Error

The **On Error** command lets you tell Visual Basic where to go when an error occurs. Each subroutine or function in which you want to trap errors needs to have an **On Error** statement in it. The syntax for **On Error** is pretty straightforward:

```
On Error Goto <Line>
```

Where **<Line>** is a label that you have defined. For example, take a look at this subprocedure:

```
Sub Division()
    On Error Goto ErrorHandler
    Print 12 / 0
Exit Sub

ErrorHandler:
   MsgBox Str(Err) & ": " & Error, , "Error"
   On Error Goto 0
Exit Sub

End Sub
```

The first line, **On Error Goto ErrorHandler**, tells Visual Basic that in the event of an error it should **Goto** the label **ErrorHandler**, which is defined a little later in the subprocedure. Take a look at the code from **ErrorHandler:** onwards.

Visual Basic has two built-in variables to help you deal with errors. The **Err** variable is a numeric variable which holds the unique number of this error. You can find a complete list of all the error codes that Visual Basic generates in the back of the Visual Basic Reference manual. The second is **Error**, which is a string describing the error itself.

In our code example above, a **MsgBox** is used to display both the error number and the error message.

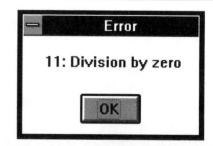

After the message box, the line **On Error Goto 0** cancels the error. This is the only way to turn off error trapping. Finally **Exit Sub** tells Visual Basic that as soon as the error handling code has done its bit, the subroutine should be exited.

Did you notice the **Exit Sub** above the **ErrorHandler:** label as well? Normally Visual Basic trots through the code in a subprocedure or function line-by-line, starting at the top and working its way down. Obviously you wouldn't want the error handling code to run if no errors were met, so **Exit Sub** is used here to get out of the subroutine without displaying a pointless message box.

Try It Out - Forgetting the Diskette

1   Load up the **CONTROL.MAK** project.

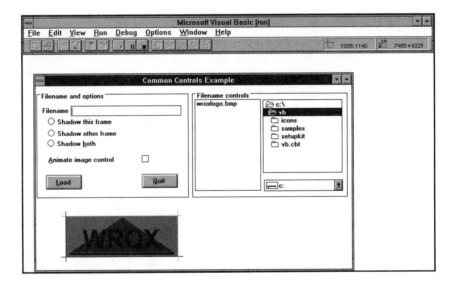

2   This is the same project that we met earlier in the book. There are problems with this program that we need to sort out. For instance, the program will let you select a floppy disk drive when there is no floppy in the drive. If you are running on a network, you could select a network drive only to have that drive go off-line. Both are problems which would normally crash the program. Both are also problems that you can work around with Visual Basic error handling.

3 We want to trap errors that occur when a user selects an unavailable drive. To do this we add code to the **drvDrives_Change** event. Double-click on the drive control to bring up its **Change** event code.

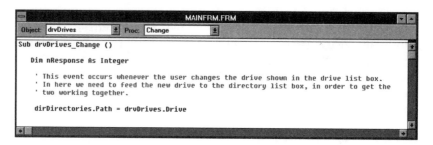

4 Change this event so that it looks like the code below. I have excluded the comments from the source here, so don't let that catch you out:

```
Sub drvDrives_Change ()

    On Error GoTo DriveError

    Dim nResponse As Integer
    dirDirectories.Path = drvDrives.Drive

    Exit Sub

DriveError:

    If Err = 71 Or Err = 68 Then

        nResponse = MsgBox("Whoa - drive problem. Click OK to try again!", 17
    , "Drive Error")
        if nResponse = 1 then Resume Else Resume Next

    End If

    Exit Sub

End Sub
```

5 Now run the program and use the drive control to select the A: drive, without a disk in it. The **MsgBox** statement you just entered should appear.

6   Click on the OK button and the program will try to access the drive again, giving you the same error you just got. Click on Cancel and the routine aborts; the drive control shows A: but none of the other controls have updated in response.

How It Works

The two error conditions we want to trap are error 71 and error 68. These are Device Unavailable and Drive Not Ready respectively. Look them up in the back of the reference manual if you don't believe me!

In the code, all we have to write is:

```
On Error Goto DriveError
```

Then at **DriveError:** we check the value of the **Err** variable to see if we have caught error 71 or 68. If we have, then the message box is popped up. Now we come to the interesting bit.

When the message box appears there are two buttons in it, one for OK, the other for Cancel. If you click the OK button then the program tries to access the disk again, but how? The secret is the Resume command:

```
if nResponse = 1 then Resume Else Resume Next
```

Once you have got an error trapped, you can use Resume to tell Visual Basic what to do next. **Resume Next** tells Visual Basic to go to the line directly after the one with the error and carry on from there. **Resume** on its own tells Visual Basic to retry the command that gave us the error in the first place.

In our example, if the user presses **OK** then **Resume** is used on its own to tell Visual Basic to try and run the line of code again. If you still hadn't inserted a floppy at this point then the same error message would pop up again. If on the other hand you clicked the **Cancel** button then Visual Basic would execute the line following the one with the error. In this case that line is **Exit Sub**, so the procedure ends.

There is one more interesting feature of the **Resume** command worth covering here. Not only can you use **Resume** to tell Visual Basic where to go after an error, you can also use it to ignore errors totally. For example:

```
On Error Resume Next
```

This informs Visual Basic that should an error crop up, it shouldn't worry about it but just move on to the next line.

> This is not the best programming style, although the Visual Basic Programmers Guide even manages an excuse for why this form of programming is acceptable: something to do with **deferring** errors. If an error occurs you really should deal with it, not put it off.

Debugging - Kill All Known Bugs Dead!

Let's lay our cards on the table. Programming any computer with any language can be a real pain in the backside. Sure, when things go well everything's rosy. You type the code in, design your forms, run the program and everything works first time. The reality is somewhat different.

A more likely scenario is that you start to type the code in and Visual Basic keeps beeping at you and flashing up annoying message boxes telling you that you missed a bracket, or misspelt a Visual Basic keyword. If you have been faithfully following all the **Try It Outs** so far you will undoubtedly have come across this already.

Visual Basic Debugging Tools

Annoying it may be, but automatic syntax checking is also an incredibly useful feature of Visual Basic. It is actually only one of a number of useful gadgets that come with Visual Basic to help reduce, and hopefully eradicate, bugs in your systems:

> When your programming is running, Visual Basic provides you with a **debug** window that your code can display messages on for only you to see.

> A **Watch** window lets you see how the variables in your program change as it runs. You can even run the program a line at a time to see where it goes and when.

> You can also change the way the program runs, while it is running, by placing new values into variables or by changing the properties of controls and forms.

We'll examine all of the debugging aids that come with Visual Basic by working through a buggy version of the **MSGBOX.MAK** project we covered in Chapter 7 - Dialogs. Let's start by taking a look at the **debug** window itself.

The Debug Window

In design mode there is a window hidden out of sight, behind your application, called the **debug** window.

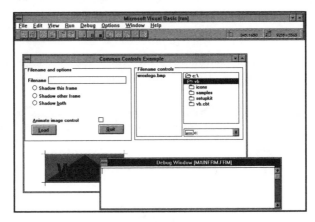

Using the debug window you can view the contents of variables and properties, and display information about your program even while it's still running. You can even change the way your program executes by changing the value of variables and properties on the fly, and by running individual procedures and functions directly.

The first stage in debugging a project is to find out exactly what the problem is.

Try It Out Part I - Running the Buggy Project

1   Load up the **DEBUG.MAK** project and run it.

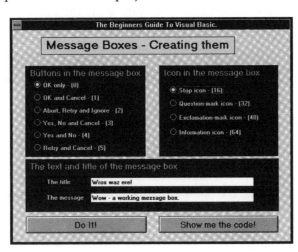

2   At first it seems that the code is running OK. The form loads all right and everything looks normal.

3   By default the program is set up to display a message box with the user's title and message, and also with a single OK command button, and the stop icon.

4   Click on the Do It! command button and the message box appears, just as you would expect. Everything seems to be working fine.

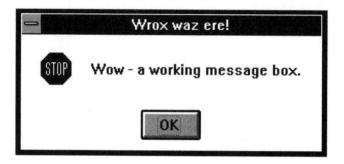

5   Close down this message box by clicking OK. Now try selecting a new type of message box by selecting the OK and Cancel option button.

6   Show the message box by pressing the Do It! command button again.

7   This time the message box appears with the command buttons we want, but the stop icon has vanished.

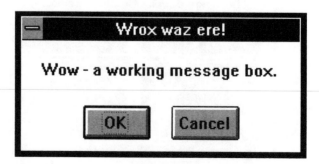

8   Select the option button for the question mark icon and hit the Do It! command button again. This time the message box appears with the right icon, but only one command button instead of two.

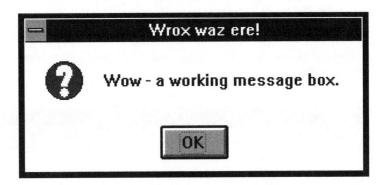

This is an example of a classic bug - there is a fault in the program somewhere that is causing the problem to behave erratically. Try playing around with the option buttons some more and clicking the Do It! command. There is no logical pattern to what the program is trying to do. Imagine the situation if this was one of your own programs and was due for release to an eager user. The program is acting really weird and it isn't obvious what has gone wrong.

Try It Out Part II - Using the Debug Window to Examine Buggy Code

1   With the **DEBUG.MAK** program still running, pause it. You can do this by: selecting the pause icon on the Visual Basic toolbar, selecting the Break item on the Run menu, or by pressing *Ctrl* and *Break* together.

2   Now press *Ctrl-B* and the debug window pops up.

```
━━━━━━━━━━━━━━━━━━━ Debug Window [MSGBOX.FRM] ━━━━━━━━━━━━━━━━━━━
------------------------------------
Go Button Click Event
mnButtonCode = 0
mnIconCode = 48
------------------------------------
------------------------------------
Go Button Click Event
mnButtonCode = 0
mnIconCode = 48
------------------------------------
```

There will be some text in the debug window, as you can see, which shows you the contents of two variables the program uses, mnButtonCode and mnIconCode. This text is displayed in the debug window using the Print command. However, instead of printing onto a form or control, the text is output to the debug window.

3 You can see the code responsible for this by pressing *F7* to bring up the code window and then using the code window's combo boxes to locate the `cmdGo_Click` event:

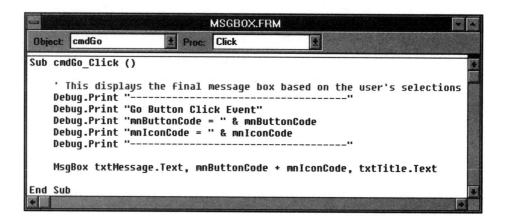

```
Sub cmdGo_Click ()

    ' This displays the final message box based on the user's selections
    Debug.Print "-----------------------------------"
    Debug.Print "Go Button Click Event"
    Debug.Print "mnButtonCode = " & mnButtonCode
    Debug.Print "mnIconCode = " & mnIconCode
    Debug.Print "-----------------------------------"

    MsgBox txtMessage.Text, mnButtonCode + mnIconCode, txtTitle.Text

End Sub
```

4 The top five lines of code all starting with **Debug.Print** tell Visual Basic to display some text onto the debug window. In this particular case they print information about the event that's being watched, as well as the values of the two suspect variables.

The usefulness of the debug window goes far beyond simply viewing a program's output though. You can even run commands in it.

5 Click in the debug window and type the command:

```
Print mnButtonCode
```

Press *Return* when you've finished.

6 Visual Basic runs this line of code as if it were in a subroutine or event procedure somewhere, displaying the contents of the **mnButtonCode** variable on the line immediately following your command.

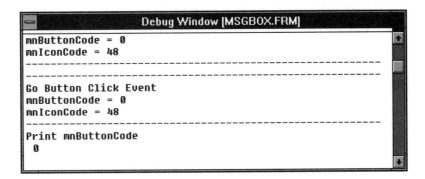

```
─  Debug Window [MSGBOX.FRM]
mnButtonCode = 0
mnIconCode = 48
------------------------------------------------------------
------------------------------------------------------------
Go Button Click Event
mnButtonCode = 0
mnIconCode = 48
------------------------------------------------------------
Print mnButtonCode
  0
```

7 You can even run subprocedures and functions from here. Type in **cmdGo_Click** and press *Return*. This runs the Do It! button click event, which results in some more information appearing in the debug window, and a message box popping up onto the screen.

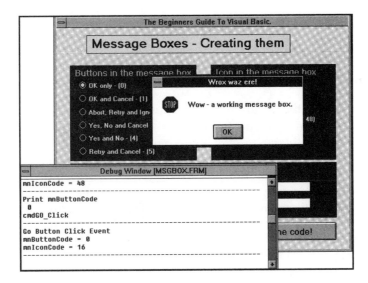

8 When the message box appears, click on the command button in it to get rid of it and return to the debug window.

Try It Out Part III - Changing Program Variables in Debug

In the same way that you can run commands and code from the debug window, you can also change variables and properties.

1   Type this in and press *Return*:

```
cmdGo_Click
```

2   This runs the Do It! button click event which results in some more information appearing in the debug window and a message box popping up onto the screen.

3   When the message box appears, click on the command button in it to get rid of it and return to the debug window.

4   In the same way that you can run commands and code from the debug window, you can also change variables and properties. Type this in and press *Return*:

```
frmMsgBoxes.Visible = False
```

5   As soon as you hit *Return*, the main form of the program vanishes, the same as it would if you used code to change the **Visible** property with code to **False** at run-time. To bring it back type:

```
frmMsgBoxes.Visible = True
```

6   So far the program is still paused in a state of limbo. It's still ready to run and carry on from where it left off, but it does nothing in its present state. To start it running again, just click on the run icon, or press *F5*.

On with the debugging. We still haven't nailed the problem yet. Try changing the option buttons around and clicking the Do It! button afterwards. If you keep referring to the debug window you will soon see that the value of the **mnButtonCode** variable is always the same as **mnIconCode**. It's obviously not being set up properly somewhere, but where? The best way to find out is to step through the code line-by-line to see what happens

The Step Commands

The Step commands in Visual Basic allow you to run a program a line at a time, or even a function or subprocedure at a time. Each time a line of code is run, the program pauses waiting for you, the programmer, to tell it if it should carry on to the next line, or whatever.

Try It Out - Stepping Through Code

1 Pause the program once again, and we will try these Step commands out.

This icon selects **Single Step** mode, or press *F8*.

This icon selects **Procedure Step** mode, or press *Shift F8*.

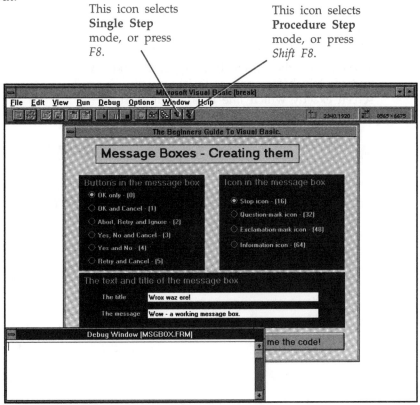

Both commands step through the code in your program a line at a time, pausing after each line. **Procedure Step** treats all lines of code exactly the same. If you come to a line of code that calls a procedure or function you have written, it runs the entire procedure in one step, then pauses. In **Single Step mode**, when a call to a procedure or function is found, Visual Basic steps into the code that makes up that procedure and starts to run it, line-by-line. This particular example program has no procedure calls and so we will stick to the Single Step command.

2 Make sure that you still have the **DEBUG.MAK** project paused while in run mode.

Try It Out!

3 Press *F8* to select single step mode to start the debugging process off.

4 At first it will seem as though nothing has happened. This is a very simple application and the only code in it is contained in event procedures. For Single Step to really start work you need to trigger an event.

5 Click one of the button option controls. This triggers an event that starts to run the option button's event code. Visual Basic stops it immediately before any code is actually executed, showing you on screen exactly which line it is about to run.

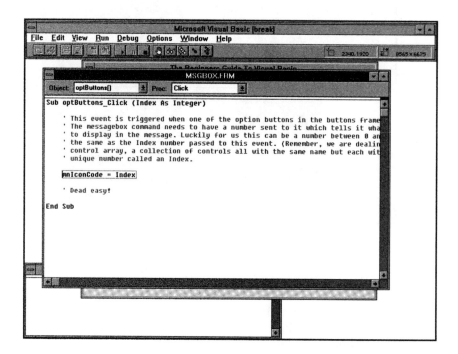

6 Voilà! We have also found our bug. The **Buttons** option button code is setting up the wrong variable. The code as it stands is this:

```
mnIconCode = Index
```

The code in the event *should* say:

```
mnButtonCode = Index
```

The **Index** is the index number of the option button that was pressed, which should be used to identify which buttons we want. Instead this is going straight into the **mnIconCode** variable, which controls the icons that appear. The message box parameters that control the button layout use the numbers 0, 1, 2, 3, 4, and 5, so you can place the index directly into the button code variable. When dealing with the icon selection, it's a little more difficult, as the numbers we use are 16, 32, 48 and 64. Instead of placing the index directly into **mnIconCode**, we place the **Tag** property of each of the option buttons, which is set to the right value at design time:

```
mnIconCode = optIcon(Index).Tag
```

We can correct the **mnButtonCode** value while the program is paused:

7 Click on the line in the code window and change it to the line shown.

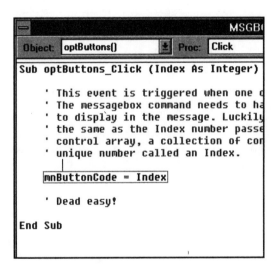

8 When you have changed the code, select single step again, *F8*. The highlight moves to the next command, **End Sub**.

9 To start the program running normally again, just press *F5*.

10 Now the program is behaving as it should.

Break-Points

So far we have paused the program to do our tests by either selecting the pause icon on the toolbar, or by pressing *Ctrl-Break*. Visual Basic provides a way of pausing a program automatically for you when a certain line of code is reached. This is called a **break-point**.

Try It Out - Setting Break-Points

1 Bring up the code window for the **cmdGo_Click** event again. Stop the program if it's still running, and double-click the Do It! command button.

2 Click on the **MsgBox** command to move the cursor there.

Set a break-point on this line by pressing *F9*.

Or select **Toggle Breakpoint** from the **Debug** menu.

Or click on the hand icon on the toolbar.

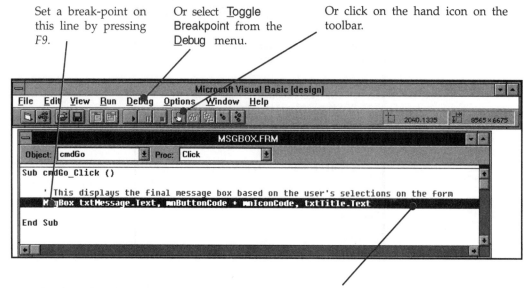

The line that the cursor is on turns red to indicate that this line is a break-point - the line at which Visual Basic will pause the program, just as if you had pressed *Ctrl-Break* while it was running.

If you press *F9* again or select the hand icon on the toolbar, then the red highlight vanishes. It's a toggle switch. Also, you can set the color yourself in the Options Environment dialog.

3   With the break-point on, run the program.

4   When the form appears, click on the Do It! command button once again. This time, instead of a message box being displayed, a code window appears showing you that the program has stopped, and highlighting the line at which it stopped.

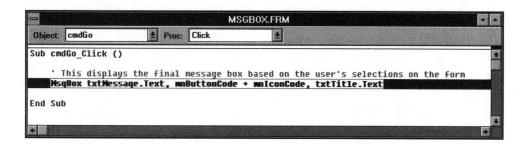

5   You can start the program running normally again by pressing *F5*, or jump into step mode if you so desire. As soon as you do either of these things, the highlighted line is run, resulting in our message box appearing as normal. From now on though, every time you click the Do It! command button the program halts, popping up the code window as it does so.

In a big and buggy program you may have quite a few break-points set. Toggling them all off by hand can be an arduous task so Visual Basic thoughtfully provides a menu option to clear them all for you. Stop the program from running and select Clear All Breakpoints from the Debug menu to turn all the break-points in the program off.

Watches

Just as break-points enable you to automatically pause a program on a certain line of code, the **Watch** window lets you automatically see the contents of variables without having to bring up the debug window and enter cumbersome **Print** commands to display them.

Try It Out - Watching Variables

There are two types of watches you can put into Visual Basic: instant watches and normal watches. Let's look at normal watches first.

1 With the program stopped properly, not paused, bring up the code window.

2 To add a normal watch, select Add Watch from the Debug menu.

3 The following dialog appears:

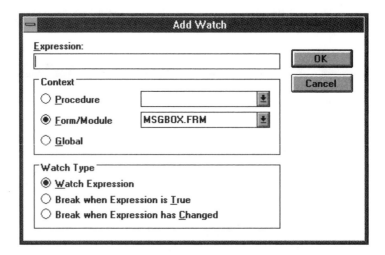

4 The top text box, Expression, is where you enter the name of the variable you want to watch, or an expression that you want to watch for. For example, you may have tracked down a bug where the system only crashes when a variable called **sAge** = **9999** is entered. You can enter this into the watch window by typing **sAge** = **9999** into the Expression text box. For now though we just want to watch what happens to the **mnIconCode** variable.

5   In the Expression text box enter mnIconCode.

The three radio buttons beneath the Expression box are used to tell Visual Basic some information about the variable.

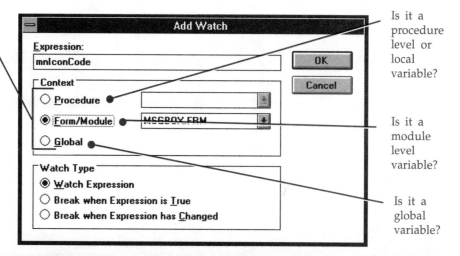

Is it a procedure level or local variable?

Is it a module level variable?

Is it a global variable?

Here it is a module level variable. I defined it in the form declarations section using the word **Dim**. If the variable is actually dimensioned in a procedure or function then you would need to select Procedure and then tell the watch dialog which procedure the variable is actually declared in.

6   Once you have clicked the Form/Module option button, make sure that the name of the module displayed is MSGBOX.FRM. In this example the project only has one form, so if the variable is a form or module level one then there is really only one place that it could be declared. In a larger project though you would have to use the combo box to select the name of the form or module in which it is declared.

7   The bottom three option buttons tell Visual Basic how to carry out the watch. The top option Watch Expression means that you want to watch the expression manually. The variable contents are displayed in the debug window whenever you manually pause the program.

8   The second option, Break when Expression is True, means that the program will automatically pause whenever the expression entered is true. If you had entered mnIconCode = 64 then whenever something happened in the program that set mnIconCode to 64, the program would stop, displaying both the debug window and the line of code that made the offending change.

9   The third option, Break when Expression has Changed, means the program will stop running whenever the variable changes. Select this option.

10 Run the program and select one of the icon option buttons. The program stops straight away.

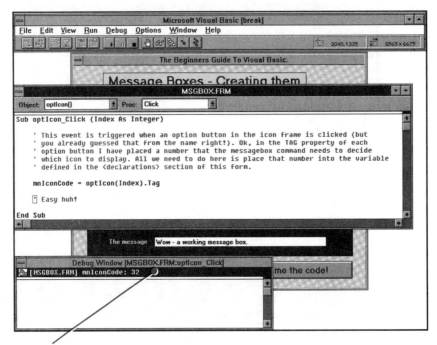

The top line of the debug window now shows you the contents of the variable that we are watching. When the debug window is displayed you can double-click on the watch variable to bring up the watch dialog box again and change the details that you previously entered.

11 Call up the watch window again now and change the Expression to mnIconCode = 32. Then select Break when Expression is True.

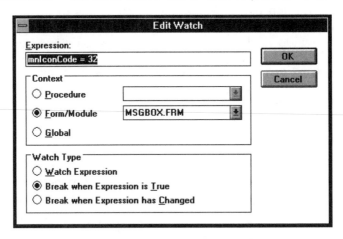

12 Select OK then hit *F5* to continue the program.

13 The program will now halt automatically when you select the question mark icon button, which is when mnIconCode = 32.

Try It Out - Using an Instant Watch

Instant watches are very similar but can be set up much more quickly. They can only be set up when the program is paused. You cannot set up an instant watch in design mode.

1 Since the program just halted itself, the code window should be visible.

Press either *Shift-F9*, or select the instant watch icon from the toolbar to set up the instant watch.

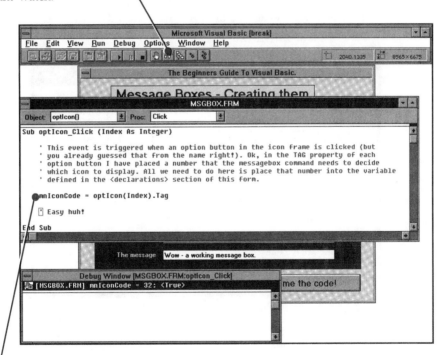

In the code window, double-click on mnIconCode to highlight it.

Try It Out!

2 The instant watch dialog box appears showing you the current value of the variable you selected.

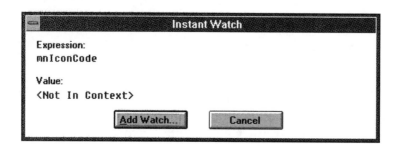

3 From here you can either click on the Add Watch ... button to add this as a normal watch, or click Cancel to get rid of the instant watch screen. Click Add Watch ... and the familiar edit watch dialog comes up to confirm the selection.

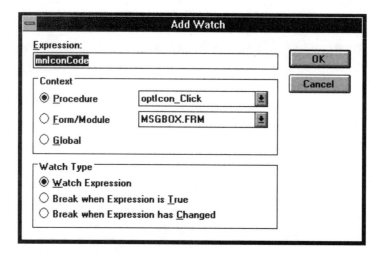

4 Just accept these settings by clicking OK. The line that shows the value of mnIconCode is then added to the debug window. This doesn't change as you continue to run the program. It just reveals the value of the variable at the time you set the watch. To get a continuous read out, you have to insert **Debug.Print** commands in the code at strategic points like we did at the start.

```
┌─────────────────────────────────────────────────────────────┐
│ ─      Debug Window [MSGBOX.FRM:optIcon_Click]               │
├─────────────────────────────────────────────────────────────┤
│ 🖰 [MSGBOX.FRM] mnIconCode = 32: <False>                      │
│ 👓 [MSGBOX.FRM:optIcon_Click] mnIconCode: 32                  │
│                                                           ▲  │
├─────────────────────────────────────────────────────────┬───┤
│                                                         │   │
│                                                         │   │
│                                                         │   │
│                                                         ▼  │
└─────────────────────────────────────────────────────────────┘
```

The Call Window

The final debugging tool is the call window. With the program paused, the call window shows you the current procedure that you are in, and any other procedures that were called in order to reach this one.

For example, you may have triggered a command button click event, then a Validate procedure to validate some controls on your form. In this case the call window would show you both of these procedures with the most recent procedure names at the top of the list, and the earliest ones called at the bottom.

Try It Out - Calling Procedure and Functions in the Call Window

1   Stop the program **DEBUG.MAK** running and then run it again, but in single step mode, by pressing *F8*.

2   After a short pause the form **Load** event will appear on screen. The highlight is positioned on the call to our **CentreForm** function.

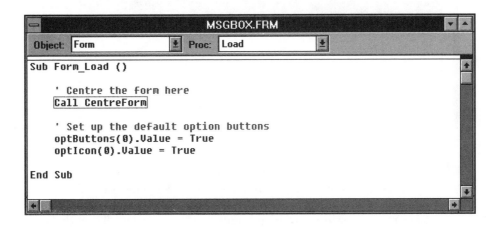

3   Select single step again to move into this procedure.

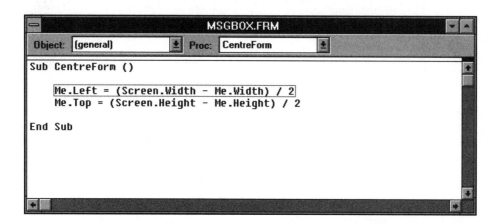

4   Think about what we just did. First we stepped into the form **Load** procedure, then we stepped into a separate procedure to center the form.

5   You see both of these by bringing up the calls window. Click the calls icon on the toolbar, press *Ctrl-L*, or select <u>C</u>alls from the <u>D</u>ebug menu.

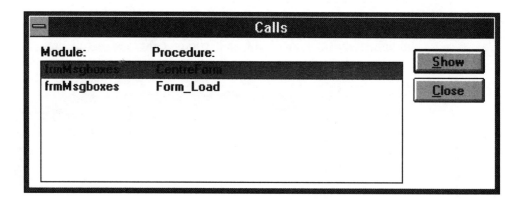

6   This window shows the path you have taken to get to the line of code you are presently at. The route is defined by the procedures and functions you executed, and the forms and modules that they belonged to. You can select any of the entries shown in the list and then click the Show button to actually see the code for that procedure on screen.

Summary

In this chapter I've tried to introduce some of the tools that can increase the chances of you ending up with a working program. There is no single solution to this age old programming problem. However, there are lots of individual things you can do that together should help you get there in the end.

The steps to producing programs that work are, in summary:

▶ Break your programs into parts that have a single purpose.

▶ Use tried and tested code when you can, and build a library of routines to do that.

▶ Put error trapping code into your program to allow it to survive in real world environments.

▶ Be prepared to debug your code and make full use of the tools that Visual Basic provides.

Now we'll go on and take a look at a couple of more advanced techniques with Visual Basic. First up is a look at how Visual Basic and Windows work together in such perfect harmony (almost!).

Chapter Eleven

Interacting with Windows

CHAPTER 11

Interacting With Windows

Visual Basic does an effective job of shielding developers from the nitty-gritty details of Windows. However, there comes a point where you can no longer hide behind the safe walls of Visual Basic. Windows is out there and waiting to talk to your program.

In this chapter you'll learn:

- ▶ How to interact with the Windows Clipboard system

- ▶ How to declare API and DLL functions in your programs and utilize the underlying power of windows

- ▶ How to use API calls to deal with **INI** files

- ▶ How to find out exactly what a resource is and how to write resource-friendly programs

Inside Windows - Outside Visual Basic

It might seem a strange thing to say but you're not reading this book to learn about Visual Basic! What you really want to do is write Windows programs. Visual Basic is a quick and easy way of doing this. It's easy because it puts a friendly face on, and an intuitive wrapper around Windows.

The radical and exciting part of Visual Basic is not so much the procedural code you write to handle events (which is a lot like QuickBasic) but the way you can easily build Windows interfaces. Visual Basic is rather like a nice control panel on the Windows machine with friendly knobs for you to turn.

That's fine up to a point, providing you can achieve everything you want to inside Visual Basic. The truth is though, that Visual Basic only encompasses a proportion of the functionality that Windows provides. If you want to go that extra mile you have to go *outside* Visual Basic and extend its capabilities by using the facilities at your disposal in Windows.

This chapter gives you an idea of the kind of things you can do with Windows beyond Visual Basic's direct capabilities. In reality it's a mammoth subject, as big as Windows itself. The aim here is to provide you with some guiding principles and some examples.

The Clipboard

One of the most common facilities that Windows provides is the **Clipboard**, which allows users to cut and paste data from one application to another. Familiar menu items such as Cut, Copy and Paste simply must appear in your application if it is to survive in the commercial world. In this chapter we'll take a look at how you can program the Clipboard from inside Visual Basic, even though it's a part of Windows.

The Windows API

Another feature of Windows, exploited more and more frequently these days by Visual Basic programmers, is the somewhat loftily named Windows Application Programmer's Interface (API). This is a group of about 1000 ready-made procedures and functions that are the base components of Windows. While many of them require an in-depth knowledge of Windows itself, there are a number which can be used 'off-the-shelf' to enhance your applications and to extend the power of Visual Basic. We'll look at a good example of using the Windows API to do something that's otherwise tedious if you use Visual Basic alone: reading and writing **INI** files.

Windows Resources

Aside from being able to exploit these features of Windows, you must also learn to respect the Windows system itself. This means you must write programs that behave themselves, so you don't disrupt any other programs which are running at the same time. To be safe, your programs must be resource-friendly, neither hogging too much memory nor too much processor time as they do their work.

The Clipboard

The Windows Clipboard has been with us since the heady days of Windows 2, many years ago. The Clipboard allows a user to transfer information 'by hand' from one application to another, or from one part of an application to a different part of the same application.

Think of your code window in Visual Basic. You can drag the mouse over a chunk of code to select it, then pick either Cut or Copy from the Edit menu to place the information onto the Clipboard. Once you've got something on the Clipboard, be it a piece of code, part of your latest blockbuster novel, or a work or art from Windows Paint, it can be Pasted into any other application that supports both the Clipboard as well as the type of data you've cut or copied onto it.

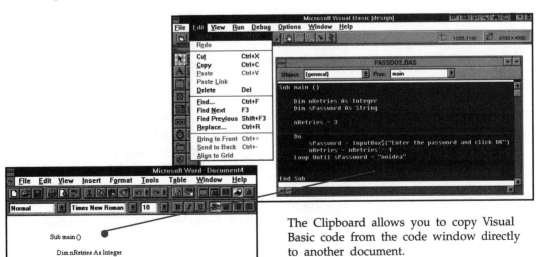

The Clipboard allows you to copy Visual Basic code from the code window directly to another document.

With the standardization of the Windows interface, users will expect applications you write in Visual Basic to support cutting to and pasting from the Clipboard. In order to implement these features, you need to understand how the Clipboard works.

Talking to the Clipboard

In Visual Basic the Clipboard is a special object, very much like the screen special object that we covered back in the chapter on forms. It has no properties of its own, and isn't something you can see or interact with in design-mode, unlike most of Visual Basic's other objects. However, it *does* have six methods which we can use within our program code.

Clipboard Method	What It Does
Clear	This clears the Clipboard of all data.
GetData	This enables you to pull non-text information into a control. For example, pulling a graphic from the Clipboard into a picture or image control.
GetFormat	The GetFormat method, Clipboard.GetFormat, provides you with a number which indicates the type of data held on the Clipboard. We cover the different values for this number a little later.
GetText	This gets text from the Clipboard, assuming it's holding text. You can then assign this text to a variable or control, or do anything else you may want to it; for example: sString = Clipboard. GetText
SetData	The Clipboard is able to hold information other than straight text. For instance, it can also be used to store graphics, sound, OLE objects and so on. SetData provides you with a method of copying such information to the Clipboard, whilst making it clear to the Clipboard exactly what format that data is in.
SetText	This copies a string (either one you specify or one held in a control or variable) onto the Clipboard. For example Clipboard.SetText txtControl.SelText copies the selected text from the txtControl textbox onto the Clipboard.

Writing to the Clipboard

The Clipboard is the ideal place to temporarily store text. Wordprocessors use the Clipboard to allow their users to move large blocks of text around with ease within their documents.

Try It Out - Writing to the Clipboard

1 Load up the **CLIPTEXT.MAK** project and run it. I've already done the leg work on the project and created the main form and menu.

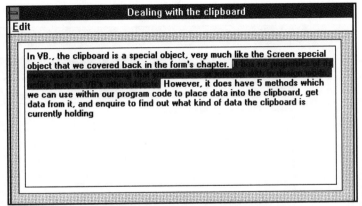

2 The form that appears has an <u>E</u>dit menu which lets you interact with the Clipboard. You can cut and copy data to it, and paste data from it.

3 The actual data you want to place on the Clipboard is entered into the large multi-line text box in the center of the form.

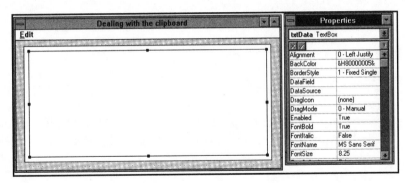

4   You can enter text, highlight some or all of it and then select the required menu option to put the selected text into the Clipboard. That's the theory any way - at the moment only the Copy function on the Edit menu works. You'll notice that the code is missing to implement the rest of these menu items. That's what you're going to do next!

Try It Out - Coding the Cut Function

1   Bring up the code window for the Edit menu Cut function. In design-mode, select Cut from the Edit menu and the code window will appear.

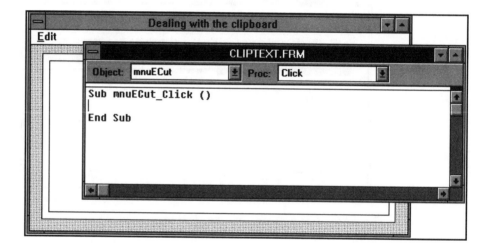

2   Type the following code into the Cut function click event:

```
Sub mnuECut_Click ()

    Clipboard.Clear
    Clipboard.SetText txtData.SelText
    txtData.SelText = ""

End Sub
```

3   Now try running the program. Type some text into the text box, highlight it by dragging the mouse over it, and select Cut from the Edit Menu.

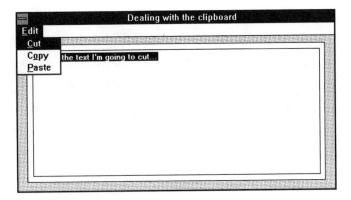

4 The selected text will disappear and be placed, out of sight, on the Windows Clipboard.

5 To see where the text has gone, launch Clipboard Viewer from Program Manager.

Clipboard
Viewer

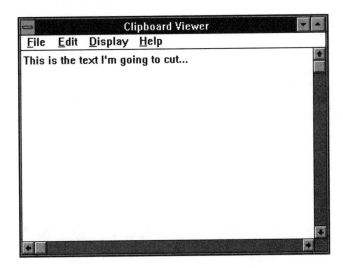

6 The text is there on the Clipboard.

How It Works

Let's take a look at the code for the Cut command. The first line **Clipboard.Clear**, does just what it says: it clears the Clipboard! Any information that was previously held in the Clipboard is thrown away, ready for us to place our own information into it.

Copying information to the Clipboard clears it automatically. So why have I used the `Clear` method here? Purely for my own personal reference. I find that being explicit about a statement like `Clipboard.Clear` in your code makes it obvious what's going on. In this case it signals that the Clipboard only contains whatever you're about to put in it. If this is the case, why include a `Clipboard.Clear` method in Visual Basic at all? Because it allows you to remove things from the Clipboard that you might not want to be pasted or viewed, such as passwords.

The `SetText` method on the second line places the selected text onto the Clipboard.

```
Clipboard.SetText txtData.SelText
```

Let's look at this line in two parts. Firstly, the `SetText` method. This places whatever text follows onto the Clipboard. For example, if the line had read:

```
Clipboard.SetText "This is a test"
```

then the text This is a test would have been placed into the Clipboard.

In our example we use the `SelText` property of the text box to identify which text we wanted to cut or copy. A text box has two text properties: `Text` and `SelText`. The `Text` property always contains an exact copy of all the text in the text box, whether visible or not. `SelText` contains a copy of any highlighted information.

When you type something into a text box you can hold the mouse button down and drag a highlight over some or all of the text. The text covered with this highlight is held in `SelText`, making it very useful for implementing Cut and Paste operations in your program.

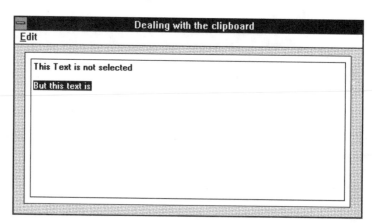

The line that follows:

```
txtData.SelText = ""
```

deletes any highlighted text from the text box. This is the code for the Edit menu Cut event. After copying the information to the Clipboard, the Cut event normally deletes whatever it's just copied.

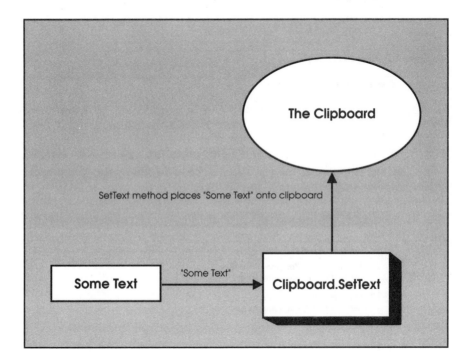

Reading From the Clipboard

Once the information we want is in the Clipboard, the user can switch to another application to paste it out, or paste it back into our own application using the Paste option on the Edit menu. From our program's point of view, the ability to paste text from the Clipboard requires no more than a few taps on the magic keyboard and a single line of code. All courtesy of the **GetText** method.

GetText is a Clipboard method which simply gets hold of the text held in the Clipboard object and places it into whatever container you have waiting, most commonly a text box. Let's now code the Paste function on the Edit menu.

Try it Out - Coding a Paste Option

1 If you don't still have the last project loaded and ready, you'll find it on the disk called **PASTE.MAK.**

2 Bring up the code window for the Paste function. In design-mode, click on the Paste item on the Edit menu.

3 Add code to the Paste menu **Click** event so that it looks like this:

```
Sub mnuEPaste_Click ()

    txtData.SelText = Clipboard.GetText()

End Sub
```

4 Try out the code by running the program, typing and cutting some text to the Clipboard, then pasting it back in using the paste menu item. Do it over and over again if you like.

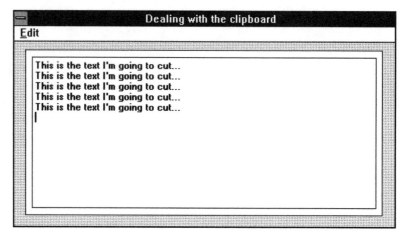

How It Works

The first thing to notice about the **GetText** method is that it's a function. Any code that you can place an equals sign in front of can be considered a function. Because **GetText** is a function remember to place the **()** after the function name.

In the code in this section, **GetText** is always used like this:

```
Clipboard.GetText()
```

No parameters are passed to the function. In reality you can tell **GetText()** to pull text from the Clipboard or from another application via something known as a DDE link. I'll tell you more about DDE later on. If you call **GetText** without any parameters then it defaults to the Clipboard.

If you set the **SelText** property of a text box to hold the text contained in the Clipboard it pastes this text into the text box at the current cursor position. This position is determined by the **SelStart** property. Imagine you have this string in a text box with **SelStart** set to 6:

```
Peter Wright
```

Then you paste the following words into the **SelText** property:

```
The Dude
```

You'll end up with this in the text box:

```
Peter The Dude Wright
```

Clipboard Data Formats

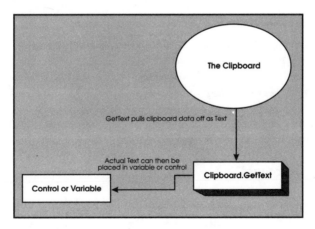

Clipboard is equally well suited to storing graphics images of various types and qualities.

Detecting the Data Type

The **GetFormat** method is how we tell exactly what kind of information is currently held on the clipboard. **GetFormat** is a function: you pass it a number telling it what kind of data you are interested in and it returns either a **True** or **False** value if the type of data you are after appears on the Clipboard.

The numbers for the types of data are all defined in the **CONSTANT.TXT** file and are all long integers, which means that they must be suffixed with an **&** sign. For example **2&** turns the number two into a long integer number 2. Don't suffix the constants with & though since VB would then treat the constant as a long variable.

CONSTANT.TXT Clipboard Data Types

CF_LINK	Used for DDE conversations between two programs.
CF_TEXT	Used for text, like the stuff we've already dealt with.
CF_BITMAP	
	Used for bitmap image, such as an icon, or a screenshot.
CF_METAFILE	Used for special-format drawing, which like the bitmap can be placed in an image or picture box.
CF_DIB	Used for device independent bitmap. Don't panic, it's just another form of bitmap.
CF_PALETTE	Used for color information.

Graphics and the Clipboard

In our example above, before using the **GetText** method to paste information back into the text box we should really have said:

```
If Clipboard.GetFormat(CF_TEXT) then txtData.SelText = Clipboard.GetText()
```

This would mean that the <u>P</u>aste function would only work if the data held on the Clipboard was text. What if we're dealing with picture boxes or image controls though? How do we get graphics bitmaps, metafiles or DIBs from the Clipboard into the control?

That's where the **GetData** method comes into play. Take a look at this:

```
If Clipboard.GetFormat(CF_BITMAP) then picPictureBox.Picture =
    Clipboard.GetData()
```

You can even extend this a little further if you add code to check which type of control is currently active, and match that against the data held on the Clipboard. We'll look at this in a little more detail in the next chapter when we examine the **ActiveControl** property of the screen, and the **TypeOf** clause, which can be used to determine the **TypeOf** a control.

System Objects in Visual Basic

Clipboard is just one of a number of built-in objects that Visual Basic supports, the others being Printer, Screen, and **App.**

The Screen Object

You've already seen how we can use the screen object to determine the width and height of the screen in order to center a form. Like other Visual Basic objects the screen object has a number of properties.

Screen Properties

Property	Description
ActiveControl	Lets you gain access to a control's properties without having to know the name of the property, for example:
	Screen.ActiveControl.Tag = "This is the current property"
ActiveForm	As with **ActiveControl, ActiveForm** gives you access to the controls on the current form, and the properties of the current **ActiveForm**. For example,
	Screen.ActiveForm.Caption = "This is the active form"
FontCount	Gives you the total number of displayable fonts available for the form.
Fonts	Lets you get at the names of all the fonts available for display on the screen. This is an array, so to display them all in a loop:
	For nFontNumber = 0 to screen.FontCount - 1
	Print Screen.Font(nFontNumber)
	Next
Width	The width of the screen, very useful for positioning forms and such like.
Height	The height of the screen.
MousePointer	Gives you a number representing the current mouse style. For example, **11** is an hourglass. There is a complete list of these numbers available through Visual Basic help by searching for **MousePointer**.

The App Object

The **App** object, or more importantly its properties, provides you with a way to get at useful information about the application itself.

Property	Description
Exename	The name of the executable of the program. For example, **Progman.Exe, MsgBox.Exe** or whatever name you give to your application.
Path	The full path where the executable is located. This is a very useful property, as you may want to store files in the same directory as the program itself, but not know the path to that directory. This property shows you that path.
PrevInstance	This is a **True/False** property which tells you whether or not there is another copy of this program running.
Title	The title of the application. This is the name that appears on the applications window if you minimize it.

The printer object lets you get access to the printer currently set up as *default* under Windows. We cover this in a lot more detail in the penultimate chapter of the book, where we look at printing from a complete application.

OLE & DDE

There are two other methods of transferring data between applications besides the Clipboard: Dynamic Data Exchange (DDE) and Object Linking and Embedding (OLE). To describe both in detail is way beyond the scope of a beginner's guide such as ours. To help you decide whether or not you want to find out more about these strange creatures, a brief discussion of them both follows.

Unlike the Clipboard, which provides a way for you to manually transfer information from application to application, DDE and OLE are both automated transfer systems.

What is DDE?

DDE is a way of linking controls in your application to controls in other applications, and also a way of transferring information between the two. For example, you may have a customer details form which contains, among other things, a certain customer's name and address. Using DDE you could link these areas of your form to data fields in a Word document, or cells in an Excel spreadsheet. This would then allow you to implement a very simple mail merge system.

For each customer in the database, your Visual Basic application could send the details across the link to the Word document. This would enable you to produce personalized letters. DDE goes a little further in not only allowing data to be sent across the DDE links, but also commands and keystrokes, to control the application receiving the data.

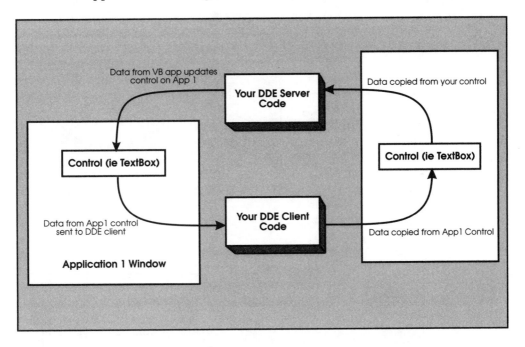

The difference between a straight cut and paste and a DDE link is that the DDE link will update the information in the receiving application whenever the original is changed.

What is OLE?

The alternative to DDE is OLE, which comes in two flavors: OLE 1 and OLE 2. OLE 1 is the simpler of the two, so we'll look at this first.

With OLE 1 you can paste icons into your programs, which when clicked invoke a complete application and display the data created with it. You could, for instance, use OLE to embed a complete Word document in a customer order system. As soon as the icon is double-clicked, the application which originally created the object is loaded, overlaying your application and allowing the user to edit the data in the object.

This presents a number of problems. Firstly, your users would need to be able to access the application that created the object on their system. Secondly, if your application is big and resource-hungry, your user's system performance will deteriorate dramatically.

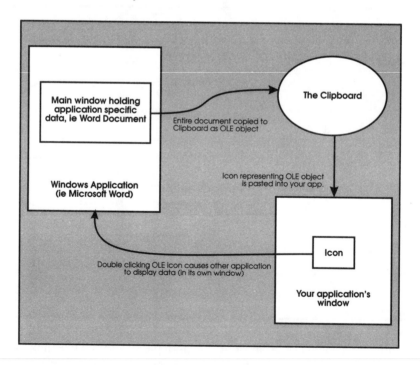

With OLE 2, not only can a program such as Word or Excel export its data as an object, it can also export its functionality. Using OLE 2 you could display a Word document and then re-format it, all with code, by invoking Word's formatting codes.

OLE 2 also allows something called in-place editing. With OLE 1 you see an icon representing the data that will be displayed when the icon is clicked. OLE 2 actually *displays* the data; your user can click on the data and edit it in-place in your applications own forms and windows. The program that produced the data, be it Word or Excel or whatever, handles all of the actual editing in response to the user's key presses, but there is no screen-flipping because Windows loads up the application to facilitate editing.

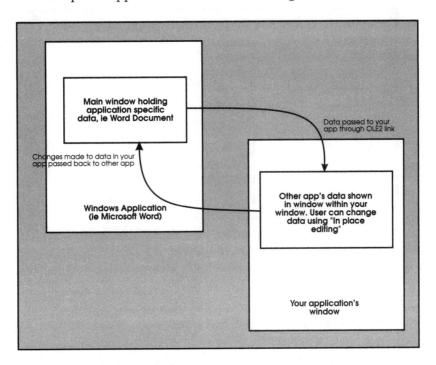

OLE 2 also lets you drag and drop data from one application straight into another, completely by-passing the need for the Clipboard. Unfortunately, the price for all this functionality is as high as it is with DDE; a great deal of technical information and knowledge is needed before you can start doing anything useful. Your users also need access to the programs that produced the OLE objects, as well as needing to know how to use them in addition to your own application.

Microsoft are putting a great deal of investment and hype into OLE 2, and it's something that will directly affect the way all of their Windows applications work and talk to each other over the coming years. Ignore it at your peril!

Dynamic Link Libraries

There's a growing market for VBX add-ons which extend the power of Visual Basic itself, and enhance your productivity as a Visual Basic developer. However, there is one enormous add-on for Visual Basic that is already sitting on every Visual Basic system waiting to be used: the Windows API.

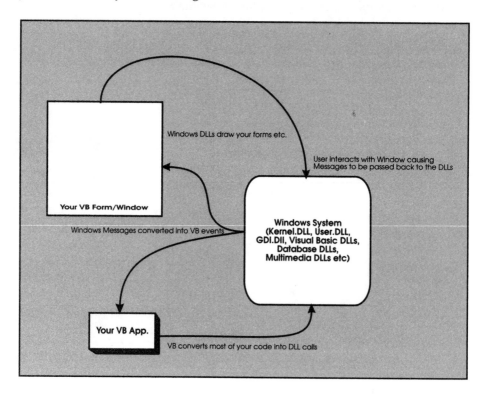

The Application Programmer's Interface (API) is a collection of just over 1000 ready made functions and procedures which are typically used by C and C++ programmers to add functionality to their programs. In general C and C++ development packages are nowhere near as friendly or intuitive to use as Visual Basic. They require the traditional 'write a thousand lines of code to do something' approach to programming, as opposed to Visual Basic's 'you want it, just draw it' approach.

Most of the API calls are already implemented in Visual Basic in the form of Visual Basic commands, keywords, methods and properties. However, there are still some API functions which Visual Basic has no substitute for. For example, there's no way to deal with **INI** files other than by writing a page or two of code to open the **INI** files as sequential files, and trotting through them line by line. We'll look at this example in more detail later.

First of all, let's look at some of the most common API calls that Visual Basic programmers use:

Function	DLL	Description
GetPrivateProfileString	Kernel	Gets a string from a named **INI** file.
WritePrivateProfileString	Kernel	Adds or rewrites an entry in an **INI** file.
mciSendString	Mmsystem	Plays sounds, music and video.
SetParent	User	Moves controls in and out of container objects at run-time. Can even put a form inside a container object such as a picture box.
SetClassLong	User	Allows you to modify the style of a form or window like removing the caption on MDI forms.
FlashWindow	User	Flashes the caption of a window. Good for grabbing the user's attention.
GetActiveWindow	User	Finds out which window the user is currently interacting with in any program.
RemoveMenu	User	Allows you to remove items from the control box menu on your forms.

To describe fully all the API functions that are available to you as a Visual Basic developer would take a book the same size as this one. What we'll do here is examine the general issues involved when dealing with API calls.

If you need further information on API calls you'd be well advised to purchase a copy of the excellent *Visual Basic Programmer's Guide To The Windows API* by Daniel Appleman, published by Ziff Davis Press.

What is a Dynamic Link Library?

The hundreds of API calls that provide Windows with its functionality are contained in DLLs. If it helps you, think of each API call as a subroutine. Given the number of API calls that make up Windows, Microsoft wisely decided to group them together into three main libraries. There are many other smaller, less frequently used DLLs which provide specialist services to applications.

Dynamic Link Libraries	
KERNEL	The main DLL, **Kernel**, handles memory management, multi-tasking of the programs that are running, and most other functions which directly affect how Windows actually runs.
USER	Windows management library. Contains functions which deal with menus, timers, communications, files and many other non-display areas of windows.
GDI	Graphics Device Interface. Provides the functions necessary to draw things on the screen as well as checking which areas of forms need to be redrawn.
MMSYSTEM	Provides multimedia functions, for dealing with sound, music, real-time video, sampling and more.
VBRUN300	The Visual Basic DLL. All your Visual Basic commands and methods are translated into call to functions in this DLL at run-time.

This last DLL, **VBRUN300,** is not part of Windows but is added to Windows by Visual Basic. You can see these files in your **WINDOWS\SYSTEM** directory.

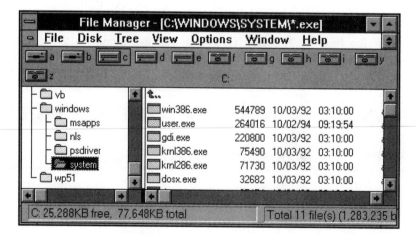

There are other smaller DLLs in Windows, but those were the big ones. In Visual Basic terms, a DLL is nothing more than a ready-compiled code module, which contains a set of pre-written functions and subroutines to cover a wide range of subjects.

A Brief Look Inside Windows

Before we go any further, and before you flick to the next chapter, let's get rid of some major myths. Many Visual Basic programmers steer well clear of API calls because names like Application Programmer's Interface (API), or Dynamic Link Library (DLL) put them off!

In reality, using the API (and the DLLs within it), can be a lot easier than getting to grips with some VBX add-ons. Indeed, using most of the API calls is as simple as calling a standard Visual Basic function or procedure that you have written yourself. Using DLLs isn't difficult; it won't melt your brain and you won't have to take a month's C programming course to get the hang of things.

You've already used a DLL in your Visual Basic programming: **VBRUN300.DLL.** This file must be present in order to run any Visual Basic programs. It translates the output from Visual Basic, (partially compiled **P-Code** as it's known), into instructions that your machine can execute. Rather than build this code into every Visual Basic program, and thereby increase its size by about 400K, it's far more efficient to put it together with your program at run-time. Hence the term 'dynamic linking'.

Compare this to static linking, traditional in the DOS world, where all the object libraries needed for your program are combined with your source code only once, at the time you create the original program. Of course, the drawback of dynamic linking is that all the files you need must be present on each machine the program runs on.

Declaring Functions in a DLL

Before a DLL routine can be used it needs to be declared. Visual Basic needs to be told:

- The name of the DLL
- Which DLL file it can be found in
- The parameters it expects to receive
- The type of value that it can return if the routine is a function

The whole process is very similar to the one where you'd declare a function or subprocedure in Visual Basic code, except that instead of using the word **Sub** or **Function** to start the code off, you use the word **Declare**.

Let's take a look at how this works using a quick example. The code uses an API call to flash the current window colors to the user. This is much easier than fiddling around with the form's **BackColor** property.

Try It Out - Flashing a Window With an API Call

1   Create a new project in Visual Basic.

2   Draw a timer control on the form and set the timer **Interval** property to **10**. This will cause a timer event to occur every 10 milliseconds.

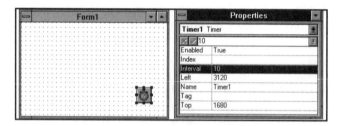

3   Double-click on the timer control you have just drawn to display its code window. Then type in code so that it looks like this:

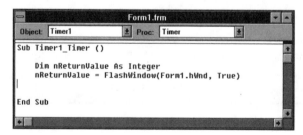

4   Now select (general) from the Object list box at the top of the code window.

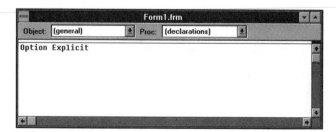

5 In this window declare the **FlashWindow** function as follows:

```
Declare Function FlashWindow Lib "User" (ByVal hWnd As Integer, ByVal
↳bInvert As Integer) As Integer
```

When you type the declaration, make sure you put all the code onto a single line in the code window, and not two (as shown here). It'll look strange at first because most of the line is hidden from view.

6 Now run the program. You should see the form appear, but with the caption of the form flashing.

It's a very simple program, but flashing the caption of a window using pure Visual Basic code is extremely difficult and requires a number of lines of code; something that a single API call can do in one!

Understanding the API Declaration

▶ The function declaration itself is fairly straightforward once you understand its constituent parts.

The word **Declare** tells Visual Basic that we're declaring a DLL routine, since DLL can only ever be used to define links to functions and subprocedures in external DLLs.

Immediately following **Declare** we could use either the word **Sub** or **Function** to declare either a subroutine or a function. Of course, you can't declare subprocedures and functions indiscriminately. It helps to have a Windows API reference manual handy to determine whether the API call you're about to use is a function or subprocedure, which DLL it's contained in, and what the parameters to be passed to the call should be.

The **Lib** keyword tells Visual Basic which DLL the function we want is contained in. In this case it's the **User** DLL file.

Finally, the parameters which are to be passed to the function are declared, along with the type of value that the function will return to us when it's done.

```
Declare Function FlashWindow Lib "User" (ByVal hWnd As Integer, ByVal
↳bInvert As Integer) As Integer
```

The parameters we're passing here are:

```
(ByVal hWnd As Integer, ByVal bInvert As Integer) As Integer
```

The first parameter, **hWnd**, is a **handle** that identifies the window we want to blink. It's important that you understand the concept of handles in Windows, so we'll come back to it later. The second parameter, **bInvert**, switches the flashing property on and off. If **bInvert** is set to **True** by the calling statement, then the bar flashes. To return it to its original state you need to call the function again, with a value **False**.

Calling the API

In the example program we call the function in this way:

```
nReturnValue = FlashWindow(Form1.hWnd, True)
```

Once you have declared an API call it's used in almost exactly the same way as a normal call to a Visual Basic function or subprocedure. In the above example, the **FlashWindow** call is a call to a function held in a DLL. Just as with Visual Basic functions, API functions return values to us which must then be stored somewhere. Since the **FlashWindow** function returns an integer at the end of the line (you can see this from the **Declare** statement which has the words **As Integer**), we store the value in an integer variable, called **nReturnValue**.

Again, just as with Visual Basic functions, you don't have to do anything with the values returned by API functions. But you *do* need to store them somewhere, even if you intend to ignore the return value. Most API functions return numeric error codes which you can use to see if everything worked correctly.

Windows Handles

Visual Basic provides you with a nice soft buffer between your code and the underlying Windows DLL calls. One of the areas where this is most evident is in a control's properties.

Take the form as an example. Windows uses something called a **structure** to hold information about a form. This information is almost identical to the information discovered through the form's properties window. However, whereas you and I can simply click on a form and press *F4* to bring up its properties window, Windows stores each window's structure in a large list of structures which relates to every window of every program actually running. It uses something called a **handle** to determine which structure relates to which window.

As you start to use API calls more and more, particularly those that deal directly with your Visual Basic forms, you'll find handles cropping up more and more. Conveniently, Visual Basic stores this handle as a **read only** property which you can use to pass to Windows functions when required.

This property is called **hWnd** (handle to a Window) and can only be accessed at run-time. The property means nothing to your Visual Basic code, but can be read and passed to API calls as a parameter to those functions that need it.

Declaring Parameter Types

When you declare the types of parameters that a DLL subprocedure or function needs, it's important to make sure that the **ByVal** keyword is used whenever necessary.

With regular Visual Basic code, if you pass a parameter to a function **ByVal** it tells Visual Basic that the function can only deal with a copy of the parameter you pass it. This is how you do it with a regular function:

```
Function Square (ByVal Number)
```

For example, if you pass a variable **ByVal** to a function, the function doesn't receive the whole variable, it simply gets a copy of whatever's stored in the variable. The alternative to **ByVal** is to pass by reference. Here, you pass the whole variable to the function, and not just a copy of its contents. Therefore, if the function changes the parameter, those changes are also reflected in the original variable. Where you don't specify **ByVal**, the default is by reference, so almost all the function and procedure calls we've made so far in the book have been done in this way.

Once your internal Visual Basic function or subprocedure has been written, as long as you pass the correct number of parameters to the code nothing serious will go wrong. Sure, you may get cases where variables passed as parameters are changed, causing weird result to come out of your program, but nothing really serious will happen. Windows won't crash, for example!

However, with DLLs, the situation is a little more serious. If you omit the **ByVal** keyword, Visual Basic actually passes a pointer to the variable. This is a long number which tells the function being called where in memory the variable is stored. It's then up to the function to go to that memory location and retrieve the value held within it for itself. This is also what happens in Visual Basic-only situations, but since the functions and subprocedures there are all written in your Visual Basic code, Visual Basic can cope. DLL code, written in a language like C for example, expects things to happen in a certain way, and can get quite upset when they don't.

547

If a DLL function expects a number, let's say between 0 and 3, and you pass it a variable by reference, the actual value passed could be something like 1,002,342, which would be the address in memory where your variable lives. The DLL function would then try to deal with the number 1,002,342 instead of a number between 0 and 3, the net result of which would be that your system **crashes.**

> There are no nasty error messages here; you know when a DLL call is wrong because your system locks up!

> One of the golden rules of messing about with API calls is *save your work*! Because you're venturing outside the protected world of Visual Basic, when things go wrong it can easily result in the whole system crashing, and you losing your work. Always save your project *before* running code with API calls in it. The best way to do this is to change **Save Project Before Run** to **True** in the Options Environment menu.

Declaring the Easy Way

Don't panic! If you're using the Professional Edition of Visual Basic, the file **WIN30API.TXT** in your **\VB\WINAPI** directory contains the API declarations for all the standard API calls.

It's common practice to copy the API declarations directly from this file rather than type them in by hand yourself. However, don't try to add this file to your project as it's far too big and Visual Basic will give you an error message if you attempt it.

Unfortunately, if you're using the Standard Edition of Visual Basic and you want to move into big-style API calling, then you're out of luck, as you don't get the file. If, after reading this book, you're serious about Visual Basic, then the first thing to do is go out and upgrade to the Pro Edition. Alternatively, invest in one of the API books, such as the VB Programmer's Guide to the Windows API, which list all the information you need.

Putting the API to Work

Having learnt about the downside of using the API, that is, getting the code right, let's look at the upside, the great things you can do with it. The example we're going to use is of handling **INI** files, something that's really hard to do with Visual Basic alone.

Talking to INI Files

Windows **INI** files are text files that tell a program certain details about how it should work, or where its data lives. The operation of Windows itself is governed by two such files:

▶ **WIN.INI** tells Windows things like which printer to use, what country the user is in, and which programs can deal with which files.

▶ The **SYSTEM.INI** file determines the way Windows itself works. It contains information such as the size and location of your swap file, which video resolution you're running, whether or not you have a sound card, and so on.

> To see these files, just double-click on the filename in File Manager, and the file will load into Notepad.

Actually reading values from and writing values to these files without help from the API is an horrendous task, requiring in-depth knowledge of flat-file handling, loops, string handling, and so on. However, if you use API calls, one line of code will enable you to read specific lines from these files, or write a specific line to them.

Reading and Writing WIN.INI

The **GetProfile** and **WriteProfile** API calls are designed to work specifically with the **WIN.INI** file. If you use these calls it's a very simple way of finding out information about your system. Changing parameters in this file can actually change the way in which Windows works - for better or for worse!

All the **INI** files, **WIN.INI** included, are actually straight text files, so if you have a fear of using API calls then you can write Visual Basic code to deal with the files manually. The result, however, would be about 3 screens full of code, which runs fairly slowly. With just one API call you can find and read values from an **INI** file very quickly.

All **INI** files, be they one of the major Windows **INI** files (**WIN.INI** and **SYSTEM.INI**) or an **INI** file of your own, have a standard format which enables them to be dealt with quickly and easily by the API **INI** calls. Take a look at the excerpt from **WIN.INI** below:

```
[Desktop]
Pattern=(None)
GridGranularity=0
IconSpacing=70
TileWallPaper=0
wallpaper=(None)
IconTitleWrap=1
```

The **INI** file is broken down into sections, with the section name being held in square brackets [ ]. In the above example the section name for this snippet is **Desktop**.

> Strangely, the API refers to this section name as an **App**lication name. Originally, I think Microsoft had planned for there to be one **INI** file for all Windows apps which would be broken down into separate applications using the square brackets.

The entries underneath the **App**lication name heading are known as keys. The text to the left of the **=** sign is the keyname while the section to the right is the keyvalue.

The actual values for the section names and keynames have no standard and vary from application to application. Windows doesn't really care what you call section names in your own **INI** files, nor what you call the keys, just so long as you know what they are and what you want to use them for. The **WIN.INI** file is rather special to Windows since it contains the global, or public, settings for how Windows looks and talks to the other components of your PC. This includes such things as which printer is connected, which fonts are installed, and so on.

For this reason, the API has three important calls just for dealing with the **WIN.INI** file and nothing else. These are **GetProfileString**, **GetProfileInt**, and **WriteProfileString**. These allow you to read and write keys in the **INI** file which contain strings and integers respectively.

Try It Out -Reading INI Files

Time to look at some code.

1   Load up the **SYSTEM.MAK** project into Visual Basic and run it. **SYSTEM.MAK** enables you to examine the **WIN.INI** file by searching for key sections of it and displaying them.

```
┌─────────────────────────────────────────────────────────┐
│ ─   Using GetProfileString to search Win.INI      ▼ ▲   │
│                                                           │
│              ┌──────────────────────────┐                 │
│              │    Reading WIN.INI        │                 │
│              └──────────────────────────┘                 │
│   ┌─Find what in Win.Ini────────────────────────────────┐ │
│   │                                                      │ │
│   │ Application (Section) Name  ┌─────────────────────┐  │ │
│   │                             │ Desktop             │  │ │
│   │                             └─────────────────────┘  │ │
│   │ Key Name (Entry Name)       ┌─────────────────────┐  │ │
│   │                             │                     │  │ │
│   │                             └─────────────────────┘  │ │
│   └──────────────────────────────────────────────────────┘ │
│   ┌──────────────────────────────────────────────────────┐ │
│   │         Search Win.Ini for the specified values        │ │
│   └──────────────────────────────────────────────────────┘ │
└─────────────────────────────────────────────────────────┘
```

Try It Out!

2 When you run it, the program asks you to enter the section name, and/ or the keyname for the parts of the **WIN.INI** file you want to look at. You don't have to enter a keyname if you don't want to. The result will be that the program displays a list of the valid keynames in a message box, from which you select one.

3 For the application name, enter Desktop then hit the Search button. A message box appears showing you a list of valid keynames for that section of the **INI** file.

4 Now try typing in WallPaper for the keyname and hit Search again.

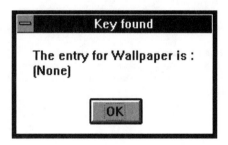

5 This time the message box appears showing you the line in the **INI** file you were after. Personally, I hate Windows wallpaper, so it says (None).

How It Works

The code behind all this is extremely simple. One of the advantages of API calls is that they can reduce your coding time dramatically. However, the time it takes to find the API call you're after in the first case can frequently offset any advantages in the short term.

```
Sub cmdFind_Click ()

Dim sReturnString As String * 4000
    Dim nReturnCode As Integer
    Dim sMessage As String, nCharacter As Integer

    If txtAppName.Text = "" Then
        MsgBox "You must enter a section name to search.", , "Missing
↳Parameter"
        Exit Sub
    End If

    If txtKeyName.Text = "" Then
        nReturnCode = GetProfileString(txtAppName.Text, 0&, "NONE",
↳sReturnString, 4000)
    Else
        nReturnCode = GetProfileString(txtAppName.Text,
↳CStr(txtKeyName.Text), "NONE", sReturnString, 4000)
    End If

    If Left$(sReturnString, 4) = "NONE" Then
        MsgBox "Either the application name or the keyname could not be
↳found.", , "Search Failed"
        Exit Sub
    End If

    If txtKeyName.Text = "" Then

        sMessage = "Valid keynames are : " & Chr$(10)

        For nCharacter = 1 To nReturnCode
            If Mid$(sReturnString, nCharacter, 1) <> Chr$(0) Then
                sMessage = sMessage & Mid$(sReturnString, nCharacter, 1)
            Else
                sMessage = sMessage & ", "
            End If
        Next

        MsgBox sMessage, , "Valid keynames"

    Else

        sMessage = "The entry for " & txtKeyName.Text & " is : " & Chr(10)
        sMessage = sMessage & Left$(sReturnString, nReturnCode)
        MsgBox sMessage, , "Key found"

    End If

End Sub
```

There are comments about the code on the disk which will give you more information.

Only one line of code is needed to actually run the API call. The format of the **GetProfileString** function call is:

```
GetProfileString ( <ApplicationName>, <KeyName>, <Default>, <Your string
variable for the results>, <Size>) as Integer
```

Like many API functions **GetProfileString** returns an integer to your program which tells it how many characters were returned in the string variable you passed to it. The actual string you were after is returned in the string variable which you pass to the routine. Take a look at the declarations section of the example program and you'll see that this particular parameter doesn't use the **ByVal** keyword and is therefore passed by reference and not by value.

<ApplicationName>   This is the name of the section you want to search. Therefore, if you were to pass **DeskTop** as the application name, then you would be searching the **DeskTop** section of the **WIN.INI** file.

<KeyName>   This is the name of the key that you want to search for. You can either pass the keyname itself, or a long 0 (**0&**). Passing a long 0 in this way returns in the return string a complete list of all the keynames in the section that you specified in the **ApplicationName** parameter.

The keynames in this returned string are all separated by character **0**, which in API terms is commonly called the **NULL** character. You can use a **ForLoop** to walk through the characters in this string pulling out the keynames. The number returned from the function tells us exactly how many characters were placed in the return string, and this is used to make sure that we only check as much of the returned string as necessary.

```
sMessage = "Valid keynames are : " & Chr$(10)

For nCharacter = 1 To nReturnCode
    If Mid$(sReturnString, nCharacter, 1) <> Chr$(0) Then
        sMessage = sMessage & Mid$(sReturnString, nCharacter, 1)
    Else
        sMessage = sMessage & ", "
    End If
Next

MsgBox sMessage, , "Valid keynames"
```

There is also code in the example to check whether or not the user actually typed in a keyname. If they did, then the name they entered is converted to a string and passed to the API call using **Cstr**; otherwise a long **0** is passed.

```
If txtKeyName.Text = "" Then
    nReturnCode = GetProfileString(txtAppName.Text, 0&, "NONE",
↳sReturnString, 4000)
Else
    nReturnCode = GetProfileString(txtAppName.Text, CStr(txtKeyName.Text),
↳"NONE", sReturnString, 4000)
End If
```

Beware when reading API and DLL reference manuals! Their definition of **NULL** is usually character **0**, which is *very* different to Visual Basic's **NULL** constant.

Should the call fail to find the section or key you asked for, then the value specified in **Default** is returned back to your application. In the above example we checked the returned string to see if it was equal to **"NONE"**, that being the value passed to the DLL function as the default value:

```
If Left$(sReturnString, 4) = "NONE" Then
        MsgBox "Either the application name or the keyname could not be
↳found.", , "Search Failed"
        Exit Sub
```

<Size>   This is the size of the string variable that you're passing. In our example we declare a string variable to be a fixed length string, capable of holding 4000 characters. So the value of the **<Size>** parameter is set to 4000.

The **GetProfileInt** call is almost identical to the **GetProfileString** call, the only difference being that a string variable is not passed to the routine. Instead, the number found is returned from the function. In the **DeskTop** section of the **WIN.INI** file, the **IconSpacing** key is actually an integer value, so to retrieve that value we could say:

```
nIconSpacing = GetProfileInt( "DeskTop", "IconSpacing", 9999)
```

Here **9999** is the default value returned if all else fails.

In general though you shouldn't really have to worry about whether or not to use **GetProfileInt** or **GetProfileString**. Just consistently use the **String** routine and check the contents at the end of the call to see if you get back a number or some text. This has the advantage that your code remains consistent when dealing with **INI** files, and because you have reduced the number of global, or module level DLL declarations, your application will use less memory and resources at run-time.

Dealing With Private INI Files

The other alternative to reading and writing values to and from the **WIN.INI** file all the time is to use your own private **INI** file. For example, if you had an application called **CUSTOMER.EXE** you could name your private **INI** file **CUSTOMER.INI**.

> It's a good a idea to use your own private **INI** files. Therefore, if you trash it your whole system doesn't collapse!

You can create **INI** files for your own programs with whichever name and information you want. Windows programs don't have to have **INI** files. There's no direct link in Windows between a program and its **INI** files. Indeed, you can have more than one **INI** file for a program to use if you want. It's up to you.

The **WIN.INI** and **SYSTEM.INI** files hold information about Windows itself, how it runs, how it looks, and the devices it can talk to. Application-specific **INI** files are normally used to hold application-specific information. For instance, a client-tracking program may use an **INI** file to hold the date the program was last used, or information about how the user of that program likes to have the Windows arranged. Shareware programs often use **INI** files to hold an expiry date which says when the user must go out and buy the full package.

There are three special API calls which deal solely with these private **INI** files. In use they are almost identical to their **WIN.INI** counterparts. They are **GetPrivateProfileString**, **GetPrivateProfileInt**, and **WritePrivateProfileString**.

When you use these calls the only difference between them and their **WIN.INI** cousins is that each has an additional parameter added to the end of the list. This is the name of the **INI** file you want to search. Therefore, if you had an **INI** file called **CUSTOMER.INI** and you needed to search the **Database** section to find the path of the application database, you'd simply write:

```
nReturn = GetPrivateProfileString( "Database", "Path", "FAILED", sPath,
    ⤷ "Customer.INI")
```

This is assuming that you have first declared the function along with the **nReturn** and **sPath** variables, like this:

```
[Declarations section]
Declare Function GetPrivateProfileString Lib "Kernel" (ByVal
  lpApplicationName As String, BYVal lpKeyName As Any, BYVal lpDefault As
  String, ByVal lpReturnedString As String, ByVal nSize as Integer, ByVal
  lpFileName As String) As Integer

Sub A_Sub()

    Dim nReturn As Integer
    Dim sPath As String
    :
    :
```

Looking After Your Resources

Computer resources, such as memory and time, are not bottomless. This is especially true in an environment such as Windows, where you can have many programs all running together vying for the same memory space, processor time, and so on.

If you write a resource-unfriendly program it can have some dire consequences: other programs start to crash, or they perform slowly and your users soon start to get upset. On the other hand, writing an efficient, resource-friendly program can make it appear head and shoulders above the rest of the crowd: the program responds more quickly to your users, forms load and seem to appear faster than in other applications, and all is generally wonderful.

What Are Resources?

The word resource actually means two entirely different things in the Windows lexicon. One type of resource is the non-program data that is contained in Windows programs in the form of icons, images and so on. That's *not* what we're talking about here. The resources that affect your program's performance, and the resources that are likely to run out, are actually sections of memory that are allocated to specific tasks.

As far as Windows is concerned there are three parts to these resources in your PC: GDI resources, User resources and regular memory. What really matters for us here are the first two, GDI and User resources. So what are they?

▶ The GDI resource maintains information about anything graphical in your program. If you use icons, different fonts, non-standard colors and so on, information about each of these is placed into the GDI resource heap. You can think of a heap as a big array.

▶ The User heap holds what windows calls 'style information', which relates to your forms and controls. In Visual Basic terms, these properties are used to determine the look and feel of the components of your program.

Each type of resource is held in an area of memory only 64K in size. When you consider that every program running must share the same two heaps, you start to realize what a fragile contraption Windows is.

Plain old memory is the area inside your computer where the rest of the information about your program lives: its code, its variables, and so on. With Windows, if you're running on 386 or higher you have something called **virtual memory**. This is an area of your hard disk set aside to *pretend* that it is memory, and not disk space. The net result is that Windows thinks you have a lot more memory than you really have. The downside is that once you run out of normal memory (RAM) and start to use the virtual memory on the hard disk your applications begin to slow down dramatically. Microsoft call it system deterioration; users call it a crap program.

Why does all this matter? It matters because it's easy to write programs in Visual Basic that gobble-up what limited resources are available in Windows. Gobbling-up too many resources means your system is slow, and that your users are prevented your user from opening other applications at the same time; and that's if you're lucky!

Checking Your Resource Usage

There is a gauge on the Windows Program Manager About screen that shows how your resources are being consumed. Open up the Help menu and select About.

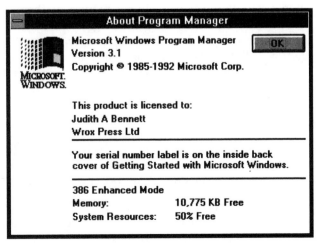

Now,. if you open up a few more applications, and look again, you'll see the amount of free resources dwindle. Incidentally, you may be wondering what happens if you run out of resources at run-time.

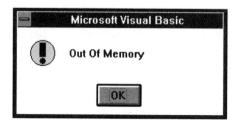

Not very dramatic, I hear you cry! Well, bear in mind that when this happens if any databases are open they'll crash and you'll need to re-boot to gain access to them. Windows has now ground to a halt, and any information the users were entering has been lost forever; any other applications running are very likely to keel over and die out of sympathy. It's at this point that your users will be rapidly sharpening knives and dialing your number!

So let's take a look at some ways of reducing the amount of resources your programs consume in their race to reach the best-seller lists.

Loading and Saving

Each form in your program consumes both GDI and User resources. This is in addition to the normal memory where the form code is held. In order to keep the use of these resources to a minimum, only load your forms as and when they're needed.

If you have a massive login screen with hundreds of controls which show the user information about the system, a hi-res picture of themselves, and an astrological forecast for the next millennium - get rid of it. I don't mean delete it from the project for ever and start again; simply unload the form once the user has logged in. All the resources consumed by the form will be released and made available for the other forms in your program, or in other programs that may be running.

The Process of Loading a Form

It's all right saying that a form uses *this* resource and *that* block of memory, but the exact point in time at which this happens isn't entirely straightforward. The following steps show how your memory is eaten when you load a form:

> Your code does a **Load** method to load a form. Visual Basic hunts around the hard disk to find where the form is, what it looks like, and how much memory it's likely to need.

▶ Visual Basic tells Windows to set aside GDI resources to hold information about graphical aspects of the form, such as its fonts, colors, patterns, and so on.

▶ Visual Basic tells Windows to set aside User resources to hold the property information for the form and every control on it. This is called style information (if you ever need to discuss it with a C programmer).

▶ Visual Basic asks Windows for memory so it can store the form variables and data, including the data that you might see in any of the form controls. This doesn't include local variables, only module level and static variables.

▶ Providing all the steps worked well up to this point, the form is displayed on the screen.

▶ The user moves the mouse onto the form and clicks, for example, a command button.

▶ Visual Basic panics. It forgot to load the code earlier. Some disk chunking occurs and Visual Basic asks Windows for some more memory, this time to hold the form code.

That's the order of events when the form loads. Notice the last step: the form's code is only loaded in when it's needed. If you load and then unload a form, its code module is never loaded providing that no events occur to invoke an event handler.

Unloading a Form

Unloading a form is a little more straightforward than loading one up, but it still has its fair share of problems. When you unload a form by using the **Unload** method on a form, the GDI resources, User resources and memory used to store the code are released and handed back to Windows. Windows says 'thanks a lot, I don't need this stuff anymore!'

Have you noticed what's missing yet? The area of memory set aside to hold the forms variables and data is still reserved. This can cause problems. If you place a value into a form level variable that is one-dimensional in the declarations section of a form, and you then unload and reload the form, the contents of that variable won't be cleared.

Luckily, this little quirk can be worked around if you set the form to **Nothing**.

```
Unload frmBigForm
Set frmBigForm = Nothing
```

This will free all the memory and the resources eaten by a form. Setting a form to something such as **Nothing** (confused? you will be!) is a whole new topic we haven't yet covered, namely, how to handle object variables. In the next chapter you'll see exactly what object variables are and how they can be used. I bet you can't wait!

Controls and Memory

There are issues to be aware of even when you deal with simple controls. Controls in Visual Basic can be categorized into **heavyweight** (list boxes, grids, data controls, text boxes) and **lightweight** (labels, images, lines and shapes). Microsoft recommend you use lightweight controls instead of the heavyweight ones wherever possible:

> If you just need to display text, don't use a text box, use a label.

> If you have an application that needs a static grid (one that doesn't scroll), you can save a lot of resources by using a picture box to store an image of the grid. A lot of screen capture programs allow you to take screenshots of portions of a form and store them as images. You can use one to grab an image of the grid and store it as a graphic. In your program you can display the grid graphic using a picture box and then use the **Print** method to print data into the grid. This saves a lot of memory, but it's not an easy thing to do.

> If you have a tool bar which consists of a number of command buttons with picture boxes on to hold the images, use a single image control to represent all the buttons. In the **MouseDown** event, work out where in the image the mouse appears and draw a solid black border over the white and gray borders of a command button. At mouse-up time just redraw the image control as it was. This gives an illusion of a button being depressed, but it only uses 1 lightweight control instead of 10, 20 or even more heavyweight ones.

> If you have many data controls, one of which displays bound information, the others being used to feed list boxes, combo boxes and so on, replace them with two data controls, one to display the bound information, and one to build all the list boxes. In the **Load** event change the **RecordSource** property of the second data control to build each individual list box. This is better than using 4 data controls for 4 list boxes.

```
datLists.RecordSource = "Select * from Jobs"
datLists.Refresh
' Build the Jobs list box here

datLists.RecordSource = "Select * from company"
datLists.Refresh
' Build the companies list box here

datLists.RecordSource = "Select * from SalaryBand"
datLists.Refresh
'Build the salary band list box here
```

All these techniques do mean that you have to put a lot more thought and code into your applications. However, with a big application that appears to run very slowly and eat lots of resources, these techniques can really pay off.

Well-Behaved Multi-Tasking

One of the reasons that people use Windows is for its multi-tasking. This means that it's possible to run more than one program at once, and those programs can run side by side, seemingly working away in parallel.

Traditional multi-tasking environments manage this by giving each program a time-slice: a small period of time in which the application can do something, before a time-slice is given to a second program. These time-slices are so small that the illusion given is that the programs are running together, when in reality they are not. This method, where the processor calls all the shots, is known as **pre-emptive multi-tasking**, and it's the way that Windows NT and OS/2 does it.

Windows doesn't use this method. Instead, it gives a program as much time as it needs to finish a single operation. However, as soon as a program asks Windows to do something else for it, such as redraw a form or display some text, then Windows transfers control to other programs that are waiting to execute an instruction sequence of their own. This is known as co-operative multi-tasking. It relies on each application having suitable breaks in its own processing to enable Windows to pass control to another active application.

This can cause some major problems, primarily in the areas of loops and large calculations. Take a look at the following little gem.

Try It Out - A Processor Hog

1   Create a new Visual Basic project and bring up the code window for the default form, Form1.

> Before you start typing the following code, be warned that you should not run the program without first making your system safe.

2   In the code window, add this code to the form load event

```
Sub Form1_Load()
    Dim nNumber as Long
    Do
        nNumber = 2
    Loop
End Sub
```

> STOP! Don't run the project yet ! Firstly, make sure that you save it, and close down all your other applications. Don't say I didn't warn you!

3   Now run it and your system will lock up. Sorry, but it's *Ctrl-Alt-Del* time.

All this code does is assign the number **2** to a variable, over and over again. It doesn't display any values on screen or do anything that would normally require the use of Windows itself. For this reason this particular piece of code will freeze Windows. This means that while it's running, no other applications will be able to do anything. More importantly, if you'd written this code in your program by accident it could be very hard to spot.

DoEvents

A way around processor hogging is to use the **DoEvents** method. By inserting it into your code, particularly into loops, Windows gets a chance to pass control around. Let's see how it works.

Try It Out - Using DoEvents

1   Reset your machine.

2   Reload the last project.

3   In the code window, add the statement **DoEvents** so the form **Load** event looks like this:

```
Sub Form1_Load()
    Dim nNumber as Long
    Do
            nNumber = 2
            DoEvents
    Loop
End Sub
```

4   Try running the code again. Notice how nothing seems to happen. The **Load** event never ends, but at least all the other applications work fine. For example, try pressing *Alt-Tab* to switch between Visual Basic and Program Manager.

How It Works

Superficially, the code appears very similar to the earlier example which had such catastrophic results on the system. However, the addition of the **DoEvents** line makes it much more system-friendly. **DoEvents** tells Windows that it can do anything it's waiting to do, if it wants to. Therefore, if you hit *Alt-Tab*, Windows knows that you want to switch applications, and that means redrawing the screen, and so on. When our code hits the **DoEvents** line, Visual Basic says to Windows 'Do you have anything you need to do?' Windows replies 'Yes' so that Visual Basic lets it go away and do it.

This cuts both ways. Not only does it mean that other Windows applications get a look in, it can also make your application seem much more rapid. You may be trying to do a large calculation in your code at the same time as Visual Basic is trying to draw one of your forms. Normally, the form would appear slowly, bit by bit, as Visual Basic and Windows fight against your looping code. If you use **DoEvents** the form appears to load and display much faster, which is a psychological boost for the user.

Idle Loops

You can use **DoEvents** to produce idle loops. This is a loop which only runs when Windows has nothing better to do. This is a good way to make effective use of your computer's time.

Computers can perform hundreds of thousands of small tasks every second. A user typing in information will only ever expect the computer to do something every 1/4 of a second when a key is pressed. This leaves a lot of time in that second when the computer is not actually doing anything. You can use idle loops to do something constructive in that time, such as building up large listboxes. To do this you need to use the **DoEvents** function, as opposed to the straight **DoEvents** statement.

The DoEvents Function

The **DoEvents** function serves two purposes. Firstly, it returns a value to you which indicates the number of open forms in your application. A **DoWhile DoEvents()** loop will run on and on until your application unloads all its forms.

In reality, it's rare to want to have a loop run forever, or at least until the application closes. A better use for this kind of idle loop is to combine it with another condition. For example:

```
Sub Form_Load()

    Dim BoxNotBuilt As Integer

    BoxNotBuilt = True

    Do While DoEvents() And BoxNotBuilt

            : Code to build a list box
            : When the build is complete, BoxNotBuilt is set to False

    Loop

End Sub
```

Here the form **Load** event starts up an idle loop in order to build up a list box. The loop runs in idle-time until the list box has been built.

The other affect of the call is that, along with the **DoEvents** statement, control is passed to Windows if an event is waiting to happen. This happens if, for example, a form needs repainting, or the user very thoughtlessly hit the wrong keys and Windows wants to tell them off.

At first glance this seems pretty useless. Why not just use the **DoEvents** statement instead? To see how useful it is we need to do some coding.

Try It Out - Idle Loops

1   Load up the **SLOW.MAK** project supplied on the examples disk with the book.

2   Run the program. The program does nothing more than load a form with three combo boxes on, each containing 2000 items in its list portion.

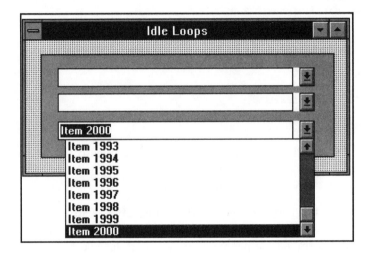

3   When you run the program watch the form as the program tries to display it. On a slow machine the form will appear corrupted and remain that way until the combo boxes are ready. On a faster machine you'll notice a 2 or 3 second delay between the form appearing and you being able to do anything.

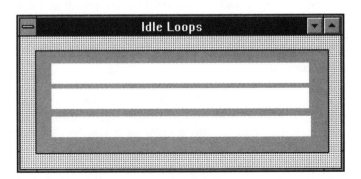

4 Stop the program from running and bring up the form code window to view the form **Load** event. We're going to enter some code to speed this load process up:

```
Sub Form_Load ()
    Static nindex As Integer

    frmMain.Show

    nindex = 0
    Do While nindex < 2001
        nindex = nindex + 1
        comFirst.AddItem "Item " & nindex
        comSecond.AddItem "Item " & nindex
        comThird.AddItem "Item " & nindex
    Loop

    frmMain.Refresh

End Sub
```

5 Change the **Do While nIndex < 2001** line so that it looks like this:

```
Do While DoEvents() and nIndex < 2001
```

6 Run the program again. This time, after Visual Basic has sorted itself out, you'll see the form appear instantly on *any* machine. As soon as the form has appeared you can start to select items from the combo boxes, whilst the **Do While** loop continues to add items to the combo boxes in the background.

How It Works

This is a very simple but highly effective way to solve a lot of user complaints. Imagine the situation where the user is on the phone to a customer and needs to pull up customer information by selecting an item from a list. In the traditional method, the user might have to tell the customer on the phone to hold while the program loads. With this message that problem is cured. Very few users will notice that for 2-3 seconds the lists to which they have access are incomplete.

It's a bit of a programming illusion really. Run the example program and try not to think about what you're doing. Select item number 1400 from one of the combo boxes. You'll scroll to the bottom of a combo list and select an item, then when you look at the screen you'll notice that you have the wrong one.

Most users at that point won't think to blame the program, but will instead happily go back to the list again, presuming they've just selected the wrong item. Chances are that by the time they get back into the list, the list will be completely built and everything will be OK.

There's no such thing as a free lunch however, and there is one major problem with the **DoEvents** loop. Try running the program again, and then closing it straight away. It won't let you! The **DoEvents** loop will run forever, or in this case will run until **nIndex > 2000**. The only way to stop this program is to either wait until the combo boxes are all built, or go to the Run menu and select End. If you're running on a fast computer you'll have to shut the form down pretty quick to see this happening, or it will fill the list box long before you can point the mouse and fire.

If you do use this approach in your code, you may want to use a module level variable to indicate the status of the **DoEvents** loop. If the variable is set to **True**, for instance, you could make the **DoEvents** loop jump out. The variable could be set in the **QueryUnload** event of the form.

Summary

This chapter should have provided you with a glimpse of the power that lies beyond the strict limits of Visual Basic, as defined by the language itself. This is a huge subject, so all we've done is to touch on the principles of using the Windows system objects like the Clipboard, and the API.

With power comes responsibility, because once you choose to operate outside the confines of Visual Basic, you have to look after yourself. It pays to develop a deep understanding of all the components of Windows so you can write Visual Basic programs that are truly well behaved members of the Windows desktop community.

In our brief tour we covered:

- How Windows and Visual Basic fit together
- What system objects Windows provides for your use
- How to use the Clipboard
- OLEs and DDEs
- How to use the Windows API to extend the power of Visual Basic
- How resource usage can affect the performance of your programs
- How to write well-behaved Windows applications

From this point I hope you're motivated to get the Professional Edition of Visual Basic, and to delve further into the mysteries of Windows.

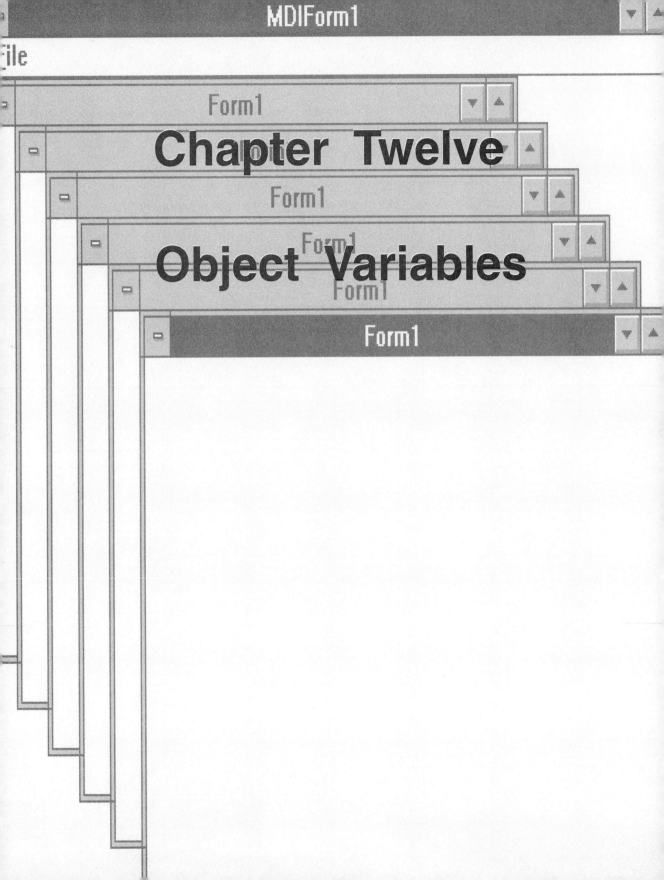

MDIForm1

File

Form1

Chapter Twelve

Form1

Form1

Object Variables

Form1

Form1

Object Variables

Almost all the objects you've come across so far that make up the components of Visual Basic, such as controls and forms, can themselves be used as variables. There are almost no limits to what you can do now.

We're going to learn about:

- Why Visual Basic is almost, but not quite, object oriented
- How to manipulate controls like variables
- What kind of object variables are available
- How you create arrays of objects
- What is an MDI application
- How to work with multiple forms in your applications

Visual Basic as an Object Oriented Language

There's a lot of talk in programming circles at the moment about **Object Oriented Programming**, or **OOP**. At its most basic this is a method where all the real world data in your program is turned into a data collection known as a **class**. You might for instance have an employee class to represent a generic employee in a personnel database.

From these classes you can derive objects which represent specific types or instances of a class. Going back to the personnel metaphor you may have an object in your code called CurrentPerson which is derived from the employee class. It contains data and functionality that is defined in its parent class, the employee class, but which contains specific data relating to the CurrentPerson.

Visual Basic 3 is not yet a true OOP development system in that you can't create your own classes and objects in the same way you can with a language such as C++. However, the link between Windows itself and Visual Basic is based along OOP lines. Here your classes are the types of controls you may use, such as text boxes, list boxes and so on. The objects are the specific instances of a class on a form, for example a text box you have drawn named txtEmployee. Think of the design environment; a class is a control in your toolbox, an object is that control drawn on the form.

Introducing Object Variables

Visual Basic lets you take control of these objects and classes in your code through special variables known as **object variables**. Using these you can:

- Create new controls at run-time

- Copy controls to produce new instances of existing ones

- Create duplicate forms, all with identical names, controls and code but each containing and dealing with different data, much like the different documents you might have loaded in a Word session

Object variables also provide a way to write general routines to deal with specific controls. You may have a text box validation routine, but it can only be used in a project by specifying the exact name of the control explicitly in the code itself. Treating that control as an object variable makes the routine independent. You can use it with any control. This makes your code so much more transportable and ultimately, useful.

Controls as Object Variables

Remember the chapter on menus? One of things we did in that chapter was to create a dynamic menu; a menu whose items grew and shrunk each time we selected a file name. Menu items are controls, the same as a text box, command button and so on. What we were actually doing back then was creating dynamic controls, controls that only exist at run-time, not at design-time. We were in effect creating and destroying instances of objects in the same way as we do with variables.

This technique can be extremely useful for applications where you need to create a great many controls of a similar type, but don't want the hassle of drawing them all by hand, for example a toolbar. You can even let your users create their own custom toolbars using object variables.

Creating Controls at Run-Time

The principles of creating controls on the fly are easy to follow. The simplest method is to create a control array at design-time, then extend that array with code at run-time.

In the same way that you can **Redim** a normal variable array, you can also extend and shrink control arrays. The difference is that you can't **Redim** a control array like you can a variable array. Instead you have to **Load** new instances of the controls into the array. When you want to remove controls you **Unload** them from the array to reduce its size.

Try It Out - Creating Controls at Run-Time

Let's put this into practice by creating a row of command buttons on a form, starting with just one command button drawn at design-time, the rest created through your program code.

1   Start a new project in Visual Basic and draw a small command button on the form.

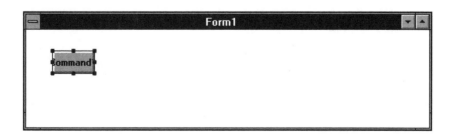

2   When you create the command button, place 0 into the Index property. This creates a control array with just one control in it.

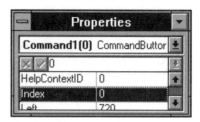

3   In the **Click** event for the command button type the following code:

```
Sub Command1_Click (Index As Integer)

  Static sNextOperation As String
  Dim nIndex As Integer

  For nIndex = 1 To 10

    If sNextOperation = "UNLOAD" Then
      Unload Command1(nIndex)
    Else
      Load Command1(nIndex)
      Command1(nIndex).Visible = True
      Command1(nIndex).Left = Command1(nIndex - 1).Left +
Command1(nIndex - 1).Width
      Command1(nIndex).Caption = nIndex
    End If

  Next

  If sNextOperation = "UNLOAD" Then
    sNextOperation = "LOAD"
  Else
    sNextOperation = "UNLOAD"
  Endif

End Sub
```

4   Run the code and click on the command button to see the new buttons get created and then deleted.

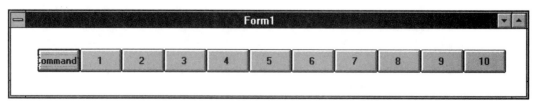

How It Works

The most important part of this code is the **For..Next** loop which actually creates and deletes the new command buttons.

```
For nIndex = 1 To 10

    If sNextOperation = "UNLOAD" Then
      Unload Command1(nIndex)
    Else
      Load Command1(nIndex)
      Command1(nIndex).Visible = True
      Command1(nIndex).Left = Command1(nIndex - 1).Left +
 ↳Command1(nIndex - 1).Width
      Command1(nIndex).Caption = nIndex
    End If

  Next
```

The contents of a variable you defined called **sNextOperation** are checked on each pass through the loop to see whether we need to **Unload** elements or **Load** them. The first time you press the command button **sNextOperation** is set to **Load.** The array is then extended by using **Load.** This takes as an argument the name of the initial command button, followed by the new Index number in brackets. In our case the index variable is **nIndex**, which is the counter for the loop:

```
    Load Command1(nIndex)
```

Once each new button has been created, its **Visible** property is set to **True** to make the buttons appear. The **Left** property is then set to position the new button directly to the right of the previous one next to it:

```
    Command1(nIndex).Visible = True
    Command1(nIndex).Left = Command1(nIndex - 1).Left +
 ↳Command1(nIndex - 1).Width
```

New controls created at run-time always appear by default in exactly the same position as the original control. They are invisible. Making them invisible at the start lets you move and resize them without the user seeing what's happening. It also stops Windows having to redraw a load of controls which can make the display appear quite messy while you're moving them about.

The last instruction in the loop puts a caption on the new command button showing its index number:

```
    Command1(nIndex).Caption = nIndex
```

Once the loop has run ten times and created the complete array, the **sNextOperation** variable is set to the opposite action. The first time around this means setting it to **Unload**, so that the next time you press a command button the whole array is unloaded button by button.

```
If sNextOperation = "UNLOAD" Then
    sNextOperation = "LOAD"
  Else
    sNextOperation = "UNLOAD"
  Endif
```

Managing Controls as Object Variables

Not only can you use objects as variables in arrays, you can then pass both object variables and object arrays to procedures as parameters. You may wonder why such an arcane sounding activity could be useful, but in fact it's a really powerful feature of Visual Basic.

Picture the scene; you have a form with thirty text boxes on it, each requiring a specific type of validation. Some need to accept only numeric information; others need to accept only alphabetic information. Still others need to accept both, but also need to check that a maximum length of data is not exceeded.

Normally, this would mean three separate routines, one for each eventuality. There would also be a line of code in each control's **KeyPress** event to pass the contents of the text box to a subprocedure for checking. The subprocedure then needs to pass information back, which may need to be written into the **Text** property of the control. This can soon add up to a lot of code. The solution is to treat each text box as an object in itself, and pass it to central procedure.

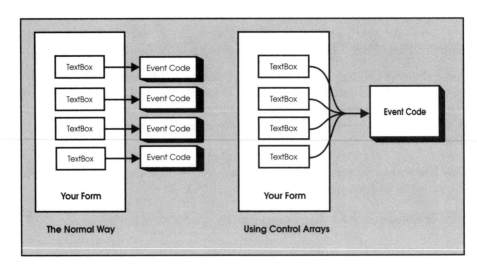

Passing Controls as Parameters

An object variable allows you to pass a complete control between code in forms and separate code modules. The procedure gets all the functionality and properties of the original control in the object variable but doesn't have to know anything too specific about it. For example it doesn't need to know the control's name, or which form it's on.

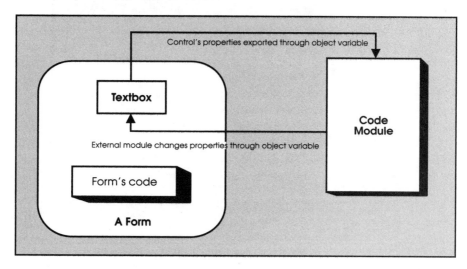

A Central Text Box Validation Routine

Wouldn't it be great to have just one routine that you could call to do all your text box validation? Such a routine would automatically know what kind of data each text box needed and what lengths the data should be. It could automatically abandon key presses that break the rules. Object variables mean that all this is possible, and with surprisingly little code.

Try It Out - Text Box Validation

1   Load up the **VALIDATE.MAK** project.

Try It Out!

577

2 Run it, and three text boxes appear on screen, one accepting only alphabetic characters, the second accepting numbers only and the third taking anything that's thrown at it. Try typing some things in.

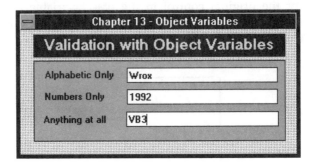

3 Stop the program. We're not really interested in what the program does, but how it does it. Double-click on one of the text boxes and bring up the **KeyPress** routine in the code window:

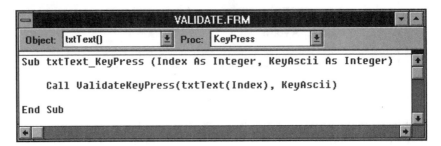

The three text boxes are in a control array and all call the **ValidateKeyPress** procedure as each key is pressed.

How It Works

Simple though it may be, the program does demonstrate just how useful object variables can be. Since the validation is all held in a generic routine to which the text box is passed for validation **as an object variable**, only one line of code is needed to handle the validation for all three text boxes.

The way the routine is called is just the same as with any other function or subroutine with parameters. However, instead of passing a value, or a variable name as a parameter in the call, you pass the name of a text box control identified by its index number:

```
Call ValidateKeyPress ( txtText(Text) , KeyAscii )
```

The text box and the code of the key that was pressed are passed to the **ValidateKeyPress** routine:

```
Sub ValidateKeyPress (txtControl As TextBox, nKeyAscii As Integer)

    Dim sMaxLength As String
    Dim sKey As String * 1

    If nKeyAscii < 32 Or nKeyAscii > 126 Then Exit Sub

    sMaxLength = Right(txtControl.Tag, Len(txtControl.Tag) - 1)

    If Len(txtControl.Text) = Val(sMaxLength) Then
        Beep
        nKeyAscii = 0
        Exit Sub
    End If

    Select Case Left$(txtControl.Tag, 1)

        Case "A"
            sKey = UCase(Chr$(nKeyAscii))

            If Asc(sKey) < 65 Or Asc(sKey) > 90 Then
                Beep
                nKeyAscii = 0
                Exit Sub
            End If

        Case "9"
            If nKeyAscii < 48 Or nKeyAscii > 57 Then
                Beep
                nKeyAscii = 0
                Exit Sub
            End If

    End Select

End Sub
```

The first line of the routine accepts the parameters from the calling statement. Here **txtText** is our object variable:

```
Sub ValidateKeyPress (txtControl As TextBox, nKeyAscii As Integer)
```

It is declared in the same way as any other variable, such as a string or an integer, only it's declared as a **TextBox** object. Thinking back to our brief discussion of classes at the start of the chapter, we are **deriving** an object from the **TextBox** class.

The second parameter is just the **KeyAscii** parameter given to you in the **KeyPress** event. Since I've missed out the **ByVal** keyword here, the parameter is passed by reference. Setting it to 0 at any point in the code means that the original **KeyAscii** variable will be reset to 0, which in a **KeyPress** event has the effect of canceling the key pressed.

The actual way the routine works centers around the **Tag** property of the text box. This is a property you can assign any value to, as long as Visual Basic itself doesn't use it. You can therefore adapt it for your own purposes. We used it in the **MSGBOX.MAK** project in Chapter 7 to hold the icon value that corresponded to a particular option button. There, as here, its use is as a general purpose private label on a control.

In this project, we use the **Tag** property to tell us what kind of data should be placed in each text box. This doesn't actually control anything itself; it's just a label. The first character in the **Tag** property is the one we want. Here, A means Alphabetic data only, 9 means numeric, and anything else means, well, anything else! You can set the **Tag** property at design-time. The numbers that follow it determine the maximum characters the text box can accept.

This is the **Tag** property of the Alphabetic Only text box:

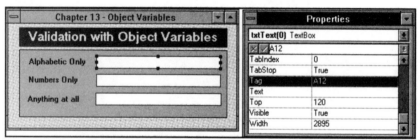

If you want to change the format of the data that a text box accepts, then bring up the properties window and change the **Tag** property.

The **ValidateKeypress** code uses the **Tag** property of the text box object variable together with the **nKeyAscii** parameter to determine exactly which key was pressed, and whether or not that key is valid.

The first stage of the program checks **nKeyAscii** for special keys (such as *BkSp* or the arrow keys) and if one of them was pressed then that key is not checked and is allowed to pass:

```
If nKeyAscii < 32 or nKeyAscii > 126 Then Exit Sub
```

After this line the code is certain that it's got a key press which needs to be checked.

The next line places the numbers from the back end of the **Tag** property into the variable **sMaxLength**. To remove the first character, the **Right** function returns all the characters in the **Tag** property (except the *first*) by counting back from the right-most one to the one next to the first:

```
sMaxLength = Right(txtControl.Tag, Len(txtControl.Tag) - 1)
```

Once we have determined the maximum length of the data in the textbox, a check is made to see if we're already at this limit.

```
If Len(txtControl.Text) = val(sMaxLength) then
```

If we are at the limit, then the **nKeyAscii** value is set to **0**. Since this parameter is passed to the procedure by reference, the **0** is automatically fed back into **KeyAscii** in the **KeyPress** event. This effectively cancels the key press.

The remaining code just checks whether the keys pressed are valid for the textbox, again based on the **Tag** property. If the **Tag** property is set to **99999**, indicating that you can only enter numbers (and even then a 5 digit number at most) then the **Select Case** statement will reject alphanumeric or punctuation keys.

> If you *do* plan to use the routine in your own code, bear in mind that it is supposed to be called from a **KeyPress** event.

Types of Object Variables

In the last program, we declared the text box that we wanted to pass to the procedure in this way: **txtControl As TextBox. TextBox** is just one of the explicit object variable types that Visual Basic recognizes. The others are:

CheckBox	ComboBox	CommandButton	MDIForm
Data	DirListBox	DriveListBox	FileListBox
Grid	Frame	HScrollBar	Image
Label	Line	ListBox	Menu
OptionButton	OLE	PictureBox	Shape
TextBox	Timer	VScrollBar	Form

These are the standard objects. If you add more controls, then they too can be used as objects variables. We'll now take a look at some general principles for working with object variables. Form objects are a bit special so we'll cover them specifically in more detail.

Declaring Object Variables

You declare an object variable **explicitly** in the same way as you would a regular variable, if you replace the data type with the control type. For example:

```
Dim txtControl as TextBox
```

Although your code is undoubtedly more efficient and usually runs faster if you declare object variables **explicitly**, Visual Basic will also let you declare an object variable **implicitly**, by simply saying that a variable name relates to a **Control**. For example:

```
Dim ctlControl As Control
```

Function and subroutine parameters can be declared in this way. This enables you to pass any control you like to them at run-time. Visual Basic provides a special clause for the **If...Then** statement which allows you to check the type of control an object variable relates to. This is the **TypeOf** statement. We'll take a look at this in more detail in the section **Collections of Controls**.

Explicit Vs Implicit Declaration

Implicit declaration is easier but has distinct drawbacks:

▶ Your code is harder to understand.

▶ Visual Basic has less chance of trapping errors.

▶ It runs slower.

Your code is harder to understand because you tell future readers of your code less about what's going on. Picture the situation where you have a function that validates data. If you simply declare the object parameter at the head of the function as a **Control** it can be very confusing. The reader can't tell instantly whether you are validating records in a data control, in text boxes, in combo boxes or the latest hi-tech widget from Visual Basic Addons Inc.

We've seen before how declaring variables explicitly can make debugging easier. The same is true for object variables. If you declare an object as a specific type, such as a **TextBox**, Visual Basic automatically knows which properties are valid for that **TextBox**.

If you declare the object variable **ctlControl** implicitly as a generic **Control**, rather than as a **TextBox**, then Visual Basic will allow you to enter the following line of code:

```
ctlControl.Peter = "Some Text"
```

Visual Basic won't spot the error until your program runs. The line may be in a function or a piece of code that you missed in testing, and there's nothing more embarrassing than having a user ring you up to tell you that the run-time Visual Basic DLL is reporting syntax errors.

> Visual Basic only checks the properties of a generic **Control** object at run-time, whereas at compile-time it reports property errors with explicit controls.

As for the difference in speed, the best way to appreciate it is to try it.

Try It Out - Comparing Implicit and Explicit Declarations

1 Load up the **CTRLTIME.MAK** project and run it.

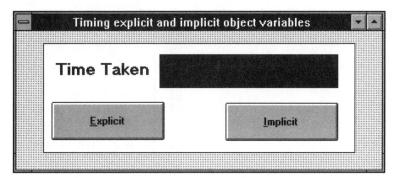

2 When the form appears on screen click on the Explicit command button. The program shows the time taken to assign 1000 different captions to the command button. The routine it uses to do this accepts the command button as an explicitly declared object variable.

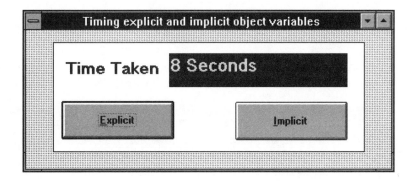

3 Click on the Implicit command button. This does the same thing, only this time the command button is declared implicitly as an object variable.

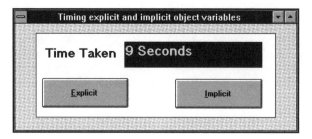

How It Works

The two command buttons have very similar **Click** events:

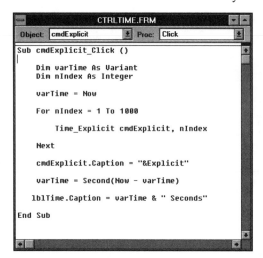

First **varTime** is set to the start time. Then the central loop calls the **Time_Implicit** or **Time_Explicit** procedure 1000 times, passing the command button and the loop counter as parameters.

The real difference is in the way the command button is accepted in the two subprocedures. Here we accept **cmdCommand** explicitly as a **CommandButton**.

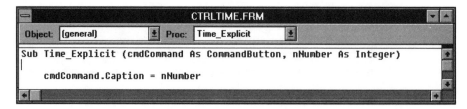

While here we accept it implicitly as a `Control`.

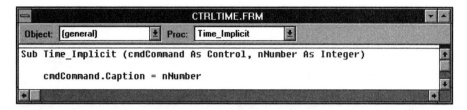

Having done this 1000 times, we reset the caption and work out the time elapsed between **Now** and the start time in **varTime**.

Collections of Controls

Every form in your application has something known as a **control collection** built in. This is simply an array which you can use at run-time to gain access to the controls on a form without having to know the name of each one, or even what type of control it is.

The elements of the control collection are accessed in the same way that you access the elements of a normal array. The obvious difference between a control collection and a variable array is that the elements of the control collection have properties which you can examine and alter at run-time.

The controls collection is useful for data entry forms. You can write a generic routine to go through a control collection looking for data controls to then change their database properties to point to the appropriate path and file name for the customer's database.

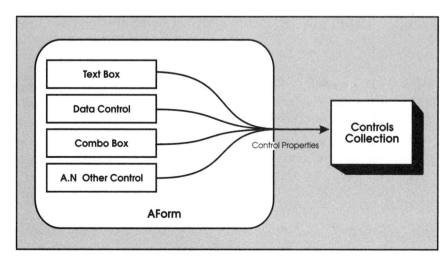

The Controls Property

You can gain access to a control collection through the **Controls** property of a form. This isn't something you can get at through the properties window; you need to do it through code. The **Controls** property is actually an array, where each element of the array is a single control; element **0** is the first control on the form, element **1** is the second, and so on.

> These numbers are assigned to the controls automatically at design-time, according to the order in which the controls are drawn on the form.

For instance, if you had a simple form with only two text boxes on it you could change the **Text** property of each with this code:

```
Form1.Controls(0).Text = "Control 0"
Form1.Controls(1).Text = "Control 1"
```

The general format for this is:

```
<formname>.controls( <number> ).<property> = <a value>
```

Here **<formname>** is the name of you form, **<number>** is the number of the control where **0** is first, and so on. To really make this useful we need to know how many elements there are in a control collection, and be able to identify the individual elements of a control collection.

Identifying Controls on the Form

The **Controls** array has a property of its own called **Count**. This lets you know how many controls are on the form. Be careful though if you use this in code. The elements of the control array are numbered from **0**. Therefore, if the **Count** property tells you that there are 3 controls on a form, these controls will be numbered **0**, **1** and **2** in the controls array, not **1**, **2** and **3**.

Unfortunately, until you run a program you have no real way of finding out which control corresponds to which number. There are two ways of identifying specific members of a control collection at run-time.

> Check the **Tag** property, as you can to loop through all the elements. This method requires that you set up all the **Tag** properties with unique identifiers at design-time.

▶ Use the **TypeOf** method to deal with groups of similar controls. This doesn't let you single out individual controls, but you'll find that most of the time you want to address all the controls of a certain type anyway. The best way to understand this is to look at some code:

```
For nControlNo = 0 to Form1.Controls.Count - 1

    If TypeOf Form1.Controls( nControlNo ) Is TextBox then
    :
    :
    EndIf

Next
```

Here we loop through each of the members of the control collection on **Form1** up to the last control, **Count-1.** For each control we use **TypeOf** to check if it's a **TextBox** or not.

Try It Out - Changing Colors Remotely

A common facility in today's applications enables the user to decide what colors he or she wants to see on the screen. Control arrays let you change the colors of controls throughout a form. That's exactly what the program **CTRLARRY.MAK** does.

1 Load up **CTRLARRY.MAK** and run it.

Try It Out!

2 Choose which type of control you want to change the colors on by clicking the appropriate check box. Then press either the Background or Foreground command button. The color dialog comes up:

3 Choose a color and the controls change on the form.

How It Works

Let's take a look at the code behind the <u>B</u>ackground command button:

```
For nControlNo = 0 To frmMain.Controls.Count - 1
  If TypeOf frmMain.Controls(nControlNo) Is TextBox Then
    If chkTextBoxes.Value = 1 Then
⤷frmMain.Controls(nControlNo).BackColor = nColour
  End If

  If TypeOf frmMain.Controls(nControlNo) Is Frame Then
    If chkFrames.Value = 1 Then
⤷frmMain.Controls(nControlNo).BackColor = nColour
  End If

  If TypeOf frmMain.Controls(nControlNo) Is Label Then
    If chkLabels.Value = 1 Then
⤷frmMain.Controls(nControlNo).BackColor = nColour
  End If

  If TypeOf frmMain.Controls(nControlNo) Is CheckBox Then
    If chkCheckBoxes.Value = 1 Then
⤷frmMain.Controls(nControlNo).BackColor = nColour
  End If

Next nControlNo
```

There is a little more code than this in the actual program. This is in order to display a colors common dialog and store the selected color in the **nColour** variable.

The code uses a **For..Next** loop to move through each control on the form using its **control collection**. The **If Typeof** statement is a specialized form of the **If** statement and is used to check the type of the control. There are actually four of these tests, one for each type of control that the program is interested in: **textbox, label, checkbox** and **frame**.

There are some points to note about the **If Typeof** statement:

▶ The **TypeOf** clause must be the only check on the **If** line if you intend to use it. You can't use it with **And** or **Or** keywords. For example, the following won't work:

```
If TypeOf Control Is TextBox and sToday = "Tuesday" then....
```

▶ Whereas normally we would use the = sign with an **If** statement, you must use the **Is** keyword when dealing with **TypeOf**.

Once a matching control has been found, a second **If** statement is used to see if the appropriate checkbox is set. This shows if this is one of the controls the user wants to set the colors on. If it is then the **BackColor** property is loaded with the color selected from the common dialog:

```
frmMain.Controls(nControlNo).BackColor = nColour
```

There are literally hundreds of uses for the **Controls** array, including setting fonts on all controls as the result of the user choosing a font. The **Database** properties of data controls can also be set, which makes it easy for the user to install the application anywhere they want to, and not necessarily in the directory that you want them to.

Creating Toolbars

It's becoming a standard among Windows applications to provide their users with a way to customize toolbars in applications, adding and removing items at their leisure. How can such a feat be accomplished in Visual Basic?

By now you know the basics of creating controls at run-time. You've already worked through an example that creates command buttons on the fly. Creating toolbars is only a small step away.

The first hurdle is the Visual Basic command button. Toolbars consist of graphical commands which show a small icon, rather than a caption. Visual Basic command buttons are no help here since they can't, under any circumstances, display graphics. To create a toolbar in Visual Basic you need to look to the image control.

Try It Out - Creating a Toolbar

Not only can the image control display graphics, it can also respond to mouse events like **MouseDown** and **MouseUp**. To create a toolbar using image controls, we just need to add code the **MouseDown** event. This loads up an image of a button when depressed, so as far as the user is concerned the image control is actually a button. The **MouseUp** event contains code to restore the picture of the button in the up position.

1   Load up the **TOOLBAR.MAK** project and run it.

2 Select the Options menu. A separate form appears in which you can select checkboxes to indicate which icons should appear on the toolbar.

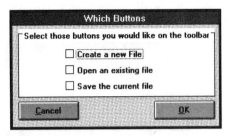

3 Click on the Open an existing file checkbox, then click OK. The options form vanishes leaving you with the main form again, and a button on the toolbar.

4 The new button is part of a control array of images (not buttons) that is created by the program as it's needed. Try clicking on the button and holding the mouse down; the image changes as you would expect.

Remember that this is an image not a command button; it wouldn't normally change the graphic as a result of you clicking on it. There is code in the background that's doing all that stuff for you.

5 Stop the program from running and take a look at the main form again.

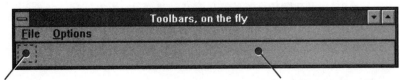

The square in the picture box is an image control with no image loaded.

The gray area beneath the menu bar is a picture box that's being used as a container. If you set its Alignment property to Top the picture box remains firmly fixed to the top of the form at all times.

6   Bring up the properties window for the image and take a look at the **Index** property. I've set the **Index** property to **0**. This tells Visual Basic that although this is the only image control on the form, it's going to be part of a control array.

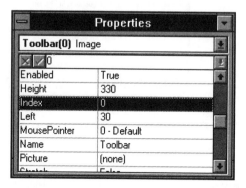

7   You can bring up the Options window if you display the project window and click on the appropriate entry in the list. Double-click the OK button to see the code that creates the control array at run-time:

```
Sub cmdOK_Click ()

    Dim nButtonNo As Integer

    For nButtonNo = 1 To gnButtons
        Unload frmMain!Toolbar(nButtonNo)
    Next

    gnButtons = 0

    For nButtonNo = 0 To 2

    If chkOptions(nButtonNo).Value = 1 Then
        gnButtons = gnButtons + 1
        Load frmMain!Toolbar(gnButtons)
        frmMain!Toolbar(gnButtons).Tag = chkOptions(nButtonNo).Tag
        frmMain!Toolbar(gnButtons).Top = frmMain!Toolbar(0).Top
        frmMain!Toolbar(gnButtons).Left = frmMain!Toolbar(gnButtons
- 1).Left + frmMain!Toolbar(gnButtons - 1).Width
        Call LoadImage(frmMain!Toolbar(gnButtons), "up")
        frmMain!Toolbar(gnButtons).Visible = True
    End If
    Next

    Unload frmOptions

End Sub
```

How It Works

Don't panic! It's nowhere near as bad as it looks. The first thing the code does is **Unload** all the image controls on the toolbar with the exception of the button we saw at design-time. It does this with a **For**..loop, going from **1** to the number of buttons on the toolbar. A global variable, **gnButtons**, defined in another module, holds a count of the number of visible buttons on the toolbar.

```
For nButtonNo = 1 To gnButtons

    Unload frmMain!Toolbar(nButtonNo)

Next

gnButtons = 0
```

Having unloaded the images, **gnButtons** is reset back to **0**, meaning that there are no visible buttons on the toolbar.

Creating the Buttons

The second loop actually creates the buttons themselves. Each checkbox on the options form is also part of a control array, so the second loop just loops through these checkboxes trying to find which ones have a value of **1** (meaning they've been selected).

```
For nButtonNo = 0 To 2

    If chkOptions(nButtonNo).Value = 1 Then
      gnButtons = gnButtons + 1
      Load frmMain!Toolbar(gnButtons)
      frmMain!Toolbar(gnButtons).Tag = chkOptions(nButtonNo).Tag
      frmMain!Toolbar(gnButtons).Top = frmMain!Toolbar(0).Top
      frmMain!Toolbar(gnButtons).Left = frmMain!Toolbar(gnButtons
 - 1).Left + frmMain!Toolbar(gnButtons - 1).Width
      Call LoadImage(frmMain!Toolbar(gnButtons), "up")
      frmMain!Toolbar(gnButtons).Visible = True
    End If
  Next
```

When a selected checkbox has been found, **1** is added to the global variable holding a count of the number of buttons:

```
gnButtons = gnButtons + 1
```

The new button is then created using the **Load** command:

```
Load frmMain!Toolbar(gnButtons)
```

Now the confusing bit. At run-time, how do the new buttons know which image to display, or which menu code should be run when they are clicked? The answer lies in the **Tag** property.

Each checkbox on the options form has its **Tag** property set up with a number which indicates the menu option to call when a button is pressed, as well as the name of a graphic file.

When the new buttons are created, the above code copies the checkbox's **Tag** property into the new button's **Tag** property:

```
frmMain!Toolbar(gnButtons).Tag = chkOptions(nButtonNo).Tag
```

Here, **gnButtons** is the name of the global variable which is counting the buttons, and **nButtonNo** is the index variable used in the **For Loop**.

Displaying the Buttons

The remaining lines of code in the loop position the button directly to the right of the previous button, and make the new image control visible. A call is also made to a routine called **LoadImage**, defined in a separate module. This routine handles loading the graphic images of the buttons in the image controls themselves.

```
Call LoadImage(frmMain!Toolbar(gnButtons), "up")
```

To see a list of all the files in the project containing code, press *F2* in the code window:

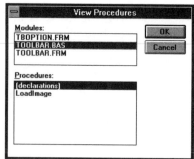

From the modules list select **TOOLBAR.BAS**. The procedures list will change to show the code in that module. Select LoadImage to see the **LoadImage** routine.

```
Sub LoadImage (imgControl As Control, sSuffix As String)

    Dim sFileName As String

    sFileName = Mid$(imgControl.Tag, 3, Len(imgControl.Tag) - 2)
    sFileName = app.Path & "\" & sFileName & sSuffix & ".bmp"

    imgControl.Picture = LoadPicture(sFileName)

End Sub
```

This code pulls the filename out of the image controls **Tag** property and uses the **LoadPicture** function to load the graphic in. The names of the images in the **Tag** property have been kept fairly simple: **Open**, **Save**, and **New**. Remember that this routine is global and can be used to display both the images for the button up and the button down.

When the subprocedure is called you need to pass a suffix to it, either **"up"**, or **"dn"**.

```
Sub LoadImage (imgControl As Control, sSuffix As String)
```

This suffix is then added onto the end of the filename, along with **".bmp"** to get a full file name. For example, if the name of the graphic in the **Tag** property was **Open**, and this routine was called with a **sSuffix** parameter of **"dn"**, then the actual graphic loaded is **Opendn.bmp.**

If you take a look at the graphics files installed from the sample disk you will see these files there: **openup.bmp**, **opendn.bmp**, **saveup.bmp** and so on.

Press *F2* to bring up the code list again. Select **TOOLBAR.FRM** from the list, and then select **Toolbar_MouseDown** from the procedures list. This shows you the event code that occurs when the user points at an image control and presses the mouse button down.

```
Sub Toolbar_MouseDown (index As Integer, Button As Integer, Shift
⬐As Integer, X As Single, Y As Single)

    Call LoadImage(Toolbar(index), "dn")

End Sub
```

When this happens, **LoadImage** is called again to display the button down image.

595

Adding Menu Code

That takes care of how the images are actually drawn. However, there's still something missing. When you click an image in the actual program, the image calls the appropriate menu routine. For example, if you put an open image on the toolbar and click it, a message box pops up from the File/Open menu click code.

As with most other elements of this program, the menus are all defined as part of a control array. Along with the name of the graphic in the **Tag** property, there is also the **Index** number of the menu item to which the graphic relates. When you click an image control, the image simply calls the menu array's click code, passing it the **Index** number of the menu item that it wants to run from the image's **Tag** property.

```
Sub Toolbar_Click (index As Integer)

    Call mnuFItems_Click(Val(Left(Toolbar(index).Tag, 1)))

End Sub
```

The **Tag** property is actually holding a string in the form of a number, followed by a space, followed by a filename. Therefore, **Val** is used to get the actual value of the number from the **Tag**. **Left** is also used to make sure that we only pull the value of the first character in the **Tag** property, and nothing else.

There you have it, a whirlwind guide to user definable toolbars, courtesy of control arrays and object variables!

MDI Applications

All the applications we have looked at so far are what Microsoft call **SDI (Single Document Interface)** applications. It's a fairly hefty name for a simple concept. All the forms in the applications we've written so far are independent of each other. Each could be resized to whichever size your users want, moved in front of or behind other applications, and so on.

It doesn't take very long before an SDI application with multiple visible forms begins to look confusing. Where did I put that customer entry form? Oh yes, it's over there behind Word for Windows, but in front of the order entry form!

MDI (**Multiple Document Interface**) tidies up these kinds of applications. Again, it's a hefty name for a simple concept. In MDI you have one large MDI form (a **parent** form) which acts as a container for all the other forms in your program. The MDI form acts like a virtual form; windows are displayed inside it (called **child** forms) which can't be moved outside of the MDI form. They can only be maximized to the same size as the MDI form, and when minimized appear as an icon on the MDI form, not on Windows itself.

Actually, it's a concept you're well used to, though you probably haven't thought about it before. Program Manager is an MDI application.

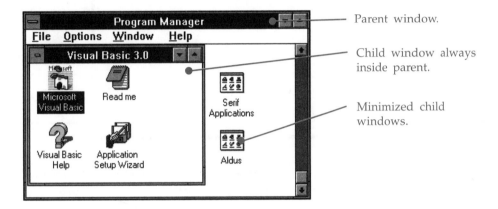

Parent window.

Child window always inside parent.

Minimized child windows.

MDI Forms With Visual Basic

MDI forms are very useful. They can bring order to your application by providing a convenient way for you to group all the forms and functions of your program into one big container window. However, despite its power, MDI under Visual Basic does have some limitations. Let's explore some of them now.

Try It Out - Limitations of an MDI form

1   Load up Visual Basic and start a new project.
    From the File menu, select New MDI Form.

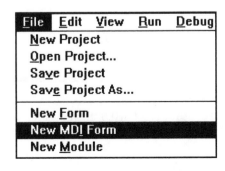

2   After a short pause an MDI parent form will appear.

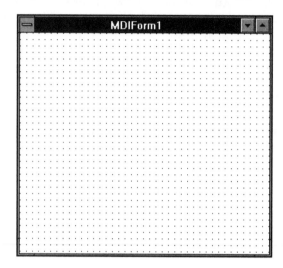

3   Let's try changing the **BackColor** property of the parent form. Press *F4* to bring up the properties window and find the **BackColor** property.

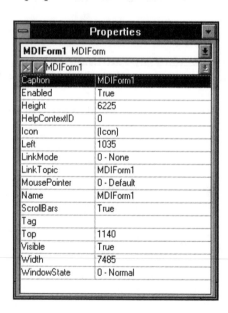

There is no **BackColor** property! MDI forms can't have their colors set directly from within Visual Basic. You have to use a series of DLL API functions to accomplish that.

4 OK, so we can't change the colors. Let's put some controls onto the form. Select a command button from the toolbox and try to draw it on the form. Nothing happens.

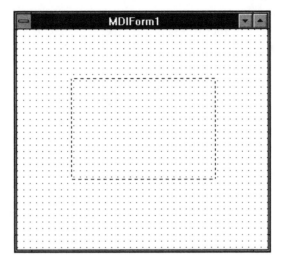

MDI forms can only have picture box controls drawn on them, or in the Professional Edition, 3D-Panels.

> The general rule is that only controls that have an **Align** property can be placed on an MDI parent form.

5 Select the picture box from the tool palette and draw that on the form.

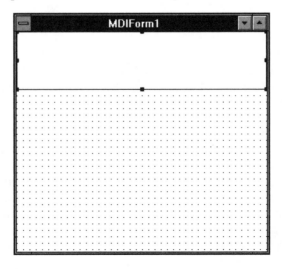

The box automatically sits at the top of the form and assumes the same width as the form. You can't change this. Picture boxes drawn on an MDI form must be the same width as the form, and must be attached to either the top or bottom of the form.

6   Go to the File menu again and try to create a second MDI form. The New MDI Form option is this time disabled.

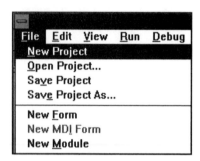

You can only have one MDI form per application.

With all these apparent limitations, MDI applications really *are* worth the effort. Imagine what Program Manager would be like if you had program groups floating around all over the place, in front of your programs, hidden out of sight behind others, and so on. Imagine what any Windows wordprocessor would be like if you could only open one document at a time, and these couldn't share the same menu structure or toolbar. At the bottom line MDI applications look good, are comfortable for your users to use, and are an all round good idea for many types of application.

Child Forms

When you start to use MDI forms, all the other normal forms in your program refuse to fit within the MDI frame. They still float about on their own happily disrupting the overall karma of windows. You need to tell a form that it is a **child** form before it starts to behave itself.

Luckily, this is a simple process. The **MDIChild** property of a form can be set to either **True** or **False** to tell it that it now belongs to an MDI form. Since Visual Basic only allows you to have one MDI form per application, the child form automatically knows who its parent is, so that when the program runs it stays within the confines of the MDI form. At design-time the child form is as free-floating as ever; there's no visible way to tell the difference between a child form and normal independent form at design-time, other than if you check the form's **MDIChild** property.

Although you can view and set the **MDIChild** property at design-time, at run-time the property is strictly off-limits. Try setting it to **True** or **False** in your code. You'll get an error from Visual Basic before your program crashes.

Try It Out - Child Forms in Action

Let's see all this in action.

1 Load up the **MDICHILD.MAK** application, but don't run it yet. Select the MDI form from the project window to display it. It's called frmMain.

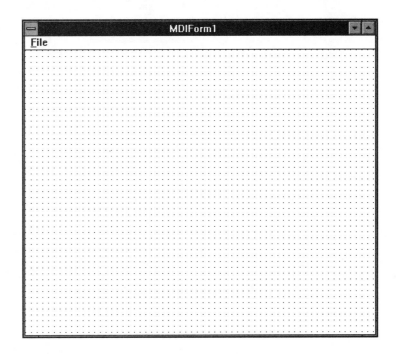

2 The form has a File menu which contains just two items, New and Exit.

3 Now display the other form, frmChild. This also has a menu bar but with a great many more options on it.

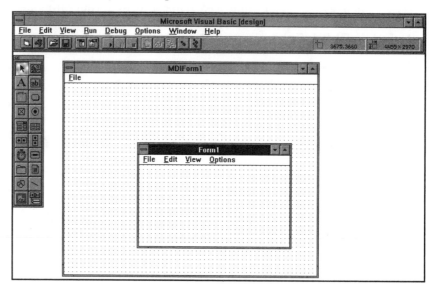

4 Run the program. When the MDI form comes into view it has no child windows so it displays and uses its own menu structure. If you select the New menu option from the File menu the child form is displayed.

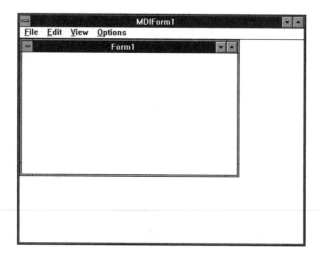

Not only does the child form come into view, but the menu structure of the MDI form changes; it becomes the menu structure of the child window.

Closing Child Windows

Child windows can't be hidden. If you want to remove a child window from view you must move it behind another child window, or minimize it so that an icon for it appears on the MDI form, or unload it using the **Unload** command.

I don't know why Microsoft decided to take this approach to child windows. It can be very annoying. What do you do if you have variables in the form which contain information you wish to keep, but you need to remove the form from the display? Doesn't **Unload**ing remove the form itself, the code, and the form's variables?

In fact, it doesn't. Any **static** variables you have in the form are kept in memory. Next time the form is loaded the **static** variables are maintained. This allows you to continue from where you left off.

Instances of Forms

The above example only lets you load one child form onto an MDI form. This isn't very useful if you are developing the next Excel.

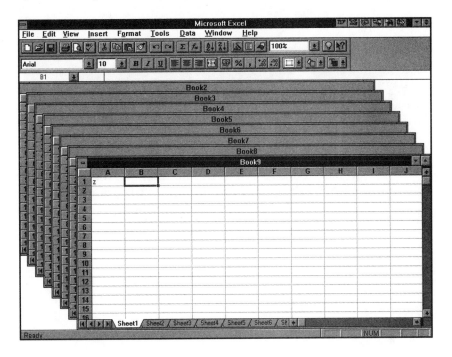

This is where form **instances** come into play. Using object variables you can create copies of a form (instances). Each copy of the form has exactly the same controls on it, and an identical menu structure, but each can hold different data. Although the code and the variable and control names it contains are identical, the actual data they deal with is stored in a different place in your PC's memory for each form.

Try It Out - New Form Instances

Let's put this into action.

1 Load up the **MDICHILD.MAK** project again. Use the project window to select the MDI form itself frmMain.

2 Select Ne<u>w</u> from the MDI form's <u>F</u>ile menu. At present the code looks like this:

```
Sub mnuFNew_Click ()

    Load frmChild

End Sub
```

3 We can create **clones** of the **frmChild** window using an object variable to create a **New frmChild** window. Change the code so that it looks like this:

```
Sub mnuFNew_Click()

    Dim OurNewForm As New frmChild
    OurNewForm.Show

End Sub
```

4 Back at the project window, this time select the child window. When the window appears, bring up the menu editor and delete all the menu items. This will make the code a little less complicated.

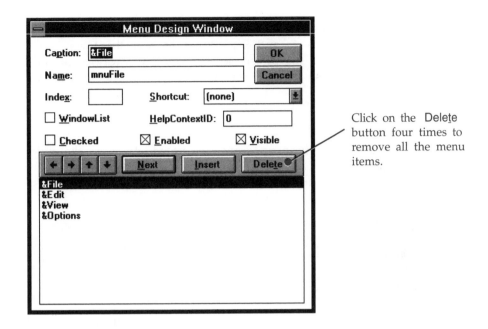

Click on the Delete button four times to remove all the menu items.

5 When all the child form's menus have gone, run the program and select New from the MDI form's File menu. Do it again, and again, and again; each time a new child window is created.

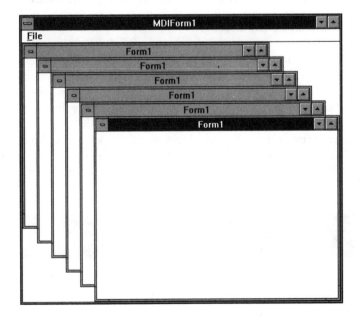

6 When you're done playing, stop the program running. You can save it if you select Save File As and Save Project As from the File menu. Rename both the form and the project so that you can always come back to the originals. We'll use the new files in a short while to look at window lists.

How It Works

Firstly, let's look at how the new forms are created. Bring up the code window and take a look at the **Click** event for **mnuFNew**. You may be surprised to see that there are only two lines of code in the event, and one of those is a simple variable declaration.

```
Sub mnuFNew_Click()

    Dim OurNewForm As New frmChild
    OurNewForm.Show

End Sub
```

The first line of code, the variable declaration, sets up an object variable for a **New** form. The form in this case is the child form in our project called **frmChild**. Confusing, isn't it! It's the same as how we created new command buttons earlier on in the chapter. We already have a form called **frmChild** in the application. What we want to do is create new copies of it. These new copies all display their own data and variables, but share the same event code:

```
Dim OurNewForm As New frmChild
```

Create a new form which just for the purpose of this event code we'll call **OurNewForm**. This new form is an exact copy of our **frmChild** form. It's a new **frmChild** form. You can do this if you declare a new object variable **OurNewForm** and tell Visual Basic that this is a new instance of **frmChild**.

So, **OurNewForm** is actually an object variable set up to hold a new **frmChild** form. Once the object variable has been set up we can treat it just the same as any other form. The command **OurNewForm.Show** shows our new form on the screen.

> Another way to look at this is to think of **OurNewForm** as being a variable of type **frmChild**. It therefore inherits the properties of **frmChild**.

Now for the tricky bit. Take another look at the object variable declaration:

```
Dim OurNewForm As New frmChild
```

It's a simple **Dim**, so that means that the object variable is a local variable; as soon as the subroutine finishes so also does the life of the variable. But why does the form you've just created stay in existence?

What we've done here is create an object variable for a new form. If you destroy the object variable you just destroy the variable itself, **not the new form that was just created**. So how do you refer to the new form and the controls on it in your code?

Addressing Your New Form or Talking to Me

Since we now have an application that could theoretically display ten identically named forms, Visual Basic kindly gives us a special keyword called **Me** which can be used in your code to refer to the current active form.

A line of code that says:

```
Me.txtEmployee.Text = "Peter Wright"
```

sets up the text property of a text box called **txtEmployee** on the current active form. In the same way, if you need to unload the form from inside one of its events just type **Unload Me**.

> I had great problems with this when I started learning. It seems too easy and logical to be right, but believe me it's fine!

Creating Window List Menus

Once you start dealing with MDI forms and child windows, things can get very out of hand on your screen. Your user can get lost in a sea of similar looking child windows, not knowing which is which, or where the first form they created has gone to.

Visual Basic provides a simple way of dealing with this problem - the **Window List Menu.**

Try It Out - Creating a Window List Menu

1 Load up the changed version of **MDICHILD.MAK** that you saved from the earlier example. When the project has loaded, bring up the main form and invoke the menu editor.

Try It Out!

2   Create a <u>W</u>indow menu that is not indented under the other menu items like this:

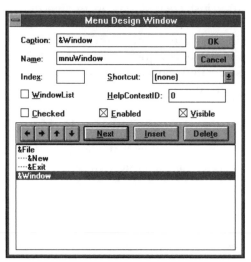

3   Underneath this new menu item create another one, set the Caption to &List and the name to mnuWList.

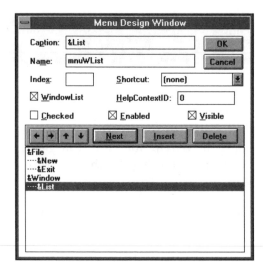

4   Click on the <u>W</u>indowList check box like I've done here. Also, make sure that the new menu item is indented underneath the <u>W</u>indow menu. Finally, press OK to accept the new menu structure and then run the program

5 Create a few child windows using the File/New menu item on the main MDI form. Now go to the new Window menu and select the List item. A list of all the child forms in the application appears, with the active window marked with a checkmark.

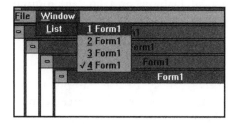

6 If you select any of the items on this list, then that form becomes the current active form. Pretty neat, huh? No code involved!

Arranging Your Desktop

WindowList is just one of a number of time saving features of Visual Basic that you have at your disposal when dealing with MDI applications. The other is the **Arrange** method.

The **Arrange** method allows you to give your users features similar to those on the Window menu of Program Manager. Using **Arrange** you can tile child windows, cascade them, and arrange the child window icons in a neat and orderly fashion.

Load up the **MDICHLD2.MAK** project and run it. Play around with the new items on the Window menu to see how they work. Don't forget to create some child windows first.

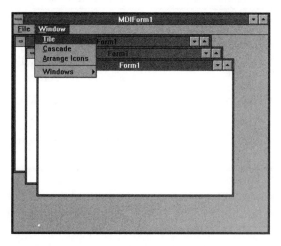

With a large number of child windows it doesn't take long before the MDI form begins to look a real mess; icons here, there and everywhere, windows overlapping other windows, each of varying sizes, and so on. The Window menu has options for Tile, Cascade and Arrange Icons. You should recognize these as being the standard items for tidying up, which automatically tile and overlay windows in a neat fashion, and line up minimized window icons in an orderly way at the bottom of the MDI form.

Different Window Arrangements

The **Arrange** method is very easy to use. Simply type the name of the MDI form, in our case **frmMDI**, in front of the **Arrange** method. After the word **Arrange** type one of the parameters which govern how the forms are arranged.

For example, take a look at the click event for the Window menu Arrange item from the **MDICHLD2.MAK** project.

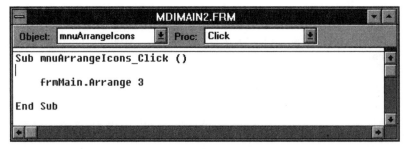

The options you have for the **Arrange** parameter are as follows:

Value	CONSTANT.TXT	What It Does
0	**CASCADE**	Cascades all open MDI child forms from top left to bottom right of the screen.
1	**TILE_HORIZONTAL**	Tiles all open MDI child forms side by side across the screen.
2	**TILE_VERTICAL**	Tiles all open MDI child forms above and below each other, down the screen.
3	**ARRANGE_ICONS**	Lines up the icons of any minimized child forms.

Those first three actions also affect any child forms you may have minimized. Although the results are not immediately visible, they can be seen as soon as the child form is resized.

Summary

In the standard edition of Visual Basic the uses of object variables are fairly simple, although it may not appear that way to you immediately. However, the Professional Edition of Visual Basic makes very heavy use of object variables. Databases in Visual Basic Pro, for example, can be dealt with through code, without the need for a data control. The tables of your database themselves are represented as object variables.

Knowing how to use Object variables provides you with the knowledge you need to write re-useable code. If you need a validation routine such as the one you saw a couple of chapters back, you can write the code to deal with textboxes in general. The code doesn't have to know the name of a specific textbox because you can pass the textbox to the validate code as an object variable.

More specifically, you have learnt:

▶ What object variables are and how to use them

▶ How to create a simple toolbar

▶ How to write efficient code that deals with a lot of controls by referring to them as object variables

▶ How to create and use an array of objects

▶ What an MDI application is

▶ How to create and manage MDI applications

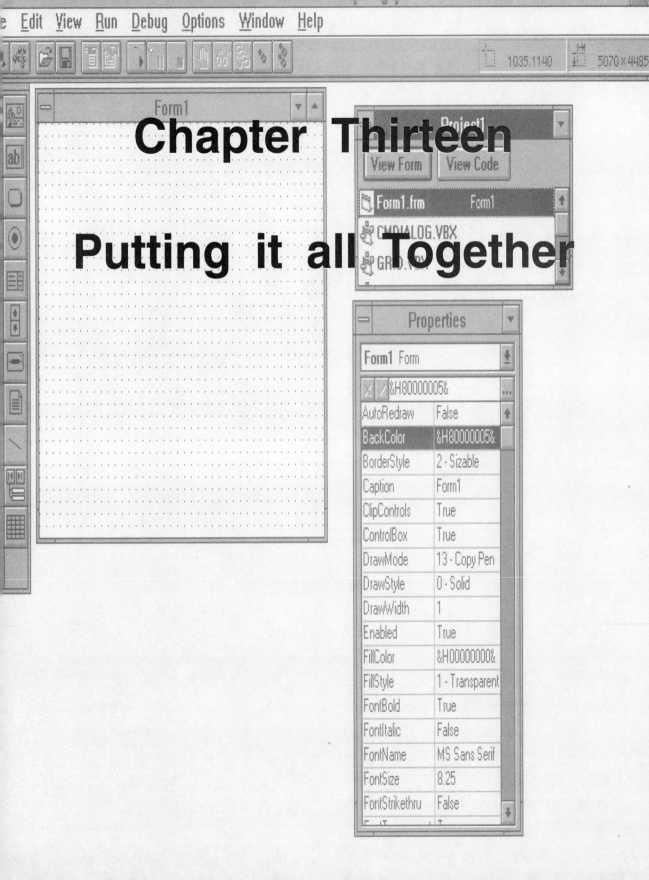

Chapter Thirteen

Putting it all Together

CHAPTER
13

Putting It All Together

By now, you should have a fairly good idea of the tools Visual Basic supplies. However, knowing where to use them and how they all fit together in a final application is a different question all together.

In this chapter we'll look at a sample application called BugTrak, which is a bug tracking and recording program. This simple database application shows you how to exploit Visual Basic's strengths in this key area. It also shows you how to overcome one of its main weaknesses, that is, its lack of a full collection of bound controls.

The aim of this chapter is to bring together everything you have learnt in this book to create a realistic working program of the kind that Visual Basic programmers produce the world over.

In this chapter you'll use and examine BugTrak to see:

▶ How to simulate bound controls, by binding combo boxes and grids

▶ Two good methods of passing records between forms in a multi-form application

▶ How to reduce the scope of the variables in a project, and minimize resource usage

▶ How to handle data entry validation to ensure that the data you get is the data you want

▶ How to print information from a database to the printer, and how to interact with the printer common dialog

▶ How to open and read straight files from the PC's hard disk

No single application can ever cover every problem you'll come across in developing a program, and BugTrak is no exception. However, by the end of this chapter we'll have covered most of the more common areas that are likely to hold you up when you come to write applications of your own.

Using BugTrak

The design aims with BugTrak were pretty straightforward. They were to produce a system to store information about projects in development (and the bugs *in* those projects). At any point in time users should be able to obtain a complete list of uncleared reports for any system, as well as link systems in the database to the current versions of the Visual Basic **MAK** files.

Users should also be able to enter new bugs, change the details of existing ones, and easily change the status of bugs from cleared to uncleared. In addition, the user must be able to enter free-form notes about both systems and bugs.

Try It Out - Using BugTrak

Before we start to pull the code to pieces, let's take a walk through the application to see how these design goals were met:

1   Load up and run the system. The project is called **BUGTRAK.MAK**. After a short pause, the main form should appear.

The grid in the center of the form shows you the bugs in the system.

You can change which bugs are shown if you select a system using the system combo box, or a file with the File combo box. In both cases, the grid will change to show only those bugs which relate to the selected system or file.

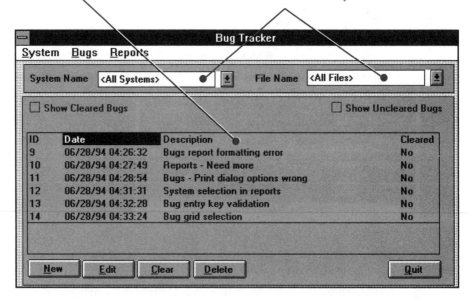

2   The two checkboxes above the grid allow you to toggle between seeing cleared bugs, uncleared bugs or both. Click one of them now to see the effect it has.

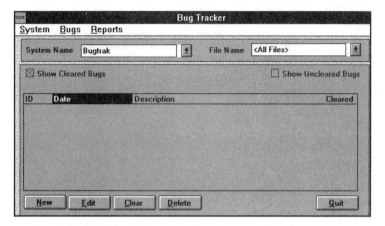

3   The buttons at the foot of the grid allow you to enter new bugs, change the details of existing ones, delete bugs, and clear them. Click on a bug in the grid and then click the Clear button. The status of the Cleared column of the grid changes depending on which bug you select.

4   Now try editing a bug. Click on one and then click the Edit button. The edit form will appear, showing you the information BugTrak is currently holding on the selected bug. You can change this and click OK to save the new information, or click on the Cancel button to get back to the main form without changing anything.

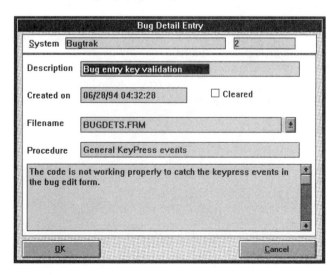

5 The same form to edit a bug you just saw is also used when you create a new one. Click on the New button in the main form and type in some details for a new bug. Don't worry about what you type in - you can't damage anything.

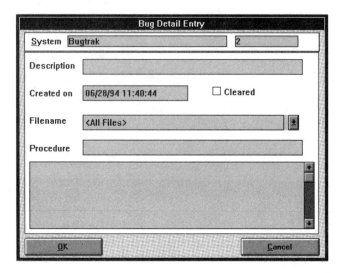

6 The system menu on the main form allows you to do for systems what you just did for bugs: create them, edit existing ones, and delete systems. Incidentally, deleting a system from the database also deletes any bugs for that system.

7 Let's try it now. Use the System combo box on the main form to select BugTrak. When you've done this go to the system menu and select Edit.

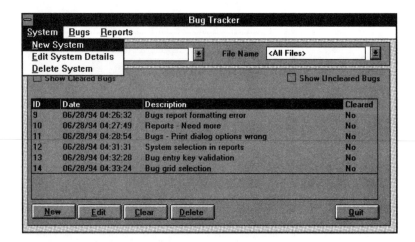

8   After a short pause the details for the system appear. The name and path of the make file are incorrect since the place you store information isn't the same as mine.

```
┌─────────────────────────────────────────────────────────────┐
│                    System Details Entry                      │
├─────────────────────────────────────────────────────────────┤
│                                                               │
│  System Name   [Bugtrak                                    ]  │
│                                                               │
│  Project Name  [D:\BOOKS\BG2VB\CHAP11\CODE\BUGTRA ]  [ File ] │
│                                                               │
│  ┌─────────────────────────────────────────────────────────┐ │
│  │ This is a small bug tracking and recording system written│ │
│  │ specifically for the purpose of the Beginners Guide To    │ │
│  │ Visual Basic.                                             │ │
│  │                                                           │ │
│  └─────────────────────────────────────────────────────────┘ │
│                                                               │
│  [    OK    ]                              [   Cancel   ]      │
└─────────────────────────────────────────────────────────────┘
```

9   Click on the File button to bring up a File common dialog, then use it to find and select the **BUGTRAK.MAK** file.

```
┌─────────────────────────────────────────────────────────────┐
│ ─              Select a project for this system              │
├─────────────────────────────────────────────────────────────┤
│  File Name:              Directories:                         │
│  [*.mak        ]         c:\vb                    [    OK    ] │
│                                                               │
│  192-111.mak         ▲   📂 c:\              ▲    [  Cancel  ] │
│  192_081.mak             📂 vb                                 │
│  autoload.mak            📁 icons                [ Network...]│
│  firstprg.mak            📁 samples                           │
│  nina.mak                📁 setupkit            ☐ Read Only   │
│  param.mak               📁 vb.cbt                            │
│                      ▼                       ▼                │
│                                                               │
│  List Files of Type:     Drives:                              │
│  [ Mak files       ▼]    [ 🖳 c:            ▼]                 │
└─────────────────────────────────────────────────────────────┘
```

10 When you've selected **BUGTRAK.MAK** click OK to return to the main form. You can now use the Files combo box to see a list of files in the BugTrak project which have code in them, and therefore those which are likely to have bugs.

11 BugTrak can also print you a hard copy report of the current bugs. Select the <u>S</u>ystem Bugs item from the <u>R</u>eports menu. Up comes a little form.

12 At the moment, we've only got one project to report on, so press <u>P</u>rint. Up comes the Print common dialog.

Now you have an idea of what BugTrak does, let's find out *how* it does it.

About BugTrak

Compared to a full-blown commercial application, BugTrak is fairly small; it consists of about twenty pages of code, five forms, and a very small, easy to manage database. However, despite its size, it *does* give you a realistic impression of what it's like to create real world programs in Visual Basic.

The Main Form

The form you see when you first run the application looks like this at design-time:

A grid is used for the main form to present the user with a list of bugs from a database. This is no mean feat. You'll remember that Visual Basic doesn't provide you with any kind of bound grid control.

Combo boxes on the main grid show you lists of information, both from database records and also from normal DOS files.

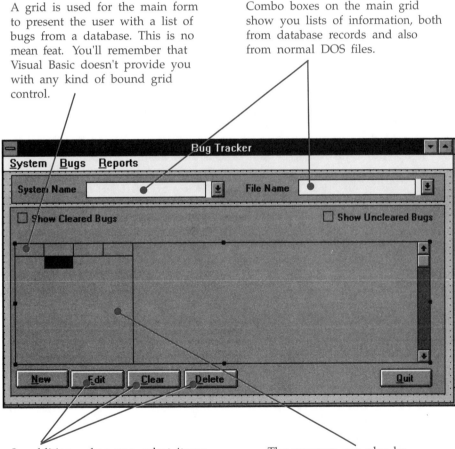

In addition, when you select items from the grid, they are passed across to separate detail forms which show you all the information on the selected record. The grid is only used to show summary information; complete information is shown on separate forms.

The program can also be configured to show information in different orders on the grid using the Select command which you saw back in the database chapter.

This brings us to another important area - passing database information between forms, and making forms talk to each other. The detail forms in the application, for example, don't use data controls at all, but they do allow you to edit and create new records in a database. You'll see how they do it in a moment.

There are also less than 10 global variables in the whole application. This, coupled with the fact that there are only two data controls in the program, makes for a very resource-efficient program, which in turn equates to a fairly fast and safe program. Before we look at the code, lets take a look at the database it interacts with.

The BugTrak Database

The database that lies behind BugTrak is straightforward and easy to use. A commercial database (one which manages payroll information or stock and inventory information for example) would typically have twenty or more tables in it. BugTrak has just two: Bugs and System.

One of the best ways to check out what's going on in the database is to load it up into Data Manager and take a look around yourself.

Try It Out - Browsing the Database Structure

1 Select Data Manager from the Window menu in Visual Basic. When it appears choose Open Database from the File menu and open up **BUGS.MDB**.

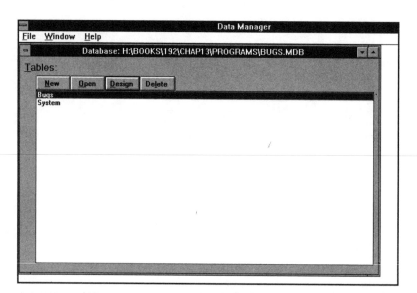

2   Firstly, let's take a look at what's in the Bugs table. Highlight Bugs and click on the Design button to bring up the table design window.

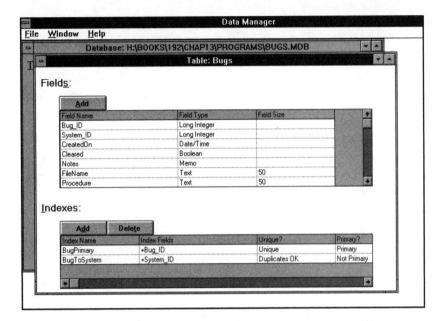

Here's a quick summary of what's in the Bugs table and what it means:

Field	Type	Description
Bug_ID	Counter	A unique number assigned to each record.
System_ID	Long	The unique number of the system to which this bug relates.
CreatedOn	Date/Time	The date and time that the bug was created.
Cleared	Boolean (Yes/No)	Has this bug been cleared yet?
Notes	Memo	A very large text field, where the user can enter notes about a bug.
Filename	String	The name of the file in the system in which the bug lives.
Procedure	String	The name of the procedure in the file in which the bug lives.
Description	String	A short textual description of the bug, for example, Invoice Reports Bug, Payroll Excess Payment.

Incidentally, if you look at the database with data manager, the counter fields will appear simply as long integers. Data manager doesn't allow you to define counter fields either, so if you want to use them in your own databases you will need to use a program like Access or Visdata (supplied with VB-Pro).

3 Each bug in the database is given a Bug_ID. This is a unique number by which it's known, and is a counter. It's quite possible that there'll be two or more bugs in a program, in the same procedure, or two bugs with the same description, so some unique way of identifying each is necessary.

To make any relational database work, you have to have at least one unique and unambiguous field in each table to identify individual entries. The best choice for this is a number, and an ID is a good name for it. Here, I've used a counter type for it. Each table in a database can have one and only one Counter field. As new records are created at run-time, the database automatically puts a unique number into the Counter field of each record that you're creating. It's this field which is used in the database to form a unique index. It's also worth bearing in mind that counter are self- updating long- integers.

A note about Counter Fields. Visual Basic makes developing database independent applications very easy. For example, you could create an Access format database, and then install the application on a user's machine to run with a totally different database format. This would involve only a small number of changes to your code original, mainly involving setting up the Connect string on your data controls.

For this reason, exercise caution when using Counter fields. Access is one of the only databases that has automatic Counter fields. Many others such as dBase, Paradox and SQL Server do not. If you use those databases you must create unique ID numbers yourself, by holding the last numbers used in a separate table, and updating them as you go.

4 In the database, each bug relates to a particular system; you can't enter a bug unless you first select a system. The System_ID of each bug relates that record to a record in the System table. This table contains information on the System from which the bug comes. Take a look at the System table by going back to the table selection window in Data Manager. Select System, and press Design to bring up the table structure.

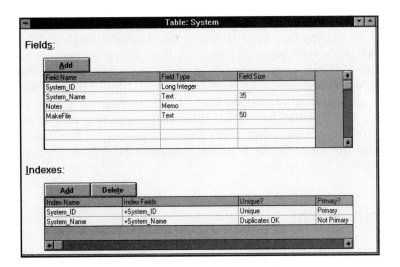

Here's a summary of the System Table:

Field Name	Type	Description
System_ID	Counter	A unique number assigned to each system in the table.
System_Name	String	A name which the user enters to make identifying the system easier.
Notes	Memo	Similar to the notes field on the Bugs table. Enables the user to enter notes about each system; for instance, to say what the system does, which stage it's at, and so on.
Makefile	String	The name of the system's **.MAK** file. This is used in the program to get a list of the modules and forms in the program, so that entering a bug and relating it to a form or module is easier.

Again a Counter field is used to give each record in the table a unique identifier, like the Bug_Id in the Bugs table.

The Makefile field is an interesting one. Normally, a database application will get all its information from tables in the database. BugTrak is slightly different. BugTrak deals with bugs in programs that you've written, or are in the process of writing. It can read a project's **MAK** file, the same **MAK** file that Visual Basic uses when you create, load and save a Visual Basic project. BugTrak uses the file to get a list of all the physical files that make up a program (for instance, the **BAS** files and the **FRM** files). This makes entering bug details a lot easier, as the user can now select a file from the project by name without having to key it in by name. To do this, BugTrak must be able to read and understand disk files.

The Main Form

Before we start to look at the code in detail, and the theory behind it, let's just remind ourselves what the main form does.

Try It Out - Checking Out the Main Form

1   Load up the BugTrak application. When you've loaded it, use the project window to take a look at the main form.

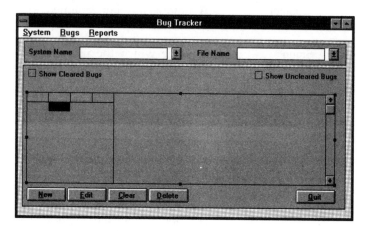

2   At the top of the form there are two combo boxes. These are used to both change the view of the grid *and* to add new bugs to the system.

3   Run the program to see how these work. If there is a project called BugTrak you want to examine, and you've already entered it as a system, then selecting it in the system box causes the grid to change so that only the bugs belonging to BugTrak are shown. Equally, if you select **BUGDETS.FRM** from the files combo box it causes the grid to change to show only those bugs which exist in the **BUGDETS.FRM**.

The grid itself lists the selection of bugs determined by the combo box contents and the state of the two check boxes.

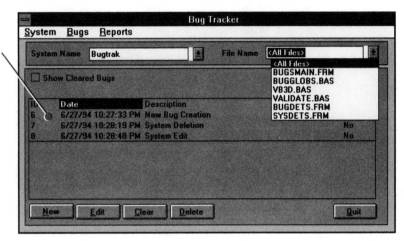

The checkboxes allow you to view those bugs in the grid which are outstanding, those which have been cleared, or both. How this works is covered in the section **Narrowing the Selection**.

I hope you noticed something unusual about the two combo boxes. They behave as though they are bound to the database, although we know very well they're not bound controls. Let's look at what's going on.

Simulating a Bound Combo Box

In design-mode, make the form slightly taller and you'll see two data controls come into view.

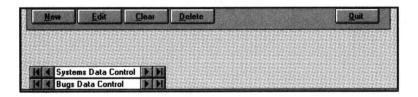

The second of these, the Systems Data Control is used to feed the System Name combo box. Visual Basic combo boxes are not bound; they can only display information that has been specifically added into them using code. How does the System combo box display data form the systems data control?

Try It Out - The Bound Combo Boxes

1 Bring up the form window and press *F2* to see a list of the procedures in the program.

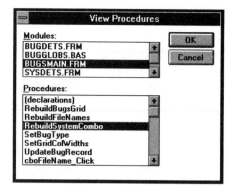

2 Select the procedure at the top of the list called RebuildSystemCombo. It's the highlighted option in the above screenshot. The code looks like this:

```
Sub RebuildSystemCombo ()

    Screen.MousePointer = 11
    cboSystemName.Clear
    cboSystemName.AddItem "<All Systems>"
    cboSystemName.ItemData(cboSystemName.ListCount - 1) = 0

    On Error Resume Next
    datSystems.Recordset.MoveFirst

    Do Until datSystems.Recordset.EOF
        cboSystemName.AddItem datSystems.Recordset.Fields("System_Name")
        cboSystemName.ItemData(cboSystemName.ListCount - 1) =
⤷datSystems.Recordset.Fields("System_ID")
        datSystems.Recordset.MoveNext
    Loop

    cboSystemName.ListIndex = 0
    On Error GoTo 0
    Screen.MousePointer = 0

End Sub
```

This code binds the data control to the combo box. Let's see how it works.

How It Works

The first thing the program does is change the **MousePointer** to pointer number **11**. When you set the **MousePointer** to number **11** you get the hourglass image which most Windows programs display when they want you to wait for something. The last line of code:

```
Screen.MousePointer = 0
```

resets the **MousePointer** back to its normal state.

The **RebuildSystemCombo** procedure is called from a number of places in the program. It's initially called when the form loads up, and then it's called whenever you add a new system to the combo list, or delete or update an existing one. For this reason, the code needs to assume that there's already data in the combo box which we don't need.

Next, the command **cboSystemName.Clear** clears everything out of the combo box. This includes all the items that have previously been added to its list, as well as any text which has been entered into the combo boxes text entry area.

Now we need to do a bit of theory. If you remember, there are two parts to the list in a combo box:

- There's the *actual* part of the list you see, which you can add items to using **Additem**, and which you can remove items from using **RemoveItem**.

- There is also an *array* attached to the list called **ItemData**, into which you can place numbers which relate to each element in the list.

A unique number, **System_ID**, is given to each system whose bugs are to be recorded in the database. The system name itself doesn't have to be unique - so what happens if there are two BugTrak systems in the database and the user selects one of them? How does Visual Basic know which record in the System table the selected item relates to? Answer - it uses **ItemData**. When a system name is added to the combo box, the **System_ID** for that name is placed in the appropriate **ItemData** slot.

The next two lines of code implement this. At the head of the list we want an option that says **<All Systems>**. This is added by the following line of code:

```
cboSystemName.AddItem "<All Systems>"
```

The next line of code sets the **ItemData** element for this entry to **0**. All system numbers in the table are therefore greater than **0**; the database takes care of this, by only ever assigning numbers to counters that are greater than **0**.

```
cboSystemName.ItemData(cboSystemName.ListCount - 1) = 0
```

The **ListCount** property of a combo box tells us how many items are currently in the list. We can use this to find out the number of the last item added to the list, and set up its **ItemData** property accordingly. The items in the list are numbered from **0**, so in the above code where there's only 1 item of data in the list, **ListCount** will equal 1. The actual number of the **ItemData** element we need to get at is **0 (ListCount - 1).**

The code that follows this actually uses the data control to copy information from the Systems table into the list:

```
On Error Resume Next
    datSystems.Recordset.MoveFirst

    Do Until datSystems.Recordset.EOF
        cboSystemName.AddItem datSystems.Recordset.Fields("System_Name")
        cboSystemName.ItemData(cboSystemName.ListCount - 1) =
datSystems.Recordset.Fields("System_ID")
        datSystems.Recordset.MoveNext
    Loop

    cboSystemName.ListIndex = 0
    On Error GoTo 0
    Screen.MousePointer = 0
```

The program needs to be able to cope intelligently with all eventualities, including the possibility that there might not be any data in the table at all. If we try to move through the records in an empty table then an error occurs. The following line of code tells Visual Basic that if an error occurs then it should ignore the error and try the next line of code:

```
On Error Resume Next
```

The most likely place in the code where an error is most likely to occur is the following:

```
datSystems.Recordset.MoveFirst
```

Here, **MoveFirst** moves to the first record in the table, and is ready for us to start looping through all the records in turn. If there are no records in the table then an error occurs, which because of our **On Error** command means that the code will simply fall down to the next line.

The next line marks the start of the code that loops through the records and builds up the combo box. The loop runs for as long as we aren't currently at the last record in the table:

```
Do Until datSystems.Recordset.EOF
```

If an error did occur, owing to there being no records in the table, then the loop wouldn't run at all. The actual code in the loop is fairly simple; it uses **MoveNext** to keep moving to the next record in the database and then copies the System name into the list box with **AddItem**, and places its **System_ID** into the **ItemData** array attached to the combo box.

When the loop finishes, the **ListIndex** property is set to **0**, which selects the first item in the list as the default. Behind the scenes this also triggers a click event for the combo box, which we'll examine in a moment.

Finally, the error handling is turned off and the mouse pointer is reset back to its normal state.

Binding Combo Boxes Step by Step

In summary, a combo box is built from a data control in a series of steps:

1   The combo box is cleared using the **Clear** method.

2   The data control is positioned at the first record in the table it's bound to.

3   If there's a chance that there are no records in the table then you need to implement some error handling to make sure that the resulting error doesn't appear on screen to the users.

4   A loop then runs until the end of the table is hit in the form:

```
Do Until <datacontrol>.Recordset.EOF
```

5   Inside, the loop code moves to the next record in the table:

```
<datacontrol>.Recordset.MoveNext
```

6   For each record **AddItem** adds one of the fields in the table to the list, while a unique number for each item is stored in the **ItemData** array. The **MoveNext** method is used after the items have been copied over.

> If you were to do a **MoveNext** first, the combo box wouldn't include the first record in the table, (you found this with the previous **MoveFirst**.)

Building the Grid From a Data Control

Grids can be bound to a data control in a similar way to combo boxes. You move to the first record, then add the field contents of each subsequent record to cells in the grid. In the code window, press *F2* again to bring up the procedures list, and select the RebuildBugsGrid procedure. The central part of the code looks like this:

```
grdBugs.Rows = 1
On Error Resume Next
datBugs.Recordset.MoveFirst

Do Until datBugs.Recordset.EOF

  sGridText = "" & datBugs.Recordset.Fields("Bug_ID") & Chr$(9)
  sGridText = sGridText & datBugs.Recordset.Fields("CreatedOn") &
⤷Chr$(9)
  sGridText = sGridText & datBugs.Recordset.Fields("Description") &
⤷Chr$(9)
      If datBugs.Recordset.Fields("Cleared") Then
          sGridText = sGridText & "Yes"
      Else
          sGridText = sGridText & "No"
      End If

  grdBugs.AddItem sGridText
  datBugs.Recordset.MoveNext

Loop

On Error GoTo 0
Screen.MousePointer = 0
```

How It Works

This isn't the complete code from the subprocedure. There's code missing from the top which changes the data control's **RecordSource** property to only show records which relate to the selected system and file, and to the values of the two checkboxes. We'll examine how this works later in the **Narrowing The Selection** section.

Although this code looks fairly complex, and somewhat different to the code for the combo box, it's actually very similar. Firstly, the grid is cleared:

```
grdBugs.Rows = 1
```

We can't use the **Clear** method to clear the grid, so instead we set the number of rows in the grid to **1**. The grid actually has a fixed row at the top which displays the heading information. If you set the number of rows in the grid to **1** it means that only the headings are left intact.

The next two lines should look very familiar:

```
On Error Resume Next
datBugs.Recordset.MoveFirst
```

The first line turns on error handling, telling Visual Basic we want to ignore any errors. The second moves to the first record of the **datBugs** data control.

Exactly as before, a **Do...Loop** is set up to move through the records in this data control. However, what actually happens within this loop is very different to the code we saw in the combo box.

Setting Up The Grid

Grids have a number of columns and we need to place information into each column. **AddItem** is used here to add rows of information to a grid, as it is to add items to a list box or combo box. However, we need to find some way of telling Visual Basic what information relates to what column. This is done by building up a string variable **sGridText**. Data for each column is added into the string variable, separated by a Tab, **Chr$(9)**. This separates the information for the various columns of the grid.

The last column in this grid is somewhat special since it displays a Boolean (**True/False**) field from the database. Normally, just copying the contents of this field into a grid would result in the grid displaying either **1** or **0**, which isn't very intuitive. Instead, a simple **If** statement is used to check the value of the field and then to insert either the word **Yes** or **No** into the grid. That way the answer to the **Bug Cleared?** question at the head of the column is always **Yes** or **No**.

```
If datBugs.Recordset.Fields("Cleared") Then
    sGridText = sGridText & "Yes"
Else
    sGridText = sGridText & "No"
End If
```

Once the string to be fed into the grid has been built up, the code follows the same pattern as it did for the combo box. The string is used with **AddItem** to place the data into the grid, and then the next record in the data control is selected using the **MoveNext** method.

```
grdBugs.AddItem sGridText
datBugs.Recordset.MoveNext
```

Finally, the error handling is turned off, and the **MousePointer** returned to normal.

633

Linking the Components Together

All the components of the BugTrak form work together. If you select a system from the System Name combo box then the File Name combo box is changed to show a list of files in that system. In turn, the File Name combo box causes the grid itself to rebuild when an item is selected, or when it's rebuilt. Likewise, both the check boxes that allow you to view cleared and uncleared bugs cause the grid to rebuild itself.

How does this all work together? Well, it's a great example of how useful subprocedures and the click event can be.

When you select an item from the System Name combo box, a click event occurs. Code in the click event calls the **RebuildFileNames** subprocedure to rebuild the files list box. We'll look at this code in a bit more detail later.

Like the System Name combo box, when the File Name combo is built up the top item in the list is automatically selected. This again causes a click event, this time for the File Name combo. Code in this click event calls the **RebuildBugsGrid** subroutine to redisplay the bugs grid.

This whole process is called **nesting** events, and has both good and bad sides. What you see here is the good side of it - one click event triggering rebuilds of two other controls on the form. However, the bad side is that if used unwisely you end up with *cascading* events rather than nested events, where one event triggers another, and another, and another, until your system crashes. We saw a good example of this in Chapter 2 with the **LostFocus** and **GotFocus** events, where control was swapped between text boxes indefinitely. You won't see focus events used at all in this application because of their nasty side effects.

The moral of the story is, if you're going to write code with nested events be very careful that you know what you're doing. The nested events in BugTrak work well; I can rebuild both combo boxes and the grid simply by calling the code to update the System combo box. However, if the code that builds up the File Name box actually triggered a click event on the system list box, our user's heaven would soon become a code writer's hell.

Calling the Detail Forms

The only data controls in this application are on the main form. There are a number of reasons for this, the primary one being the need to use system resources efficiently. Since the main form is always loaded, what's the point of loading in other forms with data controls of their own? With a little extra typing in the code window you can use the original data controls anywhere.

However, this presents us with some interesting problems, such as how do we pass record information to and from the detail forms? BugTrak tackles this problem from two angles, and which you decide to use in your own code depends on your own personal preferences. Let's look at the easiest one first, using the System maintenance window.

The System Maintenance Form

This is the easiest subform to deal with since it only has a few controls on.

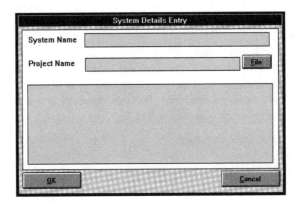

Adding a New System

Select the New System option from the System menu on the main form to see the code that loads this form:

```
Sub mnuSNew_Click ()

    Load frmSystem
    frmSystem.Show 1

    If gCancel = True Then
        Unload frmSystem
        Exit Sub
    End If

    datSystems.Recordset.AddNew
    datSystems.Recordset.Fields("System_Name") = frmSystem!txtSystem.Text
    datSystems.Recordset.Fields("MakeFile") = frmSystem!txtMakefile.Text
    datSystems.Recordset.Fields("Notes") = frmSystem!txtNotes.Text

    datSystems.Recordset.Update

    Unload frmSystem

    Call RebuildSystemCombo

End Sub
```

This loads up the system maintenance form and uses **frmSystem.Show** **1** to show the form as a modal form. The form comes into view at this point with no information on it, waiting for the user to do something.

Both maintenance forms (the bug maintenance form and the system maintenance form), use a global variable **gCancel** to indicate when the user hits the Cancel button on those forms. Since the form is shown as a modal form, the code in the menu event stops as soon as the form is shown, waiting for the form to either unload itself or hide itself. As soon as the user clicks either the OK or Cancel buttons on the form, it's hidden, rather than unloaded.

This returns control to the menu code above, but with the result that the System form, and any information entered into it, is still available to your code. An **AddNew** method is then used on the System data control to create a new record. The values of the fields on the system menu are then copied into the fields of the new record. The **Update** method then writes this information out to the System table permanently:

```
datSystems.Recordset.AddNew
datSystems.Recordset.Fields("System_Name") = frmSystem!txtSystem.Text
datSystems.Recordset.Fields("MakeFile") = frmSystem!txtMakefile.Text
datSystems.Recordset.Fields("Notes") = frmSystem!txtNotes.Text

datSystems.Recordset.Update
```

Once this is finished the form is unloaded and a call is made to the **RebuildSystemCombo** procedure which rebuilds the system combo, file combo, and the grid itself. Because the data only flows one way (out of the form) it's easy to create new system records. But what if you want to edit existing systems?

Editing Existing Systems

Still in design-mode, select the Edit System option from the System menu to see the code:

```
Sub mnuSEdit_Click ()

    datSystems.Recordset.FindFirst "System_ID = " &
 cboSystemName.ItemData(cboSystemName.ListIndex)

    If datSystems.Recordset.NoMatch Then
        Beep
        MsgBox "You must select a system first", , "System Error"
        Exit Sub
    End If
```

```
   Load frmSystem
   frmSystem!txtSystem.Text = datSystems.Recordset.Fields("System_Name")
   frmSystem!txtMakefile.Text = datSystems.Recordset.Fields("MakeFile")
   frmSystem!txtNotes.Text = datSystems.Recordset.Fields("notes")

   frmSystem.Show 1

   If gcancel = True Then
       Unload frmSystem
       Exit Sub
   End If

   datSystems.Recordset.Edit

   datSystems.Recordset.Fields("System_Name") = frmSystem!txtSystem.Text
   datSystems.Recordset.Fields("MakeFile") = frmSystem!txtMakefile.Text
   datSystems.Recordset.Fields("Notes") = frmSystem!txtNotes.Text

   datSystems.Recordset.Update

   Unload frmSystem

   Call RebuildFileNames

End Sub
```

The code here is very similar to the previous event. After loading the form, information is copied from the fields in the System table onto the new form, before the form is displayed. This means that the form comes into view with the existing system information already on it, ready to be edited. The rest of the code works in the same way as the New System event. The code waits until the user presses the OK button before copying the amended fields information back into the database.

The Bug Maintenance Form

The bug maintenance form works to demonstrate a slightly different method of updating sub forms. As you develop more and more applications in Visual Basic you'll come across code and forms that you can re-use in other applications. However, when you're dealing with database code and forms you need to approach the problem of passing information from a slightly different angle.

With the bug maintenance form, the information from the currently selected bug in the grid is copied into a variable with a custom type. This type is defined in the **BAS** file and is thus available globally.

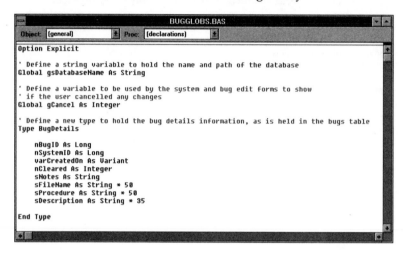

```
BUGGLOBS.BAS
Object: [general]          Proc: [declarations]

Option Explicit

' Define a string variable to hold the name and path of the database
Global gsDatabaseName As String

' Define a variable to be used by the system and bug edit forms to show
' if the user cancelled any changes
Global gCancel As Integer

' Define a new type to hold the bug details information, as is held in the bugs table
Type BugDetails

    nBugID As Long
    nSystemID As Long
    varCreatedOn As Variant
    nCleared As Integer
    sNotes As String
    sFileName As String * 50
    sProcedure As String * 50
    sDescription As String * 35

End Type
```

To actually use it you need to define a variable of the type:

```
Dim CurrentBug as BugDetails
```

Whenever you click on the New or Edit buttons this is exactly what happens; a new variable is declared with the custom type and information from the current Bug record fed into it using a global procedure **SetBugType**. The newly filled type variable is then fed to another global procedure. This loads up the Edit form and copies the information both from the type into the form, and out of the form at the end back into the type.

This is all handled by the **EditBug** procedure in **BugGlobs.Bas**:

```
Sub EditBug (CurrentBug As BugDetails, sType As String)
    Dim nIndex As Integer

    screen.MousePointer = 11

    Load frmBugs

    frmBugs!lblSystem.Caption = frmMainForm!cboSystemName.Text
    frmBugs!lblBugID.Caption = CurrentBug.nSystemID
    frmBugs!txtCreatedOn.Text = CurrentBug.varCreatedOn

    If CurrentBug.nCleared Then
        frmBugs!chkCleared.Value = 1
    Else
        frmBugs!chkCleared.Value = 0
    End If
```

```
            frmBugs!txtNotes.Text = CurrentBug.sNotes
            frmBugs!txtProcedure.Text = CurrentBug.sProcedure
            frmBugs!txtDescription.Text = CurrentBug.sDescription

            frmBugs!cboFilename.Clear
            For nIndex = 0 To frmMainForm!cboFileName.ListCount - 1

                frmBugs!cboFilename.AddItem frmMainForm!cboFileName.List(nIndex)

        Next nIndex

        frmBugs!cboFilename.Text = CurrentBug.sFileName

        screen.MousePointer = 0

        frmBugs.Show 1

        If gCancel = True Then
            Unload frmBugs
            Exit Sub
        End If

        screen.MousePointer = 11

        CurrentBug.nSystemID = frmBugs!lblBugID.Caption
        CurrentBug.varCreatedOn = frmBugs!txtCreatedOn.Text
        CurrentBug.nCleared = frmBugs!chkCleared.Value
        CurrentBug.sNotes = frmBugs!txtNotes.Text
        CurrentBug.sProcedure = frmBugs!txtProcedure.Text
        CurrentBug.sDescription = frmBugs!txtDescription.Text
        CurrentBug.sFileName = frmBugs!cboFilename.Text

        If sType = "NEW" Then

            frmMainForm!datBugs.Recordset.AddNew
            frmMainForm!datBugs.Recordset.Update
            frmMainForm!datBugs.Recordset.Bookmark =
 frmMainForm!datBugs.Recordset.LastModified
            CurrentBug.nBugID =
 frmMainForm!datBugs.Recordset.Fields("Bug_ID")
            Call UpdateBugRecord(CurrentBug)

        Else

            Call UpdateBugRecord(CurrentBug)

        End If

        Unload frmBugs
        screen.MousePointer = 0

End Sub
```

Don't be too daunted by this code, at least not by the size of it! Unlike the System maintenance code this one routinely handles both the record creation and maintenance operations. Let's take a walk through it.

The first chunk of the code, up to the line **frmBugs.Show 1** handles setting up the Bugs form. It copies information from the type variable into the controls on the Bug Maintenance form, and also loads up the files combo box on that form, to make relating a bug to a file easier for the user.

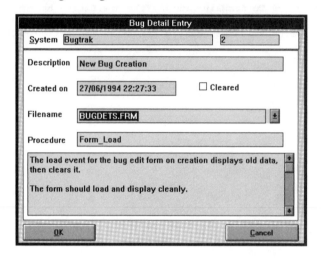

The **True/False** value obtained from the Cleared field on the Bugs record needs to be changed into either **1** or **0** for the cleared check box on the form. The form is then shown modally, in exactly the same way as the system form. Just like the system maintenance form, when the user finally clicks on OK or Cancel on the maintenance form, a **Hide** method is used to return control to our procedure. If Cancel is pressed then the global **gCancel** variable is set to **True**, causing our code to exit immediately.

Assuming everything went well, the code then goes about deciding what to do with the data it got back. Firstly, it reloads all the values from the Bug maintenance form into the type variable. In this particular application that's really a case of overkill. However, if we wanted to extend the program a little further, to add auditing for example, then we have the complete Bug record in a variable which can be thrown at any other routine we want. As I said, it's overkill time, but it could be very useful if the program had to be expanded in some way.

After the field values have been copied out, the procedure then checks to see if we are adding a new record or updating an existing one. This is determined using a parameter passed to the procedure, the **sType** parameter. If this is passed as **"NEW"** then we're asking the code to create a new record.

```
Call EditBug (CurrentBug, "New")
```

If we are simply updating an existing record then the **UpdateBugRecord** procedure is called. This copies the information in the **CurrentBug** type variable out to the database record. On the other hand, if we want to create a new record, a little more work is in needed.

```
If sType = "NEW" Then

        frmMainForm!datBugs.Recordset.AddNew
        frmMainForm!datBugs.Recordset.Update
        frmMainForm!datBugs.Recordset.Bookmark =
↳ frmMainForm!datBugs.Recordset.LastModified
        CurrentBug.nBugID =
↳ frmMainForm!datBugs.Recordset.Fields("Bug_ID")
        Call UpdateBugRecord(CurrentBug)
```

Firstly, the **AddNew** method is used to create a new record in the Bugs table (represented by the datacontrol on the main form). Immediately after the **AddNew** method has been used, an **Update** is used to save the record to the database. This gives us a blank record with a unique number, since the database assigns the **Bug_ID**s itself.

Whenever you add a new record to the database, Visual Basic automatically moves the current record back to wherever it was before the add took place. This is bad news for us since having created the new record we now want to stuff information into it.

This is where Bookmarks come in handy - remember those? There's a property of the **RecordSet** called **LastModifed** which is simply the bookmark of the last record in a table that was either changed or created. If we set the bookmark of the **RecordSet** to the value of this **LastModified** parameter we can move the data control back to the new record.

```
frmMainForm!datBugs.Recordset.Bookmark =
↳ frmMainForm!datBugs.Recordset.LastModified
```

Up to this point our code has had no idea of the ID of the new bug, so immediately after the bookmark has been set and the new record found again, the **Bug_ID** is copied into our **CurrentBug** type. All that remains now is to call the **UpdateBugRecord** procedure. At this point, everything's complete.

Although this is a very long-winded way of doing things, it *does* make the code very re-useable. If we wanted to be able to add system records from more forms in the system, then there'd be a lot more typing involved, as you'd have to copy the code out of the menu events into the new events.

We could allow the user to create more bug information in other parts of the application using only two procedure calls, **SetBugType** and **EditBug**, making this a much more efficient way of doing things in the long term.

Talking to the Database

One of the most flexible aspects of this program is the way it lets you decide what you want to see on the grid on the main form. If you only want to see cleared bugs then you can do that. If you want to see all outstanding bugs in a particular file of a project then you can do that too.

This flexibility is all handled by a command you saw briefly back in the database chapter, the **Select** command. **Select** actually belongs to a programming language called **SQL** which is included with the Access database part of Visual Basic. SQL (it's supposed to be pronounced 'sequel') allows you to tell a database exactly what information you want and how the database should get it in a language very similar to English. Unfortunately, its use in the Standard Edition of Visual Basic is limited to the RecordSource property of data controls. We used it this way in Chapter 9.

Narrowing the Selection

Before we look at the code itself, which is rather confusing, let's do some theory. **Select** works by passing it the names of the fields you want, the files they come from, and any specific criteria that you want to match those records against.

Let's suppose you wanted to select all bugs that have been marked as cleared. This is the **Select** statement you'd put into the RecordSource property to achieve this:

```
Select * from Bugs where Cleared
```

This means 'select everything' (* means everything) from the Bugs table where the Cleared field is **True**'. Simple enough! Now, what about selecting all those records from the Bugs table which belong to system number 1 and which are in the **MAINFORM.FRM** file? It's not that much harder than the statement you've just seen:

```
Select * from Bugs where cleared and System_ID = 1 and FileName
= 'MAINFORM.FRM'
```

Read it out loud. With **SQL** even a complex set of criteria like this is fairly easy to put together. Also notice that when you specify strings in a **Select** statement, like **MAINFORM.FRM**, you put them in single quotes ("). The **Select** statement always goes into the RecordSource property of a data control and so is itself enclosed in quotes. If you put normal quotes (" ") inside the RecordSource then Visual Basic gets mighty confused.

If **Select** is so easy to use, how come I said that the code that deals with it is so nasty? In BugTrak we need to build a **Select** statement at run-time, based on the values of certain controls on the form which may or may not need to be included in the **Select**. This involves quite a lot of string handling.

Take a look at the **RebuildBugsGrid** procedure, which is where the **Select** statement is used most:

```
Sub RebuildBugsGrid ()

    Dim sGridText As String
    Dim nGridRow As Integer
    Dim sSQL As String

    screen.MousePointer = 11

    sSQL = "Select * From Bugs Where "

    If cboSystemName.Text <> "<All Systems>" Then
        sSQL = sSQL & "Bugs.System_ID = " &
  cboSystemName.ItemData(cboSystemName.ListIndex) & " and "
    End If

    If cboFileName.Text <> "<All Files>" Then
        sSQL = sSQL & "Bugs.FileName = '" & cboFileName.Text & "' and "
    End If

    If chkShowCleared.Value = 0 Or chkShowUnCleared = 0 Then

        If chkShowCleared.Value = 1 Then sSQL = sSQL & " Bugs.Cleared"
        If chkShowUnCleared.Value = 1 Then sSQL = sSQL & " not Bugs.Cleared"

    End If

    If Right$(sSQL, 6) = "Where " Then sSQL = Left$(sSQL, Len(sSQL) - 6)
    If Right$(sSQL, 4) = "and " Then sSQL = Left$(sSQL, Len(sSQL) - 4)
    sSQL = sSQL & " Order By Bugs.Bug_ID"

    datBugs.RecordSource = sSQL
    datBugs.Refresh
    grdBugs.Rows = 1

    On Error Resume Next
    sGridText = ""
    datBugs.Recordset.MoveFirst
```

```
    Do Until datBugs.Recordset.EOF

        sGridText = "" & datBugs.Recordset.Fields("Bug_ID") & Chr$(9)
        sGridText = sGridText & datBugs.Recordset.Fields("CreatedOn") &
 ⮠ Chr$(9)
        sGridText = sGridText & datBugs.Recordset.Fields("Description")
 ⮠ & Chr$(9)
        If datBugs.Recordset.Fields("Cleared") Then
            sGridText = sGridText & "Yes"
        Else
            sGridText = sGridText & "No"
        End If

        grdBugs.AddItem sGridText
        datBugs.Recordset.MoveNext

    Loop

    On Error GoTo 0
    screen.MousePointer = 0

End Sub
```

This one is going to take some explaining, so bear with me. The main part of this code deals with the **Where** clause of the **Select** statement. We need to add **and** and **or** statements to the code on the fly, as well as brackets, in order to break up the conditions into nice easy-to-manage chunks.

The first part of the procedure is easy to follow. A string variable is used to hold the **Select** statement as it's built up, so the words **Select   *   from Bugs   Where** are placed into the string:

```
sSQL = "Select * From Bugs Where "
```

Next, the code checks whether or not the user has selected a system name and a file name:

```
    If cboSystemName.Text <> "<All Systems>" Then
        sSQL = sSQL & "Bugs.System_ID = " &
 ⮠ cboSystemName.ItemData(cboSystemName.ListIndex) & " and "
    End If

    If cboFileName.Text <> "<All Files>" Then
        sSQL = sSQL & "Bugs.FileName = '" & cboFileName.Text & "' and "
    End If
```

If either of the combo boxes has anything other than **<All Systems>** or **<All Files>** in it, then the appropriate values are fed in the **Select** string as well.

Take a look at the code which matches **cboFileName**. If a filename has been selected, then it's fed into the string, but enclosed in single quote marks. If you look closely enough at the code fragment you'll see that the string we append to **sSQL** says:

```
"Bugs.FileName = ' " & cboFileName.Text & " ' and "
```

The next part of the code deals with the combo boxes, translating their **Value** properties into **True** or **False** tokens which can be used in the **Select** statement. This is where things get a little complicated:

```
If chkShowCleared.Value = 0 Or chkShowUnCleared = 0 Then

  If chkShowCleared.Value = 1 Then sSQL = sSQL & " Bugs.Cleared "
  If chkShowUnCleared.Value = 1 Then sSQL = sSQL & " not Bugs.Cleared "

End If
```

The code only deals with the combo boxes if at least one of them is unchecked. There is a reason for this: if both are checked that means that the user wants to see *all* bugs, cleared or not. The program treats having both checkboxes unchecked as the same thing. Therefore, the checkbox values are only added into the **Select** statement if only one of them is checked.

At the end of all this, the **Select** statement is tidied up. There are two circumstances under which the **sSQL** string could get messed up. Firstly, if neither a file nor system are selected and neither of the checkboxes are checked then you could end up with this:

```
Select * from Bugs Where
```

Alternatively, if a file or system is selected, but again the checkboxes aren't selected, then your **Select** statement will be:

```
Select * from Bugs where Bugs.System_ID = 1 and
```

In the first example we need to lose the **Where** bit on the end of the statement so that it'll make sense. In the second example we need to lose the word **and** The next two lines of code check for just these situations and strip the offending words out of the code:

```
If Right$(sSQL, 6) = "Where " Then sSQL = Left$(sSQL, Len(sSQL) - 6)
If Right$(sSQL, 4) = "and " Then sSQL = Left$(sSQL, Len(sSQL) - 4)
```

These both check a number of characters from the right of the string for the offending statements, and truncate the string if they're found. We covered the **Right$**, **Left$**, and **Len** statements way back at the beginning of the book, so take a look there if this is all getting a bit too much.

645

Putting the Data in Order

One of the other magical abilities of the **Select** statement is ordering data. Having told the database where to get information from, and exactly what information to get, you can also tell it how that information should be ordered, using the **Order** statement. The next line of code does just that:

```
sSQL = sSQL & " Order By Bugs.Bug_ID"
```

This tells the database that we want the records in the data control to be ordered based on the **Bug_ID** field in the **Bugs** table. By default, **Order** sorts records into ascending order, but we could have said:

```
Order By Bugs.Bug_ID Desc
```

This sorts the records in descending order.

Having built a valid **Select** statement in a string variable, that variable is then copied into the data control's **RecordSource** property before refreshing the data control.

```
datBugs.RecordSource = SQL
datBugs.Refresh
```

Refresh makes Visual Basic go away and use the **RecordSource** property to rebuild its selection of records. If you simply place something into the **RecordSource** property this won't be good enough. Visual Basic will quite happily ignore everything in the **RecordSource** property until the data control is refreshed, either by loading the form again, or by doing an explicit **Refresh** on it in this way.

File Handling and the File Combo

One major topic that we haven't come across in this book yet is file handling, that is, dealing with straight files on your computer's hard disk rather than information in a database. Visual Basic has some very comprehensive file handling methods available for you to use. Since BugTrak is designed primarily to deal with Visual Basic projects, we can use these file handling methods to actually dissect the Visual Basic **MAK** file and give the user a list of files in the files combo box which are likely to contain code, and thus bugs.

All the file handling in the BugTrak program is actually contained in a single procedure, **RebuildFileNames**.

```
Sub RebuildFileNames ()

    Dim varFileNumber As Variant
    Dim sLineInMak As String
    Dim nCharacter As Integer

    screen.MousePointer = 11
    varFileNumber = FreeFile
    cboFileName.Clear
    cboFileName.AddItem "<All Files>"
    datSystems.Recordset.FindFirst "System_Id = " &
↳cboSystemName.ItemData(cboSystemName.ListIndex)

    If Not datSystems.Recordset.NoMatch Then
        On Error GoTo EndOfBuild
        If Dir$(datSystems.Recordset.Fields("Makefile") & "") <> "" Then
            On Error GoTo 0
            Open datSystems.Recordset.Fields("MakeFile") For Input As
↳varFileNumber
            Do Until EOF(varFileNumber)
                Line Input #varFileNumber, sLineInMak
                If UCase(Right$(sLineInMak, 4)) = ".BAS" Or
↳UCase(Right$(sLineInMak, 4)) = ".FRM" Then
                    For nCharacter = Len(sLineInMak) To 1 Step -1
                        If Mid$(sLineInMak, nCharacter, 1) = "\" Then
                            cboFileName.AddItem Right$(sLineInMak,
↳Len(sLineInMak) - nCharacter)
                            Exit For
                        End If
                    Next
                    If nCharacter = 0 Then cboFileName.AddItem
↳Right$(sLineInMak, Len(sLineInMak) - nCharacter)
                End If
            Loop
            Close varFileNumber
        End If
    End If

EndOfBuild:
    On Error GoTo 0
    cboFileName.ListIndex = 0
    screen.MousePointer = 0
    Exit Sub

End Sub
```

File Handles

At the start of the code three variables are declared: **varFileNumber**,
sLineInMak and **nCharacter**. The most important of these is **varFileNumber**.
Whenever you deal with a file on the disk you need to assign it a number. In
older versions of Basic this was often called a **channel** number, but you'll also
hear it refered to as a **file handle** or a **file number**.

Visual Basic gives you a function called **FreeFile** which you can use to get a valid file number. Therefore, the line:

```
varFileNumber = FreeFile
```

puts the next valid file number into the **varFileNumber** variable. This can then be used with the file handling commands a little later.

The next line of code puts the **<All Files>** item into the combo box, so that there's always this option in the box if nothing else.

Finding The File

A search using **FindNext** is then made to attempt to match any system in the database with the system currently selected in the System combo box, using the lines:

```
        datSystems.Recordset.FindFirst "System_Id = " &
cboSystemName.ItemData(cboSystemName.ListIndex)
```

If a match is found, we then drop into the main file handling code, which starts with the line:

```
Not datSystems.Recordset.NoMatch Then
```

Before we can start dissecting the **MAK** file associated with the system we need to make sure that the file actually exists on the user's hard disk. It may have existed when the system was originally keyed in to the database, but since then the user may have deleted the system or moved it somewhere else.

The name of the make file is held in the **MakeFile** field on the table. The way you check for if a file exists is by using the **DIR$** command. If **DIR$** returns **""** then the file couldn't be found.

```
If Dir$(datSystems.Recordset.Fields("Makefile") & "") <> "" Then
```

If **Dir$** is not equal to **""**, meaning the file is there, then we can go on to the proper file handling code. However, there is a problem with this command. **Dir$** assumes that the directory we want to search in exists, even if it doesn't. This is where the **On Error** code on the line above comes into play.

```
On Error GoTo EndOfBuild
```

If the directory doesn't exist then Visual Basic triggers an error. Our **On Error** statement catches this and transfers the program to the end of the **EndOfBuild** label, at the end of the procedure.

Once we get past this check the error handling is turned off:

```
On Error Goto 0
```

Examining the Disk Files

There are three commands that we can use to examine a file on the disk. The first you'll come across is **Open**.

```
        Open datSystems.Recordset.Fields("MakeFile") For Input As
⤷varFileNumber
```

This opens up the file whose filename is held in the **Makefile** field for input. **Open** needs us to give it a file number, which is where the **varFileNumber** variable we set up at the top of the code comes into play:

```
    Dim varFileNumber As Variant
```

Having opened the file we can then start to loop through the entries in it:

```
    Do Until EOF(varFileNumber)
        Line Input #varFileNumber, sLineInMak
        If UCase(Right$(sLineInMak, 4)) = ".BAS" Or
⤷UCase(Right$(sLineInMak, 4)) = ".FRM" Then
            For nCharacter = Len(sLineInMak) To 1 Step -1
                If Mid$(sLineInMak, nCharacter, 1) = "\" Then
                    cboFileName.AddItem Right$(sLineInMak,
⤷Len(sLineInMak) - nCharacter)
                    Exit For
                End If
            Next
            If nCharacter = 0 Then cboFileName.AddItem
⤷Right$(sLineInMak, Len(sLineInMak) - nCharacter)
        End If
    Loop
```

This starts a loop which runs until the end of the file is hit. This file has the handle **varFileNumber**. The **EOF** function returns **True** if the end of the file is reached, **False** for as long as everything is OK. It works much like the **EOF** property on the **RecordSet** that you can check to see when you've reached the end of a table.

The first line in the loop reads information from the file into our **sLineInMak** variable:

```
Line Input #varFileNumber, sLineInMak
```

Visual Basic **MAK** files are simply lists of filenames which go to make up the total project, such as this:

```
MAINFORM.FRM
OLE2.VBX
VBCTL3D.VBX
DETFORM.FRM
C:\WINDOWS\SYSTEM\ACTRL.VBX
```

Each entry in the file is placed on a line of its own. The **Line Input #** command reads these lines one by one.

```
Line Input #varFileNumber, sLineInMak
```

With **Line Input #** you need to specify the filenumber of the file you're reading, and the variable where you want to store the results. If we were looking at the above **MAK** file, **Line Input #** would put **MAINFORM.FRM** into **sLineInMak** first, then **OLE2.VBX** on the next pass through the loop, and so on.

Immediately after we've read-in a line, a few simple string commands are used to check whether the line just read ends in **FRM** or **BAS**.

```
                    If UCase(Right$(sLineInMak, 4)) = ".BAS" Or
⮡UCase(Right$(sLineInMak, 4)) = ".FRM" Then
```

If it matches either of these extensions then this is a file we're interested in adding to the combo box. In this case, a **For** loop moves through the string character by character, making sure that all that is added to the combo is the filename, not the full path name of the file. So if we had read in the line:

```
C:\DEVELOPS\PETER\MAINFORM.FRM
```

then the **For** loop in the code would make sure that all that gets added to the combo box is **MAINFORM.FRM**, not the **C:\DEVELOPS\PETER** section. It does this by moving through the string, character by character from the right hand side. As soon as a \ character is met then the loop is stopped there with **Exit For**, and the text directly to the right of the \ is added to the combo box.

If the loop exits without finding a \ character, then the whole string just read is passed to the combo box, since the code assumes that since it didn't find a \ character (and all that's in the line is a pure file name). After all this lot the **Do Loop** continues on its way, reading the next line from the file and repeating the whole process.

When the end of the file is reached we need to close the file, effectively severing this program's link with it.

```
Close varFileNumber
```

Again, it's a fairly easy command to use; you simply type **Close**, followed by the number of the file you want to close, which in this case is held in the **varFileNumber** variable.

File handling is rarely used in Visual Basic programs nowadays. If you need to deal with data then use a database. In fact, the most common instance where you might want to look at a file on disk is when you need to pull something out of an **INI** file. If you need to do this you really should be looking at the **GetPrivateProfile** API calls that we covered back in Chapter 11.

Printing Reports

BugTrak has a facility which produces a simple printed report. This is a summary of the uncleared bugs in a selected system. As far as BugTrak's users are concerned this is great; they can easily get a list of all the outstanding work on a system, on paper.

This is the kind of report it produces:

```
Summary of uncleared bugs as of 06/28/94 12:31:29


System     :Bugtrak  (H:\BOOKS\192\CHAP13\PROGRAMS\BUGTRAK.MAK)


ID    Description                          Created
9     Bugs report formatting error         06/28/94 04:26:32
10    Reports - Need more                  06/28/94 04:27:49
11    Bugs - Print dialog options wrong    06/28/94 04:28:54
12    System selection in reports          06/28/94 04:31:31
13    Bug entry key validation             06/28/94 04:32:28
14    Bug grid selection                   06/28/94 04:33:24
```

If you take a look at the form in design-mode you see that there's a common dialog on the form. This lets users reconfigure their printers, and decide how many copies of the report they want.

The real work behind the report takes place in the Print button's click event.

```
Sub cmdPrint_Click ()

    Dim nCurrentCopy As Integer
    Dim sOldRecordsource As String
    Dim nC2 As Integer, nC3 As Integer, nC4 As Integer

    Const PD_DISABLEPRINTTOFILE = &H80000
    Const PD_HIDEPRINTTOFILE = &H100000
    Const PD_NOPAGENUMS = &H8&
    Const PD_NOSELECTION = &H4&


    dlgPrint.Flags = PD_DISABLEPRINTTOFILE + PD_HIDEPRINTTOFILE +
 PD_NOPAGENUMS + PD_NOSELECTION
    dlgPrint.Action = 5
    screen.MousePointer = 11
    sOldRecordsource = frmMainForm!datBugs.RecordSource

    frmMainForm!datBugs.RecordSource = "Select * from Bugs where
 Bugs.System_ID = " & lstSystems.ItemData(lstSystems.ListIndex) & " and
 not cleared"
    frmMainForm!datBugs.Refresh

    For nCurrentCopy = 1 To dlgPrint.Copies

        printer.FontSize = 18
        printer.Print "Summary of uncleared bugs as of " & Now
        printer.Line -Step(printer.TextWidth("Summary of uncleared bugs
 as of " & Now), 0)

        printer.FontSize = 13
        printer.Print
        printer.Print

        frmMainForm!datSystems.Recordset.FindFirst "System_ID" =
 lstSystems.ItemData(lstSystems.ListIndex)
        printer.FontItalic = True
        printer.Print "System    :";
        printer.FontItalic = False
    printer.Print frmMainForm!datSystems.Recordset.Fields("System_Name")
 & "  (" & frmMainForm!datSystems.Recordset.Fields("Makefile") & ")"
        printer.Print
        printer.Print

        printer.FontBold = True
        printer.FontUnderline = True
        printer.Print "ID    Description
 Created          "

        nC2 = printer.TextWidth("ID    ")
        nC3 = printer.TextWidth("ID       Description
 ")
```

```
        printer.FontUnderline = False
        printer.FontBold = False
        printer.Print

        On Error Resume Next
        frmMainForm.datBugs.Recordset.MoveFirst
        On Error GoTo 0

  Do Until frmMainForm.datBugs.Recordset.EOF

    printer.CurrentX = 0
    printer.Print frmMainForm.datBugs.Recordset.Fields("Bug_ID");
    printer.CurrentX = nC2
    printer.Print frmMainForm.datBugs.Recordset.Fields("Description");

    printer.CurrentX = nC3
    printer.Print frmMainForm.datBugs.Recordset.Fields("CreatedOn")

      frmMainForm.datBugs.Recordset.MoveNext

  Loop

      printer.EndDoc

  Next

  frmMainForm!datBugs.RecordSource = sOldRecordsource
  frmMainForm!datBugs.Refresh
  screen.MousePointer = 0

End Sub
```

At first glance this amount of code looks scary. Don't panic! 90% of it is repeated over and over again. I could have put a lot of the code into subprocedures but then you'd have a chunk of code that calls the subprocedures, over and over again. There's no way out of doing a lot of typing when it comes to printing with Visual Basic.

The first thing the code does is invoke the Print common dialog. We first met this back in Chapter 7 - Dialogs. Here, I've set up the Flags property somewhat more extensively than before.

You can find a complete list of all the flags for all common dialogs, if you bring up Visual Basic on-line help and do a search for the word Flag - there are lots of them! The ones I use here allow me to turn off the **Selection** and **Pages**. Handling these options through code can be quite tricky, so if you're not confident about them, turn them off.

```
dlgPrint.Flags = PD_DISABLEPRINTTOFILE + PD_HIDEPRINTTOFILE +
  PD_NOPAGENUMS + PD_NOSELECTION
```

The common dialog is used here to get the number of copies to print from the user, and to allow them to configure their printer before actually producing the report.

After starting the dialog, the RecordSource property of the Bugs data control is saved into a variable.

```
sOldRecordsource = frmMainForm!datBugs.RecordSource
```

The **RecordSource** is then changed so that we can get access to a complete list of uncleared bugs for the currently selected system.

```
frmMainForm!datBugs.RecordSource = "Select * from Bugs where
⮑Bugs.System_ID = " & lstSystems.ItemData(lstSystems.ListIndex) & " and
⮑not cleared"
```

At the end of the code the **RecordSource** is returned to its former value and the data control refreshed to rebuild its own **RecordSet**.

```
frmMainForm!datBugs.RecordSource = sOldRecordsource
```

The actual code to print then follows inside a loop that goes from **1** to the number of copies selected using the common dialog.

```
For nCurrentCopy = 1 To dlgPrint.Copies
```

Using The Printer Object

Printing is all handled through a special Visual Basic object known as the **Printer** object. In many ways, the **Printer** object is like a form; you can set any **Font** property you want, move the cursor in it using the **CurrentX** and **CurrentY** properties, and even use graphics methods to draw onto the printout.

There are two special methods for the **Printer** object which the form doesn't have. The first is **Printer.NewPage**. At any point during the production of your report you can move to a new page by inserting this:

```
Printer.NewPage
```

Windows handles the rest for you. This report is fairly simple and doesn't use the **NewPage** method at all. It *does* make use of the **EndDoc** method though, which tells Visual Basic when we've finished printing. As soon as Visual Basic encounters an **EndDoc** method the current page is ejected from the printer ready for the next print to commence on a fresh page.

```
printer.EndDoc
```

After setting the **FontSize** properties to display some large text, the lines:

```
        printer.FontSize = 18
        printer.Print "Summary of uncleared bugs as of " & Now
        printer.Line -Step(printer.TextWidth("Summary of uncleared bugs
 as of " & Now), 0)
```

print a heading on the paper and draw a solid line underneath it using the **Line** method. Knowing where you are on the printed page and lining items up can become a bit of a bind, so you'll see the **TextWidth** function used quite a lot throughout most Visual Basic print routines.

In this example, **TextWidth** is used to get the exact width of the heading we just printed. This then controls the length of the line we draw. After printing, Visual Basic automatically moves the cursor down to the next line, so the **Line** method you see here can be used to draw a line from its current position straight out, without you having to worry about whether or not the line will be positioned correctly; it's all done for you.

After printing the main heading, the record for the currently selected system is found, which enables us to print the system's name, and the name of its **MAK** file directly beneath the page heading.

```
frmMainForm!datSystems.Recordset.FindFirst "System_ID" =
 lstSystems.ItemData(lstSystems.ListIndex)
        printer.FontItalic = True
        printer.Print "System    :";
        printer.FontItalic = False
    printer.Print frmMainForm!datSystems.Recordset.Fields("System_Name")
 & " (" & frmMainForm!datSystems.Recordset.Fields("Makefile") & ")"
        printer.Print
        printer.Print
```

This code also turns on italics to highlight the word *System:* The two lines at the bottom of the code are used for spacing:

```
printer.Print
```

After this, the column headings for the actual bug information are printed, with the **TextWidth** function being used to store the widths of each column in three variables.

When the time comes to print the actual bug information, we can set the CurrentX property of the printer object to move the cursor to the correct position across the line, without any worries about whether or not the text we're printing will line up properly or not.

Take a look at the lines in the loop which actually print the bug record information.

```
Do Until frmMainForm.datBugs.Recordset.EOF

    printer.CurrentX = 0
    printer.Print frmMainForm.datBugs.Recordset.Fields("Bug_ID");
    printer.CurrentX = nC2
    printer.Print frmMainForm.datBugs.Recordset.Fields("Description");

    printer.CurrentX = nC3
    printer.Print frmMainForm.datBugs.Recordset.Fields("CreatedOn")

        frmMainForm.datBugs.Recordset.MoveNext

Loop
```

Notice how with the exception of the last **Print**, the others all have a semi colon (**;**) at the end of each command. This tells Visual Basic not to drop down onto the next line after printing this information. This way, we only need to change the CurrentX property to line up the data in the right places across the paper, without having to worry about also changing the CurrentY property.

That's all there is too it; a stack of code for a very simple report, with only a small amount of data on it. Imagine trying to write a routine to print invoices on pre-printed stationery using the **Printer** object!

If you plan to do any serious printing with Visual Basic and databases, then you really should consider buying a professional print designer, such as Crystal Reports Pro. Professional print designers can reduce your coding time and reduce the hit and miss aspects of reporting. They could soon pay for themselves.

Summary

In this chapter we've been on a detailed tour of a stand-alone Visual Basic application. The BugTrak application is a typical standard edition database app.

My aim in walking you through the project in detail was to bring everything we've learnt during the course of the book together in a realistic way. While we haven't used every last feature of Visual Basic in BugTrak, it has made good use of the most important ones.

BugTrak shows you:

- How to structure a simple database for a real world application
- How to bind non-bound controls such as combo boxes and grids to a data base using code
- How to link multiple forms together in an application
- How to build **SQL** statements in code
- How to handle disk files with Visual Basic
- How to produce printed reports

Well, that's the end of the Beginner's Guide to Visual Basic. You should be feeling pretty pleased with yourself if you made it this far, particularly if you were able to understand BugTrak. So where do we go from here? If you look in Appendix A I've put together some personal advice about what to do next to further your career as a Visual Basic professional. Good Luck.

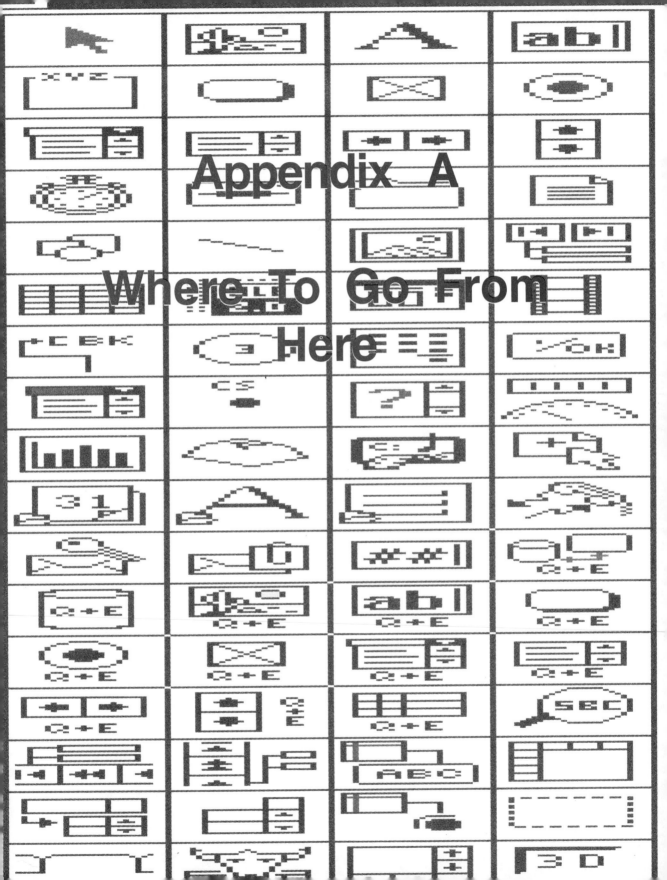

Appendix A

Where To Go From
Here

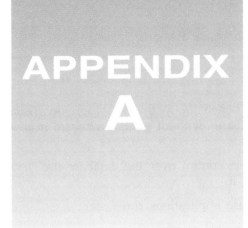

APPENDIX A

Where To Go From Here

By now you should well and truly have a feel for the Standard Edition of Visual Basic. However, as you've also seen, there are elements of the package that don't lend themselves towards certain applications. For instance creating a nice static toolbar requires an in depth knowledge of object variables and graphics controls. Programming database applications requires more than a passing familiarity with the data control, and locks you into doing things the data control way.

One of the great strengths of Visual Basic is its extendibility. Using custom controls you can add new features to the package, improving both your program's functionality and your productivity as a programmer.

In this short appendix I'll try to show you where you can go next. I'll tell you which controls I use and what are the best routes to take depending on your needs as a developer.

Let's start with the most obvious upgrade; Visual Basic Professional.

Visual Basic Professional

Visual Basic Pro is more than just an upgrade. It gives you a whole stack of new improved controls, as well as a number of new methods and functions for dealing with databases. In addition you get Crystal Reports, a report generator thrown in free as well as the Microsoft Visual Design Guide, an on-screen guide to designing better user interfaces.

By far the biggest benefit is on the database side. Visual Basic Pro developers can deal with databases without going anywhere near a data control. This has a number of benefits:

- You get more control over the database itself, and the operations you perform on it.

- Your database applications run faster.

- You can use code to index by name, making searching much faster.

- You get more SQL commands which let you do bulk updates and deletes in tables with a single command.

One of the problems with programming the data control is that you end up fighting the events. You need to use code specifically for when the data control thinks it should update records, making canceling edits and new record creations a bit of bind. In the Pro Edition you can tell Visual Basic when you want to do an update and take the whole issue out of Visual Basic's hands.

Report generation is also a lot easier, thanks to Crystal Reports. We'll look at this in more detail shortly. The general rule of thumb is, if you're serious about doing database development get the Professional Edition immediately.

The new controls you get also make life simpler. You get controls to deal with communications, sound, video and music. There are also a number of controls you can use to give your forms a 3-D look. There's also a control to display progress bars which fill up with a color as an operation takes place. There's also a new text box control which can format data as it's entered, and do validation for you.

Database Controls

You've already seen how limiting unbound controls such as grids, combo boxes, and list boxes can be when used with Visual Basic; you have to write code yourself to fill them with data from a database table. There are a number of packages available which can simplify this process.

Sheridan Systems supply a package called Data Widgets which includes a bound grid, combo box and list box, as well as an enhanced data control. These all have a 3D look about them and can be bound to data controls on separate forms. They are extremely easy to use for both you and your users.

My personal favorite has to be Truegrid. This is an enhanced grid control which can be bound or used in the same way as a standard grid. You can configure it's look between normal and 3-D, change the colors of the cells in the grid, display graphics from a database in the grid, add code to the grid itself to do different things based on the values of its cells and much more.

If you want a bound grid control for use with Visual Basic then look no further than Truegrid.

The pro-edition of Visual Basic also comes with a cut down version of Crystal Reports. However, Crystal Reports Professional, the full blown commercial version of the product, is much more powerful and easy to use.

At its most basic level it lets you draw reports on screen as you want them to appear when printed. Then by adding the Crystal VBX to your program you can load up, preview and print the final report with only a few lines of code. This is a great improvement over the leg work we had to do to create a simple report in Chapter 13.

Other Good VBXs

There are hundreds of VBXs available for a wide range of purposes, from dealing with spreadsheets to talking to barcode readers. I only use a select few:

VBTools 4

This is a collection of about 100 controls covering everything from drawing playing cards to bound grids, to pop up tips, to command buttons with images on. VBTools is the most definitive collection of general purpose controls available.

Imagestream

This is a control for loading, manipulating and writing graphics files in almost any conceivable format.

Designer Widgets

This is a collection of three controls to do the fashionable stuff you see in top flight applications, including making drag and drop toolbars, changing the appearance of a form (shrinking and enlarging the caption area, making the control menu 3-D and so on), and producing tabbed dialog boxes, like the ones in Word 6 and Excel 5.

Writing Games

At present Visual Basic is not the best platform for Windows game development. However, Microsoft have a freely available DLL for all to use called WinG. This enables you to shove graphics around the screen at phenomenal speeds, almost equal to games produced outside Windows in DOS.

If you want to do games then get hold of this now. It's on the WINMM forum on Compuserve, and available via ftp from ftp.microsoft.com.

Talking to the Wide World

Visual Basic programmers are a select bunch who love to talk to each other, share ideas and code, and generally shoot the breeze about all things Windows based. You can find a great many of them on CompuServe in the MSBasic forum. This is a section of CompuServe in which Visual Basic people regularly send each other mail for all to see solving technical problems and dealing with Visual Basic's bugs and flaws. Microsoft also actively participate in this forum.

Alternatively, you could try the Visual Basic conference on CIX, in the UK. This tends to be a much more easy going place to discuss things; MSBASIC on CompuServe can get more than a little heated at times. Check out your local on-line service providers to see what's available.

There are also a number of Visual Basic conferences on the Internet if you have access to it.

The Programmer's Library

By buying this book you've already admitted that it's helpful to have more on your book shelf than the two Visual Basic manuals. The other books I personally use are:

Visual Basic Programmer's Guide to the Windows API, from Ziff-Davis Press, by Dan Appleman.

This book tells you everything you ever wanted to know about API calls and Visual Basic.

The Database Developer's Guide, from Sams Publishing, by Roger Jennings.

This is a good guide to developing database applications with Visual Basic.

Code Complete, from Microsoft Press, by Steve McConnel.

An excellent, highly readable book covering programming practices in general, including debugging techniques, design techniques, naming and programming standards and much much more.

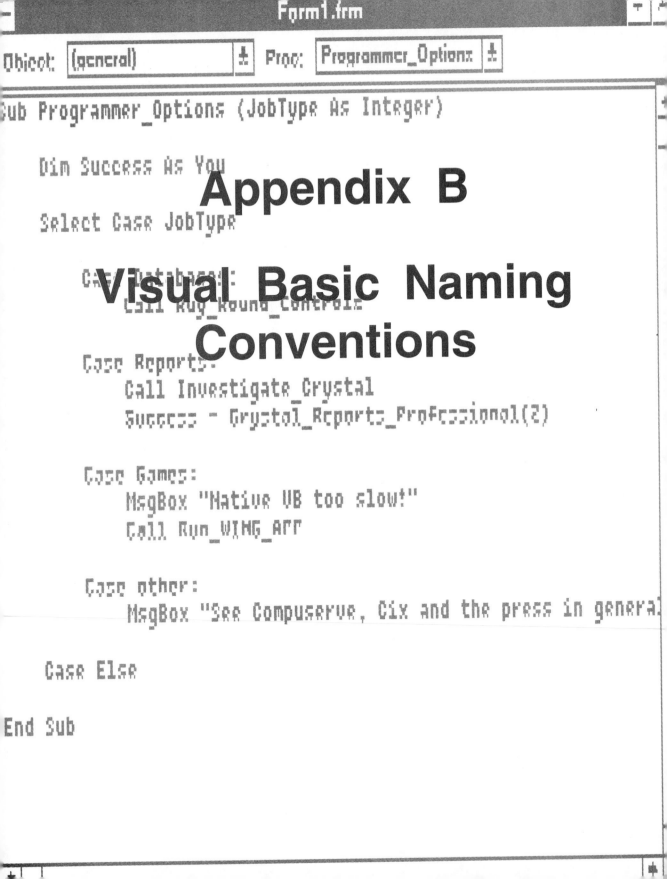

```
Form1.frm

Object: (general)          Proc: Programmer_Options

Sub Programmer_Options (JobType As Integer)

    Dim Success As You

    Select Case JobType

        Case Database:
            Call Rug_Round_Controls

        Case Reports:
            Call Investigate_Crystal
            Success = Crystal_Reports_Professional(2)

        Case Games:
            MsgBox "Native VB too slow!"
            Call Run_WING_App

        Case other:
            MsgBox "See Compuserve, Cix and the press in general

    Case Else

End Sub
```

Appendix B

Visual Basic Naming Conventions

Visual Basic Naming Conventions

This appendix introduces a scheme for naming all the objects in Visual Basic in a way that increases the safety and readability of your code. Some parts of this is taken from standards published by Microsoft, and some of it's my own.

There are three kinds of objects we need to have standard names for in our Visual Basic code:

1 Controls

2 Variables

3 Functions and procedures

Before we come to each of these in turn, let's consider why it's necessary to have a naming scheme at all.

Why Have a Standard Naming Scheme?

Naming standards can help prevent costly and embarrassing mistakes. By adopting a set of standards and by sticking to them, you're guaranteeing that in x months time when you return to debug or change some code, you'll understand what you were trying to say back when it was written.

Think about road signs. Imagine how confusing it would be if each town in the country had different designs and standards for their road signs. Each time you came into a new town you'd waste valuable reaction time trying to understand unfamiliar drawings and symbols, time that is better spent on the job - driving.

The same applies to programming. With a decent set of programming standards your code can in many ways becoming self-documenting; reading such code could be as easy as reading a book about it.

Take a look at this - it's a program your boss just gave you which has a bug in it, and you have ten minutes to fix it.

```
For a = 1 To z

    d(a) = d(a) - cv(d(a))
    q(a) = q(a) + d(a)
    v(a) = cv(d(a))

next a
```

Impossible! You can't make any sense of it. There's no indication what the code does, or what the variables are that it deals with. As a contrast, look at the same piece of code, now with some standards applied:

```
For nInvNo = 1 to nTotalNumberOfInvoices

    nPrice(nInvNo) = nPrice(nInvNo) - Vat(nPrice(nInvNo))

    nBalance( nInvNo ) = nBalance(nInvNo) + nPrice(nInvNo)

    nVat(nInvNo) = Vat(nPrice(nInvNo))

Next
```

Here, the code is spaced out to make it easier to read, and the variables now have sensible names. It's obvious that the code is dealing with invoice totals, in particular the outstanding balance of an invoice, the amount payable and the Vat (sales tax).

From this it's easy to see that the bug is in the first line. **vat** should be added to the price, not subtracted.

Naming Controls

The objective when naming a control is to help anyone reading the text to understand two things about the control that the code refers to:

▶ What kind of control is it? Each control has a unique three letter **prefix** that tells you what kind of control it is.

▶ What does the control do? Does this command button exit the form, or print the data? This function is described by the **usage identifier**.

Each control name is therefore made up of a prefix followed by a usage identifier:

Control Prefixes

A three letter prefix is used to identify the type of control, and to make it clear which names in your code are variables and which are controls.

The control prefixes I use are:

Prefix	Control
frm	Form
txt	Text box
lbl	Label
fra	Frame
pnl	Panel
chk	Checkbox
opt	Option/Radio buttons
dat	Data control
com	Combo box
lst	List box
grd	Grid
ole	OLE control
fil	File list box
dir	Directory list box
drv	Drive list box
gph	Graphic control (lines, boxes and circles)
dlg	Common dialogs

The **lin** and **shp** names that are in the Visual Basic manuals for Line and Shape have been ignored here. This is purely a question of personal taste; I rarely use the graphical controls so I might as well use the same prefix for all the them, namely **gph**.

Naming Custom Controls

There's a temptation with custom controls that you add in to projects, to use the brand name of the product as the prefix. Don't do it! If you decide later on to switch to a control from another supplier, then you'll have to change all your code. The safe way to do it is to use a name that describes the function of the control. For example, if you're using the Image Knife control, don't use the prefix **knf**; instead, use something like **imp** (**im**age **p**rocessing).

Choosing a Control Usage Identifier

In choosing the main part of the name for a control, your aim should be to convey a clear idea about what that control is used for in the code. You can use one or more English words that clearly define this usage. General rules that are worth following include:

- Use capital letters for parts of the name.

- Underscore characters can be used to separate the words of the name (this is left to your personal preference).

- You can make the name as long, or as short, as you like. Obviously, the longer the name the more typing you've got to do - a sensible limit is about 15 characters.

- If the name's too short, it probably won't tell you anything.

- If it's too long it'll be confusing and take a lot of typing each time you use it.

There are some limitations to the names you can use. For example, you can't create variables that have identical names to Visual Basic keywords. Equally, you can't start a variable name with a number, or with a special character, such as $,%,^,&,*, and so on.

Example Control Names

First the bad names. These are all too cryptic to be useful:

```
Text1       Combo      A_Form          txtDSADSXZ
Alfred      Henry      God_Knows       chkB
```

Don't laugh! I've seen all these in Visual Basic programs!

These on the other hand are much nicer:

```
txtSurname      cboEmployees        frmMainForm
chkSex          txtEmpCode
```

Naming Variables

When naming a variable there is an additional piece of information we need to include in addition to its type and a description of its usage - its scope. Controls are all local to the form on which they are placed, but variables can be either local, global or static.

The format of a typical variable name is:

Variable Scope

The scope part of the name consists of a single letter prefix to the variable name

Prefix	Variable Name
g	**Global** variables, variables defined with the **Global** keyword.
m	**Module** level variables, defined with **Dim** or **Static** in the declarations section of a Form (**.Frm**) or Module (**.Bas**).
no prefix	All Local variables, defined using **Dim** or **Static** in a function or procedure, have no prefix.

Variable Type

Just as with scope, a single alphabetic character can be used to define the type of a variable, such as string, integer, and so on. These **type** letters are as follows:

Character	Type of Variable
s	String
i	Integer
l	Long (a large integer)
f	Floating point number, both singles and doubles
c	Currency
var	Variant

Additionally, some of the data types are used to hold values that are, in fact, data types in their own right, but which can't be declared as such in Visual Basic. These include:

b/l	Boolean/Logical values held in an integer variable.
d	Dates and or Times.

Date and Time values are special-case data types since they could be held in either a String or a Variant, but both types of variables require different functions in order to work with the data.

Where you intend to store these values in variables, name the variable in the usual way and prefix it with **d** for date or **b** for boolean. For example, an integer variable called **Flag** would normally be called **nFlag**.

If you intend to store boolean values, then it's a lot more readable to write **bnFlag**.

Choosing a Variable Usage Identifier

The rules for naming variables are similar to those for controls.

Never use quick names for variables, such as the traditional **X, Y, I, J, Z**. An experienced programmer knows that **I** means an Integer index in a **For** loop, but a beginner might not. Badly named variables can lead to you using them in the wrong place in your code, such as typing **I** where you meant to type **J**, and so on. If you've taken the time to declare a variable for a particular purpose, then take the time to give it a useful name!

Example Variable Names

To summarize, some complete examples of variable names are:

gsUserName	A	global string holding a User Name
iCounter	An	integer used as a counter of some kind
bMale	A	Boolean value, True represents Male
mdvarDate	A	module level date variant, indicating the date

Declaring Variable Data Types

Although Visual Basic supports the use of type identifiers such as **$** for String, and **%** for Integer, they're really only a hang over from the original ANSI specification for BASIC. Type identifiers can easily be mis-typed. Notice how **$** is next to **%** on the keyboard. Also, they don't jump out at you when you re-read a buggy section of code for the 12th time, and they look cryptic if your code is handed to a beginner.

> When declaring data types, **always** use the data type name, such as **String** instead of **$** and so on.

> Remember never to leave the data type off a declaration as this results in you defining a variant which would probably mean your variable name is wrong, and you haven't thought about the use of the variable.

Object Variables

Most object variables are controls, so you just go ahead and name them as you would a normal control. However, object variables relating to databases are also named along the same lines as controls. The prefixes to use are:

Prefix	Variable
dyn	Dynaset
tbl	Table
snp	Snapshot
db	Database
rec	Recordset

Naming Functions and Procedures

Function and procedure names should reflect the purpose of the procedure or function using English words.

Naming Functions

Functions always return a value and where possible should be given a name that reflects the return value. A function that returns the square root of a number should simply be called **Square_Root**, or **Square_Root_Of**, rather than **Calculate_Square_Root**. You can tell if a function has been given a good name by seeing how the code reads:

```
fRoot = Square_Root_Of ( 36 )      ' This is good!
fRoot = ClcSqrRt( 36 )             ' This is bad, read aloud!
```

Naming Procedures

The same amount of thought should be given to procedure names. Procedures generally perform a task, such as clearing a list box, or changing a frame layout. The task the procedure performs should be reflected in the name.

```
Remove_Borders Frame1      ' Easy enough!
RBF1_V1 Frame1             ' No idea - bad name!
```

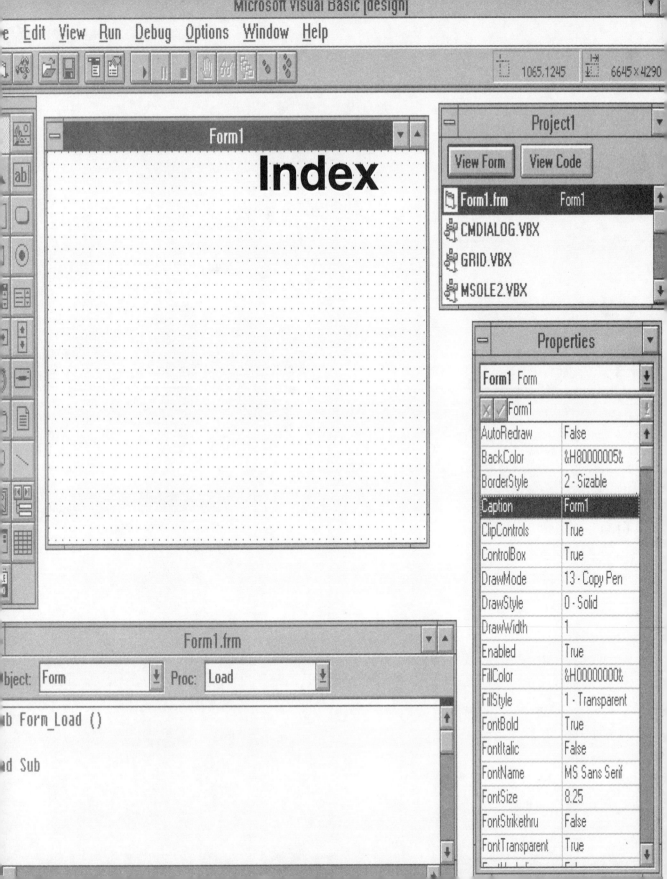

INDEX

A

U

The Beginner's Guide to Access 2

This Beginner's Guide commences with the methodology behind modern databases, proceeding through an example-driven tutorial of all the relevant basics. The second section of the book offers more advanced coverage of the topics, along with an introduction to Access Basic programming.

Author: Wrox Development
$24.95 / £22.99
ISBN 1-874416-21-4

The Beginner's Guide to Turbo Pascal

Turbo Pascal is the ideal language for the ambitious beginner in programming who wants to get into applications beyond the limitations implicit in BASIC. This book takes you on the fast track of learning, providing you with an easy and rapid route to the power of Turbo Pascal and introducing the basic concepts of the latest programming methodology - Object Oriented Programming.

Author: Oleg Perminov
Includes disk
$29.95 / £27.99
ISBN 1-874416-30-3

The Revolutionary Guide to Visual C++

The book teaches the essentials of objects to allow the reader to write Windows programs with the MFC. Section One of the book allows the C programmer to quickly get to terms with the difference between C and C++, including the concepts involved in object oriented design and programming. Sections Two and Three are a comprehensive guide to writing complete Windows applications.

Author: Ben Ezzell
Includes disk
$39.95 / £37.49
ISBN 1-874416-22-2

The Beginner's Guide to C

This is a well-structured tutorial on application programming, not merely a language reference. The author builds a complete application with the reader, step by step, leaving them with a useful tool and a sense of achievement. The ANSI C language is given comprehensive coverage in a friendly environment.

Author: G. Kesler
$24.95 / £22.99
ISBN 1-874416-15-X

The Beginner's Guide to OOP in C++

This Beginner's Guide teaches OOP to programmers from the procedural world, assuming a small amount of programming knowledge. The information is presented in a manner which teaches aspects of the language on a need-to-know basis. This gives the reader not only the tools, but also the methodology to actually use them.

Author: L. Romanovskaya
$29.95 / £27.99
ISBN 1-874416-27-3

World Class Programming